The Emergence of
the Irish Banking System
1820–1845

The Emergence
of the
Irish Banking System
1820-1845

G. L. Barrow

GILL AND MACMILLAN

Published by
Gill and Macmillan Ltd.,
2 Belvedere Place,
Dublin 1
and internationally through association
with the
Macmillan Publishers Group

    G. L. Barrow, 1975
7171 0765 5

Printed in the Republic of Ireland by
Cahill and Co. Limited, Dublin

ACKNOWLEDGEMENTS: PLATES

Illustrations are by courtesy of the following, whose permission is gratefully acknowledged:

Allied Irish Banks Ltd: Plate 1

National Museum of Ireland: Plates 2, 3, 5, 7, 9, 12, 14.

Institute of Bankers in Ireland and Central Bank of Ireland: Plates 6, 8, 10, 11, 13.

Institute of Bankers, collection of paper money: Plate 16.

Old Dublin Society: Plates 4, 15.

Contents

Preface

The primary source for any history of banking should be the records of the banks. In this we are fortunate that nearly all the principal banks discussed in this book are happily still with us, albeit some of them in recently altered form. But bankers are, by profession, a secretive lot, and rightly so since their customers' confidence lies at the heart of their business. The passing of the years (and of the customers) may bring some relaxation of the pressure for secrecy but it brings too the loss of many basic records. Most banking business is ephemeral, and once transactions have been completed and the time for litigation passed the documents concerned merely gather dust on office shelves. In time secretarial efficiency prompts their consignment to the incinerator. One such incident is recorded in the Royal Bank,[1] and in at least one Irish bank, the Belfast, the incineration was carried out by enemy bombers. But even when early papers are still in being, bank directors are naturally reluctant to expose them without the kind of internal check which their officials, concerned with the present and the future rather than the past, lack the time or the incentive to carry out.

In the light of these difficulties I owe a great debt to the directors of the different Irish banks who have allowed me to see so much of what does survive. I am especially grateful to the directors of the Bank of Ireland, and to the then governor, Mr D. S. A. Carroll, for giving me access to its minute books, an invaluable source previously used on a large scale only for Hall's history of the bank. The boards of the Provincial, National, Hibernian, Royal, Belfast and Ulster Banks all allowed me to see their deeds of settlement—for the most part formerly unconsulted—and such annual reports and early published documents as they possess. The Royal was the only one to allow a glimpse (under supervision) of its board minutes. In the case of the Northern Bank the full deed and summaries of the annual reports are printed in its centenary volume. The Munster & Leinster, yet unborn in these years, kindly let me look through the records of La Touche's which it holds. I am particularly indebted to the various officials of all these banks on whose time and goodwill I have trespassed at different times in the last six years.

Few private papers of Irish bankers dealing with their banking have come to light. Only when the banker is also a public figure, as

1 K. Milne, *The Royal Bank of Ireland*, p. 9.

with O'Connell and Spring Rice, are their papers available, and then they scarcely touch on their banking activities. I am nevertheless extremely grateful to Professor Maurice O'Connell for letting me see some of the typescript of his recent edition of O'Connell's letters; this has helped to locate the few references to O'Connell's banking that do exist. A search in the Public Record Office in Belfast failed to uncover anything from the founders of the banks in that city.

This shortage of private sources is fortunately made good in large measure in contemporary newspapers and journals which carry a great deal of banking information mainly in the form of notices and reports inserted by the banks themselves. I have relied in the main on the *Freeman's Journal* as the most readily accessible over the whole period but have consulted other papers as well at the more important stages. A search through all the newspapers might bring forth a few more snippets of information—but this is an activity peculiarly subject to the law of diminishing returns.

Among public records the most useful have certainly been the reports of parliamentary committees and other sessional papers. Other public papers consulted include the treasury papers in the Public Record Office, London, the correspondence of the chief secretary's office in the State Papers Office, Dublin, the Peel papers in the British Museum and the Goulburn papers at Kingston. This all proved helpful but less so than might have been expected. Most banking references in them are duplicated in the minute books of the Bank of Ireland, and there is little relating to other banks and not much on the preliminaries of banking and monetary legislation. The records of the Dublin Stamp Office would have been of interest but do not appear to have survived the flames of 1922.[2] Another lacuna is any direct evidence on the working of the Dublin money market.

While a good deal of information has been gathered from the viewpoint of the banks the search for any from their customers has been less rewarding. Business and estate accounts from the period are few, and those examined have little to say about dealings with the banks. The only business histories of any substance relating to Ireland in this period are Gill on the linen industry, Rebbeck's unpublished thesis on shipbuilding (mostly post-1850) and Lynch and Vaizey on Guinness's brewery; the first has some information on financial operations, the two latter very little.

Hall's history of the Bank of Ireland is the most important bank history but suffers from many inaccuracies. The only others published are the Northern's centenary volume, the Ulster's *Decades* and Milne's history of the Royal but none of them goes, or indeed claims to go, much below the surface. The same applies to the sections on Irish

2 H. Wood, *A guide to the public records of Ireland* (1919), p. 143, mentions some of these records, but the report on the destruction and reconstruction of the Record Office has no reference to them (*P.R.I. rep. D.K.* 55 (1928), app. I).

banks included in the histories of English banks with which they are associated—on the Belfast in Crick and Wadsworth's history of the Midland and on the Ulster in Gregory's history of the Westminster.

For the rest the published literature of Irish banking in this, or indeed any other, period is extremely scanty. A few works appeared in the last century—Gilbart's *Banking in Ireland* (1836), the Irish section of his *Practical treatise* (1849), Collins's *Law and practice of banking in Ireland* (1880) and Dillon's *History and development of banking in Ireland* (1889)—but on examination they all prove either superficial or inaccurate or both. Since Dillon's book (a very thin work, literally and metaphorically) the only publication claiming to be a comprehensive history of Irish banking has been Nolan's *History and mystery* of 1923 but this has small claim to scholarship. Hall's unpublished thesis in Trinity College, Dublin, which runs from the seventeenth century to 1942, is largely based on secondary sources and repeats many of their errors.

On private banks O'Kelly's book on those in Cork and Limerick is sound and informative but limited in scope, and there have been a number of useful articles in journals; those by Tenison, often treated as a reliable source, are discussed below.[3] On the monetary system as a whole Fetter's short book on the Irish pound is most valuable, but it ends where the present study begins.

On Irish affairs in general in this period there is a mass of contemporary literature—pamphlets, travellers' tales, etc.—in addition to the torrents of official reports. This all helps to fill in the background but only a small part is directly concerned with the banks. The most valuable accumulation of pamphlets is the Haliday collection in the Royal Irish Academy, which I have kindly been allowed to consult. It was given to the academy by the widow of Charles Haliday, a prominent director of the Bank of Ireland in the mid-nineteenth century, but despite this banking connection the pamphlets relevant to the subject, though useful, are few.

Most of the research for this book has been done in the National Library in Dublin and I would like to record my thanks to the reading room staff for their never failing courtesy and assistance, as also to the curators and staff of the various other institutions in which I have worked. The latter are listed in the bibliography, and I hope that all concerned will forgive my not mentioning them here by name. But I must particularly acknowledge the ready co-operation of those who have allowed me to examine their collections of bank notes, Mr John Teahan, keeper of the Art and Industrial Division of the National Museum, Dublin, Mr Basil Greer, secretary of the Institute of Bankers in Ireland, Mr P. Spiro, librarian of the Institute of Bankers, London, Mr W. A. Seaby, director of the Ulster Museum, Belfast, Mrs Brigid Dolan, librarian of the Royal Irish Academy, Mr Seamus O Coigh-

3 Below, p. 202.

ligh, curator of the Cork Public Museum, and Mr F. E. Dixon in respect of his private collection in Dublin, as well as to Mr Michael Dolley of the Queen's University, Belfast, for advice and help in this connection. To those who have allowed their notes to be illustrated acknowledgement is made above but I would like to add my thanks for their co-operation in obtaining the necessary photographs.

This work originated as a thesis accepted for an external Ph.D. by London University. I was greatly helped in its early stages by the comments and suggestions of Dr L. M. Cullen of Trinity College, Dublin, and of Dr L. S. Presnell of the London School of Economics, and in the later stages by those of Professor Oliver MacDonagh of University College, Cork. I am most grateful for this and for the encouragement and invaluable editorial advice of Professor T. W. Moody. For the opinions and errors that remain all blame rests of course wholly on the author. The author and publishers are indebted to the Bank of Ireland for their generous assistance towards publication.

G. L. Barrow

Dublin, 12 February 1974

ABBREVIATIONS

B.M. Add. MSS	British Museum additional manuscripts
B. Mag.	*The Banker's Magazine*
B. of I. Mins.	Minutes of the court of directors of the Bank of Ireland
F.J.	*Freeman's Journal*
H.C.	House of Commons sessional papers
I.H.S.	*Irish Historical Studies*
N.L.I.	National Library of Ireland
P.R.O.	Public Record Office, London
P.R.O.I.	Public Record Office, Dublin
P.R.O.N.I.	Public Record Office, Belfast
R.I.A.	Royal Irish Academy
S.P.O.	State Papers Office, Dublin
U.C.D.	University College, Dublin
Watson's Almanack	*The Gentleman and Citizen's Almanack* (Dublin)

Abbreviations of parliamentary proceedings and reports are given below, pp 234-7.

All references to present day Irish banks are to those as they were before the recent amalgamations.

Introduction

Writing in 1822 Thomas Joplin described banks as 'the fountains of our currency, the depositaries of our capital and at once the wheels and pillars of our trade'.[1] He was thinking of banking in England and Scotland, the latter as a model for the former, but his words were just as true, in a rather negative sense, of Ireland which was suffering from the interdependent weaknesses of an inadequate banking system, a shortage of currency, an outflow of capital and the stagnation of trade.

The Irish economy in these years was in the grip of depression and unemployment. Signs of improvement were sometimes detected but these were only relative. A rapidly increasing rural population was underemployed on the land but deterred from moving off it by the lack of any alternative source of livelihood. For many the only way to find employment was by emigration, temporary or permanent, to Britain or the New World. At the same time Ireland was crying out for economic development to provide things for the lack of which so many of her people were living on the fringes of starvation. Money is not the sole key to this paradox but it is the medium through which an exchange economy operates. An understanding of its supply and use is essential to an understanding of such an economy, and this means in the first place an understanding of the banking system.

The rising population needed increased production and employment. Banks could not create this but they could provide the necessary financial mechanism. As Adam Smith had put it half a century earlier, 'it is not by augmenting the capital of a country, but by rendering a greater part of the capital active and productive than would otherwise be so, that the most judicious operations of banking can increase the industry of a country'.[2] Whether such 'judicious operations' are seen as active measures of monetary reflation to draw unemployed resources into use or as passive responses to real developments, their role was central to the economy in providing a currency, mobilizing capital and financing trade.

The following pages look at banking in Ireland from the last great crisis of the private banks in 1820 at the depth of the post-war depression to the consolidation of the system under the Irish Banking Act in 1845 on the eve of the Great Famine. In politics, with the

1 T. Joplin, *An essay on the general principles and present practice of banking in England and Scotland*, p. 1.
2 Adam Smith, *Wealth of nations*, ed. Seligman, i, 285.

French wars at last out of the way, these were years of some not very successful efforts to make a reality of the Union. In economic life they were marked by what can be seen in retrospect as a series of missed opportunities for the reflation that might have averted catastrophe. One of the few positive achievements was the construction of the banking system.

1

The Banking Scene in 1820

The Eighteenth-century Background

Banks first appeared in Ireland around the end of the seventeenth century, as they had about half a century earlier in England, as off-shoots of other businesses. The point at which a person engaged in such business comes to deserve the name of banker may often be hard to identify, but the term first appears in Irish law in an act of 1709.[1] This provided that notes issued by any 'banker, goldsmith, merchant or trader' which were 'payable to any person or persons, his her or their order, shall be assignable or endorsable over in the same manner as inland bills of exchange are or may be according to the custom of merchants'. Bills of exchange were of very ancient lineage but the issue of notes payable to bearer on demand was a more recent development, and it was this that distinguished the modern banker from a discounting merchant, bill broker, deposit-accepting goldsmith or moneylender. There were, it is true, firms in Dublin, as there were in London, which issued no notes and yet were recognized as banks, but this was due to their peculiar circumstances.

During the course of the eighteenth century numerous banks rose and fell in Dublin. There were normally six or eight there in the middle decades but only three survived the crisis of 1759-60, and for the rest of the century the number never exceeded five. The only one to see the whole century through was La Touche's. Outside Dublin there were a number of banks in Cork, also in Waterford, Limerick, Clonmel and Belfast,[2] but it was not till after the suspension of cash payments in 1797 that country banking became widespread in Ireland.

Some of the difficulties under which these banks laboured are discussed below. Their operations were less riddled with scandal than is commonly supposed but they failed nonetheless to provide the country with a stable banking system. Then in 1783 the scene was transformed by the appearance of a bank of an altogether different order, designed to play a role in Ireland akin to that of the Bank of England across the water.

The Bank of Ireland

In 1782, during the full flood of the conflict over legislative indepen-

1 8 Anne, c. 11, s. 5 (Ir.).
2 F. G. Hall, *The Bank of Ireland 1783-1946*, pp. 6-14, discusses some of these banks but is not wholly accurate; L. M. Cullen, *Anglo-Irish trade 1660-1800*, pp. 155-205, deals with eighteenth-century Irish banking in general, especially its exchange aspects; see below, p. 202, for the work of C. McC. Tenison and E. O'Kelly.

dence, the Irish parliament passed with little debate a government bill to authorize the raising of £600,000 and the incorporation of its subscribers under a royal charter as the Governor and Company of the Bank of Ireland.[3] Letters patent establishing the corporation were issued in April 1783, the charter was granted on 10 May and the bank opened for business on 25 June.

The charter was, and still is, the bank's corporate constitution, analogous to the articles of a modern company.[4] Later statements notwithstanding, it did not grant any monopoly. What later critics called the monopoly, but the bank preferred to describe as its special privileges, derived, not from the charter, but from section 14 of the act which declared that no other body exceeding six persons might 'borrow, owe or take up any sum or sums of money on their bills or notes payable at demand or at any less period than six months'. This provoked little comment at the time, none of the existing banks having more than six partners and the head of the leading one, David La Touche, being a prime mover in the formation of the Bank of Ireland, but in the next century it was to become the chief target for criticism. It was modelled on a similar provision in respect of the Bank of England in an act of 1708,[5] and its effect was to confine all other note-issuing banks to a maximum of six partners.

The Bank of Scotland had been granted similar privileges on its foundation in 1695 but when its original charter expired in 1716 they were not renewed. The reason was said to be the sympathy of some of the directors for the rebels of 1715.[6] No similar taint ever fell on the loyal directors of the Bank of Ireland. Many were supporters of Grattan and opponents of the Union,[7] but in case of open rebellion there was no doubt where their loyalty lay; in 1798 on the vote of a special meeting of stockholders £20,000 was donated to the government 'for the exigencies of the state at this important crisis', and when parliament voted £100,000 for 'the relief of suffering loyalists' the court was quick to advance it against treasury bills.[8] In consequence by 1820 the bank's privileges, like those of the Bank of England, were still intact while those of the Bank of Scotland were over a century dead. This is the key to the divergence in the banking histories of the two countries.

In addition to its statutory privileges the Bank of Ireland's capital arrangements set it apart from its fellows. Under the act the £600,000 capital was advanced to government as a permanent loan with interest

---

3 21 & 22 Geo. III, c. 16 (Ir); its progress through parliament is recorded in. *Commons' Jn. Ire.*, x, 307-45, *Lords' Jn. Ire.*, v, 304-23, *Parl. reg. Ire.*, i, 295-304, 316, 320-1. See also Hall, *op. cit.*, pp. 31-4.
4 There is a copy of the charter in the N.L.I.
5 7 Anne, c. 30, s. 66.
6 W. H. Marwick, *Scotland in modern times*, p. 15.
7 J. Hone, biographical notes in Hall, *Bank of Ireland*, pp. 479-508.
8 B. of I. Mins., 6 Mar., 17 July 1798.

at 4 per cent to be paid by an annuity of £24,000.[9] The bank drew financial strength from this in two ways. By section 20 of the act the corporation could only be dissolved on twelve months' notice by the government after 1 January 1794 on repayment of all sums owing, or on a petition by the bank after the same date, while section 6 limited the bank's borrowing powers to £600,000, the stockholders being personally answerable for any excess. The loan to government therefore formed a guarantee fund to meet the full amount of authorized borrowing in the event of dissolution. No penalty was prescribed for exceeding the limit, which in practice was ignored,[10] but on the unlimited liability of the members.

The act also included a guarantee of current payments. By section 13 any judgement creditor of the bank could secure payment from the exchequer who would then deduct the sum from the next annuity. This right, never apparently exercised, must have reinforced the sense of the bank's dependability in its early years.

Between 1782 and 1820 the Bank of Ireland's capital was increased three times, by acts of 1791, 1797 and 1808.[11] The date before which it might not be dissolved, originally 1794, was extended to 1816 by the 1791 act and to 1 January 1837 by that of 1808; this was commonly but inaccurately described as extension of the charter.

These acts left the bank's capital in 1820 as £2,500,000, fully issued and paid. Against this it could set loans to government of £2,350,000 at 5 per cent, the interest on which it was obliged to pass on to the stockholders.[12] It was authorized to borrow up to £2,500,000 by note issues or otherwise, with no objection raised to its exceeding this limit on the unlimited liability of its members. It could not be dissolved without its own consent before 1837 and it was the only bank in Ireland enjoying the benefits of incorporation and the only bank of issue permitted with more than six members. Since 1783 it had been banker to the Irish government—one of the functions for which it was created—and since 1797 had also managed the national debt.[13] It was commonly known at the time as the 'National Bank' but this name is now liable to cause confusion with a later body

The bank started life in most unsuitable premises in Mary's Abbey but in 1803 purchased the vacant parliament building in College Green into which it moved partly in 1806 and fully in 1808.[14] By 1820 this was still its sole office.

9 See Appendix 1 below for a summary of the capital arrangements.
10 Hall, *Bank of Ireland*, app. E, gives note issues at the end of each quarter; they exceeded the borrowing limit from the end of 1799 and were subsequently below it only for a short period after 1808 when the limit had been raised.
11 31 Geo. III, c. 22 (Ir.), 37 Geo. III, c. 50 (Ir.) and 48 Geo. III, c. 103; see Appendix 1 below for details of the capital increases.
12 Hall, *op. cit.*, app. G, gives the rate of dividend paid each year; it was always above the rate of interest received, and from 1809 to 1839 was held at 10%.
13 Below, pp. 6-7.
14 B. of I. Mins., 27 Aug. 1803, 24 May 1808; C. P. Curran, architectural chapter in Hall, *Bank of Ireland*, pp. 457-68.

As a government-supported institution with statutory privileges the bank inevitably attracted political criticism, mainly for bias against catholics in its staffing and its discount policy. It was an undoubted creation of the protestant ascendancy and the charter required every director to take the oath of allegiance, supremacy and abjuration and to subscribe to a declaration under a penal code act of 1703[15] which no catholic could conscientiously make. Members were normally required to make a similar declaration before exercising their votes, but in their case catholics were allowed instead to take an oath of loyalty under an act of 1774.[16] The charter did not formally debar catholics from becoming directors but these requirements had the same effect while allowing them to be stockholders.

The Catholic Relief Act of 1793 permitted catholics to hold office in any lay body corporate other than Dublin University without having to make any such oath or declaration.[17] The bank was a lay body corporate but legal opinion taken in 1795 and again in 1826 differed as to whether this act overruled the charter.[18] The directors held themselves bound to follow the charter and despite efforts by proprietors, both catholic and protestant, to reopen the question[19] they stuck to this view until the passing of the Catholic Emancipation Act in 1829.[20] It specifically did not exempt catholics from making declarations of this kind but the requirement was tacitly dropped by the court and in 1830 the first catholic director was elected.[21] The anti-popery declaration was not formally abolished until the 1845 Banking Act.[22] In the 1820s a wholly protestant court all of whom had been obliged to make the declaration, were, to say the least, open to suspicion of bias against catholics.

The Government Account and the National Debt

The Bank of Ireland's domination of the monetary scene sprang as much from its functions as government banker as from its constitution. No sooner had the act of 1782 been passed than the Irish House of Commons resolved that all public monies be lodged in the bank,[23] and in June 1783 this was given effect by a government warrant.[24] The bank's links with the Irish government remained close for the rest of the eighteenth century and were only a little loosened by the Union in 1801, a change in the legislature with few immediate administra-

15 2 Anne, c. 6, s. 15 (Ir.).
16 13 & 14 Geo. III, c. 35 (Ir.).
17 33 Geo. III, c. 21, s. 7 (Ir.).
18 B. of I. Mins., 3 Feb. 1795, and *F.J.*, 6 Dec. 1824, 17 June, 10 Nov. 1826, report the conflicting opinions.
19 *F.J.*, 15 Dec. 1825, 20 Mar., 13 Nov., 12 Dec. 1826.
20 10 Geo. IV, c. 7.
21 Hone, in Hall, *Bank of Ireland*, p. 488.
22 8 & 9 Vic., c. 37, s. 7.
23 *Commons' Jn. Ire.*, x, 378-80.
24 B. of I. Mins., 7 June 1783.

tive repercussions. It was not till 1817 that the Irish exchequer was amalgamated with the British and financial dealings with the government became wholly centred on the treasury in London.[25]

The operation of the government account was regulated by an act of 1814[26] which required all revenue payments in Ireland to be made direct to the bank instead of to the teller of the exchequer, and all payments by the exchequer to be by drafts on the bank. Public accountants in Dublin were also required to have accounts with the bank into which all their receipts, including treasury issues, were to be paid and which were to be drawn on only by drafts specifying the service for which the payment was made. The organization of the treasury was further tidied up under an act of 1822;[27] this abolished the offices of auditor-general and clerk of the pells and transferred their duties in part to the vice-treasurer in Dublin and in part to the commissioners for audit in London, but it left the government account still under the control of the teller.

There were three main government accounts, known as the treasury, chancery and exchequer accounts. The last two were for funds held by the courts of chancery and exchequer, while the treasury account was the central account under the control of the teller.[28] A return by the bank of the balances in these three accounts on the first and fifteenth of every month of 1822 shows the treasury account ranging between £60,000 and £428,000 with the two court accounts fairly steady, the chancery at around £200,000 and the exchequer about £45,000.[29] In addition there were a number of public accounts for various official and semi-official purposes, kept by the public accountants referred to in the 1814 act.[30]

The aggregate of the balances in these accounts was the figure of public deposits in the bank. Annual averages of the total of treasury, chancery and exchequer accounts on the one hand and other public monies on the other for the years 1808 to 1836 were supplied to the 1837 committee on joint stock banks.[31] The other public monies varied little from year to year, and during the 1820s normally averaged something over £300,000. The three principal accounts, on the other hand,

25 Below, pp. 27-8.
26 54 Geo. III, c. 83; this gave statutory force to instructions in a treasury minute of 24 Dec. 1813 (B. of I. Mins., 31 Dec. 1813).
27 3 Geo. IV, c. 56; regulations for giving it effect are in treasury minutes of 19 July 1822 and 3 Jan. 1823 (P.R.O., T. 29/211, pp. 479-83; T. 29/217, pp. 31-6).
28 There is a statement of this account for one week in April 1821 in S.P.O., 577/524/1; the debit side has a single daily item of 'sundry drafts', totalling £127,000 during the week, while the credit side has numerous receipts in cash and bills from the customs, excise, Stamp Office and chief justice, and £15,000 from the bank itself as stamp duty for the coming year; the total is about £50,000.
29 *Bank of Ireland accounts 1823*, no. 4, H.C. 1823 (323), xvi, 61.
30 The above return in 1823 details thirty-three such public accounts on 1 Jan. 1819, totalling £160,000, but the 1837 return next referred to speaks of 'about a hundred accounts' and gives a total for 1819 of £339,600.
31 *1837 committee*, app. III-20; the figures quoted here are in Irish currency as in the return, in Appendix 8 below they have been converted to British.

fluctuated considerably, from just under £350,000 in 1820 to nearly £900,000 in 1824. The return for 1822 suggests that these fluctuations were probably in the treasury account. The total of public deposits reached a wartime peak of over £2,000,000 in 1814 and 1815 from which it fell somewhat irregularly to just over £660,000 in 1820 and rose again to over £1,200,000 in 1824.

These figures show the government accounts as much less important statistically in the bank's business than its note issues (normally well over £3,000,000 in the early 1820s; if post bills are included the total ranged between £4,000,000 and £6,500,000 from 1820 to 1825)[32] and rather more than its private deposits (which rose from £520,000 in 1820 to just over £1,000,000 in 1825).[33] But this official connection was of course much more valuable to the bank than these figures suggest. The role of the government accounts in relation to the exchanges is discussed below.[34]

For managing the government accounts the bank received no fee.[35] The profit from the use of the money, plus the annuity on the capital loan, were thought sufficient reward for this and for the management of the Irish national debt.

Up to 1797 Irish government debt was in the form of debentures on which the treasury paid interest on presentation, but an act of that year allowed holders to exchange their debentures for government stock at the same rate of interest, registered at the Bank of Ireland, transferable in its books and with interest paid there.[36] In 1806 the payment of interest on debentures was also transferred to the bank.[37] It is not clear how the bank's fees were calculated but by 1808 it was receiving £8,000 a year. In the negotiations leading to the act of that year the court offered to carry on the management without charge provided the fees as then calculated would not have exceeded £15,000 a year, but as a final concession it had to drop this proviso.[38] The act therefore included a statement that the bank would continue to manage the Irish national debt free of charge.[39]

This transfer of management to the bank has been attributed to the recommendations of the 1804 committee,[40] but this is an error. It had

32 *1837 committee*, app. III-3.
33 *Ibid.*, app. III-21.
34 Below, pp. 46-7.
35 *Bank of Ireland accounts 1823*, no. 6, H.C. 1823 (323), xvi, 61.
36 37 Geo. III, c. 54 (Ir.); B. of I. Mins., 20 Sept.-3 Oct. 1797, deal with the initiation of the new arrangements.
37 B. of I. Mins., 19 May, 9 Sept. 1806; it was arranged the next year that holders resident in Britain could receive their interest in the form of bills on Dublin from the bank's London agents (*ibid.*, 10 Mar. 1807).
38 *Ibid.*, 26 Apr. 1808, reproduces the relevant lettters between the governor and Foster, chancellor of the Irish exchequer. Hall, *Bank of Ireland*, p. 101, states that the bank asked for a fee of £15,000, which is not quite correct.
39 48 Geo. III, c. 103, s. 14.
40 G. O'Brien, 'Last years of the Irish currency', in *Economic History*, ii (1927), pp. 255-6; Hall, *Bank of Ireland*, p. 101.

been largely completed in 1797 and the committee's proposal, incidental to those about the exchanges, was merely that the bank should undertake the transmission of new loans from London to Dublin.[41] This was quite a different matter to the management of the debt which comprised the keeping of registers, registration of transfers and payment of interest—all routine matters, but the court minutes suggest that they took up a surprising amount of the directors' time.

The balance of power and of advantage between bank and government was always a delicate one. The bank depended on the government for its privileged status and the solid reputation that went with it, but at the same time the government depended on the bank for accounting and transfer services, and also for that most pressing need of all governments, ready cash. In addition to the capital loan of £2,350,000 the bank made short-term advances similar, but on a smaller scale, to those made by the Bank of England.

These advances took the form of credits to the treasury account against treasury or exchequer bills issued to the bank. The total fluctuated, particularly with deficiency loans made on three-month bills to cover shortages in the consolidated fund at the end of each quarter; these were made under an act of 1817 which specifically permitted the Bank of England and the Bank of Ireland to take them up.[42] In March 1819 the total on short loan was £2,500,000.[43] By April 1822 it had fallen to £1,200,000,[44] but since the capital loan had been increased by the funding of £500,000 in 1821,[45] the true fall was only £800,000. On the other side of the ledger the average of public deposits (owed by the bank to the government) fell from £920,000 in 1819 to £750,000 in 1822. The reduction in net government indebtedness to the bank was therefore rather less than £800,000, but the figures not being strictly comparable, we cannot say by how much.

The supply of liquid funds to the government had been of exceptional importance during the war and was now being reduced, but it was, and was to remain, an integral part of the Bank of Ireland's business, as it was of the Bank of England's. It was one of the things that gave them their strength since the government's liability to the two banks was the main backing for their liabilities to the public on notes and deposits. The banks were thus the intermediaries through whom the government performed its sovereign function of providing the community with a currency.

41 *1804 committee*, p. 13; below, p. 40.

42 57 Geo. III, c. 48; deficiency loans are referred to in B. of I. Mins., 11 Apr., 26 June, 23 Sept. 1820, 31 Mar. 1821, etc.

43 *1819 committee* (C), app. 28.

44 *Account of the total amount of debt due to the Bank of Ireland 3 April 1822*, H.C. 1822 (210), xviii, 391; of this amount £114,000 was for commercial credit advances—below, pp. 21-3.

45 Below, pp. 62-3.

Cash Payments

The Bank of Ireland in 1820 was still, like the Bank of England, prohibited from paying out specie, that is from performing the promise embodied in its notes, and was relieved of liability for such default. The restriction was imposed on the Bank of England to protect its gold reserves against an internal or an external drain arising from the war.[46] It was accepted as relieving all other banks in England and Scotland of the obligation to pay cash, but in Ireland, with an independent legislature, a separate administration and its own 'National Bank', a distinct act was required. An order in council forbidding the bank to pay cash therefore followed promptly on the English one, and was later confirmed by act of parliament.[47]

The bank was in a perfectly sound state and its directors opposed the restriction but it was needed, as Pelham, the chief secretary, explained to the Irish House of Commons, in order to 'prevent the current gold of the kingdom from being carried out of it by drafts from England'.[48] Anyone who could acquire notes or other claims on the Bank of Ireland could demand gold for them, and if this threatened to exhaust the bank's stocks the government would then have either to stop payment or to allow replenishment from the only possible source, the Bank of England. The act prohibited the bank from paying cash for sums of over 20s, except in particular cases for the armed forces, and it was accepted as relieving other Irish banks of similar obligations. It left the Bank of Ireland's circulation as a free currency unlinked to gold, to Bank of England issues or to anything else.[49] Gold coin passed out of use and strong opposition developed to its reintroduction.[50]

Irish exchanges were virtually all with England, and the lifting of the restriction depended therefore, like its imposition, on conditions in London. There was much discussion on the subject, and in 1810 the bullion committee recommended resumption,[51] but the needs of war prevented action, much of the cost of its later years being met by inflation. In 1817, when the continental exchanges looked favourable, the first moves were made. Three successive orders were made under the restriction acts to authorize payment first of notes under

46 The English restriction was imposed by an order in council which was then confirmed by act of parliament, 37 Geo. III, c. 45.
47 37 Geo. III, c. 51 (Ir.); B. of I. Mins., 2 Mar. 1797, record the actual suspension; Hall, *Bank of Ireland*, pp. 79-82, reproduces some of the principal documents relating to the passing of the act.
48 *Parl. reg. Ire.*, xvii, 405 (6 Mar. 1797); Hall, *op. cit.*, p. 82, misquotes the above statement by reading 'drains' for 'drafts'.
49 F. W. Fetter, *The Irish pound 1797-1826*, pp. 13-5; this short book gives the best account of the Irish currency during the restriction; see also the same author's 'Legal tender during the English and Irish bank restriction', in *Journal of Political Economy*, lviii, no. 3, 241-53.
50 Below, p. 25.
51 *1810 committee*, pp. 30-3.

£5 issued before 1812, then of the same issued before 1816 and finally of all notes issued before 1817. In each case orders for the Bank of Ireland followed those for the Bank of England.[52] Then, early in 1819, the exchanges turned against London, there was a critical drain on the Bank of England and both houses of parliament appointed select committees to look into the problem.[53] Both quickly recommended in interim reports that the restriction be re-imposed temporarily, and this was done for the Bank of Ireland as for the Bank of England.[54]

The final reports of both committees deal exhaustively with the position of the Bank of England but refer only briefly to Ireland. The Commons committee reported that after 'personally examining' the governor they were satisfied that there would be no difficulty about the Bank of Ireland 'carrying into effect any regulations of the same nature with those which may be adopted with respect to the Bank of England'.[55] The governor, Nathaniel Sneyd, was not a witness before the Commons committee but the reference may be to his remark before the Lords, in the course of a brief and not very informative evidence, that the bank 'would endeavour to follow any regulations imposed on the Bank of England'.[56]

For the Bank of England the Resumption of Cash Payments Act, 1819,[57] provided for resumption by stages commencing on 1 February 1820 and concluding on 1 May 1823. For the Bank of Ireland another act[58] made similar provisions but commencing on 5 April 1820 and ending on 1 June 1823. The difference in dates, which was less than the three months prescribed in the restriction act, was designed to give the Bank of Ireland time to build up its gold stocks without unduly disturbing the exchanges—a matter about which the directors had been worried.[59] Initially, like the Bank of England, the Bank of Ireland was required to pay only in gold bars or ingots of sixty ounces, with the rates per ounce reduced from £4 1s 0d (British) between 5 April and 1 November 1820, to £3 19s 6d between 1 November 1820 and 1 June 1821, to £3 17s 10½d (the mint price) between 1 June 1821 and 1 June 1823. After 1 June 1822 the bank might pay coin at its own option and from 1 June 1823 the restriction act was to cease and the contractual obligation to pay all notes in coin would revive.

The ingot scheme derived from Ricardo who envisaged it as a permanency with internal circulation supplied by notes.[60] He died in

52 B. of I. Mins., 24 Dec. 1816, 29 Apr., 16 Dec. 1817, show that all the orders were made on formal requests from the bank.
53 The reports of both committees are in H.C. 1819, iii.
54 59 Geo. III, c. 23 & 24.
55 *1819 committee* (C), p. 18; *1819 committee* (L), p. 19, was even curter.
56 *1819 committee* (L), p. 268.   57 59 Geo. III, c. 49.   58 59 Geo. III, c. 99.
59 B. of I. Mins., 5, 13, 20 July 1819; Fetter, *Irish pound*, pp. 58-9, argues that this fear was groundless and the time lag unreasonable, but in the prevailing uncertainty of the effects of resumption the directors' caution is understandable.
60 D. Ricardo, 'Proposals for an economic and secure currency' in *Works*, ed. P. Sraffa (Cambridge 1951-5), iv, especially pp. 66-7.

1823 bitterly disappointed by the Bank of England's failure to adopt it.[61] Irish developments might have pleased him better.

A favourable turn in the continental exchanges and a consequent flow of gold into the Bank of England made this gradual process superfluous. The Bank of England never cared for the ingot scheme and at its request an act was passed to allow payments in coin from 1 May 1821.[62] The very next act gave the Bank of Ireland the same permission from 1 June 1821.[63] The effect of these acts was to bring forward by a year the dates from which each bank might pay coin at its own option. From 1 May 1823 for the Bank of England and 1 June 1823 for the Bank of Ireland the full obligation to pay coin would still revive under the 1819 acts.

Popular demand for gold was negligible in Ireland but the bank nevertheless took precautions and in September 1819 instructed its London agents, Puget & Bainbridge, to buy £100,000 worth.[64] It held £2,000,000 of treasury bills due on 5 April 1820 which would normally be exchanged for new bills, but in January it gave notice that it would want up to a quarter of them in cash.[65] Vansittart, the chancellor, replied that with the current price of gold he did not expect a heavy demand on the bank and suggested that instead it take English exchequer bills which could be cashed at will.[66] The court agreed and £500,000 of exchequer bills were duly issued.[67] In April an advance of £100,000 to cover the quarter's deficiency was only agreed to on condition that it be repaid in cash in July,[68] and further deficiency advances were made in June and September against exchequer bills on the understanding that the bank could cash them at will.[69]

In the event the resumption passed off with no extra demand for gold. In July 1821 the bank decided to sell all but £5,000 of its £35,432 worth of ingots and in November it disposed of about £1,000,000 of guineas to the Bank of England.[70] By February 1822 when offered the choice of gold or exchequer bills for £1,100,000 of treasury bills due, it chose the bills.[71] Its gold holdings in fact rose from £1,100,000 at the end of 1819 to over £1,700,000 at the end of 1821.[72]

Between 1 February 1819 and 1 April 1820 the bank's circulation

61 R. S. Sayers, 'Ricardo's views on monetary questions' in *Papers in English monetary history*, Ashton and Sayers eds., pp. 76-95.
62 1 & 2 Geo. IV, c. 26; J. H. Clapham, *The Bank of England*, ii, 63-73, describes the resumption from the London point of view.
63 1 & 2 Geo. IV, c. 27.
64 B. of I. Mins., 21 Sept. 1819.
65 *Ibid.*, 4 Jan. 1820.
66 Vansittart to governor, 13 Jan 1820 (B. of I. Mins., 18 Jan. 1820).
67 B. of I. Mins., 1 Feb. 1820.
68 *Ibid.*, 11 Apr., 2, 9 May 1820.
69 *Ibid.*, 26 June, 23 Sept. 1820.
70 *Ibid.*, 19 July, 6 Nov. 1821.
71 *Ibid.*, 19 Feb. 1822.
72 *1837 committee*, app. III-2.

fell by some 21 per cent.[73] There is no direct evidence that this was in deliberate preparation for the resumption but it seems likely. The deflationary effect was noted at the time with some alarm,[74] and at the beginning of May the *Freeman's Journal* commented that 'money has never been more scarce in Dublin than at this moment'[75] which suggests that the fall was not due to any shortage of demand. With the resumption safely accomplished and gold plentiful, circulation rose during the next twelve months to reach the highest level yet in the first quarter of 1821.

The Private Banks

The Bank of Ireland was undisputed cock of the banking walk in 1820, but its failure to move out of Dublin left most of the country dependent for financial services either on private banks or on merchants or bill discounters doing what was essentially banking business. The commodity in which a bank deals is its own credit, the confidence that people have not only in the management's integrity but also in its ability to meet the bank's obligations when due. While this confidence persisted they would accept its notes and deposits as money but if, for any reason, it faltered they would want quickly to change them for some other form of money—and then would occur one of those runs which were a commonplace in the banking history of the eighteenth and early nineteenth centuries. The greater a bank's ability to pay the less likely would such a break in confidence be. The more reserves a bank held the less likely would it be to have to use them; the less it held the more likely it would be to need them.

This paradox of banking was what made the Bank of Ireland's monopoly effective. Its liabilities up to £2,350,000 were backed in the last resort by the government, and beyond that figure by the full personal estates of the holders of its £2,500,000 stock. The liabilities of any other bank in Ireland were, by contrast, backed only by its own resources and the personal property of its partners, limited by law to six. The more readily a bank's resources were available to meet its liabilities the less profitably could they be employed, and the same applied to the property of the partners. The more they put into the bank the greater its prospects of success, but at the same time the more that was tied up in the bank the less there would be to fall back on in case of trouble.

Two other restrictions were placed on private banks by an act of the

---

73 *1837 committee*, app. III-3, gives circulation on the first and fifteenth of every month 1808-36; during 1818 the total of notes and post bills was normally over £4,400,000 and rose to the highest figure yet recorded, £4,560,000, on 1 Feb. 1819, from which it fell to £3,600,000 on 1 Apr. 1820, then rose to nearly £5,340,000 on 15 Mar. 1821.

74 *F.J.*, 19 Apr. 1820.

75 *F.J.*, 3 May 1820.

Irish parliament of 1756.[76] Section 1 required the names of all partners to be stated on all notes and receipts—a small point but a troublesome one especially when partners changed. Section 2, a more substantial restriction, declared that no person or persons carrying on business as bankers might 'trade or traffick as merchants in goods or merchandises imported or exported'. Any sizeable merchant business in 1820, as in 1756, would include either imports or exports, and a banker was thus debarred from having any of his wealth so employed. The intention was to prevent the abuse of banking facilities in the merchant interest of the partners but the effect was to cut banks off from their most likely supporters. The ban even applied to sleeping partners, for the act of 1782[77] which gave them legal recognition specifically excluded bankers from its benefits. The trader-banker, familiar to English and Scottish banking, was thus denied legal existence in Ireland after 1756 unless he confined his trade to the limited domestic sphere.

When all went well private banks provided useful currency and financial services for their clients as well as profits for the partners but if any doubts arose, real or imaginary, they were wide open to catastrophe. A bank's liquid resources were, in the nature of its business, always less than its demand liabilities. They would consist primarily of coin and Bank of Ireland notes, followed in order of liquidity by bills of exchange and debts due to the bank of varying soundness and maturity dates, with the personal property of the partners as a last reserve. When a run started the readily available funds would be quickly exhausted and, unless the bank could replenish them by selling other assets or by borrowing in some form, its only recourse was to stop payment.

Once a bank had stopped the creditors might take action under one of two acts, the Irish Bankers' Act, 1760,[78] or the Bankruptcy Act, 1772.[79] Before 1760 there was no bankruptcy law in Ireland and when a bank failed it was usual to pass a special act for the relief of its creditors. The Irish Bankers' Act removed the need for this by providing that when any banker died, absconded or stopped payment, the creditors might appoint trustees, subject to approval by the court, to administer his property. The 1772 act, on the other hand, was of general application and provided that when anyone had committed an act of bankruptcy, any creditor might petition the lord chancellor to appoint a commissioner to examine him, arrange his affairs and hand over his property to trustees to administer. The creditors could then

76 29 Geo. II, c. 16 (Ir.); it is sometimes dated 1755, since it is included in the printed statutes of that year, but it received the royal assent in 1756.
77 21 & 22 Geo. III, c. 46 (Ir.).
78 33 Geo. II, c. 14 (Ir.); it received the royal assent in 1760 but is printed in the statutes of 1759 and is therefore sometimes dated, incorrectly, to that year.
79 11 & 12 Geo. III, c. 8 (Ir.).

only proceed under the 1760 act if the court agreed to supersede the commission.[80]

The Bankers' Act procedure was normally preferred as simpler, quicker and cheaper, but there was not much to choose. Pierce Mahony, a leading Dublin solicitor, stated in evidence in 1826 that he had scarcely known a case of winding up under the Bankers' Act to have been completed without the intervention of the court of chancery; in the case of the Cork bank of Cotter & Kellett, which failed in 1809 with reputed assets of 40s in the £, the winding up was still not completed in 1826, and owing to ruinous legal expenses—at one hearing he had seen no less than eighteen counsel—the total dividend was unlikely to exceed 10s.[81] Many similiar cases could be cited under both procedures.

One provision of the 1760 act which touched the daily business of banking was a prohibition, in section 4, on any banker giving 'any note, negotiable receipt or accountable receipt with any promise or engagement therein contained for the payment of any interest '. No penalty was prescribed but such notes or receipts would be null and void. Opinion differed as to whether this made it illegal to pay interest on deposits,[82] but evidence in 1823 suggests that it did in fact impede the flow of surplus funds into the banks.[83] Nothing comparable existed in English law, nor in Scotland where the payment of interest on deposits had been pioneered by the Bank of Scotland as early as 1729.[84]

The 1760 act also included an intriguing disqualification, in section 15, on anyone in charge of public money from being a partner in a bank—an evident fall-out from the affair of Malone's bank launched in 1758 with the chancellor and teller of the exchequer as partners which failed after four months.[85] The ban was not repealed until 1845.[86]

Private banks might be brought to ruin either by deflationary pressure beyond their control or by their own mismanagement or misfortune. They could always protect themselves by restricting their liabilities, in other words their business, but this would reduce their chances of profit and their usefulness to the community. One form of restriction was to refrain from issuing notes. This was the policy followed by La Touche's after 1797 since David La Touche held that

80 The decision in the case of Ffrench's bank (*F.J.*, 7 Sept. 1814) shows that such an order of supersession was almost unobtainable.
81 *1826 committee (C)*, p. 258; E. O'Kelly, *The old private banks and bankers of Munster*, pp. 55-61.
82 Below, p. 35.
83 *1823 committee*, p. 167, evidence of James Roche, a former banker of Cork.
84 W. Graham, *The one pound note in the history of banking of Great Britain*, pp. 62-4.
85 J. Busteed, 'Irish private banks', in *Cork Hist. Soc. Jn.*, liii, 38; a special act, 33 Geo II, c. 4 (Ir.), was passed to facilitate the winding up; its preamble gives the main facts about the bank.
86 8 & 9 Vic., c. 37, s. 5.

'a banker should never issue a note to bearer that he could not pay in gold'.[87] With a wealthy landed clientele and little commercial business La Touche's could afford such self-denial, but it would have gone hard for any banker in Cork or Limerick or Belfast who did the same. Wherever Bank of Ireland notes were not readily available the chief service which the public required and were prepared to pay for from banks was the supply of a currency in the form of their notes. The Bank of Ireland's monopoly and its immobility in Dublin meant that this service could only be supplied by private banks. To supply it they must be ready to take risks, to exploit their own credit and to face ruin and abuse if they failed.

When cash payments were suspended in 1797 there were four private banks in Dublin, three in Cork, one each in Limerick, Clonmel and Waterford,[88] and a small one in Belfast.[89] The Restriction Act did not properly apply to private banks but the obligation to pay their notes in gold was in practice replaced by one to pay in Bank of Ireland notes. This made running a bank a little easier and as wartime inflation gathered way there were many new formations. The number of banks paying stamp duty on their notes was eleven in 1799 but had risen to forty-one by 1803.[90] From then onward the best information is in the annual lists published in *Watson's Almanack*. These are not always reliable but they show the total fluctuating around forty for the next ten years and then steadily declining with the return of peace. By the beginning of 1820 those that remained were in three distinct groups— six in Dublin, four in the north and about fourteen in the south. Such information as is available about them is summarized in Appendix 2 below, arranged geographically.

The Dublin banks, living in the shadow of the Bank of Ireland, at once competitor, policeman and support in time of trouble, were in a class by themselves. Dublin no longer housed the money-spinning activities of a resident parliament but it was still the administrative capital of Ireland, the chief port and centre of communication.[91] Its population in 1821 was 184,000 compared to 101,000 in Cork, 59,000 in Limerick and 37,000 in Belfast. With the essential circulation supplied by the Bank of Ireland,[92] the business of the private banks centred chiefly on account keeping and exchange dealing.[93] Of the

---

87 *1826 committee* (L), p. 63, evidence of Peter La Touche, son of David La Touche.
88 *Ibid*, p. 52, evidence of Roche; he gave the Dublin figure incorrectly as three.
89 *Ibid.*, p. 26, evidence of John Houston, nephew of one of the partners.
90 *1804 committee*, apps. D to H.
91 Coal imports to Dublin in 1821 exceeded those of the next five ports together (*Return of coals imported into the different ports of Ireland 1821*, H.C. 1822 (48), xviii, 481).
92 *1826 committee* (L), pp. 59-60, evidence of Joseph Robinson Pim, a Dublin cotton merchant and manufacturer.
93 L. M. Cullen, *Anglo-Irish trade*, pp. 155-205, discusses this business in the eighteenth century.

three oldest banks La Touche's and Newcomen's had given up issuing notes of their own and Finlay's was about to. The other three, Ball's, Shaw's and Alexander's, on the other hand, all had considerable issues and their notes circulated widely outside Dublin, especially in the north.

Dublin had a tradition of banking going right back through the eighteenth century, but the same was not true of the north where the only banks on record before 1797 were two or three small firms in Belfast the last of which closed in 1798.[94] Gold, which went out of circulation in the rest of Ireland soon after the suspension of cash payments, continued in use in the north for some time thanks to the insistence of landlords on it for rent. This caused a divergence between the Dublin/London and the Belfast/London exchange rates which figures prominently in the inquiries of the 1804 committee on the Irish currency.[95] But when in 1808-9 three new banks were founded in Belfast, Gordon's, Montgomery's and Tennent's, their notes quickly ousted gold as the general currency.[96]

Outside Belfast there were seven banks founded in different Ulster towns during the restriction period but the only survivor in 1820 was Malcolmson's in Lurgan. This lack of banks was however made good by the spread of agencies of the three Belfast banks. Pierce Mahony gave the 1826 committee a list of banks operating in Ireland before the opening of the Provincial (in 1825) which included eleven agencies of Montgomery's, nine of Batt's (the name of Gordon's since 1824) and ten of Tennent's, all in Ulster towns except for one agency of Batt's just outside the province in Dundalk. Altogether he showed sixteen Ulster towns with one agency or more.[97] These figures cannot be taken as precise and they refer to agencies not full branches, but it is clear that Ulster, particularly its north-eastern half, enjoyed a better banking network in the early 1820s than any other part of Ireland outside Dublin.

The growth of Belfast as an industrial city had barely begun in 1820. Its population, less than Cork and Limerick, was only a little more than Waterford and Galway. The cotton industry which had brought factory methods to the area at the end of the previous century was still important but soon to decline in the face of English competition with the removal of the temporary Union duties after 1824.[98] The linen industry was mainly domestic, linked to agriculture, with two-thirds of its cloth produced by local craftsmen and manufacturers and sold in local markets.[99] Shipbuilding was not to become a major

94 *1826 committee* (*C*), p. 103, evidence of Houston.
95 Fetter, *Irish pound*, p. 45.
96 Below, p. 25.
97 *1826 committee* (*C*), p. 252.
98 J. J. Monaghan, 'The rise and fall of the Belfast cotton industry', in *I.H.S.*, iii (1942-3), 1-17.
99 C. Gill, *The rise of the Irish linen industry*, p. 272.

industry until after 1851,[100] while growth of the port did not really begin until 1837.[101] Development of the town centre was a little nearer; it dates from 1822 when the Donegall family, to relieve the financial embarrassments of the second marquis, offered long leases on payment of a fine, many of which were taken up between 1822 and 1831, giving business tenants security of tenure.[102]

Belfast was nevertheless the centre of a manufacturing region unlike any other in Ireland. This was of great importance for the banks. Gill, the historian of the linen industry, writes of the Lisburn bleaching firm J. & J. Richardson and its bankers, Montgomery's, that 'it is to the growth of sound banking and an organised money market that we must look for the main underlying cause of the increased exports from Belfast'.[103] But the converse is equally true. Richardsons bought brown linen in the markets, bleached and finished it and exported direct to customers in England who paid them with bills on London which they discounted at Montgomery's.[104] Payments by the firm were made either in Montgomery's notes or by drafts on the bank (i.e., cheques). The bank provided Richardsons with the vital services of credit, transfer and note issues, and received in return a steady flow of good self-liquidating bills which it collected when due. Against these it both met the firm's cheques and issued notes which were then spread around the province, chiefly through the markets.

There must have been similar links between all three Belfast banks and other firms in both the linen and the cotton industries. This industrial connection was what distinguished banking in the north in 1820 from that in the rest of provincial Ireland.

In the south the position was quite different. Industry, mainly brewing, distilling, flour milling, bacon curing and textiles, did exist but on a small scale, and essentially the banks depended on commerce and agriculture. Some seventy banks are recorded at different times during the restriction period in towns of Leinster, Munster and Connacht, but by the beginning of 1820 there were no survivors outside Dublin north of Limerick and Kilkenny, nor any in the extreme south-west. In the rest of the south—roughly from Cork and Limerick to the east coast—there appear to have been fourteen open at the beginning of the year.

Cork, still the second city of Ireland, had some industry—Beamish & Crawford's brewery for instance had greater production than Guinness's until the 1830s[105]—but its main activity was commercial.

100 D. Rebbeck, 'History of iron shipbuilding on the Queen's Island up till 1874', (Ph.D. thesis, Queen's University, Belfast).
101 E. Jones, *A social geography of Belfast,* p. 43.
102 *Ibid.,* p. 50.
103 Gill, *op. cit.,* pp. 254-5.
104 The normal terms were two months' credit, then a bill at sixty-one days, known as 'two and two months'—the same as in the cotton trade.
105 P. Lynch and J. Vaizey, *Guinness's Brewery in the Irish economy,* p. 90.

It was the main centre of the produce export trade to England, the West Indies and the continent,[106] a business that had been augmented during the war by the victualling of naval vessels with beef and butter. With the coming of peace beef exports had declined but those of butter continued to increase.[107] This trade provided the banks in Cork, and indeed all over the south, with the bulk of their business.

Some eight banks are recorded in Cork during the eighteenth century, most of them from the 1760s onwards, and another two appeared in the opening years of the nineteenth,[108] but only three, Pike's, Leslies' and Roches', and a possible fourth, Newenham's, were still in existence in 1820.

Limerick, also a centre of the produce trade,[109] had three banks at the beginning of the year, Maunsell's, Roches' and Bruce's, but in addition it had many attorneys, shipping agents and insurance agents who discounted bills and exchanged notes on commission.[110] Such people on the fringes of banking, not only in Limerick but all over the country, are a common cause of confusion. They issued no notes of their own and so were not obliged to register—and so simplify the task of later historians—yet before the emergence of a full network of banks they undoubtedly played an important role in easing the flow of money, if not necessarily in increasing its stock.[111]

On the road south from Limerick to Cork the small market town of Charleville had a branch of Bruce's and the popular watering place of Mallow was the home of Delacour's, destined to be the last private bank outside Dublin. Spread out from here to the east coast were the other seven banks—Scully's in Tipperary, Riall's in Clonmel, Sausse's in Carrick-on-Suir, Newport's and Scott's in Waterford, Loughnan's in Kilkenny and Redmond's in Wexford.

At the beginning of 1820 the country outside Dublin and the north-east depended for its banking services either on postal communication with Dublin or on these fourteen banks (fifteen if Bruce's is reckoned as two). In the early summer of that year just half of them were to go under.

The Crisis of 1820

The crisis of May-June 1820 marked the beginning of the end of private banks in the south of Ireland, but it was not quite the hurricane sweeping all before it that has often been depicted. It was sparked off

106 J. O'Donovan, *Economic history of livestock in Ireland*, pp. 148-56.
107 A. Marmion, *Ancient and modern history of the maritime ports of Ireland*. p. 536; *Account of the quantity of butter exported from each port in Ireland 1806-23*, H.C. 1826 (338), xxiii, 291.
108 O'Kelly, *Munster banks*, pp. 30-97, gives a good account of these banks.
109 Marmion, *op. cit.*, pp. 492-3.
110 O'Kelly, *op. cit.*, p. 98.
111 Below, p. 37.

B

by the closure of Roches' in Cork on Thursday 25 May, followed at once by Leslies'. On Saturday, when the news had reached Limerick, Maunsell's announced that they would not open on the Monday, and on that day Bruce's also closed in Limerick and Charleville. Pike's in Cork and Roches' in Limerick both kept open, as did Delacour's and Scully's in Mallow and Tipperary. By the end of the week the pressure had spread eastwards and on Saturday 3 June Loughnan's closed in Kilkenny. During the next week Newport's closed in Waterford on Wednesday and Riall's in Clonmel on Thursday. This left Scott's in Waterford and Redmond's in Wexford still open in the southeast, and possibly Sausse's in Carrick-on-Suir.[112]

In just two weeks seven out of the fourteen banks in the south had folded up, including some of the oldest and most respected like Maunsell's and Newport's, and confidence in those that remained was severely shaken. A contemporary letter from Cork described business being at a standstill with daily bankruptcies, while 'those who have property cannot get forward for want of money', and went on that all credit was at an end and 'even Pike's notes remain but a few days out when again exchanged for national paper'.[113] The seven survivors were joined by Newenham's later in 1820 and by the reopened Leslies' in 1822, but all were soon to close—Sausse's and Newenham's in 1824, Roches' and Scott's in 1825, Pike's and Leslies' in 1826, Scully's probably in 1827, Redmond's in 1829 and finally Delacour's in 1835. As Sir John Newport put it in 1826, the issue of paper in general circulation had 'ceased to be an object with men who had any real or personal property to rely on'.[114] Without such support there was no foundation on which small banks could establish their credit.

In the rest of the country the effects of the crisis were surprisingly slight. The principal business of banks in the south was discounting for the produce trade by the issue of their own notes, and this led to trouble when prices fell. In Dublin business was spread more widely, with note issues of less importance, and when banks ran into difficulties they could apply for, and normally receive, help from the Bank of Ireland. The only failure there was Alexander's on 12 June, the Monday after the last closures in the south.[115]

This led to a brief run on the other banks but with Bank of Ireland support they all survived.[116] On the twelfth Shaw's asked the bank

---

112 This summary is based on reports in the *Freeman's Journal* and *Saunders' Newsletter* comprising extracts from papers in the towns concerned; other contemporary accounts are in the *Annual Register* 1820, p. 221, in W. Urwicke, *Biographical sketches of James D.La Touche*, p. 266, and *1823 committee*, p. 162, evidence of Roche. See Appendix 2 below for further details.

113 O'Kelly, *Munster banks*, pp. 27-8, quoting from Crofton Croker correspondence.

114 *1826 committee (L)*, p. 44.

115 *F.J.* and *Saunders' Newsletter*, 13 June 1820, report this failure in one and three lines of small print respectively.

116 The following details are from B. of I. Mins., 31 May-16 June 1820.

for £20,000 on discount and £11,000 against government stock, with facilities to discount another £30,000 during the week if needed. They had last been helped in 1814, during the pressure following the suspension of Ffrench's bank in Tuam and Dublin, and had then promised that they would never make such a request again.[117] The court now expressed 'unqualified disapprobation of the conduct which had led to an infringement of their pledge', but agreed to help after a solemn assurance that this would enable the firm to meet all demands. The total paid to Shaw's on 12 and 13 June seems to have been £52,000. Ball's, who had given a similar pledge in 1814, were allowed £40,000 on the twelfth on the same condition.

On the thirteenth La Touche's, who had given no such pledge, were granted £29,000 on discount and £50,000 against government stock but were evidently refused anything against £8,500 of wide streets debentures. On the fourteenth they were allowed another £12,347 on discount and on the sixteenth £6,600, making a total of almost £98,000 over the four days. On the thirteenth Finlay's were allowed discounts of £70,243 and a loan of £43,800 against stock, and New-comen's were granted £12,000 by discount.

All the Dublin banks therefore were supported by the Bank of Ireland during this week with the exception of Alexander's who seem to have gone under without a cry. It must remain an open question whether any of the southern failures might have been averted by prompt access to similar support. On 31 May Joshua & Joseph Pim, Dublin agents for Newport's and Riall's, told the Bank of Ireland that they had given all the help to the two banks that they could from their own resources but they still needed more. They had credits in London but in the state of public alarm could not make immediate use of them by passing bills on the exchange. The bank agreed to take £40,000 of bills on London from them and lend a further £15,000 against government stock.[118] This help was either too little or too late for a week later the two banks closed.

On 2 June a somewhat similar request came from the Dublin firm of Gibbons & Williams. Two gentlemen from the Charleville bank had given them £4,000 of government stock for sale to raise cash to pay off its notes. Pending completion of the sale the Bank of Ireland agreed to discount their note for £4,000 at ten days. Bruce's of Charleville had already closed on 29 May so this help was merely to facilitate the liquidation.

On 16 June a loan of £11,900 on collateral security was granted

117 B. of I. Mins., 28-30 June 1814.
118 Hall, *Bank of Ireland*, p. 131, has an account of the bank's operations in this crisis which includes a number of errors; in particular the date of this application is given as 13 May instead of 31 May and the help to Bruce's as 'two weeks later', i.e., about the twenty-seventh, which puts the loan to Newport's and Riall's two weeks before the crisis instead of right in the middle, and that to Bruce's as just before its closure instead of a few days after it.

by the bank to Power & Redmond 'for the Wexford bank'. This firm were corn factors in Dublin,[119] evidently Redmond's agents, probably family connections. By that date the crisis had passed but the loan may have been what enabled Redmond's to get business going again.

These three cases seem to have been the only help given to southern banks and only the first can be called support in fighting the pressure. But a press report at the beginning of June stated that £100,000 had been transmitted by the Bank of Ireland to aid bona fide transactions of merchants in the south,[120] and more than one witness in 1826 spoke of such help.[121] The bank court's minutes make no reference to it but a letter from the lord lieutenant to the chancellor, written after consulting the governors, speaks of large quantities of small notes sent to the south and describes the bank's advances as 'nearly equal to the amount of the circulating medium that had been withdrawn '.[122] His precise meaning is not clear—possibly was not even to himself. The banks that failed in the south had some £636,000 in circulation plus some £540,000 of deposits.[123] Additional issues by the Bank of Ireland even approaching the value of the notes could never have been made without discussion in the court. The total help to southern banks referred to above was only £70,000, the total to all banks (mainly in Dublin with little business in the south) some £420,000. The bank's support for the system in Dublin was considerable and effective but its help to the south seems to have been much less than the government was led to believe.

In the north the effects were even less than in Dublin. The linen industry gave the northern banks a more stable source of business than the produce trade gave their fellows in the south, and there seems to have been no general pressure.[124] Alexander's connections were chiefly in the north and after its failure a writer in the *Annual Register* commented bleakly that there had been no crash there yet 'but you may well conceive what is now to be expected'.[125] The same writer put Alexander's outstanding notes at £500,000, an oft-quoted figure that is just four times too high; he was equally astray in his fears about the north.

On 16 June a manifesto by 271 landowners, merchants, traders and others expressed confidence in the three Belfast banks and pledged the signatories to accept their notes on all occasions; it was reissued on 20 June with fifty-three more signatures and on 23 June with

119 *Wilson's Dublin Directory 1820*, p. 124; they were at 127 Townsend Street.
120 *F.J.*, 6 June 1820.
121 *1826 committee* (*C*), p. 74, evidence of Hunt of Waterford; *ibid.* (*L*), p. 41, of Callaghan of Cork.
122 Talbot to Vansittart, 19 June 1820 (B.M., Add. MSS 31232).
123 Below, pp. 33, 35.
124 *1826 committee* (*C*), p. 78, evidence of John Acheson Smyth, agent in Londonderry for the Belfast Bank; *ibid.* (*L*), p. 13, of Leonard Dobbin, agent in Armagh for the Northern; *F.J.*, 20 June 1820.
125 *Annual Register 1820*, p. 230.

another three.[126] On 15 and 16 June the Bank of Ireland allowed Montgomery's £14,000 on discount and £21,000 on collateral security,[127] so there evidently was some pressure, but the underlying position must have been sound since this help proved effective. Malcolmson's in Lurgan stood firm during the crisis[128] but closed later in the year.

The collapse of the banking system in the south was the kind of thing that, even under the prevailing orthodoxy of *laissez-faire,* was held to warrant government intervention. Immediately after the closure of Roches' and Leslies' a memorial to the lord lieutenant was drawn up by 'the merchants, manufacturers, traders and country gentlemen of Cork'. It stated the notes of the two banks outstanding to be about £350,000, comprising some four-fifths of the circulating medium of Cork, Kerry and parts of adjacent counties, and went on,

> That, in consequence, all confidence, as well as trade, is suspended, there not being a sufficient currency to represent property in its transfer—that the manufacturers, and other employers of the industrious population, are obliged to dismiss their workmen, that the merchants, unable to dispose of imported goods, cannot purchase the produce of the country brought to market, and the people are deprived of the means of paying the king's duties, rates and taxes.

His excellency was begged to intervene with the Bank of Ireland to grant loans on good security so as to 'reanimate industry, restore confidence and sustain credit'.[129]

This memorial, with its concise exposition of the influence of monetary conditions on economic activity—and on government revenue—was handed in at Dublin Castle by a deputation of Cork merchants on 1 June. It had to be forwarded to the chief secretary, in London for the session of parliament, but after only a week's delay some interim help was approved from the remains of funds voted for relief in 1817. A new act was then put through which authorized advances to a total of £500,000,[130] the figure inserted by the Commons in place of the £300,000 proposed by the government. Commissioners would receive applications from 'merchants, traders and manufacturers in Ireland' and make advances to those approved at 6 per cent[131] either with sureties or on good security.

126 Quoted in E. D. Hill (ed.), *Northern Banking Company centenary volume*, p. 14.
127 B. of I. Mins., 15, 16 June 1820.
128 *1826 committee* (*L*), p. 25, evidence of John Houston.
129 O'Kelly, *Munster banks*, pp. 158-60, gives the full text of this memorial and related correspondence.
130 1 Geo. IV, c. 39; this was modelled on the act of 1817 (57 Geo. III, c. 34) under which the interim aid was granted.
131 5% of this was to be passed on to the treasury and 1% retained by the commissioners to cover expenses, any balance left being paid in at the close of operations.

Two amending acts were passed during 1822, the first in May to allow repayment by instalments up to 1830,[132] the second in August to reduce the rate of interest to 5 per cent and to allow further time for payment.[133] By the middle of 1823 conditions were thought to have improved sufficiently to bring the scheme to an end,[134] and an act was passed to prohibit further loans after the end of July.[135] The total advanced had been £286,750 Irish (£264,962 British);[136] the £300,000 would therefore have been enough but the extra sum authorized may well have helped to restore confidence. Of the balance left £100,000 was set aside by the 1823 act for assistance to public works and fisheries.

The loans ranged, in Irish currency, from £300 to £80,000. Forty-seven were granted totalling £286,750. By 1838 all but £37,583 had been repaid, and of this sum over £20,000 was on one loan of £30,000 to Nowlan Shaw & Co., woollen manufacturers in Co. Kilkenny, which had been granted by the commissioners with extreme reluctance; they doubted the firm's solvency, its prospective profitability and the soundness of its sureties, and only approved the loan on a peremptory directive from the chief secretary.[137] The event proved their doubts only too well founded; almost the only sums recovered were by sale of the goods deposited as part security, while all but two of the twelve sureties who guaranteed the rest were, by 1838, either untraceable, insolvent or dead leaving no property.

Loans to bankers who had recently stopped payment were frowned on at first as objectionable in principle and of doubtful security,[138] but in January 1821 this opinion was reversed and three

---

132 3 Geo. IV, c. 22.

133 3 Geo. IV, c. 118.

134 Chief secretary to loan commissioners, 28 May 1823 (S.P.O., Abstract of outgoing correspondence, chief secretary's office).

135 4 Geo. IV, c. 42.

136 Two returns were made to parliament; the first (H.C. 1823 (415), xvi, 81), just before the passing of the 1823 act, listed the names of the recipients, the sums lent and the state of repayment; the second (H.C. 1837-8 (723), xlvi, 407) in 1838 has the same list plus the loan to Riall's (see below) and the state of repayment then, with the names and addresses of sureties of loans still overdue.

137 *Letter . . . respecting a loan to Nowlan Shaw & Co. in 1821*, H.C. 1823 (414), xvi, 69; to qualify for the loan the firm had to clear its debts with the Bank of Ireland, paying off £3,500 of short bills and arranging for £10,000 of long to be taken over by the endorsers (B. of I. Mins., 31 Oct. 1820). *F.J.*, 3 Jan. 1817, has an account of the philanthropic purposes of this firm; see also W. J. Pilsworth, 'The merino factory', in *Old Kilkenny Review*, no. 2 (January 1949).

138 Vansittart to Talbot, 2 Aug. 1820 (B.M., Add. MSS 31232) gives this opinion after consultation with Liverpool, the prime minister. The chief secretary repeats it in a letter to the commissioners of 8 Aug. 1820, but in another of 12 Jan. 1821 he tells them to carry on as though no such communication had been received (S.P.O., abstract of outgoing correspondence, chief secretary's office). A later judgement in Leslies' case (O'Kelly, *Munster banks,* p. 146 n. 25) held such loans to be within the 1820 act; the second act of 1822 added bankers to the list of persons to whom loans might be made, but by that date this loan had already been granted.

such loans were made—£80,000 to Leslies', £33,000 to Riall's and £20,000 to Sausse's.[139] Between them they made up nearly half the total; apart from the Nowlan Shaw loan the next largest was £13,000 and there were only four others over £5,000. The loan to Leslies' enabled them to reopen but only for four years, and when they closed in 1826 the repayment of £50,000 still due, for which the commissioners successfully claimed priority as a debt to the crown, left little for the other creditors.[140] Riall's, on the other hand, were able to pay their creditors in full and repaid the loan from the subsequent sale of property, Sausse's were also enabled to repay their creditors but by 1838 only half of their loan had been repaid; the commissioners were satisfied with the security they held for the rest, so it may well have been paid in the end.[141]

The recipients of the remaining forty-four loans, totalling just over £150,000, were presumably merchants and manufacturers, but information on their occupations is incomplete, as it is also on their places of business. The purpose of the act was to relieve distress in the south but loans were allowed to any part of Ireland and the first approved was £13,000 to a merchant firm in Dublin. Possibly they traded in the south, but it is hard to believe the same of other recipients in Belfast and Londonderry. As far as can be judged from the records most of the loans did however go to the south,[142] but the difficulty was to find suitable applicants. The Nowlan Shaw case indicates what could happen when standards were relaxed to encourage enterprise.

The purchasing power injected by these loans may have done something to revive commercial life in a community which had suddenly lost half its banks, but they were no substitute for a reconstruction of the banking system—a subject to which we will return in Chapter 3.

139 Hall, *Bank of Ireland*, p. 133, states that Leslies' were the only bank to be helped, an error evidently due to consulting only the 1823 return which omits Riall's loan and spells Sausse as Sause.
140 O'Kelly, *Munster banks*, p. 28; below, Appendix 2.
141 Treasury to chief secretary, 13 Apr. 1836 (P.R.O., T. 14/26, p. 230). *Saunders' Newsletter*, 11 Oct. 1839, has a notice of sale of estates near Carrick-on-Suir in the case of John Galloway (secretary to the loan commissioners) v Richard Sausse and others.
142 Sundry letters from the chief secretary to the loan commissioners, 10 June 1820-8 Mar. 1826 (S.P.O., Abstract of outgoing correspondence, chief secretary's office) approving loans, some of which give occupations and addresses of the recipients; the above comments rely on this information and such details as there are in the returns to parliament.

2

The Monetary System

The Currency and Coinage

The unit of account in use in Ireland in 1820 was the Irish pound, a notional standard which had arisen out of the monetary disorder at the close of the seventeenth century. A proclamation of 1701 fixed the English shilling at 1s 1d Irish and another of 1737 fixed the English guinea on the same basis at 22s 9d. This rate of 12 English to 13 Irish still prevailed as the par of exchange in Dublin; £100 English (or British as it was more commonly called by 1820) exchanged for £108 6s 8d Irish and the exchanges were said to be at par when the rate, quoted as the surplus per cent of Irish currency exchanged for British, was $8\frac{1}{3}$.[1]

Despite this 'Irish currency' the lawful coinage was the same gold coin as in Britain—guineas worth 22s 9d Irish and sovereigns (first minted in 1817) worth 21s 8d.[2] Gold had however passed out of circulation over most of the country after the suspension of cash payments in 1797. In the north it continued in use thanks to the insistence of landlords that rents be paid in it, but when the banks were founded in Belfast in 1808-9 it was soon replaced there too by notes.[3] By the 1820s there was some demand from emigrants and an unknown quantity was hoarded but there was virtually none in general use.[4]

Though not in circulation gold retained its importance in bank reserves, partly for psychological reasons, partly from uncertainty as to when payments might be resumed. The Bank of Ireland held some £1,000,000 of specie, predominantly gold.[5] Private banks held some but there is no means of knowing how much; even when a bank failed the figure of its assets normally lumped coin and notes together in one total of cash on hand.[6] During the restriction their own notes were in

1 Fetter, *Irish pound*, pp. 9-10; Cullen, *Anglo-Irish trade*, pp. 155-8.
2 B. of I. Mins., 14 Oct. 1817, record the appearance of sovereigns in Ireland; a proclamation of 20 Nov. 1820 fixed their value, and that of half-sovereigns, crowns and half-crowns, in Irish currency (*Dublin Gaz. 1820*, p. 1295).
3 *1810 committee*, p. 134, evidence of Wakefield; *1826 committee* (*C*), pp. 76, 103, 243, evidence of Smyth of Londonderry, Houston of Belfast and Dobbin of Armagh. See also Fetter, 'Legal tender during the English and Irish bank restriction', in *Journal of Political Economy*, lviii, no. 3, pp. 248-50.
4 *1826 committees, passim*; nearly all the Irish witnesses, drawn from all parts of the country, gave evidence to this effect.
5 See Appendix 6 below.
6 A rare exception was Newcomen's who held £1,400 of specie compared to £37,000 in bank notes when they closed in 1825 (*F.J.*, 25 Jan. 1825); Pike's in 1826 held 'a few thousands' of gold (*1826 committee* (*C*), pp. 264-5, evidence of John Cotter).

practice payable in Bank of Ireland notes and often stated so on their face,[7] for it was notes that everyone wanted not guineas or sovereigns.

If gold coin did not circulate silver and copper certainly did. With wages normally under 1s per day, and market purchases on a corresponding scale, they were the most familiar form of money to the bulk of the population.[8] During the restriction period they had been a continual problem.[9]

Since 1804 the principal silver had been tokens issued by the Bank of Ireland for the treasury, in values of 6s, 30d, 10d and 5d Irish.[10] Something over £1,300,000 worth had been minted of which about half were thought still to be in circulation in 1823.[11] Tokens were receivable in payment of revenue, and from the date of the ending of the restriction the bank was authorized to charge any received to the government account.[12]

This last provision was not mandatory but it was treated as meaning that the tokens were not to be reissued. Consequently during 1824-5 they were all replaced by new British silver coin. This coin was supplied by the treasury to the Bank of Ireland who at first paid it out only in normal transactions, leaving the tokens to come in through the revenue collectors. During 1824 this process was speeded up,[13] and in July 1825 an act was passed to demonetize the tokens from 6 January 1826;[14] they were no longer to circulate or be received for revenue and the bank was relieved of any liability under them. The final exchange was arranged by the government in the closing months of 1825 at centres all over the country.[15] From then on silver in Ireland meant the standard coin of the United Kingdom—crowns, half-crowns, shillings and sixpences. In May 1826 its circulation was described as very satisfactory.[16]

Copper pennies and halfpennies in Irish currency were in circulation

---

7 *1804 committee*, pp. 93-4, evidence of Beresford; *1810 committee*, p. 133, of Wakefield. The wording of surviving notes confirms this.

8 *1823 committee*, pp. 65, 117, 119, 140, 150; wages as low as 4d or even 2d were quoted from Connacht and west Munster but rose to 1s in towns like Carlow for superior types of labour; estate accounts show similar ranges.

9 *1804 committee*, pp. 16-8, discusses this problem; *1810 committee*, pp. 134-7, has a summary of money then in use submitted by Wakefield.

10 B. of I. Mins., 16, 17 Jan. 1804, 15 Feb.-11 June 1805, deal with the original issue; 7 May 1813 with a further coinage in 1813; their forgery was made a felony by 44 Geo. III, c. 71 and 45 Geo. III, c. 42. Tokens had also been issued by private firms but were prohibited by an act of 1812 (52 Geo. III, c. 157).

11 Treasury to Bank of Ireland, 17 May 1823 (B. of I. Mins., 22 May 1823).

12 45 Geo. III, c. 42, s. 4.

13 Treasury to Bank of Ireland, 29 Apr. 1824 (P.R.O., T. 14/23, p. 279); B. of I. Mins., 22 May 1823, 4 May 1824, 14 Sept. 1824; chief secretary to Bank of Ireland, 19 Oct. 1824 (S.P.O., Abstract of outgoing correspondence, chief secretary's office).

14 6 Geo. IV, c. 98.

15 Proclamations in *Dublin Gaz. 1825*, pp. 665, 769, 837, 937, 973.

16 *1826 committee* (C), p. 88, evidence of J. R. Pim of Dublin; p. 92, of James Marshall of the Provincial Bank; *ibid.* (L), p. 10, of John M'Namara of Limerick.

in 1820[17] and a further coinage was made in 1822.[18] Demand for it was overestimated and by April 1823 the Bank of Ireland was complaining to the government that supplies were excessive.[19] The Assimilation Act, passed in June 1825 to take effect from 6 January 1826, required that Irish copper be called in and exchanged for British,[20] but supplies of the latter proved insufficient and Irish copper was allowed to continue in circulation for a time at the old value.[21] By May 1826 there was still 'a great want of copper' so that much retail trade continued in Irish,[22] but by July the position had improved to the point where the remaining Irish copper could be assimilated to the British.[23]

From 1826 therefore silver and copper coins were common currency for the whole United Kingdom. This would only affect the monetary position in Ireland to the extent that they were taken in and out of the country. Some certainly were, in the pockets of travellers including harvest labourers bringing home their wages, but it is doubtful if the amount was appreciable at this date. Any large sums would be carried in gold, and the export and import of silver and copper may for practical purposes be ignored.

The simultaneous use of British and Irish currency was an anomaly in a single United Kingdom and a cause of much confusion in Ireland. It was one of the things left over for settlement at the time of the Union, and assimilation of the currencies was recommended by, among others, the 1804 committee.[24] As long as the war lasted nothing was done but in 1816 the first step was taken with an act to amalgamate the two exchequers from 6 January 1817.[25] One chancellor was to be responsible for the finances of the whole United Kingdom and control was centralized in the treasury in London with a vice-treasurer acting for it in Dublin. Irish accounts were required, by section 26, to be kept in such a way that they could be laid before parliament in

---

17 B. of I. Mins., 31 July 1810, has a letter from the Dublin corn merchants that describes copper as the sole circulating medium of the Liberty, the main working class area; it was received by bakers for bread, exchanged by them for bills from pawnbrokers who then fed it back into circulation while the bakers paid the corn factors with the bills.

18 Treasury minute of 19 July 1822 (P.R.O., T. 29/211, pp. 477-8), approves coinage of £30,000; a proclamation of 19 Dec. 1822 (*Dublin Gaz. 1822*, pp. 733-4), fixes the value.

19 B. of I. Mins., 8 Apr. 1823; Irish office incoming correspondence, 10 Apr. 1823 (P.R.O.I.); the bank had just received £50,000 and been advised of £10,000 more on the way.

20 6 Geo. IV, c. 79, s. 12.

21 Proclamation of 26 Dec. 1825 (*Dublin Gaz. 1826*, p. 5).

22 *1826 committee (C)*, p. 88, evidence of Pim; *ibid. (L)*, p. 42, of Daniel Callaghan of Cork.

23 A royal proclamation of 12 July 1826 (*Dublin Gaz. 1826*, pp. 534-5), required that it pass at twelve pence to the shilling.

24 *1804 committee*, p. 11.

25 56 Geo. III, c. 98.

British currency, but a year later this was still not being done and the treasury had to order its officers in Ireland to comply.[26]

These changes applied to the accounts kept by the treasury, not to the government accounts in the Bank of Ireland nor to official dealings with the public nor even to the government's dealings with its own departments. Salaries continued to be fixed in Irish currency and treasury issues in Dublin made in it. This led to further complications in the chief secretary's office when funds for the expenses of its London section (the Irish office) had to be transferred there in British currency. This was done by buying bills on London at the day's rate of exchange, so that salaries received by the London staff varied with this rate, while transfers to meet expenditure in London (for which funds had been issued in Dublin at the par rate) led to some profit or loss in each case. The accounting ingenuity to iron out these anomalies was evidently not thought worthwhile.[27]

The Irish currency was finally abolished from 6 January 1826 under the Assimilation of Currencies Act, 1825.[28] Peel, then home secretary, and Goulburn, chief secretary for Ireland, were both critical of the measure, but mainly because they had not been sufficiently consulted.[29] The chief issue of principle arose over army pay. Troops stationed in Ireland had formerly been paid the same sum in Irish currency as they were paid in British currency when stationed in Britain. As they were liable to serve anywhere this was an anomaly which, partly on Peel's insistence, was rectified by changing their rates to the same figure in British currency, that is making rates uniform throughout the United Kingdom. Allowances for local expenses on the other hand were converted from Irish to British on the grounds that the prices involved would be similarly altered. Apart from adjustments for impractical fractions the pay of the forces was the only case in which the value of money was changed in real terms—the soldier received the same

---

26 Treasury minute of 23 Jan. 1818 (P.R.O., T. 29/157, pp. 445-9). The papers of Sir George Hill, the vice-treasurer at this date, include correspondence from treasury officials explaining the difficulties of interpreting and applying this section (P.R.O.N.I., 642/93-102). R. B. McDowell, *The Irish administration*, p. 92, n. 3, refers to this minute but leaves its meaning a little obscure.

27 S.P.O., Irish office incoming correspondence, has many letters covering such payments—see especially Taylor to Flint, 20 Nov. 1820. Bills were drawn on firms or persons in London by firms in Dublin for the equivalent at the day's rate of the amount due in Irish; this applied even to payments due to government departments in London. Payments the other way, by London departments to persons in Dublin, were similarly transmitted by bills on Dublin houses drawn in Irish currency in London—see Taylor to Trundle, 24 Nov. 1823, acknowledging one such payment. This practice continued for some time after 1826 but with all bills drawn in British currency.

28 6 Geo. IV, c. 79; a treasury minute of 5 Dec. 1825 (P.R.O., T. 29/252, pp. 84-91) gives directions for putting the act into effect; there is a copy in S.P.O. 588E/593/6.

29 Peel to Goulburn, 12 Nov. 1825; Goulburn to Peel, 15 Nov. 1825 (B.M., Add. MSS 40331); Goulburn to Peel, 10 Aug. 1826 (*ibid.*, 40332).

number of pounds but they were worth more. For the rest the assimilation was an alteration in the unit of account not a revaluation.

The act passed with little discussion and no opposition.[30] It provided for British currency to run throughout the United Kingdom with prior debts in Irish settled at the rate of 12 : 13. Further note issues in Irish were prohibited but existing notes kept their value and there was no obligation to withdraw them. The Bank of Ireland promptly altered its accounts;[31] the Northern did the same,[32] and so presumably did all the banks. Other institutions took their time; Dublin Corporation only changed in 1829,[33] while on the Dublin stock exchange stocks denominated in Irish currency continued to be quoted in Irish until 1830.[34]

References to 'late Irish currency' recur for some years, and the shortage of new copper coin meant that much retail trade was carried on for a time at the old standard, but the change was generally welcomed in business circles and by May 1826 all wholesale trade was being transacted in British.[35]

Note Issues

In theory the assimilation established a common currency for the United Kingdom but this was not so in practice since the major element in the Irish money supply was the note circulation of the Irish banks. In England notes for less than £5 had been prohibited by an act of 1777, made perpetual by another of 1787,[36] but had been allowed as an emergency measure under the restriction acts. With the repeal of the latter the ban would revive but in 1822, alarmed by the post-war deflation, parliament continued its suspension to 1832.[37] No such ban existed in Ireland—or in Scotland—and the right to issue small notes therefore continued. A bill to prohibit it in Ireland by banks other than the Bank of Ireland was introduced by the government in May 1820 but was not proceeded with.[38]

Though legally permitted to issue notes for under £5 the Bank of Ireland had not done so before 1797 but commenced with the coming of the restriction.[39] Private banks issued some small notes

30 Fetter, *Irish pound*, pp. 60-1, describes the proceedings.
31 B. of I. Mins., 29 Nov. 1825.
32 E. D. Hill (ed.), *Northern Banking Company*, p. 44.
33 *Calendar of the ancient records of Dublin*, xviii, 388.
34 Public notice, 5 Jan. 1830, in Dublin stock exchange lists.
35 *1826 committee (C)*, p. 88, evidence of J. R. Pim.
36 17 Geo. III, c. 30; 27 Geo. III, c. 16.
37 3 Geo. IV, c. 70.
38 H.C. 1820 (295), i, 747; *Commons' Jn.*, lxxv, 454-66, records its progress to the report stage but has no further reference.
39 *1804 committee*, pp. 86, 90, evidence of William Colville and Jeremiah D'Olier, directors of the bank; Colville stated that the bank issued no notes under £10 before 1797 but B. of I. Mins., 20 Jan. 1784, has a resolution to issue notes of 5 guineas. Hall, *Bank of Ireland*, app. E, gives the bank's issues 1783-1844, distinguishing small from large for the first time in 1802.

before 1797[40] and greatly increased their issues after it. In 1799 a measure of control was attempted by an act which prohibited all notes payable to bearer for less than 5 guineas other than those for 9s, 6s and 3s 9½d issued by bankers outside Dublin.[41] Many of the latter, the so-called silver notes, were issued between 1799 and 1804 when all notes for less than 20s were declared void.[42] This prohibition, repeated by an act of 1805,[43] was the only statutory restriction on note issues in force in 1820.

The distinction between large notes of £5 and over and small notes of under £5 had therefore no legal significance in Ireland, but it was commonly made and had some monetary importance since the large notes were used mainly for commercial payments and remittances while the small passed from hand to hand as currency.

In addition to notes both the Bank of Ireland and the private banks issued post bills. They were designed to allow time to stop payment in the event of loss in transit and were therefore made payable some days after issue, normally seven but sometimes five, ten or twenty-one.[44] To some degree they were more analogous to bills of exchange than to notes but the many endorsements on those that survive indicate that they did pass from hand to hand as currency.[45] Circulation figures sometimes include them, sometimes do not.

Notes and post bills were always denominated in Irish currency until just before the assimilation.[46] The word 'sterling', commonly added after the amount, did not indicate British currency but seems to have been no more than a promise of sound value. When British currency was intended, as in bills or promissory notes payable in London, the words 'British sterling' were used.[47] Many notes were in guineas but this was solely a British unit and the promise to pay was always stated in Irish at the rate of £1 2s 9d to the guinea. Notes for pounds and fractions of pounds on the other hand were always

---

40 *1826 committee* (L), p. 46, Sir John Newport stated that he believed small notes of private banks to have been in circulation as far back as 1770; Cullen, *Anglo-Irish trade*, pp. 198-201, gives some interesting but incomplete figures of private issues before 1797.

41 39 Geo. III, c. 48 (Ir.); the curious denomination of 3s 9½d was one-sixth of a guinea in Irish currency.

42 44 Geo. III, c. 91.

43 45 Geo. III, c. 41.

44 The collections in the National Museum and the Institute of Bankers in Ireland include post bills of all these dates.

45 See for instance La Touche post bills in the Royal Irish Academy.

46 Hall, *Bank of Ireland*, app. E, shows issues in British currency commencing in the first quarter of 1825.

47 The National Museum has a promissory note for '£135 British sterling' issued in Dublin in 1823, payable in London at three months. Cork Museum has two notes issued by Leslies', one just before the assimilation in 1825 for '25/- sterling', the other just after it in 1826 for '25/- British sterling'.

denominated in and payable for the same amount, both being Irish currency.[48]

English and Scottish notes were sometimes seen in Ireland but did not circulate. All those in use were therefore issued either by the Bank of Ireland or by one of the private banks, their acceptability depending on the credit of the issuing bank. Bank of Ireland notes, commonly designated as 'national paper', were held to be as good as gold but to the bank's critics they were too scarce. Good banking entailed the issue of notes only on sound security so that they were always scarce in the sense that people offering security which a bank did not consider sound could not procure them, but in the case of the Bank of Ireland, complaint was magnified by its refusal to move out of Dublin.[49] It was only in 1824 that discount accounts were authorized for 'respectable persons in the interior of Ireland' and arrangements formalized to transmit notes and post bills to them through the mail.[50] Prior to that date notes were issued only over the counter in Dublin and merchants in the country had to employ agents to collect and dispatch them.[51]

The Bank of Ireland's issues were described in 1804 as being 'for service of government, for the discount of bills and for loans upon government security',[52] and a statement by the bank in 1819 said the same in rather more detail.[53] Issues by the withdrawal of deposits were not mentioned, possibly because they merely meant the exchange of one liability for another, but in 1826 Arthur Guinness included them when he described issues to the public as being by discount of bills, in payment of cheques drawn on the bank by people who had previously made deposits, and in discharge of ordinary demands.[54] Deposits and notes were the two types of money made available by the bank and the holders could exchange one for the other or for coin

---

48 Examples of both types are to be seen in many collections. Hall, *op. cit.*, p. 98, and O'Kelly, *Munster banks*, p. 80, have photographs of notes in guineas; O'Kelly, pp. 88-9, shows notes for £1 5s 0d and £1 10s 0d. See plates 2, 4 and 5.
49 *1823 committee*, p. 162-6, evidence of Roche, gives the fullest and best-informed criticism of the bank's policy.
50 B. of I. Mins., 22 June, 7 July 1824.
51 *1823 committee*, p. 166, evidence of Roche; *1826 committee* (L), pp. 9-10, of M'Namara of Limerick; *ibid.* (C), p. 74, of Hunt of Waterford.
52 *1804 committee*, p. 87, evidence of Colville.
53 *1819 committee* (C), app. 29, states the mode of issue to be
   (1) occasionally for the purchase of exchequer or treasury bills;
   (2) to government on the security of treasury bills alone;
   (3) to individuals upon discount of mercantile bills or notes very seldom exceeding a period of sixty-one days to run, and occasionally upon discount of notes not exceeding a period of sixty-one days to run, with a collateral of government stock alone.
   Ibid. (L), p. 268, Nathaniel Sneyd, governor of the bank, added some very guarded comments.
54 *1826 committee* (C), pp. 235-6; Guinness was governor 1820-2 and remained a director until 1847; he was the second Arthur Guinness, son of the first who founded the brewery.

at will. The statistics indicate their relative importance, with average note issues in 1820 at just over £3,000,000 (of which rather over half were large notes) plus some £1,230,000 of post bills, while private deposits were only £520,000 and public deposits £660,000. All these figures were abnormally low, with higher averages in both earlier and later years.[55]

Private banks had no government transactions. Their issues were therefore entirely to private customers, the bulk by discount of bills —in the south mainly for produce merchants, in the north for both linen traders and produce merchants. Prior to the 1820 crisis southern banks used to allow book credits to merchants after seeing their orders, in other words loans against which they issued notes with which the merchants made their purchases and repaid when the produce had been sold.[56] Private banks in Dublin and the south also issued by way of mortgage loans[57]—a method forbidden to the Bank of Ireland by the 1782 act[58]—and there is evidence from Limerick of loans secured on life assurance policies.[59] In the north, on the other hand, mortgage loans were held to be 'foreign to the business of banking'; all issues by Batt's (also presumably by the other banks) were by discount of bills for merchants; the proceeds might initially be credited to accounts but these could be drawn on at will.[60]

Private bank statistics are most inadequate. Peel, as chairman of the 1826 committee, tried to collect figures of their circulation but the results were incomplete and not very informative.[61] The only reliable figures are the numbers of notes stamped at the Stamp Office. It may be assumed that virtually all notes stamped were issued, but with no record of cancellations we cannot estimate the numbers in circulation. An act of 1815 allowed notes to be reissued for three years after stamping,[62] and in Belfast small notes were said to be

55 *1837 committee*, app. III-4, 20, 21; these figures are all in Irish currency but in appendix 7 below have been converted into British.
56 *1823 committee*, pp. 161-2, evidence of Roche.
57 Liquidation accounts normally lumped mortgage loans in one total of secured debts—e.g., Leslies' balance sheet in O'Kelly, *Munster banks*, p. 67. There is evidence of mortgage loans by La Touche's, or at least by members of the firm, to the Newcomen estates in 1814-7 in the King Harmon papers, and by Alexander's in 1816 in the McKenzie brewery papers (both in P.R.O.I.).
58 21 & 22 Geo. III, c. 16, s. 7 (Ir.); the Bank of Ireland made vain efforts to have this restriction lifted (B. of I. Mins., 28 Apr. 1824, 20 Jan. 1825); it was finally repealed in 1860 (23 & 24 Vic., c. 31).
59 O'Kelly, *Munster banks*, p. 106, in reference to Maunsell's.
60 *1826 committee* (C), pp. 105, 107, evidence of Houston; see above p. 16 for Montgomery's transactions.
61 S.P.O. 588E/574 has Peel's request to Goulburn, the chief secretary, for these figures, and the questionnaire circulated to the banks and discount houses. Of nine banks only six replied and only two gave the full information asked. Details are lacking but the maximum and minimum total circulation for 1815, 1821, 1823, 1824 and 1825 and the latest figure for 1826 are given in the *1826 Commons committee report*, p. 15, and the *Lords' committee*, app. A2.
62 55 Geo. III, c. 100, ss. 8, 9.

normally worn out after fifteen months,[63] but there is no firmer evidence on the subject.

The Stamp Office supplied the 1826 committee with figures of stamping from 1817 to 1826[64] which showed the total number stamped to have been over 1,000,000 in 1817 and 1818, dropping each year to just over 280,000 in 1823. The bulk were small notes—a little under 90 per cent of issues each year by banks in Dublin and a little over 90 per cent by those elsewhere. In 1817 and 1818 total stampings were about equally divided between Dublin and the rest, but from then on the Dublin figures form a steadily smaller portion of the total. There are no firm figures for the values of these notes, but the Stamp Office did produce their estimates of it for each quarter. By guessing at the likely proportion of different denominations they put the total value of notes stamped at nearly £1,000,000 during 1820, falling to under £600,000 in 1821, a little over it in 1822 and under £500,000 in 1823.

The only bank for which we have any individual figures is Gordon's (Batt's) whose annual circulation from 1811 to 1825 averaged about £300,000.[65] For the rest the only figures are those of notes outstanding at the time of bank failures. The eight banks that failed in 1820 had a total of some £760,000 between them.[66] From their respective sizes we might assume that the other banks in Dublin and the south had about the same or a little less, making a total of some £1,500,000. If Montgomery's and Tennent's had each a similar circulation to Gordon's, again a reasonable assumption, the circulation of the Belfast banks was about £900,000, making a total private bank circulation for all Ireland of around £2,400,000; of this some £760,000 disappeared in May/June 1820, and more soon afterwards as the southern banks contracted.

These are very tentative guesses, but they are not incompatible with the stamping figures. They suggest rather higher circulation than the figures collected by Peel in 1826. Bank of Ireland issues of notes and

63 *1826 committee* (L), p. 26, evidence of Houston.

64 *1826 committee* (C), app. 4, 10; the committee asked for figures from 1790 but they were only available from 1817, a consequence of the 1815 act which required the use of specific stamps for bank notes.

65 *1826 committee* (L), p. 25, evidence of Houston, one of the partners; the highest figure was £412,000 in 1819 from which the total fell to £300,000 in 1820 and £268,000 in 1822, then rose steadily to £351,000 in 1825.

66 This total is made up as follows, mainly from liquidation accounts:

Leslies' ⎫ Roches' ⎭	350,000 Memorial in O'Kelly, *Munster banks*, p. 158.
Maunsell's	74,500 *Ibid.*, p. 104.
Newport's	96,000 Burke, in *Cork Hist. Soc. Jn.*, iv (1898), 282.
Riall's	70,000 Burke, *History of Clonmel*, pp. 188-90.
Loughnan's	26,000 *Leinster Journal*, 17 June 1820.
Bruce's, say	20,000 no record.
Alexander's	126,000 *F.J.*, 28 June 1820.

762,500

post bills in 1820 were £4,230,000. Private issues before the crisis were therefore a little over half this.

Deposits

To most contemporary theorists money comprised coin and bank notes only—and some would not even include bank notes. Deposits were regarded as book entries of money lodged with a bank. It was often recognized that payments were made by their transfer but the idea that they should be regarded as money in the same sense as notes, created by a bank against bills or other assets, was generally over-looked.[67] Yet there is little doubt that this is what they were, even if still to a limited degree. Like bank notes they were promises to pay and were accepted as money out of confidence in the bank's integrity and capacity to honour them. They were created either by the lodgement of notes or coin or by some banking transaction such as the discount of bills in just the same way as notes.

The Bank of Ireland held its liability on deposits to be the same as on notes, subject of course to notice where appropriate, and that it could not refuse notes tendered for lodgement to accounts.[68] The two were interchangeable forms of bank money. Printed cheque or draft forms were in use,[69] and already in 1793 merchants who discounted £200 and over were authorized to have it paid to their accounts and to draw on the bank for it at will.[70] In 1824, when the opening of discount accounts for country customers was approved, withdrawal by draft was specifically provided for but only on due notice and in minimum sums of £100.[71] It was not till 1834 that drafts were allowed down to £5, and 1858 before they were allowed down to £1.[72]

In private banks the keeping of accounts was obviously important but information is meagre. A clear distinction was usual between permanent deposits and cash accounts. In Gordon's, payments into the former had to be at least £20 and were normally over £50, with ten days' notice formally required for withdrawal but not insisted on, whereas the latter were operated by merchants who sent in bills for credit to the accounts to be drawn on at will. Overdrawing was not allowed and interest was paid on permanent deposits but not on cash accounts.[73] Montgomery's operated in much the same way, and payments by their linen trade customers to other parts of the country were made by drafts on their accounts.[74] In the south the main evidence is from liquidation balance sheets, most of which include both per-

---

67 Lloyd Mints, *History of banking theory*, pp. 42-3, analyses the ideas of the period on this point.
68 *1826 committee* (L), p. 68, evidence of Guinness.
69 See plate 10; similar cheques of 1803 and 1812 are in the National Museum.
70 B. of I. Mins., 8, 12 Jan. 1793.
71 *Ibid.*, 7 July 1824.
72 *Ibid.*, 6 May 1834; *F.J.*, 5 July 1858.
73 *1826 committee* (L), pp. 26-7, evidence of Houston.
74 Above, p. 16.

manent deposits (or lodgements) and current (or cash) accounts. Banks
in the Cork area were said to take large sums in lodgements on which
they normally paid interest.[75] Surviving forms of cheques or drafts
suggest that they were in fairly common use.[76]

There was some debate as to the legality of interest on deposits. The
1760 act prohibited a banker from issuing a receipt with any promise
to pay interest,[77] but most bankers got round this by making no mention of interest on their receipts. Customers might have difficulty in
enforcing payment at law but obviously a bank's good name would
suffer if it refused.[78] The Bank of Ireland, on the other hand, held
interest to be illegal under any circumstances and paid none.[79] This
made the distinction between permanent and current deposits of little
significance, and it does not in fact seem to have been made by the
bank at this date. The main attraction in holding such deposits must
have been their security and the facility of making payments from
them and drawing out notes.

There are quite good statistics of deposits in the Bank of Ireland for
the years 1808-36 in the form of annual averages of public and private
deposits submitted to the 1837 committee.[80] They show private deposits
rising to £650,000 in 1817, dropping to £520,000 in 1820 and then
rising steadily to over £1,000,000 in 1825. Public deposits fell from
over £1,000,000 in 1818 to £600,000 in 1820 and then rose to over
£1,200,000 in 1824 and 1825.[81]

The only figures for private banks are those in liquidation accounts.
Alexander's had deposits of £40,000 when they failed in 1820,[82] while
the seven banks that failed in the south had perhaps £540,000 between
them.[83] Nothing is known of the volume of deposits in the other Dublin

75 *1823 committee*, p. 167, evidence of Roche.
76 A cheque drawn on La Touche's by the duke of Leinster on his own printed
   form in 1783 is in the National Museum; another drawn on Ewing Holmes & Co.
   of Belfast (the bank known as the Four Johns) in 1792 is in the Ulster Museum.
   O'Kelly, *Munster Banks*, p. 101, refers to one of Maunsell's of 1818. See plate
   11 for one of Shaw's of 1830.
77 33 Geo. II, c. 14, s. 4 (Ir.).
78 *1826 committee* (*C*), p. 248, evidence of James Orr of the Northern Banking
   Company.
79 *Ibid.*, p. 236, evidence of Guinness.
80 *1837 committee*, app. III-20, 21; below, Appendix 7.
81 It is a matter of definition whether public deposits in the Bank of Ireland should
   be treated as part of the money supply; see below, p. 47.
82 *F.J.*, 28 June 1820.
83 This figure is arrived at as follows:

Leslies'	64,000	O'Kelly, *Munster banks*, p. 66.
Roches', say	120,000	no record.
Maunsell's	104,000	O'Kelly, *op. cit.*, p. 104.
Newport's	128,000	Burke, in *Cork Hist. Soc. Jn.*, iv (1898), p. 282.
Riall's	86,000	Burke, *History of Clonmel*, pp. 188-90.
Loughnan's	16,000	*Leinster Journal*, 17 June 1820.
Bruce's, say	20,000	no record.

538,000

banks,[84] nor in those in Belfast, so it is not possible to hazard a guess at the total for the whole country even as tentative as that made above for circulation, nor can we estimate the proportion of deposits held by other banks and so not strictly part of the money supply. All we can say is that deposits and balances by accounts formed a significant part of the liabilities of the private banks. They circulated by transfers between accounts in payment of bills and on orders by cheques or drafts, but it is doubtful if this was yet common.[85] For the most part deposits, temporary as well as permanent, seem to have been treated as a reservoir from which to draw notes at need. This does not mean that they were not money but they were a less liquid form than notes, with a lower velocity of circulation.

Bills of Exchange

Notes and deposits were money by reason of their general acceptability, which rested on the credit of the banks whose liabilities they were. Bills on the other hand were liabilities of the parties to them and they became assets of the banks when they were discounted. Discount of bills was one of the two chief ways by which money was fed into circulation—the other was government payments—and they therefore played a major role in the monetary system. They were also themselves a common means of payment, particularly between parties at a distance.

Virtually all bills discounted by Irish banks were drawn in Ireland but they were classified as English or Irish according to where they were payable.[86] Irish bills were similarly divided into Dublin and country bills. What a banker looked for in a bill was certainly that it would be paid when due. To some degree this depended on the soundness of the names on it but the best guarantee was if it were based on a real transaction whose completion would produce the funds to meet it. The bills that best satisfied this test, and were always preferred by Irish bankers, were English bills, drawn by exporters on reputable English buyers.

Bills were discounted by banks either for notes and coin over the counter or for credit to accounts. In either case the transaction was an exchange of debts. The bank's debts were accepted as money which the consumer could use to carry on his business, and for the service of supplying this money the bank was paid by the discount it deducted. The debt received by the bank in the form of the bill was either sold

84 Newcomen's in 1825 had liabilities of £200,000 with no note issue, but this included large sums owed on mortgage (*F.J.*, 25 Jan. 1825).
85 *1837 committee*, Q. 4092, Pierce Mahony agreed that cheques had scarcely been used in the south before the establishment of the Provincial Bank (in 1825)—but 'scarcely' is a relative term.
86 This terminology was often misunderstood in England; in 1848 the governor of the Bank of Ireland had to explain it to the Lords' committee on commercial distress (*1848 committee (L)*, Q. 4163).

direct to someone who needed funds at the place of payment or was sent to the bank's correspondent there to collect.[87] English bills collected for an Irish bank were normally credited to its London funds which could then be drawn on to meet other bills and drafts by the bank's customers. Irish bills similarly established a credit for the bank at their place of payment but they were less favoured by reason of the limited scale of internal trade.

Where there were no banks, or sometimes to supplement the services of banks by taking bills which they might refuse, private firms and individuals often discounted in the same way, using Bank of Ireland notes.[88] Goulburn, as chief secretary, tried to collect statistics of issues by such discounters for Peel in 1826 but the results are not known; they evidently included lottery offices in Dublin who must have found this a profitable way to employ their funds.[89] James Marshall, chief accountant of the Provincial Bank, spoke of private discounters in Limerick and Galway charging 10 to 15 per cent, but when pressed he agreed that they did not exceed the legal limit of 6 per cent discount and that the full cost, with commission, etc., can never have exceeded 9.[90] Mahony, on the other hand, mentioned a firm in Armagh that tried discounting with Bank of Ireland notes but found that it did not even cover the cost of postage.[91]

Bills, whether English or Irish, were also a common means of remittance. Within the banking system agents naturally remitted to their principals by forwarding the bills they had discounted,[92] while outside it merchants and land agents with surplus notes on hand used them to buy bills for remittance, normally to Dublin.[93] Gordon's, whose notes were payable by its Dublin agent, kept him in funds by remitting bills which he collected himself if payable in Dublin or sold on the exchange if payable in England, in either case receiving payment in Bank of Ireland notes.[94] Externally payments to England were normally made by bills purchased either on the Dublin exchange or from the banks or direct from persons with funds available there.[95]

87 *1823 committee*, pp. 161-7, evidence of Roche, gives the best account of bill transactions in the south; *ibid.*, p. 63, evidence of Thomas Oldham, a Lancashire linen merchant, speaks of agents buying linen for him in Ireland and having no difficulty in discounting bills drawn on him at twenty-one days; *1826 committee* (*C*), p. 105, evidence of Houston, discusses the practice in Belfast.
88 H. Dutton, *Statistical survey of County Galway* (1824), p. 418, records two such discounting houses in Galway; they gave bills on Dublin or Bank of Ireland paper for 'bills of undoubted security'.
89 Goulburn to Gregory, 14 Apr. 1826 (S.P.O., 588E/574).
90 *1826 committee* (*C*), pp. 94-5.
91 *Ibid.*, p. 251.
92 See below, p. 68, for the practice of the Northern Banking Company.
93 *1826 committee* (*L*), p. 12, evidence of Dobbin; p. 71, of Humphrey Evatt, a land agent in Co. Monaghan.
94 *1826 committee* (*C*), p. 108, evidence of Houston.
95 See above, p. 28, n. 27, for a discussion of such remittances from the chief secretary's office in Dublin to its London section.

Whether bills so used should be regarded as money or as orders to pay money is a matter of definition; if the former they represent an increase in its volume, if the latter a rise in its effective velocity of circulation. Prior to the full development of cheques and banking transfers, and of the branches through which to pass them, they were a most important means of payment. They undoubtedly circulated but it is not possible to measure how much. In Belfast small bills were never used for wages or business payments, and large bills were always promptly discounted.[96] In the south the circulation of bills was described as much diminished after the 1820 crisis;[97] this reference is apparently to normal discounting by the drawers but the same presumably applied to circulation amongst the public.

Bills were also used for accommodation by drawing and accepting where no real transaction had taken place. The acceptor of such an accommodation bill was legally liable to pay it when due but the drawer undertook, whether by formal agreement or simple understanding, to provide him with the means to do so, the parties often keeping running accounts with each other of their transactions.[98] The bills were either discounted at a bank or taken by others in payment. Their use was probably considerable, and with reliable names they might be more secure than real bills. Banks disliked them but often felt obliged to take them to help valued customers.[99]

The discount that might lawfully be charged was still limited by the usury laws. In England the maximum was 5 per cent but in Ireland it was fixed at 6 per cent by an act of 1731.[100] The Bank of Ireland however was restricted to 5 per cent by the 1782 act,[101] and its discount rate remained at this from its foundation until May 1824 when it was reduced for the first time to 4 per cent. From the beginning of 1825 the bank quoted separate rates for English and Irish bills but they were in fact the same until March 1831 after which the rate on Irish bills was normally higher than on English by as much as a point.[102]

96 *1826 committee (L)*, p. 30, evidence of Houston.
97 *1823 committee*, p. 162, evidence of Roche.
98 Robert White papers (N.L.I., MSS 8855) deal with such bill operations between Dublin and the country and between Dublin and Paris in the 1830s, treated as normal procedure, perfectly honourable if faithfully carried through. The O'Connell papers have many references to them throughout this period—see especially U.C.D., MSS 63.15, where the accounting method is explained. *1826 committee (L)*, p. 70, evidence of W. P. Lunell, director of the Bank of Ireland, deplores the practice.
99 B. of I. Mins., 8 June 1830, 5 Jan. 1831, show that they were sometimes taken by the Bank of Ireland if of 'undoubted security'.
100 5 Geo. II, c. 7 (Ir.); this was a reduction from earlier levels. G. O'Brien, *Economic history of Ireland in the eighteenth century*, p. 358, states that the rate was reduced to 5% in 1788 but this is incorrect; a bill to that effect passed the Commons after long debate (*Parl. reg. Ire.*, viii, 237-345 *passim*) but was rejected by the lords (*Lords' Jn. Ire.*, vi, 155-65 *passim*).
101 21 & 22 Geo. III, c. 16, s. 7 (Ir.).
102 Hall, *Bank of Ireland*, app. D, gives a full table of rates 1783-1946.

This restriction and the discrimination between the Bank of Ireland and the rest continued until 1833 when the Bank of England Charter Act abolished all limitations on rates charged on bills or notes with not more than three months to run.[103]

The significance of interest rates in the control of credit had been emphasized by Henry Thornton as early as 1802,[104] but the usury laws prevented them having much effect. Higher expectations of profit might well increase the demand for credit but its price could never rise above 6 per cent. The differential of 1 per cent in rates between England and Ireland might have been expected to attract capital from the former to the latter but there is no evidence that it did.[105]

The Anglo-Irish Exchanges

Bills were the chief medium through which the exchanges operated between England and Ireland. Payments to England were normally made by buying bills on London drawn by Irish exporters on their English buyers; sometimes the bills might be drawn by banks or others on their London correspondents but since the latter would have been supplied with funds by collecting bills on London this was merely a delayed form of the same operation. The exchange rate in Dublin on London was the percentage premium or discount at which such bills could be bought.[106] Essentially the bills on London and elsewhere in Britain represented one side of the Anglo-Irish balance of payments and the demand for them represented the other. When the two were in equilibrium the exchanges stood at par; they rose above it when Irish payments (the demand for funds in London) exceeded Irish receipts (the proceeds of bills on England) and fell below it in the opposite case.

Prior to the assimilation of the currencies in 1826 the par rate was $8\frac{1}{3}$ per cent,[107] but during the restriction the actual rate fluctuated violently either side of this.[108] These fluctuations were the main theme of the inquiries of the Irish currency committee in 1804. The suspension of cash payments had broken the link between the English and Irish currencies and had left the issues of the Banks of England and

---

103 3 & 4 Will. IV, c. 98, s. 7.

104 H. Thornton, *Paper credit of Great Britain,* ed. Hayek (London 1939), pp. 253-9; below, p. 51.

105 The prospectus issued by the National Bank in 1834 put this as one of its attractions (*F.J.,* 1 July 1834), but by that date the restriction had been abolished.

106 The market for bills was in the Royal Exchange in Dublin; no direct account of its working has come to light.

107 Above, p. 25.

108 Fetter, *Irish pound,* p. 20, gives a graph of fluctuations 1794-1823 in the London rate on Dublin, for which fuller records are available than for the Dublin rate on London.

Ireland free of any direct restraint.[109] The committee pointed out that the relationship between them was reflected in the state of the exchange and that the recent high rate against Ireland arose because the Bank of Ireland's issues were excessive relative to those of the Bank of England.[110] The two Bank of Ireland directors who gave evidence, William Colville and Jeremiah D'Olier, while agreeing that increased circulation might raise prices, refused to concede that this could turn the exchanges against Ireland,[111] but the committee, guided by Henry Thornton, were not impressed.[112]

The proper way to keep the currencies in line, the committee argued, was to restore the link through gold by ending the restriction. If war needs made this politically unacceptable it recommended instead that the Bank of Ireland should establish a fund in London from which to redeem its notes with those of the Bank of England. This proposal was based on the practice adopted by the Scottish banks after 1763 which had successfully stabilized the exchanges between Edinburgh and London. The fund would be opened with the proceeds of a loan recently raised in London by the Irish government and with the investment of the bank's surplus specie, and might be augmented by treasury bills specially issued for the purpose and perhaps by an increase in capital. It would then be fed by bills on London taken by the Bank of Ireland and would be drawn on to meet bills on London which the bank would supply against its notes in Dublin at rates gradually reduced to par.[113]

D'Olier argued that this scheme would oblige the bank to give bills in exchange for its notes equal to the whole of the balance of payments against Ireland—which would mean 'the ruin and shutting up of the Bank of Ireland'.[114] This view followed logically from his premise that the reduction in circulation would do nothing to correct the exchange, but it was precisely this correction that the committee looked for. The bank court, of which Colville and D'Olier were leading members,[115] turned the scheme down on the grounds that 'the misconstruction which might and would be affixed to their conduct' would tend to

---

109 Above, p. 8.

110 *1804 committee*, pp. 7-8. See also Fetter, *Irish pound*, pp. 32-48; this book reprints the full report and parts of the evidence.

111 *1804 committee*, pp. 90, 98, 118-22, evidence of Colville; pp. 115, 118, of D'Olier.

112 The minutes do not identify the questioners but Thornton's incisive intellect can often be detected; see also Fetter, *op. cit.*, p. 31.

113 *1804 committee*, pp. 11-5.

114 *Ibid.*, pp. 115, 123-5; the same view was expressed by John Puget—*ibid.*, p. 21.

115 Both had been members of the original court in 1783; D'Olier was governor 1799-1801, Colville 1801-3; Colville retired in 1813, D'Olier in 1817 (Hone, in Hall, *Bank of Ireland*, pp. 483, 486).

destroy public confidence in the bank.[116] In 1805 the proposal was repeated in connection with another loan and again rejected.[117]

Loans continued therefore to be transferred either in Bank of England notes and post bills which were sold by the treasury in Dublin,[118] or by the Irish treasury selling bills to merchants in Dublin on Puget & Bainbridge in London, or by Pugets using the loan funds to buy bills on Dublin and sending them to the treasury there to collect.[119] These methods were strongly criticized by the 1804 committee for their destabilizing effect.[120] In 1810 sufficient bills were not available to transfer the current loan and the Bank of Ireland agreed instead to receive part of it in Bank of England notes provided it was guaranteed against exchange loss (when it resold the notes) and was paid 5 per cent interest on the notes deposited.[121] It was then asked to receive exchequer bills instead and have them deposited at the Bank of England to form a fund for making payments in London but only agreed to take them if delivered to Dublin and covered by the same guarantee against loss.[122]

This was the thin end of the wedge and in 1813 when the treasury asked the bank to undertake the transfer of funds from Dublin to London the court at first refused, quoting its letter of 1804, then agreed provided it was guaranteed against loss, and finally consented to bear all risks itself at a commission of $\frac{1}{4}$ per cent.[123] In 1814 a further step was taken when the court, after arranging another remittance to London, agreed to continue to remit whatever funds were necessary to relieve the market from depression, and the treasury undertook that it would subsequently issue a warrant for the amounts transmitted and would pay $\frac{3}{4}$ per cent commission against risks and $\frac{1}{8}$ per cent for management costs.[124] This meant that the bank would buy bills on London whenever the rate was unduly low, the proceeds of the bills being paid to the treasury in London and the bank reimbursed by the treasury in Dublin. This was not quite the full equalization scheme proposed in 1804 but it was a long way from the bank's flat refusal to be involved in exchange dealings.

An incident at the beginning of 1821 may possibly have spurred the

116 B. of I. Mins., 29 Aug. 1804, reproduce both the letter from Foster, chancellor of the Irish exchequer, of 27 Aug. proposing the scheme and the court's reply of 30 Aug. rejecting it. *Hansard 1*, iii, 260, has Foster's statement in the House of Commons on the subject.
117 B. of I. Mins., 24 Apr. 1805.
118 *Hansard 1*, iii, 260-1, statement by Foster, 5 Feb. 1805.
119 *1804 committee*, pp. 125-7, evidence of Puget.
120 *Ibid.*, pp. 13-4.
121 B. of I. Mins., 25 Sept., 9, 16 Oct. 1810, reproduce the letters between Foster and the governor.
122 *Ibid.*, 18 Oct., 20 Nov. 1810; the suggestion came from Spencer Perceval passed on by Foster.
123 *Ibid.*, 26 June, 19, 21 Aug. 1813.
124 *Ibid.*, 25 Mar., 22 Nov., 6 Dec. 1814.

bank to take the final steps. In June 1820 the court resolved not to receive any specie either in lodgements or in exchange for notes, their reason being that the bank was debarred from issuing it and so would have to hold it as a useless deposit.[125] This ruling aroused little public comment until February 1821 when Ricardo and Francis Baring asked questions about it in parliament and Vansittart, the chancellor, called on the bank for an explanation so that he could answer.[126] The bank was trying at this date to build up its gold stocks in preparation for the resumption of payments[127] and he could not understand this refusal to accept gold from the public, a policy directly contrary to that of the Bank of England.

After consideration by a special court the governor, Arthur Guinness, replied that the ruling was designed to frustrate speculators who might import gold from England and pay it into the bank, which would be profitable whenever the exchange rate fell below par by more than the cost of transport. He agreed, as Ricardo had pointed out in the House of Commons, that such a low exchange rate pointed to the need for more circulation, but he argued that this could be better achieved by the bank itself taking good bills for discount. Yet he asserted that no one who could exhibit 'such property as the bank could legally lend upon' had been disappointed[128]—in other words that any deficiency in circulation was due to a shortage of sound demand not to the policy of the bank.

This letter hardly answers the complaint that the bank had rejected the opportunity to expand the circulation by issuing notes against gold imported at someone else's expense, and there was evidently some division of opinion in the court. It was immediately after this that Guinness and Sneyd began the discussions in London on 'several points to be settled between the government and the bank'[129] which led to the 1821 act. The court's minutes have no further reference to the ruling of June 1820, and it is not too much to assume that the bank's role in the exchanges was one of the several points. If the bank wanted to prevent speculative movements of gold the right way was to regulate the circulation so as to keep the exchange rate steady. This obligation it now proceeded to adopt.

First of all an agreement was made with the Bank of England to

125 B. of I. Mins., 7 June 1820. Hall, *Bank of Ireland*, p. 106, attributes the court's action to a desire to discourage the circulation of gold, but the evidence suggests the opposite.
126 *Hansard 2*, iv, 339-42; parliamentary report in *F.J.*, 7 Feb. 1821; Vansittart to governor, 3 Feb. 1821 (B. of I. Mins., 6 Feb. 1821). Vansittart to Grant, 31 Oct. 1820 (B.M., Add. MSS 31232), shows Vansittart critical of the bank's policy three months before it was raised in parliament.
127 Above, p. 10.
128 Guinness to Vansittart, 7 Feb. 1821 (B. of I. Mins., 7 Feb. 1821); *F.J.*, 15 Feb. 1821, has an anonymous letter defending the bank's action in such similar terms that it must have originated in the court.
129 Vansittart to Guinness, 10 Feb. 1821 (B. of I. Mins., 13 Feb. 1821); below p. 62.

act as agents for the Bank of Ireland in London. During his visit Guinness had 'many interviews' with his opposite number, Charles Pole, and on 14 September wrote to him asking to open an account for the Bank of Ireland. Dealings, he expected, would be extensive and would include the remittance and drawing of bills, the supply of Bank of England post bills, the investment of funds in exchequer bills and the shipment of coin and bullion in both directions. The Bank of England agreed, and Guinness wrote to Puget & Bainbridge explaining regretfully that the new arrangements would 'limit to a great degree' the Bank of Ireland's dealings with them.[130]

Two years later, when the question of the agency fee was causing some difficulty, the purpose of opening the account was described by the Bank of Ireland as being[131]

> to enable them by a judicious course of operations in the taking and passing of bills to prevent considerable fluctuations in the exchanges between England and Ireland, hoping thereby to render essential service to the commercial intercourse between the two countries—and likewise to facilitate the pecuniary transactions of the government.

The bank had in fact adopted the 1804 committee's scheme, using the agency account at the Bank of England as the exchange fund.

In November 1821, just before the opening of the account, the court made new regulations for the taking of English bills.[132] Three types were specified as admissible: 1. Bank of England notes and post bills, 2. Bills drawn on London, accepted or unaccepted, 3. Bills on any part of the United Kingdom, payable in London and accepted. Bills must be for a minimum of £100 and have at least six and not more than sixty-seven days to run. All were to be taken at the rate of exchange fixed by the Bank of Ireland with no deduction in the case of Bank of England notes and accepted post bills but with discount for the days left to run in all other cases.[133] The rate then fixed by the bank was $7\frac{5}{8}$ per cent; it was raised by two stages to 8 in November 1822,[134] and finally the next month the court resolved both to take and to pass English bills at the par rate of $8\frac{1}{3}$.

This last resolution of December 1822, which followed a review by the treasury committee, explained the reasons for the new policy.[135]

130 B. of I. Mins., 23 Oct. 1821, reproduce these letters.
131 Governor of the Bank of Ireland to governor of the Bank of England, 11 Nov. 1823 (B. of I. Mins., 11 Nov. 1823).
132 B. of I. Mins., 20 Nov. 1821.
133 Three days grace were added on all bills, plus three more for transit on unaccepted post bills and on unaccepted bills drawn after sight; the six to sixty-seven days therefore meant anything up to sixty-one plus these extra six.
134 B. of I. Mins., 9 Nov. 1822.
135 *Ibid.*, 17 Dec. 1822; Hall, *Bank of Ireland*, pp. 107-8, reproduces this resolution in full but wrongly dated as November.

Before 1797 both the bank and the government had been forced from time to time to import guineas to make good the loss of currency due to exchange fluctuations. Since the resumption such losses had recurred; in the seven months to October 1822, £233,000 in gold had been withdrawn though the exchange rate had never been higher than $8\frac{3}{4}$.[136] This was despite the interventions by the bank in taking and passing bills on London to check fluctuations; during the period it had passed a total of £980,000. More payments were now being made by way of exchange, that is by the purchase of bills on London, which meant that if the bank declined to discount them its discounts would form a very small portion of the trade of the country. The court announced therefore that the bank would in future take English bills at par, less only the discount, and pass bills payable at the Bank of England at thirty days at par.

The first part of this announcement simply meant that the Bank of Ireland was continuing its previous practice but at the par rate. It had not in fact 'declined' to discount bills on London but by offering too low a rate—£$107\frac{3}{4}$ Irish for £100 British when the market offered £$108\frac{3}{4}$—it had clearly secured little business. It had just put the rate up to £108, and now to £$108\frac{1}{3}$, at which it could hope for a fuller share.

But it was the second part of the announcement that was the real innovation. The bank had on occasions passed bills on London, as in the transfer of loans referred to above, and during the seven months to October 1822, when it offered them at a lower rate than that ruling in the market, had sold £980,000 worth, but this was the first time it had made a firm offer to do so and at the par rate. Any holder of notes or deposits could now use them at any time to buy bills on London at par which would be paid on maturity at the Bank of England. As long as it upheld this undertaking the Bank of Ireland must therefore regulate its liabilities according to the assets it had available in London. The idea that its own circulation had no bearing on the exchanges was thus finally laid to rest.

Ricardo's plan for a national bank, drafted in 1823 and published posthumously in 1824, provided for control of issues by agents outside London on lines similar to these; notes would be exchanged by the agents only for bills payable in national notes in London, while anyone depositing coin or notes in London could obtain bills payable by agents in the country.[137] Ricardo's ideas had been maturing for some time before that but there is no evidence either that he influenced the Bank of Ireland or that the bank's experience influenced him.

In his evidence in 1826 Guinness explained how the system worked

136 This referred to the market rate; the rate fixed by the bank during the same period was a whole point lower at $7\frac{3}{4}$.
137 D. Ricardo, 'Plans for the establishment of a national bank', in *Works*, iv, P. Sraffa ed., especially p. 288.

in practice. The London fund was held in exchequer bills built up during the export season from the proceeds of bills on London or elsewhere in England payable in London or Liverpool (where by that date the bank had agents), which were taken by the bank in Dublin at par less the discount. During the rest of the year when the trade balance was reversed this fund was drawn on to meet bills on London at twenty-one days at par which the bank was always ready to sell to persons having remittances to make to England. If the bank needed gold it drew on the Bank of England for it against this fund but in practice it seldom did since its customers preferred bills payable in London.[138]

This arrangement effectively ended any private movement of gold. Transport between London and Dublin cost something under 10s per cent.[139] Shipment would therefore only be profitable, as it had been early in 1821, if the exchange rate moved either side of par by more than this. The effect of the Bank of Ireland's policy was therefore that fluctuations in the balance of payments were reflected neither in the exchange rate nor in the movement of gold but in changes in its London funds.

Irish private banks, particularly those in Dublin, had conducted extensive bill dealings with London from the early eighteenth century.[140] A large part of their business centred on the discount of bills on England which they either sold or forwarded to correspondents to collect. The balance of these operations, together with those of non-bankers, had been reflected in the exchange, but now any excess supply of bills at par would be taken by the Bank of Ireland and any excess demand for bills met by it. The volume of the bank's business, augmented by government transactions, was so much greater than that of any private banks that it had effective control of the market.

It is not clear to what extent private banks held funds in London. La Touche's certainly did in the 1830s; when funds accumulated there beyond their needs they used to give drafts to the Bank of Ireland for cash in Dublin.[141] Of the banks that failed in 1820 the only one whose liquidation accounts showed English balances was Newport's.[142] With the exchange rate held steady such balances would have been in effect auxiliary pools to the reservoir of the Bank of Ireland's funds.

138 *1826 committee* (C), pp. 238-9, evidence of Guinness; see also *ibid.* (L), p. 69, evidence of W. P. Lunell.
139 *1804 committee*, p. 4, found that it 'does not amount to 1 per cent'; *1819 committee* (L), p. 261, Thomas Bainbridge gave the cost of 1,000 guineas via Holyhead as 4½ guineas, and rather less by direct ship; *1826 committee* (L), pp. 34-5, the Provincial Bank put the cost at 8s per £100.
140 Cullen, *Anglo-Irish trade*, pp. 158-74.
141 La Touche letter book (Munster & Leinster Bank, Dame Street, Dublin), especially letters of 9 Dec. 1837 and 26 Apr. 1839.
142 *Cork Hist. Soc. Jn.*, iv (1898), 282; the balance sheet shows credits of £18,415 at Harman's and £18,840 at Puget's, out of total assets of £125,000.

The assimilation of the currencies in 1826 did not, as is sometimes suggested, bring the Anglo-Irish exchanges to an end. Bills drawn by Irish exporters continued to be sold to persons with payments to make in England, the only difference being that the par of exchange became £100 for £100. The rate could now vary little,[143] but that was due to the stabilization brought about by the Bank of Ireland's policy four year earlier.

Four main influences had operated on the exchange rate and now operated instead on the Bank of Ireland's London funds. They were the commercial balance, the transactions of government, the movement of specie and dealings in government stock.

The first was simply a reflection of the Anglo-Irish balance of trade, including in that term such invisible items as absentee rents and the expenditure of travellers. On the one hand, the funds were fed by the proceeds of bills drawn by Irish exporters, discounted at the Bank of Ireland in Dublin and forwarded to the Bank of England to collect from the drawees on maturity; on the other hand, they were drawn on to meet the cost of Irish imports and invisible items over and above those paid for with bills purchased in Ireland. The seasonal nature of the produce trade caused the funds to be built up during the export season and drawn down during the rest of the year.

Government transactions affected the funds whenever transfers were made from Dublin to London or vice versa. Government payments in Ireland were normally made out of receipts there. Extra funds when required were advanced by the Bank of Ireland against exchequer or treasury bills issued in London. They had formerly been either dispatched to the bank in Dublin or deposited with Puget & Bainbridge. It now became normal to deposit them with the Bank of England against advances in the Bank of Ireland's books in Dublin.[144] In December 1823 the chancellor, finding himself short of exchequer bills, proposed instead to pay the amount to the bank's credit at the Bank of England—unless the bank preferred to have it shipped in specie to Dublin, which it did not.[145]

This method, a simple book transfer in the Bank of England from the treasury account to the Bank of Ireland agency account, would seem to the modern eye the natural way to make such payments and it became more and more common in the future.[146] Whether made in

---

143 Irish office incoming correspondence from chief secretary's office, Dublin, (S.P.O.), shows some transfers in January 1826 at $\frac{1}{8}$ per cent premium, after which they all seem to have been at par; increasingly these payments were made in Bank of England post bills or by Bank of Ireland bills on the Bank of England but as late as 1831 some were still being made by bills on private firms.

144 B. of I. Mins., 1 Oct., 24 Dec. 1822, 1 Apr. 1823, etc. This was the method previously rejected by the bank—above p. 41.

145 *Ibid.*, 19 Dec. 1823.

146 Treasury to Bank of Ireland, 26 July, 21 Sept. 1825 (P.R.O., T. 14/23, 372 & 391), deal with two such payments in 1825.

cash or bills these transfers increased both the bank's London funds and its liabilities in Ireland—initially to the government, then to the recipients of government payments. When funds were transferred the other way the bank's public deposits were reduced by the same amount as the decrease in its London funds.[147] In this way the balance of government receipts and payments had its effect on the Irish money supply. If public deposits in the Bank of Ireland are treated like those in the Bank of England as money withdrawn from circulation only when paid into the Bank of England, the deflation and a surplus of payments became effective at once; if, on the other hand, they are treated as part of the money supply, withdrawn from circulation only when paid into the Bank of England, the deflation and inflation took place with the remittances between the exchequers.

Movements of specie between London and Dublin were normally between the two banks. When the Bank of Ireland had surplus coin it shipped it to the Bank of England for payment to the agency account and when extra was needed the Bank of England supplied it against the account.[148] The supply of Bank of England notes and post bills was a similar means of drawing on the London funds, but they did not circulate in Ireland and were used only for exchange purposes, by sale to persons with payments to make in England; they were therefore treated as analogous to bills of exchange rather than coin.[149]

Government Stock

The fourth source of fluctuation was the transfer of stock. There was still a clear distinction between English and Irish stocks, the former issued by the treasury in London and transferable at the Bank of England, the latter by the treasury in Dublin and, since 1797, transferable at the Bank of Ireland. Irish stocks were originally loans raised by authority of the Irish parliament but they continued to be issued down to, and even after, the amalgamation of the exchequers in 1817. Sometimes they were raised in London,[150] but they were nonetheless Irish loans, charged on the Irish revenue.

147 *Return of remittances 1795-1854*, H.C. 1864 (569), xxxiv, 153; this consolidates earlier returns, the first made in 1833. During the years 1795-1817 £3,500,000 was transferred from Britain to Ireland and £17,590,000 the other way, the bulk of it in 1810-16; there were no transfers either way in 1818-9; during the 1820s transfers were all from Britain to Ireland—1820 £1,300,000, 1821 nil, 1822 £1,600,000, 1823 £877,000, 1824 £100,000, 1825 £470,000, 1826 £400,000, 1827-9 nil; from 1830 to 1845 the transfers were again overwhelmingly from Ireland to Britain—below, p. 173 The mode of transfer is not stated but the bulk, possibly the whole, must have been by the method described above.
148 B. of I. Mins., 6 Nov. 1821, records a transfer of about £1,000,000 of guineas to the bank of England; *ibid.*, 1 June 1825, has a request for shipment of sovereigns in lots of £20,000 until further notice.
149 See above, pp. 43-4; below, p. 172.
150 The mode of transfer is described above, p. 41.

In 1817 the first of a series of acts was passed to make British and Irish stocks interchangeable.[151] Holders of certain specified British stocks were given the right to transfer into certain Irish stocks at rates (after allowing for any difference in interest) equivalent to the par of exchange. The Bank of England on application would transfer the stock to the national debt commissioners for cancellation and would issue a certificate to the Bank of Ireland to write the same amount of Irish stock into its books in the name of the holder.[152] The British stock was thus reduced and the Irish stock increased by equivalent amounts. In 1818 two further acts extended this facility to other stocks,[153] and in 1821 the same principles were applied for a trial three years to transfers from Irish stocks into British.[154] By 1824 these acts had been found so beneficial that they were consolidated into a new permanent act covering transfers both ways.[155] It provided for transfers between stocks at the same rate of interest and on the same terms, £100 British transferring into £108 6s 8d Irish, and vice versa. From 1826 the latter automatically became £100 British, and the switch was identical.

The governor of the Bank of Ireland in 1838 described this act as 'a great means of regulating the exchanges',[156] but its importance in this respect had already been noted before the 1821 act had been passed.[157] At the time of the acts of 1817 and 1818 Irish stock prices had been rather higher than British, and large sums had in consequence been transferred from Ireland to buy British stocks to be switched at par into Irish.[158] This caused a temporary swing of the exchanges against Ireland but once this had been corrected the effect was to equalize the prices of stocks and steady the exchanges. If excessive money supplies in Ireland pushed Dublin prices above London, operators would buy stock in London for transfer into Irish stock and sale in Dublin. Such stock would pass from English hands into Irish and be balanced by a rise in English circulation (by the amount paid for it in London) and a fall in Irish (by the amount received for it in Dublin). When money

151 57 Geo. III, c. 79.
152 *1804 committee*, app. B, gives a plan submitted by John Puget on lines similar to this, designed to reduce remittances from Ireland to Britain for purchase of stock.
153 58 Geo. III, cc. 23, 80.
154 1 & 2 Geo. IV, c. 73, extended to other stocks by 3 Geo. IV, c. 17.
155 5 Geo. IV, c. 53.
156 *1838 committee*, Q.745, evidence of Thomas Wilson. See also J. W. Gilbart, *A practical treatise on banking* (1849 ed.), p. 659: *F.J.*, 6-9 July 1849, report of commission of inquiry into the Dublin stock exchange.
157 Governor to chancellor, 2 Feb. 1821 (B. of I. Mins., 6 Feb. 1821).
158 *1819 committee (L)*, p. 261, evidence of Thomas Bainbridge; p. 269, of Nathaniel Sneyd. Both attribute the recent rise in the exchange to transfers of funds for this purpose and for rents; Sneyd put the total transfer for stock at £3·6 million, Bainbridge at £4 million. The preamble to the 1824 act stated the total British stock transferred into Irish by that date to have been over £8 million, with 'a certain amount' from Irish to British.

was relatively scarcer in Dublin than in London the operation would take place in reverse. In either case the effect was to bring the monetary positions in the two countries back into line.

Payment by Irish buyers for stock bought in London would be either by bills on London purchased in Ireland or by drafts on bank funds in London. In the other direction payment by English buyers of stock in Dublin for transfer to London might be by bills, by Bank of England notes or post bills sent to Dublin or by drafts on the Bank of Ireland purchased by payment into its account at the Bank of England; the first two methods would influence the exchanges directly, the third indirectly through increasing the bank's London funds.

These provisions applied of course to the bank itself as much as to anyone. Its holdings of public securities were around £4,000,000 from 1817 to 1820 and over £5,000,000 from 1821 to 1825.[159] These totals include varying amounts of short-term treasury and exchequer bills but the holdings of government stock were certainly large.[160] Notes were sometimes issued against collateral of stock,[161] the court fixing the proportions from time to time.[162] Some stock may therefore have come to the bank by forfeiture of such collateral. This stock was presumably all Irish, but in January 1824 the bank started to invest part of its London funds in British stocks.[163] This became routine policy and from June 1824 was supplemented by the conversion of exchequer bills held in London into longer stocks.[164]

Such purchases were merely for the better employment of funds held in London where the stock could always be sold again in case of need, but in October 1825 the bank began the rather different policy of selling stock in Dublin to obtain funds with which to buy in London.[165] In December of that year there was a further variation. Prices were then lower in London than in Dublin, which created a demand in Dublin for drafts on London to buy stock. To relieve this pressure the Bank of Ireland exchanged £200,000 of exchequer bills for $3\frac{1}{2}$ per cent stock to be transferred to Dublin for sale on the stock exchange there.[166]

All these operations show the use of stock for arbitrage purposes

---

159 *1837 committee*, app. III-2; below, Appendix 6.
160 Above, p. 7, shows treasury and exchequer bills as £2,500,000 in March 1819 and £1,200,000 in April 1832, compared to total public securities of £3,860,000 on 30 June 1819 and £5,520,000 on 30 June 1822.
161 Above, pp. 19-20, 31 n. 53.
162 B. of I. Mins., 11 May 1824, fixes £85 against £100 of $3\frac{1}{2}\%$ stock and £95 against £100 of 4%.
163 *Ibid.*, 23 Jan., 3 Feb., 16, 23 Mar. 1824, show a total of £600,000 invested in consols in the first quarter of 1824.
164 *Ibid.*, 1, 8 June, 20 July 1824, authorize such conversions.
165 *Ibid.*, 18, 25 Oct. 1825, record the sale of £20,000 of $3\frac{1}{2}\%$ stock in Dublin and an order to buy £50,000 in London; such transactions are a regular weekly feature from then on.
166 *Ibid,.* 17 Dec. 1825.

C

which kept prices at the same level in Dublin and London. The value of money into which stocks were readily exchangeable could not then diverge by very much. Stock was a rather less liquid form than money in which to hold wealth, and the ease with which funds could be switched in or out of it in Dublin or London as a matter of indifference was an important factor in the working of the system.[167] When the balance of other payments was against Ireland so that, as Colville had put it in 1804, she owed more than she was able to pay,[168] the exchanges, instead of turning against Ireland as they had then, were kept in equilibrium by the import of capital in payment for stock. To put it another way the surplus of imports was paid for with stock instead of cash. Conversely when Ireland had a surplus on all other transactions it was used to buy stock in England for transfer to Ireland.

In the twenty years from 1826 to 1845 nearly £23 million of stock was transferred from England to Ireland and over £14 million the other way.[169] These figures are the nominal value of the stocks transferred and there is no record of the amount of money paid for them, but in all but five of these years the net transfer of stock was from England to Ireland. The net movement of capital was therefore from Ireland to England; the significance of this for the economy is discussed below.[170]

Credit Control

During the restriction, in England and Ireland alike, credit instruments —notes, bills and other orders or promises for payment—accounted for the great bulk of monetary transactions and their control was the subject of vigorous debate.[171] Prior to 1797 the volume of notes had been controlled by the obligation on bankers to pay gold for them on demand. This had been suspended by the restriction acts but replaced for private banks, in practice though not in law, by an obligation to pay in Bank of England or Bank of Ireland notes. Issues by the two banks, on the other hand, were restrained solely by the directors' sense of public duty. The court minutes of the Bank of Ireland leave

167 This emphasis on the balance of asset holding is now associated with the *Radcliffe report on the working of the monetary system* 1959 (Cmd. 827), especially paras. 370-75, 388-95; J. Tobin, 'Money, capital and other stores of value', in *American Economic Review,* li, no. 2 (May 1961), pp. 26-56, discusses the theory.
168 *1804 committee*, p. 118.
169 Annual figures of stocks transferred are available from 1826, in H.C. 1830-1 (250), v, 353 for 1826-30, H.C. 1841 (361), xiii, 219 for 1831-40, H.C. 1847-8 (196), xxxix, 571 for 1837-47; they give the annual totals of each stock transferred in each direction.
170 Below, pp. 58-9.
171 The monetary debates of the period have been well described as 'the happy hunting ground of every monetary specialist since Jevons' (J. K. Horsefield, 'The duties of a banker', p. 17, in Ashton & Sayers eds., *Papers in English monetary history*); they have been summarized in Lloyd Mints, *Banking theory*, pp. 42-60, in Hayek, Preface to Thornton, *Paper credit*, pp. 36-58, and elsewhere.

no doubt that its directors were conscious of this duty, often to the point of pomposity, and if their policy was open to criticism, as by the 1804 committee, this was for lack not of public spirit but of understanding.

To many conservative bankers any regulation was unnecessary provided banks issued only by discount of sound bills for real transactions. Their operations would then be a passive response to the needs of trade; if they issued more than the community needed the surplus would return to them and, with no real demand for it, would not be reissued. This real bills, or needs of trade, doctrine was most fully stated by Adam Smith,[172] and its inadequacy most clearly exposed by Henry Thornton.[173] Surplus notes would not, in Thornton's view, return to the banks but would press on prices. He saw no substitute for judicious management according to the state of the economy, in particular to the relationship between the rate of interest charged by the banks and the rate of mercantile profit.

The real bills doctrine was particularly inadequate as a guide to the Bank of England or the Bank of Ireland who had large issues to government in addition to commercial discounts, yet the Bank of Ireland directors were largely relying on it in 1804 when they refused to admit that their issues could cause the currency to depreciate. Colville, unconsciously it seems, referred to another weakness when he spoke of the great difficulty of distinguishing between bills for genuine transactions and others;[174] for the soundness of bills presented for discount—and the same applied to applications for loans—was a matter of degree and judgement in each case. If the banker's judgement on the economic outlook was cautious issues would be restrained, if optimistic they would be expanded.

Both the 1804 committee and the bullion committee in 1810 pointed to the state of the exchanges as the critical indicator of excessive or deficient money supply. This was a relatively simple matter for Ireland since virtually all her exchanges were with Britain and any monetary distortion would quickly be reflected in the rate for bills on London.[175] By the early 1820s the Bank of Ireland had, as we have seen, accepted the view that its issues must be regulated by the exchange position. Its undertaking to give bills on London at par for its notes (and deposits) had transferred the critical fluctuations from the exchange to its London funds.

With virtually no local demand for gold the bank's issues, even

---

172 Smith, *Wealth of nations,* i, 269. Mints, *Banking theory,* pp. 37-8, discusses the doctrine's limitations.
173 Thornton, *Paper credit,* especially pp. 253-9; the last paragraph on p. 259 is possibly as good a summary as has ever been penned of the correct policy for control of credit by an institution like the Bank of England.
174 *1804 committee,* p. 87.
175 *1826 committee (L),* p. 35, evidence of Thomas Spring Rice.

after cash payments had been resumed, depended not on its gold stocks but on the state of Anglo-Irish payments. In a sense it was following the needs of trade principle on a grand scale; on the micro level (of issuing notes only against individual securities judged sound) it was an inadequate basis for banking policy, but on the macro level (of regulating total issues by the state of the country's external transactions) it had the great merit of ensuring that the external and internal values of the currency were kept in line. There were certain domestic drawbacks in tying the circulation to the balance of payments but in a country so dependent on external trade they were probably unavoidable.

The position regarding private bank notes was rather different. In the north and, up to the 1820 crisis, in the south as well, they provided the main circulation, but not in the midlands or west where Bank of Ireland notes predominated.[176] D'Olier in 1804 based his denial of the Bank of Ireland's power to influence the monetary situation largely on the thesis that any reduction in its issues would be made good by the private banks and any increase would be at their expense.[177] If this had ever been true it was certainly not so by 1820. Notes of private banks were paid in Bank of Ireland notes; their holdings of them and the possibility of obtaining more were therefore crucial factors in their discount policy. John Houston explained in 1826 how Batt's notes were always paid in Bank of Ireland notes, and he agreed under questioning that when the Bank of Ireland contracted its issues other banks were obliged to follow, and if the Bank of Ireland were acting 'upon a liberal principle' they were induced to 'deal largely also'.[178]

In time of pressure private banks certainly looked to the Bank of Ireland for help, and in giving it the bank pressed for stricter standards by the private banks concerned—essentially what would later be considered a central banking function. We have seen how the Bank of Ireland gave support to private banks in difficulties in both 1814 and 1820 but not without strictures on their conduct and assurances that no further help would be needed.[179] Bank of Ireland spokesmen before the 1819 committee, referring to pressure in the south in 1815-6, explained that 'although the applications were very considerable the caution necessary to be observed did not induce us to discount to the amount desired', and they added that trade had been slack at the time.[180] In other words the help was conditioned by the Bank of

176 *1826 committee* (C) & (L), *passim;* the west had depended on Bank of Ireland notes since the collapse of Ffrench's in Tuam and Joyce's in Galway in 1814.
177 *1804 committee*, p. 116.
178 *1826 committee* (C), pp. 105, 108; Batt's always held £80-100,000 of $3\frac{1}{2}\%$ stock to sell if necessary, and could get £20,000 from the Bank of Ireland on this security at any time.
179 Above, p. 19.
180 *1819 committee* (L), p. 268, evidence of Sneyd and M'Call.

Ireland's view of the monetary situation. Private banks were normally expected to preserve their own equilibrium—as Guinness put it, 'a private banker ought not to borrow money'.[181] The Bank of Ireland's authority over them really derived from it being the only available source when they did need to borrow. Even a bank with funds in London could only use them in Ireland in time of pressure by offering them as security for advances from the Bank of Ireland.

The control which the Bank of Ireland had over the monetary system was always conditioned by the need to preserve convertibility in London, but combined with its special privileges and its role as government banker it did give it a powerful influence over the economy. Most of the criticism of the bank in this period centred on its restrictive use of this influence.

Money and the Economy

The Irish economy at the beginning of the 1820s was in a state of depression. Since the middle of the eighteenth century the population had soared; Connell estimates that it increased by 17 per cent each decade from 1781 to 1821 and doubled between 1781 and 1841.[182] In England a similar population explosion had been accompanied by the expansion of the industrial revolution but nothing of the kind had happened in Ireland. The English experience gave the lie to the Malthusian theory that a population rise was bound to be self-reversing by straining resources to the point of famine, but Ireland from the mid-eighteenth century to the mid-nineteenth was one country that seemed to prove Malthus right. This has often been explained, according to the writer's viewpoint, in terms of English misrule or Irish fecklessness,[183] but it still awaits an adequate economic analysis. We are concerned here only with its monetary aspects.

In 1822 there was a partial famine in the south and west, and the following year the House of Commons appointed a select committee under the chairmanship of Thomas Spring Rice[184] to inquire into its

---

181 *1826 committee* (*C*), p. 242.
182 K. H. Connell, *The population of Ireland 1750-1845*, p. 25; M. Drake, 'Marriage and population in Ireland', in *Econ. Hist. Rev.*, xvi, No. 2 (Dec. 1963), p. 313, suggests that the rise may have started rather earlier. Statistics are unsatisfactory before 1821; they become more reliable from the census of 1841.
183 G. O'Brien, *Economic history of Ireland from the Union to the Famine*, written significantly in 1921, is an outstanding example of the former; T. Campbell Foster, *Letters on the condition of the people of Ireland*, reprinted from *The Times* 1845-6, an influential specimen of the latter.
184 A leading Irish Whig from Co. Limerick; under-secretary in the Home Office in charge of Irish affairs 1827-8, secretary to the treasury 1830-4, chancellor of the exchequer 1835-9; in 1825 he was one of the founding directors of the Provincial Bank and gave evidence in that capacity in 1826, remaining on the board till 1837; in 1839 on retiring from active politics he was created Lord Monteagle by which name he was a prominent figure in the famine years (*Dict. of Nat. Biog.*).

causes. This committee on the employment of the poor in Ireland heard much evidence on conditions in the south and west.[185] Its most important conclusion was that, while the proximate cause of the distress was the failure of the potato crop, there was no general shortage of food and the true cause was a want not of food but of the means of purchasing it—in other words 'the want of profitable employment'.[186] Press reports of the time tell a similar story.

A large part of the population lived on potatoes grown on land rented with their own labour and made little use of money. This was especially true of the poorest sections but even among the slightly less poor the account system of paying wages by setting them off against rent left many people with little to fall back on when the potatoes failed. This system was used not only by landlords and larger farmers for their own work but also for works under grand jury presentments, for which a landlord would employ his own tenants and set off their wages against rent. Though commonest in the more over-populated parts of the south and west there is also evidence of the practice from counties like Carlow and Westmeath. It was unsatisfactory and inefficient but from the labourer's point of view it had the great merit that it gave him what he needed most, a patch of ground on which to put up a shack and grow potatoes, in exchange for the only thing he had to sell, his own unskilled labour.[187]

To the landlords and the larger farmers there was the corresponding advantage that they obtained the labour they needed in exchange for the use of land they had to offer rather than for money of which many of them had little. During the war they had done well from the export of produce, whether on their own account or by their tenants who were able with high prices to pay high rents, but with the fall in prices from 1813 they had become steadily more embarrassed.[188] Their estates were often encumbered both with mortgages and with annuities to relatives under the wills of previous owners, so that, as one witness put it in 1823, many were little more than 'agents and receivers for the family and their creditors'.[189]

This was a classic case of the effects of deflation—those with incomes fixed in money terms (the mortgage holders and annuitants)

185 *Select committee of the House of Commons on the condition of the labouring poor in that part of the United Kingdom called Ireland . . . 1823*, H.C. 1823 (561), vi, 331 (hereinafter referred to as *1823 committee*).
186 *ibid.*, p. 5.
187 *ibid,, passim*, especially pp. 27, 45, 67, 108-9, 118, 140, 158, 182. The Paul papers (N.L.I., MSS 12982) include rent accounts 1821-4 from an estate in Waterford in which the great majority are paid by work. The Bateman papers (P.R.O.I,,1a/37/51) have rent books from a large estate near Tralee 1824-33 where the bulk are paid in cash but with a fair number by work in the years 1825, 1827 and 1833. Payment by work was probably commoner on smaller estates and farms, for which accounts are less likely to survive.
188 *1823 committee*, pp. 55, 70, 106, 121, 159, 182.
189 *ibid.*, p. 152, evidence of Gerard Callaghan of Cork.

benefited; those dependent on falling market prices with outgoings still fixed in money terms (the agricultural producers) suffered; those in between (the landlords and middlemen) suffered to the extent that their incomes were derived from agricultural production while they were obliged to pay out at fixed rates but avoided this to the extent that they were able to pass on the cost by keeping up their rents. The evidence is conflicting on the landlords' success in keeping up their rents, but they were obviously helped by the pressure of a rising population with no source of livelihood but the land.

Several possible cures for this chronic condition were put to the committee. One which would have appealed to the landlords was that country gentlemen paying 6 per cent interest on their mortgages should be lent money by government at 4 per cent to enable them to live.[190] A similar view was expressed by Goulburn, the chief secretary, later the same year.[191] At the other extreme Robert Owen, who had recently spent seven or eight months in Ireland propagating his ideas, declared that no amount of capital would suffice to create employment under the existing system since everything above the needs of bare subsistence went in rent, a large part of which left the country. He had found the peasantry to be in the lowest state of degradation and attributed this to 'the want of means to enable them to apply their industry to their own benefit'; the former view was widely shared, the latter much less so. His remedy was the organization of self-supporting communities employing the whole of the communal product either for consumption or for internal investment, and he submitted detailed plans for one.[192] The committee commended Owen's public spirit but considered this rural application of the ideas of New Lanark to be 'irreconcilable with the nature and interests of mankind'.[193]

They gave even shorter shrift, by simply ignoring it, to a suggestion from John Brackenridge, an experienced farmer from Scotland and the north of England who had recently toured Ireland, that the impetus for agricultural and industrial expansion could come from 'raising the price of labour and consequently creating an additional demand for the produce of land', to be achieved by 'the people living better and consuming more'. He had found the range of wages to be

190 *1823 committe,* pp. 56-7, evidence of William Furlong, an Irish chancery solicitor largely employed in borrowing English money for investment in Irish estates.
191 Goulburn to Peel, 7 Nov. 1823 (B.M., Add. MSS 40329).
192 *1823 committee,* pp. 70-103; the only attempt to put Owen's ideas into practice in Ireland was in 1831 at Ralahine, Co. Clare, but with the fatal defect that the land remained the property of the landlord and when he lost it at the gaming table the experiment collapsed; E. T. Craig, *An Irish commune, the history of Ralahine,* is a full account of the society by its secretary; see also James Connolly, *Labour in Irish history,* pp. 129-44.
193 *1823 committee,* p. 9.

6d to 8d per day, sometimes 10d in the case of larger proprietors, which was only about a third of the rates prevailing in Britain.[194]

James Roche, the former Cork banker, pleaded for a revival of the banking system. He explained in some detail how the loss of facilities in 1820 and the difficulty of replacing them by those of the Bank of Ireland had left the southern merchants seriously short of working capital and the south in general starved of purchasing power, and he appealed for the opening of branches by the Bank of Ireland and the establishment of corporate banks like those in Scotland to fill the vacuum.[195]

The committee cared for none of these things, neither the subsidization of landlords, the communization of rural society, reflation by a rise in wages nor even improved banking services. What did engage their attention was capital investment. Much of their questioning of witnesses was on how it might be promoted. All the witnesses agreed that capital was desperately short, both in the real sense of implements, farm buildings, storage facilities, spinning wheels, fishing gear, etc., and in the financial sense of the money to run farms employing labour on a viable scale in place of the existing fragmented holdings.[196] Industries to employ the surplus population were few and small; where they existed the distress of 1822 had been much less, and it had of course not affected the linen areas of Ulster at all.

For investment to make good these deficiencies the committee looked to England but found that English capitalists were deterred by the disturbed state of the country, itself in large measure the product of lack of employment. They pointed to this dilemma in their report. In the very preceding paragraph they had noted the reduction in landlords' incomes by remittances to England of head rents, interest and annuities at rates fixed during the war and now forming a higher proportion of total income,[197] but if the link between these two sets of facts was noted it was not commented on. What was happening was that a part of the community's income was leaking away at each round of expenditure; these 'savings' were not being invested back in the economy and therefore exerted a deflationary pressure on top of that from the fall in export prices. A century before Keynes the situation would not have been described in these terms, but the repeated complaints about absentee payments and the demands for British investment show that the two sides of the equation were understood even if the link between them was overlooked.

194 *1823 committee*, pp. 131-43; this range of wages was confirmed by other witnesses. See also Barbara M. Kerr, 'Irish seasonal migration to Great Britain 1800-38', in *I.H.S.*, iii, pp. 369-70.
195 *1823 committee*, pp. 161-7.
196 *Ibid., passim,* especially pp. 26, 110, 122, 162.
197 *Ibid.*, p. 7.

The current orthodoxy of *laissez-faire* stood in the way of any solution to this problem. If individuals had the right to do as they would with their own property, and a hidden hand ensured that in pursuing their own interests they served those of the whole community, then any interference with the movement of money would do more harm than good. This outlook and its impact on the peculiar Irish situation was well exemplified in the following exchange between Richard Wellesley in the chair and Maurice Fitzgerald, the knight of Kerry, giving evidence at the close of the hearings: [198]

Wellesley, 'Do you not think that when the people of an extensive empire are left to their own exertions that they will of their own accord seek to place their funds in those occupations which are most advantageous to them, and therefore most advantageous to the community generally?'

Fitzgerald, 'In a natural state of things, in a well constituted empire, I would agree to that principle, but I do not agree that Ireland is in a natural state. Ireland is impoverished by withdrawing a great part of its income entirely from it; that is not the state of things in England or in France or scarcely any other country in the world.'

The 1823 committee was concerned primarily with the areas afflicted by the 1822 distress, almost by definition the poorest in the country, but their findings were nevertheless of general interest. The sufferers in 1822 were those at the bottom of the economic ladder living on the margin of employment. When activity contracted, or failed to expand to provide for the increase in population, those at the bottom were pushed below the margin and left to scrape a living as best they might. The monetary economy covered the whole country geographically but not always in depth;[199] money penetrated only a certain way down the ladder. In the more developed areas of the north-east with its linen industry and Leinster with the consumer economy of Dublin, banking facilities were better, money was more plentiful and it penetrated further. In the less developed parts of the south and west banking facilities were few—after the middle of 1820 fewer than ever—money was relatively scarce and large numbers were forced to live by bartering their labour for plots of marginal land on which to squat and grow potatoes.

Ireland as a whole was in a state of deflation, an aggravated form

198 *1823 committee*, p. 197.
199 P. Lynch and J. Vaizey, *Guinness's brewery in the Irish economy*, pp. 9-17, describes Ireland in this period as divided between a maritime economy, commercial, monetary and linked to Britain, and a subsistence economy on which it was steadily encroaching with the spread of trade and the use of money; this seems a needless and unjustified dissection of an organic, if sickly, whole. J. Lee, 'The dual economy in Ireland 1800-50', in T. D. Williams (ed.), Historical Studies, viii, pp. 191-201, gives the best criticism of this thesis.

of the general post-war deflation. The fall in prices was often attributed to 'Mr Peel's Act' (for the resumption of cash payments), but Thomas Oldham, a Lancashire linen merchant who bought Irish linen for export to South America, insisted that it was due entirely to German and Russian competition in foreign markets—as he put it, 'it is the reduction in price that has withdrawn the circulating medium'.[200]

While less money came in for exports it continued to leak out for unrequited payments, and whatever savings there were tended to find their way into government stock. As noted above some £8 million of stock was transferred from England to Ireland in the years 1817-24 with only 'a certain amount' the other way; from 1826 onwards the balance was normally from England to Ireland.[201] The money to pay for it may be regarded either as an Irish capital export (if Ireland is treated as a distinct economy) or as a flow of savings from the perimeter to the centre (if it is treated as part of the United Kingdom economy). On either view Irish savings were not being used for productive investment in Ireland. They were not lost to Ireland since the stock remained with Irish holders who received income from it, but this was a very different thing to investment that would create employment, circulate money and improve the economy. To put it another way, the money used to buy the stock in England would have been better employed in importing capital goods for development.

From 1820 to 1826 this drain was partly offset by exchequer remittances of some £4,750,000 from Britain to Ireland. There were no remittances from 1827 to 1829 but from 1830 to 1845 they were overwhelmingly the other way, a total of £9,565,000 being transferred from Dublin to London which swelled rather than offset the drain for stock.[202]

The evident fact was that investment prospects in Ireland were not attractive to holders of investible funds and they preferred to put them into government stock. They may also have put some into industrial projects in England (as they certainly did later into railways) but in the absence of records this can be only a matter of conjecture. The difficulty of finding suitable recipients for commercial credits in 1820 suggests that what held development back was the scarcity of good business projects rather than of money. In the north-east the three Belfast banks had grown with the linen industry in mutual dependence, the banks supported by the sound business of the industry, the industry by the financial services of the banks. Elsewhere business depended mainly on the less stable produce trade. With the improvements in cross-channel transport and the removal in 1824 of the interim pro-

200 *1823 committee*, pp. 58-65.
201 Above, p. 58; from 1826 to 1832 the balance of transfers of stock was from England to Ireland in every year but one, with a net transfer of almost £3 million over the seven years.
202 Above, pp. 46-7; below, p. 173.

tective duties imposed at the time of the Union, such industries as did exist tended to be undermined by the cheap factory products from Britain, and new developments were frustrated by lack of power and mineral resources.[203]

But whether the banks and the money which they generated and circulated are seen as prompting the growth of business or merely responding to the plans and operations of entrepreneurs there is no doubt that the expansion of the system was essential to Irish economic progress. We must now turn to the developments proceeding to that end.

203 Lynch and Vaizey, *Guinness's brewery*, pp. 21-32, gives a good account of Irish industry at this date, marred only by some serious errors of monetary fact, notably the assumption (pp. 26, 36) that paper money was suppressed in Ireland in 1826, and the statement (p. 29) that English and Scottish notes were in general use in Ulster. See also E. R. R. Green, 'Industrial decline in the nineteenth century', in L. M. Cullen (ed.), *The formation of the Irish economy*, pp. 89-100.

3

The First Joint Stock Banks

The Monopoly Breached

The financial catastrophe of 1820 in the south occurred because the community depended for banking on private banks obliged by law to be small and weak or on the distant Bank of Ireland. Even in the north where there was no collapse the banks were finding the needs of the expanding linen industry hard to satisfy.[1] England and Wales were in a similar situation, and only in Scotland was there a sound banking system at this date.[2] After the termination of the Bank of Scotland's special privileges in 1716 two other chartered banks appeared, the Royal Bank of Scotland which dated from 1719 but was only chartered as a bank in 1727, and the British Linen Company which was formed in 1746 to help the linen industry and quickly adopted banking as the most effective means of doing so.[3] In addition, by 1826, there were twenty-nine other banks of varying sizes with a total of over three thousand partners, and all the principal banks operated branches.[4] After some earlier troubles they were all firmly established by the 1820s.[5]

The authorities were evidently conscious, as they could hardly fail to have been, of the contrast between the stability of banking in Scotland and its instability in England and Ireland. In England there was strong pressure for reform, but strong pressure too not to disturb the existing machinery. It seems that the government determined first to experiment in Ireland,[6] and in February 1821 discussions were opened with the Bank of Ireland on restricting its privileges.[7]

Under the 1808 act the bank could not be dissolved without its

---

1 Below, p. 65.
2 W. H. Marwick, *Scotland in modern times*, pp. 14-7, 49-50, gives a brief summary of Scottish banking in this period.
3 Gill, *Irish linen industry*, p. 82, commends this method compared to the direct efforts of the Irish board.
4 *1826 committee* (*L*), app. Cl, C3.
5 *1826 committee* (*C*), app. 6, shows only one Scottish failure between January 1816 and February 1826, a small Falkirk bank in 1816; W. Graham, *The one pound note in the history of banking of Great Britain*, pp. 167, 197, mentions others before and after those dates.
6 This is deduced from the order of events; there is no direct evidence.
7 Vansittart to Guinness, 10 Feb. 1821 (B. of I. Mins., 13 Feb. 1821), states that Sneyd who was in London had informed him that he could look forward to seeing Guinness in England when 'we shall enter into discussion of several points to be settled between the government and the bank'; this is the first reference to the discussions in the court's minutes.

own consent before 1838 but this did not necessitate the special privileges being continued until then. They derived from section 14 of the 1782 act which parliament could repeal or vary at will. The government had therefore a strong bargaining counter, but as against this it owed the bank over £4 million and depended on it for valuable services of accounting, transfer and management.

The discussions proceeded between Arthur Guinness, the governor, and Nathaniel Sneyd, a director and former governor, for the bank, and Nicholas Vansittart, the chancellor of the exchequer, and treasury officials for the government, with Lord Liverpool, the prime minister, taking an occasional hand. In April their conclusion was marked by an exchange of letters, subsequently laid before parliament when their subject was significantly described as 'an advance of £500,000 for the public service'.[8]

The opening letter, dated 13 April 1821, from Liverpool and Vansittart to Guinness, stated that the proposition most acceptable to parliament and the public would be to ask parliament to authorize an increase of £500,000 in the bank's capital and to allow a modification of the charter to permit banks of over six partners beyond fifty miles from Dublin[9]—not in fact a modification of the charter at all but an amendment to the 1782 act which the bank had no power to dispute.

In his reply to Vansittart on 19 April Guinness acknowledged the letter 'in which his lordship and you were pleased to agree to propose to parliament' that the bank be permitted to increase its capital on condition that the extra £500,000 be lent to the government at 4 per cent and the restriction on other banks relaxed. The court accepted these proposals and he would put them to the stockholders as soon as formally requested to. Vansittart replied the same day asking for early submission to the stockholders, and promised that the new banks would not be allowed any privileges 'beyond those to which common law partnerships are by law entitled' other than the right to sue and be sued in the name of the treasurer or secretary if the number of partners made this necessary and if parliament authorized it.

The next printed letter is an earlier one of 17 April from Vansittart to the deputy governor, Nathaniel Hone, in Dublin. In the absence of Guinness in the country, Vansittart forwards a draft of the proposed bill modelled on an act of 1816 relating to the Bank of England,[10] and suggests that the £500,000 be paid by the funding of treasury bills of which the bank held £1,500,000. The two final letters are from Hone to Vansittart conveying the agreement of the court

8 *Correspondence with the Bank of Ireland respecting an advance of £500,000*, H.C. 1821 (450), xix, 163.
9 B. of I. Mins., 25 Apr. 1821, has a copy of this letter, the first reference there to any possible reduction in the privileges.
10 56 Geo. III, c. 96.

to the proposed mode of payment and of the stockholders to the whole scheme.

These last letters possibly reach the heart of the matter, for the chancellor anyway, for the act of 1816 had nothing to do with special privileges or the rights of other banks; it authorized an advance of £3 million by the Bank of England to the government with a similar increase in capital to be credited to the stockholders, and declared Bank of England notes to be receivable for revenue. It is hard to escape the conclusion that in this period of financial stringency the government's chief concern with the Bank of Ireland was to secure the funding of half a million of short-term debt.

This is suggested too by the heading of the act which is entitled 'An act to establish an agreement with the governor and company of the Bank of Ireland for advancing the sum of five hundred thousand pounds, Irish currency; and to empower the said governor and company to enlarge the capital stock of the said bank to three millions'.[11] The relaxation of the monopoly may well have been the price of parliamentary approval for this extra-budgetary finance. The bank gave its consent in a petition praying parliament to enact the bill.[12]

On the model of the 1816 act the Bank of Ireland was authorized to advance £500,000 to government at 4 per cent and to increase its capital to £3,000,000 by crediting £500,000 to the stockholders. This loan to government was to be repaid by 1 January 1838 and as long as it was outstanding the bank's notes were to be receivable by the revenue authorities for all sums payable in Ireland other than fractions of 20s. The total capital loan was thus raised to £2,850,000 while a boost was given to the acceptability of Bank of Ireland notes (which they scarcely needed) and another link created with government finance.

Thus far the act followed that of 1816, but it then went on to break ground that was not to be broken in England until 1826. Section 6 provided that any number of persons in Ireland united in societies or partnerships and 'having their establishments or houses of business at any place not less than fifty miles from Dublin' might borrow on bills or notes payable on demand at any place over fifty miles from Dublin, on the unlimited liability of all the partners.

The Bank of Ireland's monopoly as a note-issuing bank of more than six partners was thus restricted to within fifty Irish miles of Dublin. The choice of this distance seems to have been quite arbitrary.[13] It approximated to sixty-five statute miles, and when the government in 1822 suggested a similar restriction for the Bank of England there was some argument as to whether the distance from

11 1 & 2 Geo. IV, c. 72; *Hansard 2*, v, 655-6, reports the debate on the second reading, its sole reference to the bill.
12 B. of I. Mins., 30 Apr. 1821, has a draft of this petition.
13 *1838 committee*, Q.763, evidence of Thomas Wilson, the then governor.

London in statute miles should be fifty or sixty-five;[14] the latter was finally incorporated in the 1826 Banking Act. By reason of the respective geographical positions of London and Dublin this gave the Bank of England a rather larger monopoly area than the Bank of Ireland.

As an evident sop to the Bank of Ireland for this loss of privilege the next two sections confirmed those that remained; section 7 declared that no power, privilege or authority would be granted, before 1 January 1838 or until all debts owed by government to the bank had been repaid to any partnership or society contrary to the laws in force in 1820 with reference to the Bank of Ireland, except the power to take actions in the name of a public officer if granted by parliament; and section 8 declared that nothing in the act authorized bodies of over six partners to issue notes, etc., within fifty miles of Dublin contrary to the act of 1782.

That the real purpose of the act was relief for the exchequer rather than reform of the banking system is perhaps confirmed by the purely negative character of the crucial section 6. Banks of issue with more than six partners were no longer illegal as long as they kept themselves fifty miles from Dublin, but nothing was done to ease their establishment or operation. They would still suffer from a number of legal disabilities, the most serious being that, without special statutory authority, all legal actions would have to be conducted in the names of all the partners. Not only was this cumbersome but it meant that any change of partners during a case would entail starting it all over again. For banks of not more than six partners this was troublesome enough; for those with partnerships in hundreds or thousands it would be paralytic.

New banks would still be subject to the sections of the 1756 act requiring the names of all partners to be on all notes and receipts, and debarring any banker from engaging in import or export trade.[15] The former obligation was clearly impractical for large partnerships while the latter would lose its *raison d'être* where members would be suppliers of capital and guarantors of liabilities rather than active managers; its main effect was to cut banks off from their most likely supporters.

Another impediment was included, perhaps inadvertently, in the 1821 act itself. The right, under section 6, to set up banks of issue outside the fifty-mile limit applied to any number of persons 'in Ireland'. This was interpreted to mean that all the partners must be Irish residents, and so scotched any hopes of English capital flowing into Irish banks. Had the government seriously intended to encourage

---

14 *Correspondence with the Bank of England on the subject of the charter 1822,* H.C. 1822 (316), xxi, 35. See also Clapham, *Bank of England,* ii, 87-8. The distinction between Irish and statute miles was not always kept in mind—even by Clapham (*ibid.,* pp. 105-7).

15 Above, p. 12.

the growth of joint stock banks it is hard to believe that this section would not have been more carefully drafted and that something would not have been done about the first two sections of the 1756 act and about legal procedure.

The 1824 Act and the Northern Banking Company

For three years this statutory relaxation brought no change to Irish banking. During 1824 a number of joint stock companies were launched for other purposes[16] but before one could be formed for banking the law needed further amendment. The first move for it came, not from the bank-starved south and west, but from the north where the growing linen industry needed stronger banks to provide its financial services[17]—a case of monetary expansion responding to the pressure of physical development.

In March 1824 a petition was presented to Parliament by Sir Henry Parnell on behalf of 'several wealthy and respectable merchants and bankers of Belfast'. It pleaded in particular for repeal of the first two sections of the 1756 act as essential to make the 1821 act effective, and it proposed that partners' names, in lieu of being shown on all notes and receipts, be enrolled in the court of chancery or with the clerk of the peace.[18] The 1821 act left only the south-east corner of Ulster (the south of Down and Armagh and the eastern parts of Monaghan and Cavan) within the monopoly area, and the fifty miles measured along the coach roads just included Newry[19] but no other sizeable Ulster town. A joint stock bank of issue would therefore be quite lawful in Belfast, but the other difficulties remained.

The petition was presented on 12 March but the bill was not introduced for another three months—which gave time to look into the effects on the Bank of Ireland. The law officers found nothing inconsistent with the existing law but suggested that the bank be asked to point out anything that appeared so to it. The directors could not cite any specific infringement but they did protest strongly against the whole thing. They had agreed in 1821 to the bank's privileges being relaxed in the light of the existing law 'which presented wholesome checks on the prevention of establishments such as that which is the

16 *F.J.*, 1824, *passim*, has prospectuses for two mining companies, a bog drainage company, two gas companies, several insurance companies and at least two companies for granting different types of loans.
17 Gill, *Irish linen industry*, pp. 315-6.
18 *Hansard 2*, x, 944-5; parliamentary reports in *F.J.*, 16, 18 Mar. 1824. B. of I. Mins., 12 May 1824, has a copy of a memorial to the treasury which seems to be the same as the petition.
19 The Bank of Ireland successfully prevented the opening of branches in Newry by the Provincial (B. of I. Mins., 26 June, 17 July 1827) and by the Belfast (*ibid.*, 28 Aug., 4 Sept., 18 Sept. 1827). *1837 committee*, Q.4111, Pierce Mahony stated that the shifting of the milestone following road improvements left the town centre outside the fifty mile limit, but to avoid trouble that the Provincial did not take advantage of this.

object of the memorialists'; all that had been contemplated had, in the bank's eyes, been rather stronger versions of the old private banks. The directors were obviously on weak ground, and the chancellor, Frederick Robinson, after waiting till the bill had been passed, replied curtly that it had been constructed with due attention to the agreement with the bank.[20]

After a quick passage through parliament without amendment the bill was enacted on 17 June and became the Irish Banking Act 1824.[21] It opened with the repeal of the first two sections of the 1756 act and then went on, in section 2, to require every banking firm of over six members having 'its establishments or places of business at any place not less than fifty miles from Dublin' to register annually at the stamp office in Dublin specifying the officer in whose name it would sue and be sued and the places of issue and payment of its notes. A certificate would then be granted for each place, and without it the issue of notes by such banks was declared to be illegal. The rest of the act dealt with legal actions; they could be taken against the specified officer and judgement against him would operate against the partnership and might be executed against any member; the society as a whole was obliged to reimburse the officer for all costs incurred and the act was to continue to apply to a partnership despite any changes in its members. Banks registered would legally be partnerships not corporations but they would nevertheless enjoy most of the benefits of corporate identity and perpetual succession.

No sooner had news of the royal assent to the act reached Belfast than, to quote the *Northern Whig*, 'the Northern Bank took the ball on the hop, and instantly announced its determination to open its establishment to the public on that plan'.[22] This meant admitting the public to partnership, and on 1 August 1824 this was accomplished when 264 persons signed a deed of settlement which established the Northern Banking Company to take over Montgomery's as a going concern on 1 September, or 'as soon after as the necessary arrangements can be completed'.[23] The preparations took longer than anticipated and business under the new style did not commence till 1 January 1825, but this was soon enough for the Northern to be the first joint stock bank in Ireland—or indeed in the United Kingdom outside Scotland.

One cause of delay may have been doubt about the legal position on members' residence. The great bulk of the original members came from Belfast and its environs but four gave addresses in England and two in Scotland. The 1824 act did nothing to determine whether mem-

---

20 B. of I. Mins., 12, 19 May, 30 June 1824.
21 5 Geo. IV, c. 73; the parliamentary proceedings are in *Hansard 2*, ii, 786-90; and in *F.J.*, 22 May, 12, 21 June 1824.
22 *Northern Whig*, 24 June 1824.
23 Hill (ed.), *Northern Banking Company*, pp. 269-76, gives a full list of signatories: pp. 277-301, the full text of the deed.

bers had to be resident 'in Ireland' and the issue of whether the residence of six in Britain put the company outside the 1821 act, and so still subject to the restrictions of the 1782 act, was never tested in court. The act of 1825 soon put it beyond dispute.

Another point that evidently worried the promoters was whether the ban on establishments within fifty miles of Dublin applied only to the society or to all the partners as well. Section 6 of the 1821 act might, by a strained interpretation, be held to mean the latter, and the deed of settlement therefore provided, by article 24, that any proprietor residing or having a place of business within fifty miles of Dublin must have his shares sold by public auction, in the same manner as prescribed for bankrupts and insolvents—but this may well have been put in as a safeguard to local independence.

Management was retained firmly in the hands of the partners of the old firm. Article 7 of the deed entrusted the business to three directors to be appointed for life, advised and supervised by a committee of seven, the chairman also appointed for life and the other six elected annually by the proprietors. The deed then went on to appoint three of the partners in Montgomery's as the first three life directors and the fourth as life chairman of the committee. These four were allowed maximum holdings of two hundred shares, which they all took up; other members were confined to one hundred each and only two took this number; the great majority took twenty or less.

The appointment of permanent directors with an annually elected supervisory committee was unusual, and seems to have been devised by the promoters of the Northern. It was copied later by the other two joint stock banks to be formed in Belfast but it did not spread elsewhere. One of the directors in evidence in 1858 agreed that the system differed from that in England and Scotland but claimed that the public had strong objections to dealing with a bank under fluctuating management[24]—a view which does not seem to have been shared elsewhere but which certainly produced well-run banks in Belfast. In effect the directors were more like the general managers of other banks, with the committee filling much of the role of the normal board.

The deed fixed the capital at £500,000 in 5,000 shares of £100. Applications for over 5,000 were received but only 4,891 were issued. Two calls of £10 each were made in January and March 1825 and a third of £7 1s 8d in December to make a total of £27 1s 8d Irish, the equivalent of £25 British into which it was converted in January 1826, making the total paid up capital £122,275.[25]

The committee's annual reports are summarized in the bank's

24 *1858 committee*, Q.5214-5, evidence of James Bristow.
25 *1837 committee*, app. I, no. 58.

centenary volume,[26] but in the early years they tell little. For the first ten years dividends were paid at 5 per cent, with extra bonuses in 1827 and 1832; then from 1835 the rate was raised by one point each year to reach 10 per cent in 1839, and remained so until 1845. In 1835, from an accumulated reserve of £53,327, £24,455 was capitalized by crediting £5 per share to make them £30 paid up. Profits are not stated as such but seem to have averaged a little over £10,000 up to 1836 and to have ranged from about £13,000 to nearly £18,000 from then to 1845. In the latter year the reserve stood at just under £40,000.

The only office of the Northern in 1825, as of Montgomery's before it, was in Belfast. A Stamp Office return of 1826 shows in addition twelve 'branches', presumably the places of issue registered under the act, but these were agencies run by agents, not true branches staffed by bank employees. All were in Ulster and only one (Londonderry) was more than fifty miles from Belfast.[27] The agent in Armagh, Leonard Dobbin, was a witness before the 1826 committees and explained how he worked. Every week he received notes from the bank, used them to discount bills for linen merchants and others, and sent the bills to the bank each Tuesday with his account of how he had employed the money. His discounts at that date were about £4,000 each week in bills on England, Ireland and Scotland. He never accepted deposits; they could be made only at the bank itself in Belfast.[28]

For its first ten years the Northern operated from its head office and agencies only. Then in 1835, to meet growing competition, eight branches were opened, with two more in 1836 and one in 1840, after which there were no more till 1856. All were in Ulster and only two were over fifty miles from Belfast.[29]

The Hibernian Joint Stock Company

While the Northern was being formed in Belfast another bank was in gestation in Dublin. Its origins were described thus to the 1826 Commons committee by Joseph Robinson Pim:[30]

A number of Roman Catholic gentlemen finding they were continued to be excluded from the direction of the Bank of Ireland met together and obtained the signatures not only of Roman Catholics but of a number of others, amongst the rest myself, to the establishment of this bank; many merchants signed it as con-

---

26 Hill (ed.), *Northern Banking Company*, pp. 122 ff.
27 *1826 committee (C)*, app. 9; *ibid. (L)*, pp. 61-2, evidence of James Orr, the senior director, gives nine agencies issuing notes at eleven places, one agent serving three; the list is the same as in app. 9 less Monaghan.
28 *1826 committee (C)*, pp. 242-7.
29 Hill (ed.), *Northern Banking Company*, pp. 249-50; below, Appendix 3.
30 *1826 committee (C)*, p. 83.

sidering by having an opposition bank in such a city as Dublin, advantages would frequently be derived from it and not altogether looking to the emoluments which they would receive as subscribers to the bank, but looking to it as citizens generally.

The proprietors were by no means all catholics—Pim for instance was a quaker—but it had undoubted catholic leanings. O'Connell was a stockholder and at a later meeting described the grand object of the bank as 'the putting down of the monopoly of the Bank of Ireland and the supporting of liberality among catholics and protestants'.[31] Many members were prominent in the emancipation movement and several were involved in current efforts to remove the anti-catholic clauses from the Bank of Ireland's charter.[32]

A promoting committee was elected at a meeting in Dublin on 5 March 1824 which also approved a petition to parliament for a private bill. Two deputies were sent to London to see it through and try to have the right to issue notes included.[33] They saw Robinson, the chancellor, and Huskisson, president of the Board of Trade, but failed to persuade them on this point. The right of issue would, they were told, contravene the government's undertaking to the Bank of Ireland in 1821. Ignatius Callaghan, one of the deputies and later a director and governor of the bank, asserted later that they had nevertheless been given a distinct pledge, without which they would not have proceeded, that when the undertaking expired in 1838 the charter would not be renewed and they would be allowed to issue.[34] Robinson denied that there had been, or could have been, any such pledge,[35] and it seems that the deputies must have attached more precision to the words of politicians than they were intended to bear.

With no note issue the bank would be perfectly lawful with any number of partners, and would have been so even before 1821, but the difficulty over legal actions remained and could only be removed by legislation. The public bill had not yet been enacted, and anyway would apply only to banks fifty miles or more from Dublin. The private bill was therefore promoted to secure similar rights, and it became law on 25 June 1824.[36] The bank is sometimes described as founded under this act but it had in fact already been formed as a common law partnership and the act was passed solely 'to obviate difficulties' over legal actions.

'Several persons' had already agreed to form a company under the

31 *F.J.*, 4 Dec. 1827, speech at general assembly.
32 *F.J.*, 15 Dec. 1825 *et. seq.*
33 Hibernian Joint Stock Company deed of settlement, preamble.
34 *1838 committee*, Q.1179.
35 *Hansard 3*, xxxix, 831-2; by that date (1839) Robinson was earl of Ripon, after a period as viscount Goderich.
36 5 Geo. IV, c. 159 (Local and Personal).

name of the Hibernian Joint Stock Company,[37] and the act authorized them to sue and be sued in the name of their governor or secretary. The names of governor, secretary and members were to be
enrolled in the court of chancery and judgements against governor
or secretary might be executed against any member, who could then
claim to be reimbursed by the company. The liability of members was
not to be restricted, and the act specifically did not imply incorporation or relief of members from any individual responsibility. Its sole
purpose was to simplify litigation and it was to take effect when four-
fifths of the capital of £1 million had been engaged for and 25 per
cent of it either paid into the Bank of Ireland in the company's name
or invested in government stock.

As required by the House of Lords the first directors were named in
the act; their authority was confirmed by a meeting of subscribers in
Dublin on 15 July 1824.[38] Unlike the promoters of the Northern they
had no private bank on which to build, and they seem to have under-
estimated some of the consequent difficulties. The first was to find
subscribers to the £1 million capital—in shares of £100 of which £25
was to be paid up. They looked primarily to the Dublin business
community, but to spread interest they also allocated blocks of shares
to towns in the provinces and obtained subscriptions of some £255,000
from them.[39] The total subscribed by November was still some
£100,000 short of the £800,000 (four-fifths of £1,000,000) required to
bring the act into force, and to make up the difference they arranged
for the subscription of £100,000 by investors on the London stock
exchange, with an option, which was taken up, on a further £200,000
to make up the full £1,000,00U. When the bank finally opened on 20
June 1825 its capital was therefore fully subscribed with £25 Irish
paid per share; £2 1s 8d more was called in January 1826 to make
the equivalent of £25 British.[40]

The Hibernian's original premises were at 81 Marlborough Street,
close to the new catholic pro-cathedral; in 1831 it moved to the
Newcomen Bank building in Castle Street, purchased in the Newcomen bankruptcy.

The deed of settlement as originally drafted was approved in
November 1824[41] but had to be amended to meet the wishes of the

37 This remained the official style until 1885 when it was altered to the Hibernian
   Bank Limited—which may explain the initial refusal of the Bank of Ireland to
   receive its drafts on the grounds that 'the bank does not receive drafts but on
   bankers' (below, p. 91).
38 F.J., 7, 16, 17 July 1824.
39 F.J., 22 Nov. 1824; the principal subscriptions were Cork £40,000, Kilkenny
   £32,600, Waterford £32,400, Galway £27,150, Limerick £25,300, Wexford £16,500,
   with the rest all below £8,000.
40 1837 committee, app. I-no. 57; F. J., 8 Jan. 1825, 2 Jan. 1826.
41 There is an abstract of this draft in R.I.A., Haliday 1308.

London subscribers and was finally signed, by 1,063 members, in April 1825.[42] The preamble states that the shares are divided into two classes, 6,750 subscribed by Irish residents to be designated Irish shares and 3,250 subscribed by English residents to be designated English. All matters relating to the latter were to be dealt with by the London agents, originally H. & J. Johnstone & Co., later the London & Westminster Bank. Shares might be transferred from London to Dublin but not back again, the intention clearly being to encourage their gradual transfer into Irish hands. This was how in fact it turned out. By 1844 only eighty English shares remained,[43] and by 1846 out of five hundred members all but ten were resident in Ireland, mainly in or near Dublin.[44]

The various financial activities that the bank might undertake were set out in article 2 of the deed. As things turned out its business seems to have been confined to the receipt of deposits and the discount of bills. Pim in 1826 described the whole of the deposits plus the paid-up capital as being fully employed in discounts; rates charged followed those of the Bank of Ireland and the money used was Bank of Ireland notes and occasionally gold.[45] Callaghan in 1838 spoke of the bank's customers as almost entirely Dublin businessmen; it discounted their bills and kept their accounts but neither accepted bills on its own account nor dealt in securities; apart from the necessary reserve (held in Bank of Ireland notes) all its funds were employed in discounts.[46]

The 'business affairs and concerns' of the company were entrusted by article 27 of the deed to a board of management of seventeen made up of a governor, deputy governor and fifteen directors, to be elected each December by the general assembly. The number of directors was reduced to eleven in 1826 and to nine in 1831. In practice the company adopted the Bank of Ireland's custom of electing the same governor and deputy for two years in succession and then electing the deputy as governor for the next two. All the members of the board had to be resident within twenty miles of Dublin, and in fact all those elected up to 1845 gave addresses in the city centre.[47]

In origin and purpose the Hibernian was a Dublin bank but its early years were bedevilled by the question of expansion into the provinces. The board was authorized by article 45 of the deed to

42 The original deed, signed first in London and then in Dublin and dated 11 April 1825, is in the bank's head office in Dublin; the preamble relates the history of the bank to that date and summarizes the act; *F.J.*, 1, 3 Dec. 1824, 8 Jan., 27 Apr. 1825, reports its progress.

43 *F.J.*, 3 Dec. 1844, report of general assembly.

44 *Dublin Gaz. 1846*, pp. 273-81; this gives a list of members with their addresses but not the size of their holdings.

45 *1826 committee (C)*, p. 82.

46 *1838 committee*, Q.1123-33.

47 General assembly minute book, *passim*.

select places at which to carry on business by deputies and agents, and the prospectus issued in July 1824 included among the company's objects the establishment of branches in the principal trading towns of Ireland over fifty miles from Dublin.[48] This was stated to be under the 1824 Banking Act but the promoters seem to have overlooked the fact that that act did not apply to any bank operating within fifty miles of Dublin. There was no legal impediment to the Hibernian opening branches anywhere in Ireland provided they did not issue notes, yet the welcome given to the project in towns like Cork, Limerick, Galway and Sligo obviously envisaged branches issuing notes,[49] and stock was certainly subscribed in that expectation.

On this issue the interests of the three groups who made up the proprietary conflicted. The Dublin merchants wanted a soundly based bank in Dublin as an alternative to the Bank of Ireland. The provincial subscribers, on the other hand, wanted a note-issuing bank with branches in their own towns, but this would only have been lawful if the bank abandoned Dublin. The third group, the English shareholders, were investors looking for a good return and evidently expected the quick development of a branch system on the Scottish model despite the differences in banking laws. Experience in joint stock banking at this date was confined to Scotsmen, and the board's lack of it may have led it to promise more to all parties than it was able to perform.

The first trouble arose at the end of 1825. The shares were at a discount and the English shareholders, feeling perhaps the pinch of the current English banking crisis, asked the board to use the bank's funds to buy them in the market. This was quite lawful but in direct conflict with the purpose of the promoters to employ the funds for banking in Dublin, and the proposal was rejected.[50] The next year the English shareholders called for the bank's dissolution, but the board pointed out that, except in case of the proved loss of a certain proportion of the capital, this required unanimous consent. In June 1826 a deputation of English shareholders visited Dublin for the general assembly, and after lengthy discussion of their grievances they reached the conclusion that the bank had been 'most unjustly cried down' in London. The report which they carried back evidently satisfied their fellows for the moment.[51]

With the country members in Ireland the prospect of branches had been the bank's chief attraction. Defending itself against their complaints at the general assembly in December 1825 the board pleaded that its plans had been overtaken by events—it had intended to open branches but since then the Provincial had appeared with branch

48 *F.J.*, 17 July 1824.
49 *F.J.*, 8 Sept., 15, 30 Nov. 1824.
50 *F.J.*, 1, 6 Dec. 1825; General assembly minute book, 5 Dec. 1825.
51 *F.J.*, 23 May, 6, 7, 27 June 1826.

banking as its sole purpose, the Bank of Ireland had begun to open
agencies, the new banking act had done nothing to improve the
Hibernian's legal status, and commercial affairs and the money market had taken a discouraging turn. It concluded with the sound comment that 'banking concerns above all others require time and experience to place them upon a secure and solid foundation'. The best it
could offer country members was to open accounts for respectable
traders 'to afford every accommodation to country parts'.[52]

The issue of notes was considered essential to the profitable operation of branches, and at the beginning of 1826 another bid was made
to get the law amended. Fifty merchants and others in Dublin
petitioned parliament to give banks there the same rights as those
elsewhere,[53] and at the same time a bill was brought in to extend
the Hibernian's powers to cover the issue of notes, but the government opposed it following a strong protest from the Bank of Ireland
and it was dropped on the second reading.[54]

Having failed to get the law relaxed the board tried to find a way
round it. First it issued tokens with no obligation to pay but withdrew them when officially advised that this did not make them lawful.[55] Instead it proposed to issue notes payable six months after issue
—and so not subject to the ban—but in the face of public distrust
this scheme was dropped before any had been issued. Of the tokens
£16,000 were issued but by 1828 all but £200 had been paid off.[56]

By November 1827 many country members had given up hope of
either branches or notes, and meetings at various towns called for the
bank to be dissolved for having failed to fulfil its promises.[57] The
general assembly the next month, on the other hand, after a vigorous
speech of faith in the bank by O'Connell, gave the board almost unanimous support.[58] This did not end the agitation for in March 1828
a private bill was promoted by twenty-four shareholders from Cork
to dissolve the bank.[59] Their legal adviser was Pierce Mahony, solicitor to the Provincial Bank, and in 1838 Callaghan described this incident, aptly by contemporary accounts, as 'the time Mr Pierce
Mahony brought in a bill to dissolve us'.[60] It was supported by peti-

52 General assembly minute book, 5 Dec. 1825.
53 *1826 committee* (*C*), app. 3; *F.J.*, 1 Mar. 1826.
54 *F.J.*, 20 Feb., 6 June 1826; 22 Apr. 1828; B. of I. Mins., 7, 14 Mar., 4 Apr. 1826.
55 B. of I. Mins., 22 Aug., 5 Sept. 1826, refer to the Bank of Ireland's protests
against the tokens. See plate 16.
56 *F.J.*, 22 Apr. 1828, statement by Callaghan to meeting of English shareholders
in London. The Institute of Bankers holds examples of both types.
57 *F.J.*, 10-27 Nov. 1827, reports such resolutions from Cork, Limerick, Kilkenny
and Waterford.
58 *F.J.*, 4 Dec. 1827.
59 *F.J.*, 25 Mar. 1828.
60 *1838 committee*, Q.1167.

tions from some other provincial towns and by some of the English shareholders[61] but provoked a powerful reaction in Dublin. An extraordinary general meeting condemned the move with indignation,[62] and so did a public meeting called by the lord mayor on the requisition of 342 citizens, described by the *Freeman's Journal* as including 'almost all the traders and merchants of respectability in the city', nine-tenths of them unconnected with the bank.'[63] After scraping through the second reading on the Speaker's casting vote the bill was dropped in committee.[64]

With the failure of this bill the wave of internal troubles receded. That they had not prevented steady progress is evident from the annual reports presented to the general assembly each December. As required by article 72 of the deed these included a statement of the financial position on 1 November. It gave the value of the assets and the total due to the public, with the difference between them, from which the paid-up capital was deducted to leave the balance in the profit and loss account. Callaghan described these statements to the 1838 committee 'as far as my memory serves me',[65] but had the liabilities added to instead of subtracted from the assets—a lapse of tongue or of memory for which his capacity as a banker was later held up to ridicule by Professor Longfield of Dublin University.[66]

Up to 1837 profits seem to have averaged some £12,500 per year, and from 1838 to 1845 about £16,500. Dividends were paid at the rate of 4 per cent from the second half of 1825 to 1839, with the exception of 1826 when only 2 per cent was paid. From December 1839 the rate was raised to 5 per cent and remained so until 1851. By November 1845 the reserve, which was limited by the deed to £100,000 beyond which all profits must be distributed, had reached £66,000.[67]

As the Hibernian neither issued notes nor accepted bills its liabilities to the public must have consisted almost wholly of deposits. From 1825 to 1829 total liabilities fluctuated between £84,000 and £125,000 and from 1838 to 1845 between £127,000 and £285,000. The board's policy, described by Callaghan in 1838, was to hold about a fifth of its total resources in reserve and employ the rest in discounts; he did not state it as a fixed proportion but said that if the bank had £250,000 of deposits, making £500,000 with its paid-up capital, it would hold

61 *F.J.*, 22, 23 Apr. 1828, reports the meeting of London shareholders; 28 Apr., 5, 22 May, the petitions from the provinces.

62 General assembly minute book, 5 May 1828; *F.J.*, 2, 6 May 1828.

63 *F.J.*, 14, 17 May 1828.

64 Parliamentary reports in *F.J.*, 28 Apr., 5, 20, 22 May 1828.

65 *1838 committee*, Q.1146.

66 *Dublin University Magazine*, xv, 226; below, p. 141.

67 General assembly minute book includes the statements for the years 1825-9 and from 1842 onwards; reports published in the *F.J.*, each December include them from 1837 onwards.

£100,000 in Bank of Ireland notes against emergencies and employ £400,000 in discounts.[68] It does not seem to have made any loans,[69] so that essentially it was a discount house using Bank of Ireland notes and its own deposits. Its contribution to the volume of money in use was limited to the excess of its deposits over its reserves, an amount which as far as can be reckoned seldom exceeded £100,000 during the first twenty years. The bank's main influence on the monetary system was therefore to increase the velocity of circulation of the money passing through its hands.

The legality of establishing the Hibernian within the monopoly zone never appears to have been questioned—always provided it refrain from issuing notes. The Bank of England's monopoly was assumed, by contrast, to prohibit banking of any kind by firms of more than six partners. It was only after the declaration in the 1833 Bank Charter Act[70] that this was not so that the first non-issuing joint stock bank, the London & Westminister, opened in London.[71] With the precedent of the Hibernian in Dublin it is surprising that this view took so long to prevail.

It is interesting to note that when the London & Westminster promoted a bill in 1834 to procure the right of action by a public officer it passed the Commons but failed in the Lords from opposition mustered by the Bank of England.[72] The Bank of Ireland seems to have made no such effort to defeat the Hibernian's bill of similar intent ten years earlier; it only intervened in 1826 to contest the grant of issuing rights.

The Provincial Bank of Ireland and the Act of 1825

Neither the Northern in Belfast nor the Hibernian in Dublin did anything to meet the needs of the south and west, but another company was being formed in London for this very purpose. The promoters were a group of Irish M.P.s and others and their first meeting seems to have been on 11 June 1824; on 18 August they issued their prospectus for the Irish Provincial Banking Company. Its purpose was to open 'establishments for business in the principal towns of Ireland which are distant over fifty miles from Dublin', and it was to be run on Scottish lines by a board of directors in London. A pro-

---

68 *1838 committee*, Q.1236.

69 *F.J.*, 26 July 1834, has a letter from John Reynolds, a shareholder in the Hibernian soon to be secretary of the National Bank, attacking the board for, *inter alia*, its failure to make loans against government stock or goods; he was answered, not very effectively, by Callaghan in *F.J.* 19 Aug. 1834, but without denying the fact.

70 3 & 4 Will. IV, c. 98, s. 3.

71 T. E. Gregory, *The Westminster Bank through a century*, i, 32-62, deals with the English position in detail.

72 *Ibid.*, pp. 122-43.

motion committee of twenty-six was appointed and applications for shares were invited in both London and Dublin.[73]

The scheme was inspired by Thomas Joplin, the timber merchant from Newcastle-upon-Tyne who was the most outspoken proponent of joint stock banking.[74] His contacts with Scotland had impressed him with the merits of its banking system and he battled for years against the Bank of England's monopoly. His ideas roused much interest in England but his recent efforts to found a joint stock bank in London had failed.[75] Later he was to be active in the promotion of banks in England but his first success was the Provincial in 1824-5. He became secretary of the promotion committee and later of the bank, but by May 1826 had given up this post to devote himself to 'other objects'.[76]

The name finally adopted was The Provincial Bank of Ireland. Its purpose being to introduce English capital into Ireland, the bulk of its members would be resident in England. The legal issue of residence must therefore be settled and this required a new act. The promoters hoped to incorporate in it two other matters, the right to operate in Dublin and limited liability for the members, both of which brought them into conflict with the Bank of Ireland. On a visit to Dublin in 1824 Joplin approached the directors of the Bank of Ireland about a Dublin branch but was told brusquely that they could not negotiate with anyone respecting the charter. In December he was back with two of the committee. They sought the Bank of Ireland's consent to the inclusion of a limited liability clause in the proposed bill but were told that their company was not such as had been contemplated in the 1821 act and that any limitation on liability would be a direct violation of the government's pledge. In January 1825 the court returned a draft of the bill with a similar comment.[77]

On 15 March 1825 the House of Commons gave leave for the introduction of two bills, one by Thomas Spring Rice for the regulation of a company called The Provincial Bank of Ireland, the other by Sir George Hill on behalf of the government for the regulation of banking copartnerships in Ireland in general.[78] Press reports over the next three months often confuse the two but the House of Commons journal has no reference to the former after the first reading. The public bill received a number of amendments both in committee and in the

---

73 *F.J.*, 12 Oct. 1824, has a copy of the prospectus; other details are from documents in the bank's head office in Dublin.

74 His *General principles and present practice of banking in England and Scotland* (R.I.A., Haliday 1224) was published in 1822.

75 S. E. Thomas, *The rise and growth of joint stock banking*, p. 76; this book gives much information on Joplin's activities in England. *B. Mag.*, vi, 70-80, has a brief account of his life.

76 *1826 committee* (L), p. 57, his own statement.

77 B. of I. Mins., 12 Oct., 30 Dec. 1824, 18 Jan. 1825.

78 The Provincial's bill was in fact introduced by T. P. McQueen, chairman of the promotion committee, on 21 March, and the public bill by Sir George Hill on 28 March (*Commons' Jn.*, lxxx, 237, 274).

Lords, some of which may have come from the Provincial's bill.[79] The debates were peppered with attacks on the 'illiberal' policy of the Bank of Ireland, but it defended itself with energy and the government refused to allow any violation of the charter without what the chancellor called 'the most solid and sufficient grounds'. The bill finally received the royal assent on 10 June. The Bank of Ireland directors seem to have been satisfied for they thanked the deputation they had sent to London for the great zeal, talent and skill with which they had 'upheld the rights and privileges of this chartered company' against the attempts to invade them.[80]

The stated objects of this act of 1825 were to remove doubts as to the meaning of the 1824 act and to encourage the introduction of British capital into banking establishments in Ireland.[81] The 1824 act was repealed without prejudice to things done under it or acts repealed by it. The only significant thing done under it had been the formation of the Northern Banking Company which therefore remained valid, as did the repeal of the two sections of the 1756 act. Section 2 reworded the authorization for joint stock banks to read that partnerships of more than six not having an establishment or place of business within fifty miles of Dublin could carry on the trade and business of bankers in the same manner as partnerships of not more than six might lawfully do and might issue notes and bills outside the fifty miles on the full liability of all their members. Section 3, inserted in committee, cleared up a small doubt by specifically authorizing such a partnership to appoint agents to do anything it might lawfully do itself. Section 4, without naming the Bank of Ireland, confirmed the continuation of its privileges within fifty miles of Dublin; the original wording was expanded, evidently at the Bank's instance, to make this more explicit. Section 5 removed the doubts about residence by declaring that nothing in this or any other act was to prevent any residents in Great Britain or Ireland from being members of banking partnerships in Ireland; it was inserted in committee and may well have come from the Provincial's bill. The rest of the act repeated in more detail and with a few modifications the provisions of the 1824 act on annual registration and legal procedure. The transfer of shares was permitted with the consent of the directors but transferors were to remain residually liable for three years.

The most significant part of the act was section 5, which was what

---

79 The original government bill is in H.C. 1825 (176), iii, 35, and that as amended in committee in H.C. 1825 (262), iii, 129. No copy of the Provincial's bill appears to be extant.

80 *Commons' Jn.*, lxxx, 203-428 *passim;* B. of I. Mins., 23 Feb.–24 May 1825; *F. J.*, 19, 25, 31 Mar., 12, 17 May, 11 June 1825, parliamentary reports; the latter repeatedly refer to the Irish Provincial Banking Bill when the government bill is the one under discussion. *Hansard 2*, xii, 1039-45, reports the introductory debate on 15 Mar. 1825 but has no further reference.

81 6 Geo. IV, c. 42.

the promoters of the Provincial had been waiting for, and on 1 August they proceeded with the signature of their deed of settlement. It was prepared in two copies to be signed in London and Dublin respectively, with the secretary authorized to sign each as attorney for the signatories of the other. The London copy has 414 names with addresses mostly in or near London, some elsewhere in Britain and a few in Ireland; the Dublin copy has 275 signatures, all but five with Irish addresses.[82] On both copies several names appear more than once. The Dublin holdings were generally smaller with only five for a hundred shares or more compared with forty-five in London, while large numbers in Dublin and very few in London were for less than ten shares. The bulk of the original capital was therefore held in Britain. By 1846, however, the position had changed and out of 900 shareholders about three-fifths had Irish addresses.[83]

The deed fixed the nominal capital at £2 million in 20,000 shares of £100. By January 1827 £25 had been called per share to make the total paid-up capital £500,000.[84] In 1836 this was increased to £540,000 by a bonus issue of 4,000 fully paid shares of £10.[85]

In July 1825 three directors toured Ireland with the accountant and the solicitor to finalize arrangements, and the first branch was opened in Cork on 1 September. Three more followed by the end of 1825, five in 1826, four in 1827 and two in 1828. By 1845 there were thirty-seven and of thirteen towns over fifty miles from Dublin with populations of more than 10,000 only one had no branch—Carrick-on-Suir which had branches close by at Clonmel and Waterford. Of the branches thirteen were in Munster, three in Connacht, sixteen in Ulster and five in the limited area of Leinster that was open.[86] The bank's stated aim of opening branches in all the principal towns of Ireland over fifty miles from Dublin had therefore been effectively achieved.

Some eight months after the Provincial's opening the evidence of its spokesmen, James Marshall the chief accountant in particular, before the 1826 committees gives a valuable picture of how it worked.[87] As prescribed in the deed the head office and the seat of the court of directors were in London. The original plan was for each branch to be a separate company with the London board holding half the shares, a favourite idea of Joplin's but one which never really worked.[88] In this

82 Both copies are in the Provincial Bank's head office in Dublin.
83 *Dublin Gaz. 1846*, pp. 141-56; it does not specify the shareholdings.
84 *1837 committee*, app. I, no. 85.
85 *Provincial Bank of Ireland annual report* 1836.
86 Below, Appendix 3.
87 *1826 committee* (C), pp. 71-5, Henry Hunt, local director Waterford; 88-102, James Marshall; 249-61, Pierce Mahony, solicitor; *ibid.* (L), pp. 15-21, H. A. Douglas, director; 30-40, T. Spring Rice, director; 41-2, D. Callaghan, local director Cork. See also annual report 1826, reprinted in Gilbart, *Banking in Ireland*.
88 Gregory, *Westminster Bank*, i, 335-53, discusses one such case; another was the National Bank of Ireland—below, p. 120.

case it was dropped in favour of giving each branch a board of local directors, normally three to five, appointed by the court in London from among the local business community. Their principal function was to advise the manager on bills presented for discount and they also had certain duties like checking the cash and certifying the cash book.

Each branch had a manager and an accountant under the direct control of the court. The initial appointees were recruited in Scotland after 'the most minute and scrupulous inquiries'.[89] The manager, with the consent of the local board, could grant discounts up to £1,000 to any customer but larger application must be referred to London as must any disagreement between the manager and the local board. Notes were printed in London, numbered and signed by a clerk there, then sent to Dublin to be stamped and dispatched to the branches where they were signed by the manager before issue.[90] They were payable at the issuing branch, and every branch held a stock of gold for this purpose. No general limit was fixed for discounts or issues by any branch but the manager had to send a weekly statement to London and if this indicated the need, instructions would be sent to him.

The Provincial's system was almost identical with that of the Scottish banks and one important proposal was to introduce the Scottish form of advance by cash credit, that is on a credit bond signed by the borrower and two sureties without deposit of security.[91] Interest was charged at 5 per cent on the amount actually drawn. The bank could withdraw the loan at will, and would do so if it were not kept active with payments in and out to circulate notes. Such credits were only for mercantile purposes and were the forerunners of the modern guaranteed overdraft. They were occasionally granted by the Northern Bank,[92] but as a general policy it was the Provincial who introduced them to Ireland. They did not however prove an immediate success as borrowers tended to use them as fixed loans.[93] There was an added difficulty that in Ireland, unlike Scotland, the bond had to be registered in court and so became an encumbrance on the property of the surety, which was unpopular.[94]

Another Scottish practice which the Provincial claimed to have

---

89 *Annual report 1826; 1837 committee*, Q.4320-33, evidence of Marshall.
90 The head office in Dublin has the first £1 note issued in Cork in 1825 (see plate 1) and another issued in Banbridge in 1833; they are the same basic design with small variations.
91 Graham, *One pound note*, pp. 61-2, describes the initiation of cash credits by the Royal Bank of Scotland in 1727; *1841 committee*, app. 21, shows that the Bank of Scotland adopted them in 1729.
92 *1826 committee (C)*, p. 247, evidence of James Orr.
93 *1837 committee*, Q.4424-9, evidence of Marshall; soon after 1826 he changed from accountant to secretary.
94 *1841 committee*, Q.3054, evidence of Robert Murray, inspector of branches and agent in Dublin.

pioneered in Ireland was the payment of interest on deposits.[95] Despite legal doubts several of the private banks paid interest; so did the Northern who calculated it daily on both sides of the account with the depositor entitled to call for his money including the interest at any time.[96] On the other hand, neither the Bank of Ireland nor the Hibernian paid any, the former holding it to be illegal, the latter not respectable.[97] The Provincial made no reference to interest on its deposit receipts but it was credited daily to all accounts, current as well as permanent, at the same rate—2 per cent at all branches except in the north where the northern banks' rate of 3 per cent was paid. Though not an innovation this was certainly an important feature of the banking methods introduced by the Provincial. The purpose was to attract idle money back into the banking system where it could be employed at a higher rate of interest to the benefit of all concerned.

The Provincial was legally incapable of opening a branch in Dublin, but section 3 of the 1825 act permitted the appointment of agents to do anything that the bank might lawfully do itself and this was interpreted to mean that it could appoint an agent in Dublin provided he did not issue notes. La Touche's were therefore appointed as agents— and a hard-fought legal battle ensued with the Bank of Ireland.[98] In 1836 this arrangement ended when the Provincial opened its own office at 60 South William Street as permitted by an act of 1830.[99] Robert Murray, the inspector of branches, was put in charge of this office. His duties, as described by him in 1841, covered payments of drafts on Dublin issued by the branches, retirement of their notes, collection of bills and receipt of lodgements for them, and superintendence of the bank's funds in Dublin; all his transactions passed through his account at the Bank of Ireland.[100]

The board's annual reports were presented to the general meetings held in London each May.[101] They covered the year to the end of March and contain a fair amount of information on the bank's operations and comments on the Irish economy, but the only figures they give are the net profit of the year and the undivided balance in the reserve. Net profits stayed a little over £20,000 for each of the five

95 Graham, *One pound note*, pp. 62-4, describes the origin of this in the Bank of Scotland in 1729; see also *1841 committee*, app. 21.
96 Above, p. 35.
97 *1826 committee* (*C*), p. 236, evidence of Guinness; p. 82, of Pim. Section 4 of the 1760 act, the source of this trouble, has never been repealed but the House of Lords in 1856 ruled that its definition of bankers did not cover partners in joint stock banks (O'Flaherty v M'Dowell, reported in *F.J.*, 26 Nov. 1856, court of chancery, and 11 July 1857, House of Lords; see also *1858 committee*, Q.5793). *Hansard 4*, clxvi, 683, reports the last abortive attempt to repeal the whole act in 1906.
98 Below, pp. 92-3.
99 11 Geo. IV & 1 Will. IV, c. 32; below, pp. 93-4.
100 *Annual report 1837; 1841 committee*, Q.2902-6, evidence of Murray.
101 The head office in Dublin has a printed volume of the annual reports 1826-50.

years to 1830, rose to over £61,000 in 1834/5, fell to £46,000 in 1836/7 and ranged from £45,000 to £60,000 over the next ten years. Dividends of 4 per cent were paid for the first four years, then raised gradually to 8 per cent in 1835 and remained so until the 1850s, with bonuses of 4 per cent paid in 1839 and 1842. The reserve rose steadily to £124,000 in 1836 when £40,000 was capitalized by the bonus issue of £10 shares. From then on it fluctuated around £100,000; whenever it rose above it, as in 1839, 1842 and 1847, a bonus was paid in addition to the dividend.[102]

The Provincial was certainly the pioneer of branch banking in Ireland. In 1838 the Drummond report on the development of railways held it up as a model for others to follow; it had 'afforded the extended accommodation required by the increasing business of the country, and through its numerous branches greatly assisted, without unduly stimulating, commercial enterprise'.[103] In the course of a lengthy and informative evidence in 1837 James Marshall attributed its success to three things—the 'exceedingly respectable board of directors', the sound system of accounting and inspection and the good field of banking open in Ireland when it commenced.[104] It also undoubtedly owed a great deal to the professional ability of the same James Marshall. He had been twenty-five years in Scottish banks before his appointment,[105] and most of his colleagues were also Scots.

The Belfast Banking Company

After the formation of the Northern Banking Company two private banks remained in the north, Batt's (the Belfast Bank) and Tennent's (the Commercial Bank). Shortly after the passing of the 1825 act Tennent's proposed that they amalgamate to form a new joint stock bank. In 1827 this was done under the style of The Belfast Banking Company.[106]

The deed of settlement followed that of the Northern so closely that it must have been modelled on it. Control was entrenched in the hands of four directors, with a board of superintendence of seven whose duty it was to audit the accounts, strike a half-yearly dividend, prepare an annual report to the proprietors and join with the directors in various specified matters of management. The first four directors, appointed for life in the deed, were two partners each from the two private banks, while a third partner in Tennent's was appointed

102 M. Dillon, *The history and development of banking in Ireland*, p. 28, gives a table of these figures, 1827-88, drawn from the annual reports.
103 *Drummond report*, pp. 18-9; see also *B. Mag.*, v, 202-8, for another tribute to the bank.
104 *1837 committee*, Q.4537.
105 Annual report 1846, in *B. Mag.*, v, 173-4, has tributes on his retirement which seem to have been well earned.
106 *Belfast Banking Company deed of settlement*, preamble; the head office in Belfast has a copy of the deed. Many of this bank's early records were lost in a wartime bombing raid.

D

auditor of accounts and a member of the board of superintendence, also for life. These five were allowed a maximum of two hundred shares each, all other members being limited to one hundred. Directors could be removed by a two-thirds vote of the annual general meeting, failing which they held office until death or retirement. Members of the board of superintendence, on the other hand, apart from the initial life appointee, were to be elected annually, and when a director-ship fell vacant it was to be filled by the remaining directors from among the members of the board.

In all this the deed was essentially the same as that of the Northern. Directors' salaries were fixed initially at a somewhat lower level—£600 to £800 in the Belfast as against £900 to £1,100 in the Northern—but later directors were limited to £500 in both banks subject to alteration by the annual general meeting. The Northern's ban on proprietors having a residence or place of business within fifty miles of Dublin was redundant since the rewording of the law and was omitted. The only other significant difference was the omission of the bar on any member of any other bank in Ireland from holding office or from speaking or voting at a general meeting. The Hibernian's deed included a similar clause, and one can only speculate on why its promoters and those of the Northern thought this necessary and those of the Belfast did not.

The deed was signed on 2 July 1827 by 337 persons. Business by the new firm commenced on 1 August. The capital was £500,000 in 5,000 shares of £100 of which £25 was called in the first two years to make a total of £125,000 paid up.[107] Here again the arrangements were almost identical with those of the Northern.

The new company took over the agencies of the two private banks but where they overlapped they were presumably merged. Batt's agency in Dundalk, within fifty miles of Dublin, must have been closed, as was one at Newry after protest from the Bank of Ireland.[108] Batt's also had agents in London, Liverpool and elsewhere in Britain to get bills accepted,[109] and the Belfast Banking Company presumably continued these. The first full branch seems to have opened at Coleraine in 1828 and the second at Londonderry in 1833, with two more in 1834, ten in 1835 and two in 1836. In 1845 the bank returned to Newry following the end of the monopoly, and this brought the total branches to seventeen, compared to eleven of the Northern.[110]

107 *1837 committee*, app. I-no. 82.
108 B. of I. Mins., 28 Aug., 4, 18 Sept. 1827; being on the extreme edge of the zone the exact site of the agency was significant.
109 *1826 committee* (*C*), p. 108, evidence of John Houston, a partner in Batt's.
110 Stamp Office returns to parliament were based on places of issue which may have been either branches or agencies; they often disagree with the bank's records which are followed in Appendix 3 below. *Dublin Gaz. 1846*, p. 268, gives the same branches but no opening dates.

AUTHOR'S NOTE:—Since this work went to press three pamphlets have been discovered in the archives of the Northern Bank Ltd. in Belfast by Mr. J. N. Simpson of that bank, to whom I am indebted for bringing them to my notice. They are

1. *Extract of a letter to the Right Honourable the Chancellor of the Exchequer dated London 28th April 1824 on the want of banking establishments in Ireland; and also a copy of a letter on the same subject dated 20th May 1824*, both from Thomas MacDonnell and P. L. Patrick, London, in support of the 1824 bill;

2. *Observations on the bill for the regulation of banking partnerships in Ireland . . . 1825*, in support of the 1825 banking bill and pleading for inclusion in it of repeal of the Irish banking act 1760 and other matters

3. *Statement by the directors of the Bank of Ireland and observatio·s in answering thereto*, undated but from internal evidence written in mid-1825, criticizing the Bank of Ireland's policy from 1820 to 1825.

These all plead for more liberalization of the law relating to joint stock banking. They fill out some of the details in this chapter but do not conflict with any of the views or statements.

4

The Expanding System

Bank of Ireland Agencies

For forty years the Bank of Ireland, like the Bank of England, had held that branches were too difficult to manage and control. Before the coming of the railway and the electric telegraph this was a tenable view but it had not deterred the Bank of Scotland which opened its first branches in 1774 and had sixteen by 1826.[1] The Bank of England had doubts about its power to operate branches and did not open its first until specifically authorized by the 1826 Banking Act,[2] but no such doubts ever seem to have been raised in regard to the Bank of Ireland.

If the Bank of Ireland was fourteen months ahead of the Bank of England in branch banking the reason was undoubtedly the challenge of competition, from the Provincial in particular. In 1829 the deputy governor, William Peter Lunell, writing to Horsley Palmer of the Bank of England, tried to contradict this widely-held view. After the failures of 1822 (*sic*) the Bank of Ireland, he maintained, had hoped to see new private banks opened but, when disappointed in this, took the first steps towards supplying the wants of the country itself by opening accounts for country customers; subsequently and long before the establishment of the Provincial the court had discussed 'with much pains', and finally adopted, the more effective measure of appointing its own local agents.[3]

Lunell does not seem to have had a very good memory for dates. It was on 22 June 1824 that the court resolved to open accounts for country customers, five days after the royal assent to the 1824 act and eleven after the first meeting to launch the Provincial. The directors may not have known of the latter but they certainly knew how things were moving. It was not till 4 January 1825 that they resolved to appoint agents 'in the principal outports and some other considerable towns of Ireland for transacting such business of the bank as shall be entrusted to their care'. The Northern had then just opened in Belfast. Only a few days earlier a deputation from the promotion committee of the Provincial had supplied the court with a copy of its prospectus with a request (which was refused) for an interview to discuss 'such

---

1 *1826 committee* (C), app. I; C. A. Malcolm, *The Bank of Scotland*, pp. 157-9; branch banking was pioneered by the British Linen Company employing the offices which it had established to aid the linen industry.
2 7 Geo. IV, c. 46; Clapham, *Bank of England*, ii, 110-6.
3 Lunell to Palmer, 16 Apr. 1829 (B. of I. Mins., 14 Apr. 1829).

arrangements as will be beneficial to both banks'.[4] If the court had any discussion about branches before that date it was too nebulous for record in the minutes.

The sub-committee appointed to work out details wasted little time and on 10 January presented its report.[5] It was adopted by the court and two directors were promptly dispatched to the south to put it into effect. The first agency was opened in Cork at the end of March, five months ahead of the Provincial and three months before the Hibernian opened in Dublin. Six more were opened by the end of the year, two in 1827, two in 1828 and one in 1830. All but two of the towns concerned had Provincial branches by the end of 1828; only one, the borderline town of Newry, was within fifty miles of Dublin. By 1845 the bank had opened eleven more, five of them within the fifty-mile limit. By then every town in Ireland of over 10,000 population had an agency with the single exception of Carrick-on-Suir which significantly had no Provincial branch either.[6]

Joint agents were normally appointed, two sometimes three, and they were chosen for their local standing and commercial experience. The Provincial by contrast selected branch managers for their banking experience and provided them with local boards to supply local knowledge. One of the court's criticisms of the Provincial was in fact the lack of local knowledge among its managers.[7]

In two cases private bankers were appointed—Thomas Scott and his two sons to the combined agency of Waterford and Clonmel, and John Redmond, with his brother Patrick, to Wexford. In both cases the private banks were wound up and the premises taken over. In Armagh the senior agent was Leonard Dobbin, formerly agent there for the Northern and before that for the Belfast, who had been one of the witnesses in 1826. After the 1832 Reform Bill he was elected member for Armagh and gave most of his time to politics. The agency was left in charge of the junior agent, his nephew Thomas, and this led to some sharp rebukes from the directors.[8]

The main duties proposed for agents by the sub-committee were the keeping of accounts for 'all respectable persons' who required them, the issue of drafts on the bank in Dublin and the discount of bills. Lodgements and payments were to be received in cash, Bank of Ireland notes or private bank notes, the latter to be exchanged daily. Bills discounted must be transmitted to the bank each day with an abstract of the day's transactions. The court approved these duties, and varied them from time to time by particular instructions. Internal transfers between Dublin and agencies were not taken for granted but

4 B. of I. Mins., 22 June 1824, 4 Jan. 1825.
5 *Ibid.*, 10 Jan. 1825; Hall, *Bank of Ireland*, pp. 173-4, gives the full text of the report.
6 Below, Appendix 3.
7 Governor to Goulburn, 15 Dec. 1828 (B. of I. Mins., 15 Dec. 1828).
8 B. of I. Mins., 5-26 May 1835.

were soon authorized.[9] Rules for discounting were normally the same for the agencies as for the bank itself. Initially agents were not allowed draw on Britain but this was altered in January 1826 when they were authorized to draw at thirty days sight on London and twenty days sight on Edinburgh and Glasgow.[10]

The bank insisted at first on describing its country offices as agencies. Agents were always asked, in replying to their letters of appointment, to state the name under which the agency would be conducted, and this was the style normally used; the Cork agency, for instance, was always referred to in the early years as Messrs Leycester & Cotter, never as the Bank of Ireland, Cork.[11] The term 'branch' was often used by others, including the chancellor of the exchequer, but it never appears in the court minutes until the 1830s. Even then the legal relationship continued to be that of principal and agent. When a dispute arose in 1832 between the court and the Sligo agents over excessive discounts to one customer, the issue, which was submitted to arbitration, was between the Bank of Ireland and the firm of Gethin & Dodwell who were its agents.[12] One reason for this terminology may have been to reinforce the bank's claim that its notes were legally payable on demand in Dublin only.[13]

The disadvantages of employing local businessmen rather than trained bankers soon became apparent. Their accounting methods did not always conform to those of the bank[14] and sometimes their private interests came into conflict. The most serious problem was over the volume of business. Agents were paid a commission of $\frac{1}{8}$ per cent on bills discounted but were liable for 25 per cent of any loss; the former was intended to encourage 'a spirit of adventure' on which the latter would act as 'a judicious and wholesome check',[15] but this self-regulation did not always prove sufficient.[16] In August 1833 the court decided it must be tightened up.

The Bank of England, when preparing to open branches in 1826, had sought advice from the Bank of Ireland who now returned the compliment. A detailed questionnaire was sent to the Bank of England and its answers formed the basis for a book of instructions which was

9 B. of I. Mins., 19 Apr. 1825, approves lodgements in Dublin by two customers for credit to their accounts in Cork, but it was November 1826 before general authority was given for transfers between Dublin and the agencies and from one agency to another, and for interest on government stock to be paid direct to accounts at agencies (*ibid.*, 21 Nov. 1826).
10 *Ibid.*, 24 Jan. 1826.
11 John Cotter of this agency described his operations at the *1826 committee* (C), pp. 261-5.
12 B. of I. Mins., 1 May 1832-8 Aug. 1833.
13 Below, p. 98.
14 B. of I. Mins., 19 June 1827, report of inspecting directors.
15 *Ibid.*, 6 Aug. 1833, letter to Leycester & Cotter.
16 *Ibid.*, 9 Nov. 1830, has a letter to agents to exercise caution, but a follow-up letter, 5 Jan. 1831, shows it to have been ineffective.

formally approved in December 1833.[17] It was to apply to agencies described as second class, intended for smaller towns under the direct control of the court, but in practice this term was soon dropped and all subsequent openings were under the new rules. As in the Bank of England, agents were to be paid a fixed salary and no commission and were strictly forbidden to engage in any other business or to receive any payment except from the bank. Each agency would have an agent, a sub-agent, a first clerk and other assistants as needed, all to be bank employees subject to the court's directions. Detailed duties were laid down for each post with instructions on how they were to be carried out, including an obligation on every employee to report to the court any dereliction on the part of any of the others. New accounts had to be approved by the court, with discount limits fixed for each customer. Where discretion was left to an agent clear principles were laid down for its exercise and he was held liable only for losses arising from his own negligence or default. At the close of each day a full statement was to be dispatched to Dublin.[18]

The Bank of England in choosing its agents gave more weight to banking experience than to local knowledge but the Bank of Ireland, despite the difficulties experienced, continued to favour local knowledge and the appointees in 1834 were all local men. The first outside appointment of a professional banker was not made till 1838 when the vacant agency in Limerick was filled by William Frazer from the Royal Bank of Scotland.[19] Efforts to fill junior posts from the staff in Dublin were at first coolly received,[20] but in course of time the prejudice against movement was overcome and a unified service was built up with vacancies filled by internal transfers.

Existing agencies were brought under the new rules as opportunity offered. The first converted was Sligo where the original agents were terminated after their dispute with the court and a new agent was appointed in 1834.[21] By 1845 only Derry remained under the old system and continued so until 1849 when one of the agents died.[22] The change relieved the agents of a good deal of liability but at the price of lower remuneration and closer control. They sometimes took it as a reflection on themselves but in other cases where the agents desired the change the court, for reasons unstated, demurred.[23] As part of the reorganization a fulltime inspector of agents' offices was appointed,[24]

17 B. of I. Mins., 13 Aug.-26 Dec. 1833.
18 *1838 committee*, app. 9, gives the *pro forma* of this statement.
19 B. of I. Mins., 4 Sept. 1838.
20 *Ibid.*, 22 Oct., 19 Nov. 1833.
21 *Ibid.*, 12 Feb. 1834.
22 *Ibid.*, 22 Apr. 1845, 4 Dec. 1849.
23 *Ibid.*, 1834-5, *passim*.
24 *Ibid.*, 4 Aug, 6 Oct. 1835; previous inspections had been by directors who reported back to the Court; one result of the change was that inspection reports cease to appear in the minutes.

and it is noteworthy that when in 1838 the court, working mainly through the inspector, was tightening up on the agencies, most of the difficulties concerned agents appointed under the earlier system who had allowed their private affairs to become more involved with those of the bank than was compatible with the new rules.

In evidence to the 1838 committee Thomas Wilson, the governor, spoke of these changes. The original arrangements had, he said, sometimes led the bank into transacting more business than it wished but the new system had brought uniformity between the agencies and Dublin under the effective control of the directors.[25] It is significant that the Provincial, from practical experience of branch banking in Scotland, adopted a closely controlled centralized organization from the outset, while the Bank of Ireland, thinking more perhaps of the old locally based private banks, started with loosely controlled local agents and only moved to closer regulation in the light of its own, and the Bank of England's, experience.

The Bank of Ireland's British Business

While expanding at home the Bank of Ireland was also extending its connections in Britain. These had been almost wholly with London but in January 1825 a direct correspondence was opened with the Royal Bank of Scotland in Edinburgh and Glasgow with mutual accounts for the negotiation of bills. Balances were settled from time to time by bills on London at par, which were paid by transfers between the London funds of the two banks. From then on bills on anywhere in Scotland payable in Edinburgh or Glasgow were taken by the Bank of Ireland at the same rate as bills on London.[26] In September 1825 similar arrangements were made in Liverpool with the private firm of Heywood's,[27] and in August 1827 with G. & S. Lunell in Bristol.[28] In London there seem to have been no more dealings with Puget & Bainbridge but in February 1825 an account was opened with Coutts.[29] It was used mainly for dealings in the London markets, with balances transferred to the Bank of England from time to time.[30]

The London business of the agencies was at first directed to Coutts as the Bank of England was unwilling to deal direct with them, but in June 1826, after much pressing, it agreed to undertake it. The limit on the bills which agents might draw on the Bank of England was fixed curiously at £923 1s 6d, the equivalent of £1,000 Irish, regardless of the currency assimilation then five months old.[31] The Bank of

25 *1838 committee*, Q.640-79.
26 B. of I. Mins., 10, 25 Jan., 8 Feb. 1825, 10 Apr. 1827.
27 *Ibid.*, 13 Sept., 20 Dec. 1825, 7 Feb. 1826.
28 *Ibid.*, 28 Aug. 1827, the partners were relatives of W. P. Lunell.
29 *Ibid.*, 26 Feb. 1825; the initiative came from Coutts.
30 *Ibid.*, 30 Aug., 27 Sept., 18 Oct. 1825, etc
31 *Ibid.*, 12 Jan., 6 June 1826.

Ireland proved similarly reluctant to deal direct with the branches of the Bank of England. The first were opened in 1826 but it was not till May 1829 that the Bank of Ireland agreed to receive bills and credits from them.[32] A full system of correspondence between the two banks and their respective branches was finally agreed in October that year, the Bank of England's only stipulation being that requests for specie be made only to London. With this the Bank of Ireland terminated its agreement with Heywood's and Lunell's, and from then on rates charged were uniform for all bills on London, Edinburgh, Glasgow and all places where the Bank of England had branches.[33] In May 1830 the agents were authorized to draw on Bank of England branches on the same terms as on the Bank of England itself, the par drawing being then at twenty-one days.[34]

The Bank of Ireland seems to have had no dealings with the new English joint stock banks before 1832 when an account was opened for the Sheffield Banking Company for bill dealings on strict condition that it be used only when in credit.[35] All the bank's English business was therefore effectively concentrated on the Bank of England with the Royal Bank acting for it in Scotland and settling balances through the account at the Bank of England.

For purposes of exchange stabilization it was the Bank of Ireland's total position in Britain that was important but the agency account at the Bank of England continued to be the central reservoir. In June 1825, to cover any advances that might be needed on this account, a deposit was made with the Bank of England of £200,000 of exchequer bills, increased in 1829 to £500,000.[36] At the same time the use of Bank of England notes and post bills for exchange purposes was increasing. The Bank of Ireland was always on watch to prevent their circulation but it received any that came its way and paid them out to persons with payments to make in Britain. The terms varied with the state of the market; sometimes both transactions were at par, sometimes at a charge of up to ¼ per cent.[37] When the Bank of Ireland had insufficient to meet the demand it asked the Bank of England to supply more[38]—one of the methods of drawing on the agency account to keep the exchanges steady.[39]

32 B. of I. Mins., 19, 26 May 1829.
33 *Ibid.*, 13, 27 Oct. 1829.
34 *Ibid.*, 9 Mar. 1830.
35 *Ibid.*, 22 May 1832.
36 *Ibid.*, 23 June 1825, 13 Oct. 1829.
37 *Ibid.*, 6 Jan., 21 Nov. 1826, 6 May 1828, etc.
38 *Ibid.*, 11 July 1826, directs that Bank of England notes be brought over as opportunity offered; *ibid.*, 29 Apr. 1828, records a request for £50,000 of post bills at seven days sight accepted.
39 Above, p. 47.

Inter-Bank Friction

The Bank of Ireland displayed considerable caution in its initial attitude to the Irish joint stock banks but the essentials of co-operation were soon agreed, particularly in regard to the exchange of notes.[40] In January 1825, six months before the Hibernian commenced business, an account was opened in the name of its governor and directors, presumably for receipt of capital subscriptions,[41] but in June a request for its drafts to be received on the same terms as those of private banks was rejected as 'the bank does not receive drafts but on bankers'. This rather pedantic reference to the Hibernian's style was however amended a few days later with approval for its drafts to be received as lodgements,[42] and as long as the Hibernian did not infringe the bank's privileges by issuing notes, relations between them seem to have been amicable.

With the Northern and the Belfast Banking Companies the Bank of Ireland's relations were much as they had been with the private banks to which they succeeded. The only clash was over the Belfast's agency in Newry.[43]

With the Provincial, on the other hand, there was a good deal of friction. The first serious conflict was over revenue remittance to Dublin from collectors in the country. The revenue was that of the customs, excise, stamp office and post office. In earlier years the collectors had transferred it to Dublin by various means at their own risk,[44] but latterly the treasury had ordered that it all be remitted in Bank of Ireland notes.[45] In August 1825 the bank agreed with the board of excise to accept revenue daily at twenty different centres, to be credited to the government account within thirty-one days of the end of the week, with any paid direct into the bank being credited instantly. A condition was that the excise continue to receive Bank of Ireland notes exclusively.[46]

This scheme had not yet received treasury approval when, in January 1826, the Provincial offered to undertake the remittance of all revenue. The treasury thereupon called for a joint proposal from

40 Below, pp. 97-98.
41 B. of I. Mins., 18 Jan. 1825; above, p. 70.
42 B. of I. Mins., 28 June, 5 July 1825; Hall, *Bank of Ireland*, p. 142, states incorrectly that the bank had no dealings with the Hibernian before the end of 1826.
43 Above, p. 82.
44 Cullen, *Anglo-Irish trade*, pp. 168-9, refers to transfers by exchequer acquittances, that is payments by merchants into the exchequer in Dublin against disbursements at the collecting centres—a transaction that was unpopular with merchants on account of the delays.
45 Chancellor to Goulburn, 27 Dec. 1827, referring to a treasury order of 'some time back' (B. of I. Mins., 1 Jan. 1828).
46 B. of I. Mins., 1, 11, 15 Aug. 1825; the centres were Armagh, Athlone, Clonmel, Coleraine, Cork, Drogheda, Dundalk, Castlebar, Galway, Kilkenny, Limerick, Belfast, Londonderry, Fermoy, Birr, Naas, Sligo, Tralee, Waterford, Wexford; the bank's initial offer to receive at agencies only was not accepted.

both banks with lists of the places where they could receive payments. The Bank of Ireland declined to participate in a joint proposal but offered to extend its excise scheme to cover all branches of revenue.[47] After further correspondence the treasury finally proposed that the Bank of Ireland remit all revenue from places within fifty miles of Dublin and customs revenue from all parts, the former to be credited within eight days of the end of the week and the latter within twelve, and that the Provincial remit all excise revenue (later extended to stamp and post office as well) from places over fifty miles from Dublin, to be paid into the Bank of Ireland within twelve days of the end of the week of receipt. An offer from the Northern to remit from Belfast only was rejected as too limited, and so was a proposal from the Provincial to remit only eight times a year from certain places.[48] At the same time an old regulation of 1812 that payment of troops in Ireland be in Bank of Ireland notes only was rescinded,[49] and an order seems to have been made authorizing collectors to receive Provincial notes in payment of revenue.[50]

This intrusion of its new rival into government business was seen by the Bank of Ireland as a breach of the spirit of the charter and of the government's promise of 1821, but its reiterated protests were overruled by the treasury. When the court appealed to the chancellor he pointed out that the Bank of Ireland had never remitted revenue, so no right or privilege was being invaded; the new scheme was based on that operating in Scotland and it was only the Bank of Ireland's refusal to submit joint proposals that had obliged the treasury to divide the business out itself; no exclusive claim to such business had ever been made by the Bank of England and he could not admit it for the Bank of Ireland.[51] The bank finally adopted a slightly modified version of the treasury proposal and as a gesture of conciliation declared that it would credit all payments instantly without the suggested delays of eight or twelve days.[52]

Hardly was this matter settled when a more serious dispute came to a head over the Provincial's operations in Dublin. The 1825 act allowed banks formed under it to appoint agents to do anything they might lawfully do themselves. The Provincial accordingly appointed

47 Treasury to Provincial Bank and Bank of Ireland, 25 Jan. 1826 (P.R.O., T. 14/24, pp. 78-9); B. of I. Mins., 31 Jan. 1826.
48 Treasury minutes, 31 Aug. 1827 (P.R.O., T. 29/272, pp. 507-8), 21 Sept. 1827 (P.R.O., T. 29/273, pp. 293-5); various letters in P.R.O., T. 14/24; B. of I. Mins., 11, 18 Sept., 13 Oct. 1827; *Provincial Bank annual report 1827/8*; *1837 committee*, Q.4122-4, 4385, evidence of Mahony and Marshall. Hall, *Bank of Ireland*, pp. 191-2, refers to the arrangement but dates it wrongly as 'during the 1830s'.
49 Treasury to Provincial Bank (P.R.O., T. 14/24, p. 272).
50 *Provincial Bank annual report 1827/8* refers to this; it would seem a natural corollary of the new arrangement, but such receipts were evidently at the collector's risk.
51 Chancellor to governor, 27 Dec. 1827 (B. of I. Mins., 1 Jan. 1828).
52 B. of I. Mins., 11 Jan. 1828; *1838 committee*, Q.712-3, evidence of Wilson.

La Touche's 'to conduct such business as it was lawful for the society to transact in Dublin'[53]—but the question soon arose of just what such business was. The Bank of Ireland made no difficulty about taking drafts on La Touche's from Provincial branch managers in payment of their notes, and in March 1826, when it gave £50,000 of help to the Cork branch against bills on London, this was passed through La Touche's.[54] But the payment of notes was another matter.

Payment of notes was clearly one of the things prohibited by the 1825 act within fifty miles of Dublin but the Provincial maintained that this meant payment as of legal right. Notes presented at La Touche's were therefore paid as a convenience and then returned to the branch of issue. For some two and a half years the Bank of Ireland allowed this to continue but in April 1828, shortly after the conclusion of the arrangements about revenue, the court resolved to enforce its privileges. When the Provincial rejected a request to drop the practice the Bank of Ireland took and won an action against it in the king's bench. In July 1829 the full court upheld this judgement on appeal, and added that the Provincial had disentitled itself from the benefits of the 1825 act.[55] When the Provincial then appealed to the House of Lords the Bank of Ireland asked for an injunction to stop the practice pending the hearing.

At this point the Provincial asked the chancellor, Goulburn, and the prime minister, Wellington, to intervene, and a long three-cornered correspondence ensued between Goulburn and the two banks.[56] The Bank of Ireland, with pained reflections on the change in the official view of its privileges since 1821, agreed to leave its case in Goulburn's hands. It rejected his first suggestion that the bank itself act for the Provincial in Dublin but finally agreed that the payments should continue provided they were all passed through a special account in its books.

The bank assumed that the appeal would then be dropped, but had reckoned without the legal technicality, so far apparently overlooked, that the full court judgement if allowed to stand would deprive the Provincial of all rights under the 1825 act, the legal basis for its existence. As the Bank of Ireland was unwilling to let the case go by default the only solution was new legislation. After further correspondence this was agreed on, and in 1830 an act was passed authorizing banks of over six partners to pay notes within fifty miles of Dublin by their agents provided the notes were issued and made

53 *Provincial Bank annual report 1825/6.*
54 B. of I. Mins., 6 Sept. 1825, 4 Mar. 1826.
55 Law reports in *F.J.*, 6, 8 Dec. 1828, 4 July 1829; B. of I. Mins., 12, 22 Apr. 1828.
56 B. of I. Mins., 20 Aug. 1829-Mar. 1830, reproduce the letters between Goulburn and the Bank of Ireland. *Provincial Bank annual report 1829/30* and report of extraordinary general meeting in *F. J.*, 13 May 1830, give the Provincial's point of view. Letters from Wellington to Goulburn, 22, 23 Sept. 1829 (Surrey County Record Office, Goulburn papers), show the duke taking a not very decisive hand.

payable beyond that limit and not reissued within it.[57] At the same time the Provincial agreed to make confidential returns to the chancellor every quarter of its issues and gold stocks, the gold to be not less than one fifth of the circulation.[58]

Friction between these two banks was probably inevitable. It closely resembled that between the Bank of Scotland and the Royal Bank of Scotland when the latter invaded the exclusive preserve of the former in 1727.[59] Another dispute over the payment of notes at branches is discussed below.[60] An improvement seems to have set in after a visit to the Bank of Ireland by Spring Rice and Marshall to discuss this in September 1829,[61] and by May 1830 the chairman of the Provincial was able to speak of his satisfaction at 'the establishment of a friendly and cordial intercourse' between the two.[62] They were soon to be regarded as the twin pillars of banking orthodoxy against the new waves of expansion.

The Currency Question

The expansion of Irish banking in 1825 may be seen in some degree as an overspill of the English boom of that year, but that it was meeting a real demand is evident from the few repercussions in Ireland of the wave of bank failures that swept England in November. In the two years 1825-6 ninety-three banks failed in England and Wales while seventy-one closed from other causes.[63] The Bank of England itself came within an ace of having to close.[64] The trouble originated, in parliament's view, in the issue of small notes, swollen beyond the real needs of the economy by competition between the country banks. The 1822 act[65] which permitted their continued issue was therefore repealed in 1826[66] and the ban in England and Wales under the act of 1777 was consequently revived. The government had planned to apply it also to Scotland and Ireland but this raised such an outcry from Scotland, led in prolixity if not in economic insight by the Malagrowther letters of Sir Walter Scott,[67] that it

57 11 Geo. IV & 1 Will. IV, c. 32.

58 *1837 committee*, Q.4381, evidence of Marshall; *1841 committee*, Q.2908-9, evidence of Murray, who submitted a summary of these returns, 1831-41, which forms the basis of Appendix 9 below.

59 Graham, *One pound note*, pp. 36-47.

60 Below, pp. 98-9.

61 B. of I. Mins., 1, 7 Sept. 1829.

62 *Provincial Bank annual report 1829/30.*

63 *1857 committee*, app. 21; A. Feavearyear, *The pound sterling* (2nd ed. revised by E. Victor Morgan), pp. 234-8, gives a good short account of this boom and crash.

64 Clapham, *Bank of England,* ii, 100-1.

65 3 Geo. IV, c. 70; above, p. 29.

66 7 Geo. IV, c. 6 (the Bank Notes Act, 1826).

67 *B. Mag.,* ii, reprints the letters in full; see also Clapham, *op. cit.,* p. 106.

suspended action pending the reports of committees appointed by both houses of parliament.[68]

The Irish inquiries of these two committees were less thorough than the Scottish but nevertheless give a valuable picture of the newly expanded banking system. Both reports advised against the extension of the ban to Scotland but were a little inconclusive in regard to Ireland.[69] The effect was the same—no action was taken and the issue of small notes therefore continued, by contrast with England and Wales where they remained illegal until 1914. The only statutory result of the reports was an act of 1828 which declared it unlawful to utter in England any note or bill for less than £5 issued in Scotland or Ireland.[70] Irish notes never circulated outside the country, and this act was really aimed at the infiltration of Scottish notes across the border which might undermine the English ban.

Whatever the position might be in England the great majority of Irish witnesses argued that Ireland needed monetary expansion, and so not merely the continuance but the increase of small notes.[71] Market sales, of produce and linen alike, were seldom for more than £5 and there would not be sufficient gold and silver coin with which to conduct them.[72] There was a strong popular preference for notes as being more convenient and easier to trace.[73] They were also thought more reliable than gold since coins could not be checked without scales whereas the giver of a note could always be required to sign it as a guarantee;[74] such signatures, often in large numbers, may be seen on many Irish bank notes of the period. A ban on small notes would therefore be impractical and unpopular. It would also paralyse the new banks. The Provincial considered that not more than four towns would have enough business to support branches without the issue of small notes;[75] the Northern anticipated a severe contraction;[76] the Belfast thought it might have to close.[77]

The few Irish witnesses who favoured the ban were arguing for

---

68 *Select committee of the House of Commons to inquire into the state of the circulation of promissory notes under the value of £5 in Scotland and Ireland . . . 1826,* H.C. 1826 (402), iii, 257; *the same of the House of Lords,* H.C. 1826-7 (245), vi, 377; hereinafter referred to as *1826 committee (C)* and *1826 committee (L).*
69 *1826 committee (C),* p. 17; *(L),* p. 6.
70 9 Geo. IV, c. 65.
71 J. W. Gilbart, *Banking in Ireland,* has a good summary of this evidence, in addition to a reprint of the Commons report and of the memorial submitted by the Provincial Bank.
72 *1826 committee (C),* pp. 77-8, evidence of Smyth of Londonderry, 92, of Marshall of the Provincial Bank, 242-4, of Dobbin of Armagh, 249, of Orr of the Northern Bank; *ibid. (L),* pp. 55-6, of Smith of Westport, 58, of Pim of Dublin.
73 *Ibid. (C),* pp. 236-7, evidence of Guinness, 243, of Dobbin.
74 *Ibid. (L),* p. 10, evidence of John M'Namara of Limerick.
75 *Ibid., (C),* app. 12, pp. 74, 92, 109-11, 249-51; *ibid. (L),* pp. 18-20, 35-7, 42, evidence of Provincial Bank spokesmen.
76 *Ibid. (C),* pp. 247-9, evidence of Orr.
77 *Ibid.,* pp. 104-7, evidence of Houston.

'sound money', by which they meant gold or notes so closely tied to it as to be no more than its representative,[78] but none of them explained where the gold was to come from. They assumed that it could be supplied without difficulty by the Bank of Ireland, but at this date the bank's holding of specie was around £1,000,000 and its own issue of small notes was over £1,500,000. In addition it had some £3,000,000 of large notes and post bills and about £2,000,000 of deposits, any of which might be demanded in gold.[79] It is not clear how far other banks had gold to pay off their own notes. The Provincial's position may have been similar to that of the Bank of Ireland but others in need of gold always expected to be able to get it from the Bank of Ireland and would have to do so if they were to pay off their small notes.

The Bank of Ireland could always procure more gold from the Bank of England on payment, which meant either using the proceeds of maturing bills (its private securities) for this rather than for new discounts, or selling stock (its public securities) instead of holding it as a reserve. In 1826 its private and public securities were each around £3,500,000.[80] Any reduction in them would entail a contraction in the bank's business and in its ability to meet its obligations both in London and in Ireland. The only other means by which gold could be obtained was 'by the fair effects of trade' or by 'commercial people through their remittances'[81]—in other words by Irish exports or capital imports balanced neither by import of goods nor by increases in the London funds but by gold brought in to go into circulation.

The drastic scale of the contraction necessary to introduce gold in place of small notes does not seem to have been appreciated by its advocates. When gold was in circulation there had always been great difficulty in securing enough for business needs. A merchant from Westport, Samuel Smith, when asked whether he would feel any inconvenience if gold were supplied in place of £1 notes, replied, 'Not if there were sufficiency of gold but I have never seen it in my day'.[82] Witnesses from the north, with more recent memories of gold in circulation, expressed the same view in even stronger terms. Dobbin, from Armagh, explained that shortage of gold at that time had pushed discount rates to almost double their present level—33s 4d on a bill for £100 at sixty-one days compared to 17s 1d—while tenants who had to pay rents in gold procured it from shopkeepers at a discount

78 *1826 committee* (L), pp. 43-5, evidence of Newport, 50-1, of Abraham Martin of Sligo 62-3, of Peter La Touche, 69-70, of W. P. Lunell, 71, of Humphrey Evatt of Carrickmacross.
79 *1837 committee*, app. III-2, 4, 20, 21; below, Appendices 7-8.
80 *1837 committee*, app. III-2; below, Appendix 6.
81 *1826 committee* (L), pp. 54, 69, in the words of James Roche and W. P. Lunell respectively.
82 *Ibid.*, pp. 55-6.

of 1s to 4s per guinea.[83] Houston, from Belfast, pointed out that this did not put gold into circulation since the landlord then paid it back on loan to the shopkeeper. With the great expansion of trade since then it would, he asserted, be quite impossible to carry on at the present level with gold coin alone.[84] Smyth, from Londonderry, recalled having often had to limit his purchases as a linen merchant from inability to procure sufficient gold; the normal method was to give a bill to a merchant or land agent and get the money from him as he collected it, in instalments often up to two weeks.[85] It was generally agreed that a reversion to gold would cause a severe contraction of the currency and a steep fall in prices.

Gold in circulation would be a common currency between Britain and Ireland, flowing in and out according to the Anglo-Irish balance of payments. This would make the United Kingdom a single monetary area and the free movement of men, money and goods would then, in theory, attract capital and labour to where they would be most profitably employed, and goods to where there was the greatest demand. To the government this was the strongest argument in its favour, but the economic history of Ireland under the Union is largely a record of the practical difficulties of applying uniform policies to areas of greatly divergent economic needs. England, with rapidly expanding industries and worldwide trade, needed the stabilization of its currency that the restoration of gold was designed to achieve. Ireland, with depressed agriculture and few industries, needed the stimulus, or at least the facilities, of monetary expansion.

A certain answer to this dilemma was found in the mechanism of the exchanges which tied the Irish circulation to the British yet left it free to expand on the credit base of the funds held in London by the Irish banks. The Provincial had funds in London under the direct control of its head office and was always ready, like the Bank of Ireland, to supply bills on London in exchange for its notes and deposits in Ireland. The Northern and the Belfast presumably did the same, though direct evidence is lacking. The ability of the banks to expand credit depended on the level of their London funds but, with the right to issue small notes, it did not also depend on the availability of gold. Both Guinness and Spring Rice thought this mechanism sufficient to prevent excessive circulation,[86] but there was always a danger that policies of different banks might diverge and competition would then push circulation to a higher level than the country could use at current prices. This would be checked but not wholly prevented by the regular exchange of notes, described by Sir Henry Parnell in 1827 as an

83 *1826 committee* (*C*), pp. 242-4.
84 *Ibid.*, pp. 103-4.
85 *Ibid.* (*L*), pp. 22-3.
86 *Ibid.* (*C*), p. 238, evidence of Guinness; *ibid.* (*L*), pp. 64, of Guinness, 34-5, of Spring Rice.

essential factor in the control of multiple issues.[87] In Ireland inter-bank balances were settled by drafts on Dublin,[88] not in gold as envisaged by Parnell, but in normal times this proved adequate to keep issues under control. We shall see below how it went wrong in abnormal times in 1836.

Gold Payments

While bank notes were in practice exchanged for drafts on Dublin or bills on London the legal liability remained to pay them in gold on demand. The Provincial admitted this liability at the branch of issue (which was printed on the notes) and argued that the Bank of Ireland should be under a similar costly obligation to pay its notes at its agencies. To establish this Pierce Mahony, in August 1825, presented three £100 Bank of Ireland notes to the agent at Clonmel and demanded gold, which was duly refused.[89] No place of payment was then stated on the notes but the Bank of Ireland maintained that it was liable only at the bank itself. In January 1826, when new notes were issued specifying that the sum was in British currency, this claim was emphasized by inserting the words 'in Dublin' after the promise to pay.[90] The bank, as Guinness explained, would be put under intoler-able strain if obliged to pay at the agencies; with its immense issue in Dublin anyone could draw notes there, deposit them at an agency and demand gold for the deposit. No such danger threatened the Provincial whose issues were spread around its various branches. Bank of Ireland agents were therefore instructed to give gold freely for public accom-modation but to refuse it if sought for annoyance or as a matter of right.[91]

The Northern, like the Bank of Ireland, acknowledged a liability to pay at its head office only, which no one seems to have questioned. It would not open branches at any of the eleven places where it had agencies if this entailed having to pay gold there.[92] The Belfast, whose notes were payable by its Dublin agent, agreed that it would have to pay gold in Belfast as well if it were demanded. There was in practice no such demand and it would not be able to tie up capital for payment in both places.[93] It is not clear whether this arrangement continued after the formation of the Belfast Banking Company in 1827, but there is no record of it being challenged as a breach of the Bank of Ireland's privileges.

---

87 H. Parnell, *Observations on paper money, banking and overtrading*, pp. 86-90.
88 *1826 committee* (C), app. 12, memorial by the Provincial Bank; *ibid.* (L), pp. 16-7, evidence of Douglas. B. of I. Mins., 6 Sept., 22, 29 Nov. 1825, show the Bank of Ireland's approval of such settlements by all banks.
89 *1826 committee* (L), p. 40, evidence of Spring Rice; *ibid.* (C), p. 255, of Mahony.
90 *Ibid.* (C), app. 8.
91 *Ibid.* (L), pp. 65-7, evidence of Guinness.
92 *Ibid.*, pp. 61-2, evidence of Orr.
93 *Ibid.* (C), p. 106, evidence of Houston.

In 1828, over the protests of the Bank of Ireland, an act was passed to give statutory force to the view held by the Provincial.[94] The bill was introduced by Spring Rice, then out of office, with tacit government approval.[95] It had a single clause which prohibited any bank in Ireland after 1 April from issuing any note not expressed to be payable at the place of issue; any note so issued would be valid against the bank for double the amount; notes could be made payable at several places provided one was the place of issue. The Bank of Ireland objected that this would impose an excessive burden on it and would needlessly complicate business, but Goulburn, the chancellor, was not persuaded. 'The easy convertibility of a small note circulation into gold ', he wrote, 'is the best defence of its continuance', and he refused to oppose the bill. The bank sent two directors to London, but to no avail and the bill duly became law.[96]

The act obliged the banks to hold larger stocks of specie. This must have had some deflationary effect but evidently less than had been anticipated. Neither the Northern nor the Belfast seems to have contracted its activities though the measure may well have deterred them from converting their agencies into branches. The Bank of Ireland, in preparation for the act coming into force, imported £240,000 of gold from England and distributed £490,000 to its agents, but the increase was short-lived. By January 1830 stocks were found to be excessive and £540,000 was shipped back to England.[97] Its specie holdings rose from under £900,000 in June 1827 to over £1,800,000 in December 1829 but from this level they fell steeply during 1830, fluctuated during 1831 and 1832 between £1,100,000 and £1,200,000, then dropped again and from 1833 to 1836 were always below £1,000,000, usually below £800,000.[98] In the face of these figures it is difficult to argue that the act involved any lasting increase in the specie held by the bank.

But the act did raise the problem of keeping branches supplied with gold in time of public alarm, described by the Bank of Ireland as 'a cause of most serious anxiety'.[99] It was a more serious problem for the Provincial which had inherited from the old private banks the unenviable position of chief target for runs. In March 1828 there were local runs on its branches in Kilkenny and Galway, and a more widespread run in November.[100] O'Connell was developing the promotion of runs

94 9 Geo. IV, c. 81.
95 *Commons' Jn.*, lxxxiii, 379.
96 B. of I. Mins., 27 May-29 July 1828, describe the bank's fight.
97 *Ibid.*, 10 Feb., 3 Mar. 1829, 12, 19 Jan. 1830, 26 Jan. 1831; part of this import and export was direct between the Bank of England's Bristol branch and the agencies in Cork and Waterford, and from the Bank of Ireland's agents in Liver·ool to agencies in the north.
98 *1837 committee*, app. III-2.
99 B. of I. Mins., 26 Jan. 1831.
100 *F.J.*, 6 Mar., 4 Nov. 1828; *Provincial Bank annual report 1828/9*.

for gold as a political weapon in this period and they occurred at his instigation in 1830, 1831 and 1833. In each case the brunt fell on the Provincial.[101]

After the run of November 1828 Goulburn wrote to the Bank of Ireland complaining of its failure to help. This had caused the Provincial to draw gold itself from the Bank of England and he suggested that the Bank of Ireland should make itself 'the quarter to which other bankers may confidently look for support in time of difficulty'. He attributed its failure to rivalry and jealousy, and this drew an aggrieved reply from the directors. Though always ready to help in time of crisis they questioned the wisdom of assuring other banks that whenever their excessive issues caused pressure they would automatically obtain relief from the Bank of Ireland. The recent trouble arose, in their view, from the Provincial's reluctance to depend on the Bank of Ireland and its preference for dealing direct with the Bank of England.[102]

Shortly after this Lunell, then deputy governor, visited London for talks with Goulburn and the Bank of England, and an exchange of letters followed between him and Horsley Palmer, then deputy governor of the Bank of England, which explored this question at some length.[103] Palmer did not care for joint stock banks but thought them safer than private banks and hoped, now that they were established in Ireland, that they would be 'brought into a unity of action' by correspondence through the Bank of Ireland with the Bank of England. He set out principles of management for them and then went on to outline a plan for centralizing their operations on Dublin where the Bank of Ireland would act as their agent, hold part of their reserves and, in case of need, procure extra assistance from the Bank of England by sale of securities.

Lunell cared even less for joint stock banks than Palmer. In his reply he fully endorsed Palmer's ideas about their management but 'shuddered at the responsibility' that would fall on the Bank of Ireland if it were openly to stand behind them. The Bank of England's issues were mainly on government securities but the Bank of Ireland's, he pointed out, were chiefly by commercial discounts in which it competed with the joint stock banks. Any bank offering good security could obtain help from the Bank of Ireland in time of temporary difficulty but a standing arrangement would merely engender greater confidence in joint stock banks than they merited.

Palmer was disappointed and replied that he would 'leave to time to effect those changes which appear to me to be essential'. (A comment pencilled in 1860 opposite this entry in the bank's minute book notes that by then time had done so.) He went on to question the

101 Below, pp. 121-2.
102 Goulburn to governor, 9 Dec. 1828; governor to Goulburn, 15 Dec. 1828 (B. of I. Mins., 15 Dec. 1828).
103 B. of I. Mins., 14, 21 Apr. 1829, have copies of these letters.

Bank of Ireland's right to special privileges if it did not accept the same responsibility as the Bank of England to support the rest of the system. 'Monopoly of paper issue', he wrote, 'or uniformity of action in its regulation I decidedly advocate but monopoly of the banking business I deprecate as prejudicial to the best interests of the country.' The correspondence closed on a huffy note, with mutual recriminations as to whether it was to be treated as private or official. In due course Palmer's ideas were to have some influence on the developments of 1844-5, but with reservations as far as the central status of the Bank of Ireland was concerned.

The Statistical Position

Control of note issues, and also, though this is seldom mentioned, of deposits, was therefore left to each individual bank but a major improvement was made in the collection of statistics. Several of the 1826 witnesses spoke of the need for regular returns of note issues as what Spring Rice called 'a most important corrective check',[104] and to this end another act was passed in 1828.[105] It required bankers to take out licences with the Stamp Office for their places of issue, subject to which they might issue notes unstamped in denominations up to £100. Licences cost £30 each but no bank need take out more than four, any additional places of issue being included on the fourth licence. A bank so licensed must issue all its notes unstamped, must keep accurate accounts open to inspection by the Stamp Office of notes issued and cancelled and must deliver on every 1 January and 1 July an account of its circulation on each Saturday of the previous half-year with a statement of the average circulation over the period. On this average it had to pay an annual composition of 3s per £100.

This act did not apply to the Bank of Ireland which already compounded for its stamp duty under an act of 1815.[106] The fee was agreed with the treasury on the basis of the estimated circulation of the following year, and the rate agreed was in fact much higher than 3s per cent, but with its eye on the new financial arrangements expected to accompany the renewal of the charter the bank made no move to get it altered until 1839. The abortive bill of that year[107] included the reduction of the rate to 3s per cent, and when it was abandoned the bank asked, and the treasury agreed, that the fee be calculated in future at the same rate as for other banks.[108]

Official information on circulation was therefore on a different basis for the Bank of Ireland and for the other banks, and this may

104 *1826 committee* (*L*), p. 38; see also pp. 46-7, evidence of Newport; *ibid.* (*C*), p. 87. of Pim.
105 9 Geo. IV, c. 80.
106 55 Geo. III, c. 100, s. 19.
107 Below. p. 168.
108 B. of I. Mins., 10 Sept., 26 Nov. 1839, 4, 18 Apr. 1843.

be why no information under the 1828 act ever seems to have been revealed to parliament or to anyone else. In 1833 a new act[109] required all banks in the United Kingdom to make weekly and quarterly returns of their average circulation to the Stamp Office in London, and another act in 1841[110] extended this and required monthly returns for publication in the *Gazette*. Statistics based on these returns are in the reports of the 1841 and 1857 committees[111] but they only commence in September 1833. Prior to that date statistics are reasonably good for the Bank of Ireland but, for the historian at least, most inadequate for other banks.

The fullest information on the Bank of Ireland is in the forty-one returns submitted by it to the 1837 committee.[112] They are not always directly comparable with each other but the general trends are clear. From 1824 to 1828, the first years of the agencies, the balance sheet changes may be summarized as follows:

Liabilities	£	Assets	£
Circulation : small notes	+300,000	Public securities	−1,800,000
large notes	−250,000	Private securities	+2,400,000
post bills	−650,000	Specie	− 300,000
Deposits and sundry balance	+900,000		
Total	+300,000		+ 300,000

The most striking figure here is the big rise in private securities. The great bulk of this was commercial bills. The average of bills under discount at the agencies climbed steadily from the first openings and reached £2,000,000 by 1828, which suggests that a large part of the rise represented new business secured through them.

Three-quarters of this rise in private securities is balanced by a fall in public securities. There is no information on how this came about, but to the extent that it represents a reduction in direct lending to government the effect was a switch of resources from public to private accommodation; to the extent that the reduction came from sales of stock in London the effect was an expansion of the Irish money supply by the import of capital funds to pay for it;[113] to the extent that the stock was sold in Ireland it represents no change in the money supply but a transfer of liquid funds through the bank from the buyers of the stock to the recipients of the discounts.

A further £300,000 of the rise is accounted for by the fall in specie, the net effect of which was just as if cash to this amount had been

109 3 & 4 Will. IV, c. 83.
110 4 & 5 Vic., c. 50.
111 *1841 committee*, app. 23; *1857 committee*, app. 15.
112 *1837 committee*, app. III.
113 Above, pp. 47-50.

paid out in discount of additional bills. The remaining £300,000 has its counterpart in the increase in small notes and/or deposits; the net effect again is just as if bills to this amount had been discounted and payment made either by the issue of small notes or by credit to accounts.

The remaining £900,000 increase in small notes and/or deposits is balanced by a similar reduction in large notes and post bills. The bulk of this fall was in post bills. Their circulation had risen sharply in 1821, in response presumably to the need to replace the lost transfer facilities of the private banks. It reached a peak in 1825 and then fell steadily as the branch network developed.

There are two main conclusions to be drawn from these figures. The first is the big increase in private accommodation that accompanied the coming of branch banking and joint stock competition, provided partly by a reduction in government securities and gold stocks, partly by an increase in small notes and deposits. The second is the switch in liabilities from large notes and post bills to small notes and deposits, a sign partly of circulation of higher velocity (small notes rather than large), partly of growth in the use of cheque-operated accounts in place of large notes and post bills, partly of increased savings in the form of permanent deposits.

For the other banks prior to 1833 we have to rely mainly on stamping figures, a particularly unreliable guide around 1825-6 when many banks stamped much above their normal level to issue new notes in British currency in exchange for old notes in Irish.[114] Furthermore the Provincial, in preparation for its first branch openings, stamped large numbers of notes which were not immediately issued.[115] Total numbers stamped increased, as might be expected, in 1824 and 1825 but then declined. The values were estimated at £1,120,000 in 1824, £2,110,000 in 1825, £1,190,000 in 1826 and only £660,000 in 1827. They were predominantly small notes and overwhelmingly issued by banks outside Dublin, the only Dublin issuers being Shaw's and Ball's.[116] Without details of cancellations we cannot say what additions to circulation these figures represent but when reliable statistics commence in 1833 the total for banks other than the Bank of Ireland was only £1,100,000,[117] less than half of what the private banks seem to have had out before the 1820 crisis.[118]

Statistics of deposits in these banks are not merely uncertain but non-existent. We know that both the Provincial and the Northern

114 *Return of banking establishments in Ireland 1826 and 1836*, H.C. 1836 (346), xxxvii, 373; above p. 29.
115 *1826 committee (C)*, pp. 73, 93, evidence of Hunt and Marshall.
116 *Ibid.*, app. 4, 10; *Return of number of country bank notes stamped in Ireland 1825-7*, H.C. 1828 (91), xxii, 81. See above, pp. 32-4, for earlier years.
117 Below, Appendix 10.
118 Above, p. 33.

paid interest to encourage deposits,[119] and so did the Belfast, while the Hibernian, which paid no interest, normally had deposits of about £90,000.[120] They were obviously rising in the joint stock banks just as they were in the Bank of Ireland (which paid no interest), but it is not possible to make any worthwhile guess at their total nor to give any idea of their turnover.

Taking all banks other than the Bank of Ireland it is undoubtedly true that both notes and deposits at the end of the decade were considerably higher than they had been in 1824, but it is questionable whether either had yet passed the level reached by the private banks in 1820. What had been achieved was a great improvement in stability and in geographical spread. Quite aside from any changes in the value of money as such, the notes and deposits of the joint stock banks were probably a sounder and more useful form of money than those of the old private banks. This was not a universally held view,[121] and it depended on the quality of management, but for the Irish joint stock banks at the end of the 1820s it seems a fair judgement.

119 Above, p. 80.
120 *1826 committee* (*C*), p. 82, evidence of Pim.
121 B. of I. Mins., 14 Apr. 1829, show that Horsley Palmer held it but Lunell did not.

5

The Second Wave of Expansion

Banking in the Thirties

Branch banking had been successfully launched in Ireland, but by the end of 1830 there were still only ten towns outside Dublin and Belfast with two banks and another seven with one. The population was expanding rapidly and the need for increased circulation and the banks to supply it was greater than ever. Anyone could now form a joint stock bank of issue over fifty miles from Dublin subject only to the obligation to register details at the Stamp Office, a formality without either condition or provision for refusal. Figures at Appendix 4 below indicate the change that was to take place over the next fifteen years. Most of it occurred during the middle years of the 1830s.

One of the main sources of information on banking in this period is the evidence given before a series of committees of the House of Commons. The 1832 committee on the charter of the Bank of England[1] and the 1836 committee on the working of the 1826 Banking Act in England and Wales,[2] both important in English monetary history, had no direct relevance to Ireland, but when the latter committee was reappointed in 1837 its terms were extended to cover Ireland as well. Under the chairmanship of Thomas Spring Rice, now chancellor of the exchequer, with Daniel O'Connell as one of its members, it heard seven witnesses connected with Irish banking and printed much valuable information in its appendix.[3]

The 1837 evidence was submitted to parliament with no comment and the next year the committee was reappointed. This committee of 1838 heard five Irish witnesses but its brief report merely recommended some temporary measures until parliament had had time to give full consideration to the whole question of banking legislation.[4]

1 *Report of the select committee of secrecy of the House of Commons on the Bank of England charter 1832*, H.C. 1831-2 (722), vi, 1.
2 *Report of select committee of the House of Commons to inquire into the operation of the act of 7 Geo. IV, c. 46, permitting the establishment of joint stock banks . . . 1836* H.C. 1836 (591), ix, 411 (hereinafter referred to as *1836 committee*).
3 *Report of select committee of the House of Commons to inquire into the operation of the acts permitting the establishment of joint stock banks in England and Ireland 1837*, H.C. 1837 (531), xiv, 1 (hereinafter referred to as *1837 committee*); app. I gives the answers of joint stock banks to a questionnaire on their formation; app. II lists all joint stock banks in England, Scotland and Ireland with their branches 'to the latest date the same can be made out', a useful record but not always compatible with other sources; app. III prints forty-one returns from the Bank of Ireland.
4 *Report of select committee of the House of Commons appointed to consider the same subject 1838*, H.C. 1837-8 (626), vii, 1 (hereinafter referred to as *1838 committee*).

Despite these inconclusive results there was no reappointment in 1839, but in 1840 a new committee was appointed to look into the law on banks of issue. It heard no Irish witnesses and its report which did little more than recommend its reappointment had no reference to Ireland, but it collected a number of returns from the Bank of Ireland and the Stamp Office.[5]

In 1841 the committee was duly reappointed. It heard two Irish witnesses and included more useful returns in its appendix. It made two brief reports; the first recommended the more frequent and accurate publication of circulation figures and led to the passing of the 1841 act to that end;[6] the second pleaded lack of time to give a 'well-grounded opinion' and left it to the House to decide whether a committee should be appointed next session to complete the inquiries and report.[7]

No further appointment was made, and the value of these committees lies, not in their reports, but in the evidence they collected, both a picking ground for historians and the basis on which the government of the day framed the banking legislation of 1844 and 1845. The Irish witnesses before these committees were widely drawn but unfortunately included no spokesman from the northern banks nor from the new National Bank.

The Private Banks

The first new creations of the thirties were a number of private banks in Dublin. Here a difficulty arises in deciding just what is meant by a private bank at this date. Any firm dealing in money could describe its business as banking. If it issued notes it must register under the act of 1815 but by the 1830s few private banks did. Discounting, acceptance, lending and other financial business were natural activities for many firms which could then reasonably call themselves bankers. With the bulk of traditional banking passing to the joint stock banks the genus 'private banker' merged imperceptibly with those of 'stockbroker', 'billbroker', 'land agent' and that definition-defying creature 'the merchant banker'.

Subject to these qualifications the following were the new private banks formed in this period:

---

5 *Report of select committee of the House of Commons appointed to inquire into the effects produced on the circulation of the country by the various banking establishments issuing notes payable on demand 1840*, H.C. 1840 (602), iv, 1 (hereinafter referred to as *1840 committee*).

6 4 & 5 Vic., c. 50; above, p. 102.

7 *Report of select committee of secrecy of the House of Commons to inquire into the effects produced on the circulation of the country by the various banking establishments issuing notes payable on demand 1841*, H.C. 1841 (366, 410), v, 1 (hereinafter referred to as *1841 committee*).

Robert Gray & Co., founded apparently in 1829.[8] There is little information about it before 1863 when it was incorporated as the English and Irish Bank which failed the next year. In 1836 Robert Gray was one of the largest shareholders in the new Royal Bank of Ireland,[9] and in 1849 he was a witness before the commission of inquiry into the Dublin stock exchange but had very little to say about his bank.[10]

R. S. Guinness & Co., founded some time before 1831 at 5 Kildare Street by Richard Samuel, grandson of Samuel the younger brother of the first Arthur Guinness of the brewery. The firm was mainly a land agency[11] but banking was important enough for it to be appointed agent for the Agricultural & Commercial Bank in 1834.[12] It stopped payments in 1848 and was wound up.[13]

Guinness & Mahon, formed in 1837 at 26 South Frederick Street by Robert Rundell Guinness, elder brother and former partner of the above Richard Samuel, and John Ross Mahon. This too was primarily a land agency and it was not till 1859 that banking contributed the major portion of its profits. In 1854 it moved to 17 College Green where it remains to this day.[14]

Boyle, Low & Pim, founded it seems in 1832.[15] James Pim, one of the partners, described the firm in 1838 as stockbrokers and bankers' agents, classed as bankers only because they had to take out a banker's licence.[16] As they did not issue notes it is not clear what he meant by this, but they may well have taken out a licence for the prestige of calling themselves licensed bankers. They were agents in Dublin for the Northern and English agents for the Provincial—which meant that they took English money from the Provincial and exchanged it for Irish. They employed funds in Dublin for their bank clients and did a considerable business in Bank of England post bills.[17] For a short time during 1836 they were paying agents of the new Ulster Banking Company.[18] In 1840, when moving to new premises at 35 College Green, they were described as public notaries, stockbrokers and insurance agents.[19] As time went on they concentrated more and more on stock-

---

8 *B. Mag.*, i, 369.
9 His name appears on the deed of settlement for 225 shares.
10 *F.J.*, 9 July 1849.
11 *Dublin Directory 1834* describes it as land agents only.
12 *F.J.*, 6 Dec. 1834.
13 *F.J.*, 17 July 1848.
14 The late Mr H. E. Guinness of Guinness & Mahon kindly supplied information on these two banks; the partners' place in the family can be seen in the family tree in Lynch & Vaizey, *Guinness's brewery*.
15 *Watson's Almanack 1833*, p. 159, shows it for the first time.
16 *1838 committee*, Q.360.
17 *Ibid.*, Q.408-10.
18 *Decades of the Ulster Bank*, p. 16.
19 *F.J.*, 19 Feb. 1840.

broking and their successor firm of Boyle, Low, Murray & Co. continued until 1946.[20]

Gibbons & Williams, who had been notaries to the Bank of Ireland at 21 Dame Street for many years and had acted as agents for a number of country banks and for the Northern Banking Company.[21] In a case of embezzlement by one of their clerks in 1827 they were described as solicitors and notaries public to the Bank of Ireland and at that time were evidently doing a large discount business.[22] In 1833 they commenced issuing notes[23] and the same year opened a branch in Drogheda,[24] but at the beginning of 1835 they went bankrupt[25] and are cited from time to time in joint stock bank propaganda as evidence of the instability of private banks.

While these new firms were appearing three of the old private banks disappeared. Finlay's closed in 1829, Delacour's in Mallow, the last private bank outside Dublin, failed in 1835, and Shaw's was incorporated as the Royal Bank in 1836. This left only La Touche's and Ball's. The latter still issued notes on a small scale, paying duty in 1837 on a circulation of £16,500.[26]

When Thomas Wilson, governor of the Bank of Ireland, was asked in 1838 to name the other banks doing business in Dublin he gave only the Hibernian, the Royal, La Touche's, Ball's and Boyle's.[27] His omission of the two Guinness banks and Gray's suggests that their banking business was not of great significance, or possibly was not banking at all as Wilson understood the term. A Stamp Office return for the year ending January 1836 includes Messrs Guinness & Co., which must mean the Kildare Street firm, but omits Gray's.[28]

The Agricultural and Commercial Bank of Ireland

These new private banks hardly touched the provinces but in 1834 two ambitious schemes were launched to meet their needs. The first by a short head was the National Commercial Bank of Ireland whose prospectus was issued on 21 June by a prominent Dublin firm of solicitors, William Bailey Wallace & Sons.[29] It proposed the formation

---

20 Information kindly supplied by the secretary of the Dublin Stock Exchange.
21 B. of I. Mins., 2, 15 June 1820, 1 May, 22 Nov. 1825.
22 *F.J.*, 28 Apr. 1827.
23 *Watson's Almanack 1834*, p. 159, includes the firm as bankers for the first time. B. of I. Mins., 23 July 1833, records a protest against the design of its notes. The National Museum has eleven notes issued 1833-4, those of £1-£3 payable in Dublin only, those of £10 by Jones Loyd in London as well.
24 *F.J.*, 27 Aug. 1833.
25 *Return of all banks in Ireland which have become bankrupt since 1825*, H.C. 1845 (334), xxviii, 213; *F.J.*, 27 Jan. 1835. Endorsements on a note in the F. E. Dixon collection show that they paid 10s in the £.
26 *Drummond report*, app. B 16.
27 *1838 committee*, Q.779.
28 *Return of banking establishments in Ireland 1826 and 1836*, H.C. 1836 (346), xxxvii, 373.
29 *F.J.*, 10 June 1834, has a preliminary notice; 21 June, the full prospectus.

of a company with £5 million capital on the model of the Northern & Central Bank of England in Manchester. Where existing Irish banks all had shares of £100 these were to be of £5 in order to attract the less wealthy. Subscribers desiring a branch in their town were invited to meet and elect four temporary directors. They must pay an initial deposit of 10s per share plus 1s for expenses, and after two months a second instalment of 10s. Permanent directors would then be elected and would meet in Dublin to draw up the laws of the company. Control would be vested in a court of directors sitting in Dublin.

The scheme was widely welcomed[30] and the first general meetings, of subscribers not merely directors, were held in Dublin on 18 and 25 July.[31] In the meantime the second project had been launched in London, at a meeting on 21 June of 'gentlemen interested in the foundation of the National Bank of Ireland'.[32] It too proposed the formation of banks in Irish towns with local shareholders, but with the main company in London holding half the capital in each local bank. In the chair was the dominating figure of Daniel O'Connell and he soon became the most powerful critic of the rival body.

The two schemes seem to have been independent responses to the same situation, though the respective promoters were evidently aware of each other's plans.[33] The next two years saw intense competition between them for local support all over the south and west.[34] The National enjoyed the great advantage of O'Connell's popular standing, but it was a London-based body and its rival could and did claim to be the more genuinely national concern, fully under Irish control, relying on Irish capital and retaining all its profits in Ireland. Nevertheless, to avoid confusion it altered its name, first adding 'Agricultural', then dropping 'National', and ended up as The Agricultural & Commercial Bank of Ireland.[35] It was commonly known as the Agricultural Bank.

O'Connell's great objective at this date was the repeal of the Union, yet his bank was based on just the kind of union that he was striving to break in politics. Consciousness of this may have added another dimension to the bitterness of his attacks on 'the wild scheme of what is called the Commercial and Agricultural Bank' which contained, he said, the seeds of its own destruction, no guarantee of good management and no security against panic.[36] It was a 'most absurd bubble'

30 *F.J.*, 30 June 1834, prints enthusiastic reports from eleven provincial papers and states that it could have printed many more.
31 *F.J.*, 19, 26, 27 July 1834.
32 *F.J.*, 28 June 1834; below, pp. 120 ff.
33 O'Connell to Thomas Mooney, 13 June 1834 (reprinted in W. J. Fitzpatrick, *Correspondence of Daniel O'Connell*, i, 442).
34 This has been ignored by all historians of Irish banking; Hall, *Bank of Ireland*, pp. 155-6, 158-61, is typical in treating the foundation of the two banks with no reference to each other.
35 *F.J.*, 5 July 1834.
36 *F.J.*, 21 Aug. 1834, letter to meeting of National supporters in Waterford.

and the National would be ready for its bursting.[37] The Agricultural replied with a charge that O'Connell was no more than a figurehead for two English stockbrokers and that he was trying to crush an Irish banking company in order to force an English bank on the Irish people.[38]

In attacking the Agricultural for its dependence on solely Irish support O'Connell was drawing heavily on his prestige, but in criticizing the lack of security he was picking on a genuine weakness. The unlimited liability of shareholders was of little value if they had no property to call on in time of pressure. The Agricultural claimed nevertheless that known local backers, even of limited means, provided a sounder basis for credit than unknown financiers in London. What was not reasonable was to assure members at the same time that they need have no anxiety about their liability since the bank did not intend to make any more calls and hoped for legislation to confine liability to the paid-up capital. This is just what the promoters did at one of the first meetings.[39]

In the National anyone taking shares in a local branch accepted full liability for the debts of that branch (but of no other), while shareholders in the London company, participating in all the branch companies, would be fully liable for all their debts.[40] The Agricultural on the other hand was a single company and all shareholders would be fully liable for all debts of every branch. Many members, O'Connell asserted, did not appreciate this.[41] To the charge that it was unpatriotic for his own bank to be run from London he replied that 'the best patriotism is to keep the people safe'.[42]

The weaknesses picked on by O'Connell and other critics were in time to bring the Agricultural to disaster, and it has commonly been written off as a gigantic fraud. In the end it failed, and in the world of finance few things are less easily forgiven. The charges against the promoters derive in the main from the evidence before the 1837 committee and are embodied in a series of articles in the *Banker's Magazine* of 1845.[43] They are as critical in their condemnation as they are uncritical in their acceptance of every derogatory statement and interpretation concerning the bank, and are the source of most later accounts.[44]

37 *F.J.*, 24 Nov. 1834, speech at Tralee.
38 *F.J.*, 6 Dec. 1834, statement by consulting committee.
39 *F.J.*, 26 July 1834, report of general meeting.
40 Opinions of two counsel taken by the National (U.C.D., MSS 99.4).
41 *F.J.*, 5 Dec. 1834, speech at Corn Exchange, Dublin.
42 *F.J.*, 24 Nov. 1834, speech at Tralee.
43 *B. Mag.*, iii, 65-70, 200-6, 280-5.
44 See Dillon, *Banking in Ireland*, p. 72; Hill (ed.), *Northern Banking Company*, p. 65; Hall, *Bank of Ireland*, p. 158. S. E. Thomas, *The rise and growth of joint stock banking*, pp. 270-81, deals with the bank at length but is based almost entirely on the 1837 evidence.

The first charge is that the promotion was a racket based on mistaken identity. The plan for the bank originated with one Thomas Mooney, a baker and flour factor of 149 Francis Street,[45] while one of the directors was John Chambers, a stationer of 4 Abbey Street. There was another Thomas Mooney, an ironmonger and general merchant at 40-1 Pill Lane,[46] a former and future director of the Hibernian Bank,[47] and another J. Chambers (James not John) who was a director of the Bank of Ireland.[48] Mooney and Chambers are alleged to have concocted the scheme between them and foisted it on the public by avoiding the use of their addresses and of Chambers' christian name, and so passing themselves off as their wealthier namesakes.

This theory might be dismissed out of hand as sheer fantasy but for the support of two witnesses in 1837; one, Thomas Michael Gresham,[49] a wealthy shareholder who was persuaded to join the board at a critical juncture in 1836, declared that all concerned were deceived as to the true identity of Mooney and Chambers;[50] the other, Pierce Mahony, who combined his employment by the Provincial with the representation of dissident shareholders in the Agricultural, stated in pleading for stricter provision on registration of partners that he had been deceived for two years on this point.[51] If they were not deceiving themselves in the light of later events this reflects more on their own perspicacity than on the integrity of Mooney and Chambers.

Letters in the press from this Thomas Mooney show that he had an established position in the flour trade and must have been quite well known in commercial circles.[52] Chambers ran a stationery business described as the most eminent supplier of bankers' books in Dublin.[53] Substantial advertisements for its products are frequent in the press,[54] and in 1841 it secured the contract to supply the Bank of Ireland.[55] In 1797 John Chambers, head of the firm and possibly father of this Chambers, had been a director of the Bank of Ireland.[56] The initial prospectus was not, as often stated, issued by Mooney and Chambers (without their addresses) but by the reputable legal firm of Wallaces

45 G. L. Barrow, 'Justice for Thomas Mooney', in *Dublin Hist. Rec.*, xxiv, no. 1 173-88, gives a fuller account of this enterprising gentleman.
46 *Dublin Directory 1834. F.J.*, 12, 19 June 1848 reports the firm's failure.
47 Hibernian Bank general assembly minute book, 13 Dec. 1828, 13 Dec. 1834.
48 *1837 committee*, Q.2531-41, evidence of James Dwyer; Hone, in Hall, *Bank of Ireland*, p. 483.
49 Originally a London foundling, he had opened a hotel in Sackville Street in 1817 later called after him (Ulick O'Connor, *The Gresham Hotel*, pp. 1-6).
50 *1837 committee*, Q.3289-94.
51 *Ibid.*, Q.3843-4.
52 *F.J.*, 20 Sept. 1824, 8 Aug. 1832, 7 Mar. 1833.
53 *1837 committee*, Q.2987-90, evidence of Dwyer.
54 *F.J.*, 4 Dec. 1833, etc.
55 B. of I. Mins., 2 Feb. 1841.
56 Hone, in Hall, *Bank of Ireland*, p. 483.

—acting it is true on Mooney's instructions but this was not one of the facts put before the public. Mooney's name appears for the first time in the list of fifteen committee members elected on 18 June and revised on 25 June, both times with his correct address and with no special prominence.[57] Chambers was not on this committee; he was active later in the management but seems to have taken no part in the early days. James Dwyer, then the chairman, stated in 1837 that the residence and christian names of Mooney and Chambers were always included in publications,[58] and this seems to have been the truth.

As far as Gresham was concerned Mooney pointed out in a letter to the press in 1838 that he (Gresham) had not only been present at a meeting in April 1836 which had voted to present him (Mooney) with a piece of plate in recognition of his services but had been chairman of the committee for the presentation—yet he could still state on oath that he believed him to be Mooney of Pill Lane.[59]

Mooney was the projector of the bank but he does not seem to have appeared on its behalf in public until October 1835 when he attended a meeting of National Bank supporters in Longford. This was addressed by John Reynolds, the National's secretary and agent for Ireland, and recorded its 'disgust and unmitigated contempt' for the intrusion of Mr Mooney, a baker in Francis Street, Dublin, said to be a director of the Agricultural Bank, who made an unprovoked and scurrilous attack on Reynolds and was accompanied by a drunken mob fom Roscommon.[60] A few days later in Roscommon Reynolds spoke of the efforts of the Agricultural to stop the National as like trying 'to stem the tide with a pitchfork', and told how 'a little fellow by the name of Mooney, a baker in Francis Street', had been brought to the Longford meeting by the Agricultural and had attacked the National as a humbug. Later he referred to him as 'this little pinkeen of a fellow', explaining that a pinkeen was the smallest known fish in the country and leaving it to his hearers to apply the metaphor to Mooney's financial as well as physical stature.[61]

Too much attention need not be paid to the oratorical invective which was common to much public speaking of the time, but it is clear that Reynolds, the leading publicist for the National, was in no doubt as to Mooney's identity. Had the Agricultural been deriving credit from the delusion that he was the wealthy ironmonger of Pill Lane, Reynolds would certainly have put the matter right, but the idea was never even hinted at. Mooney may have been more active in private, but anyone who knew that must also have known who he was.

57 *F.J.*, 19, 27 July 1834.
58 *1837 committee*, Q.2540.
59 *F.J.*,   1 Aug. 1838; the meeting is reported in *F.J.*, 20 Apr. 1836.
60 *F.J.*, 31 Oct. 1835.
61 *F.J.*, 13 Nov. 1835.

PLATE 1

Provincial Bank £1 note no I of 15 August, 1825. All notes of the Provincial Bank were in British currency, even before the change of currency.
(Allied Irish Banks Ltd.)

PLATE 2

A £2 note issued by Alexanders' of Dublin 26 October 1819, eight months before the bank's failure. (National Museum.)

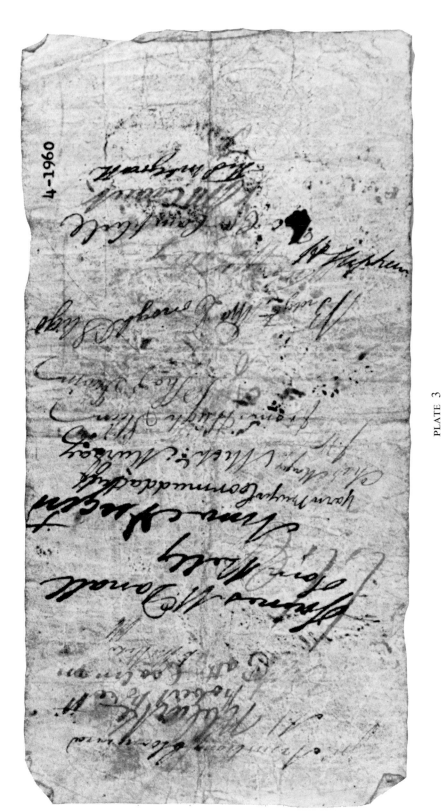

PLATE 3

The back of the same note, showing the large number of signatures of persons through whose hands
it had passed. (National Museum.)

PLATE 4

An unissued note of Finlay's of Dublin for 5 guineas. The promise to pay is in Irish currency at the rate of £1.2.9d, which indicates that the note was for issue before 6 January 1826. The partners are those registered for the years 1825-8, so the note probably dates from 1825. (Old Dublin Society.)

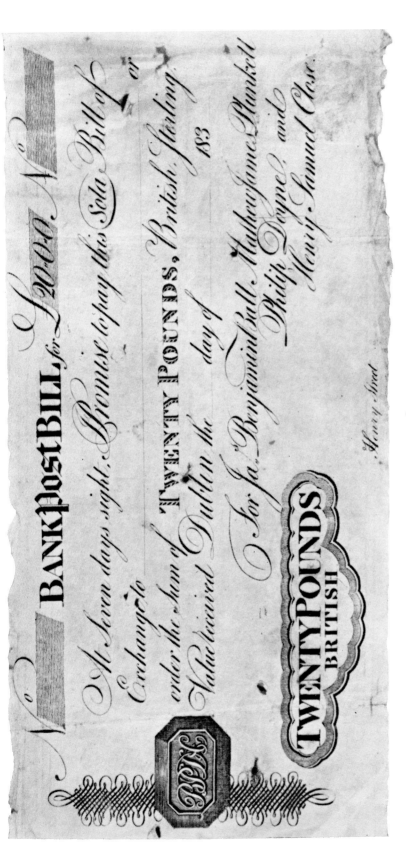

PLATE 5

An unissued post bill of Ball's of Dublin for £20, of the 1830s and therefore denominated in British currency, the word 'Sterling' added as a promise of sound value. This is payable at seven days sight, the most common tenure for bank post bills. (National Museum.)

PLATE 6

Agricultural and Commercial Bank Kilkenny £1 note of 25 May 1835, part of the original issue before the suspension of October 1836. (Institute of Bankers in Ireland and Central Bank of Ireland.)

PLATE 7

Agricultural and Commercial Bank Londonderry £1 note, a new design adopted after the bank had resumed operations. This note has been cut for transmission.
(National Museum.)

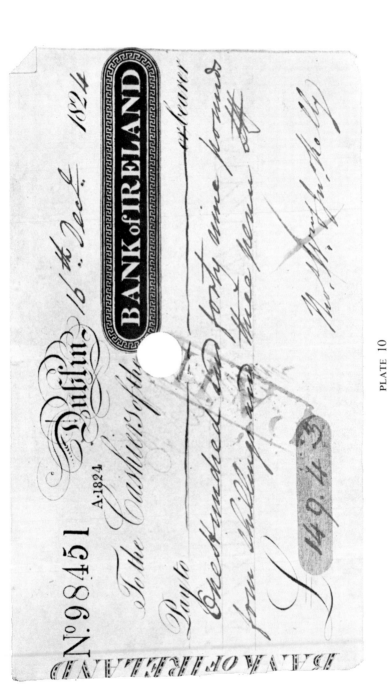

PLATE 10

A completed and paid cheque on the Bank of Ireland dated 16 December 1824.
(Institute of Bankers in Ireland and Central Bank of Ireland.)

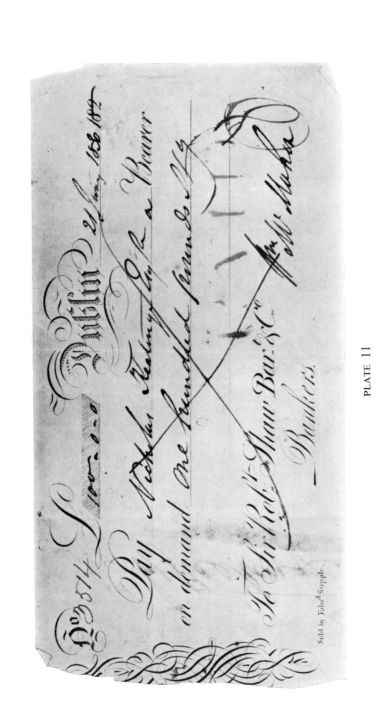

PLATE 11

A completed and paid cheque on Shaw's of Dublin dated 21 June 1830. The use of cheques was steadily increasing in these years, but few survive. (Institute of Bankers in Ireland and Central Bank of Ireland.)

PLATE 12

A joint stock bank that failed. A £1 note issued by the short-lived Southern Bank of Ireland in Cork in 1837. The design is picturesque but the note soon proved worthless.　(National Museum.)

PLATE 13

A joint stock bank that succeeded. A thirty shillings note issued by the Ulster Banking Company at Ballymoney in 1838, less ornate than the one above but of sound value.

(Institute of Bankers in Ireland and Central Bank of Ireland.)

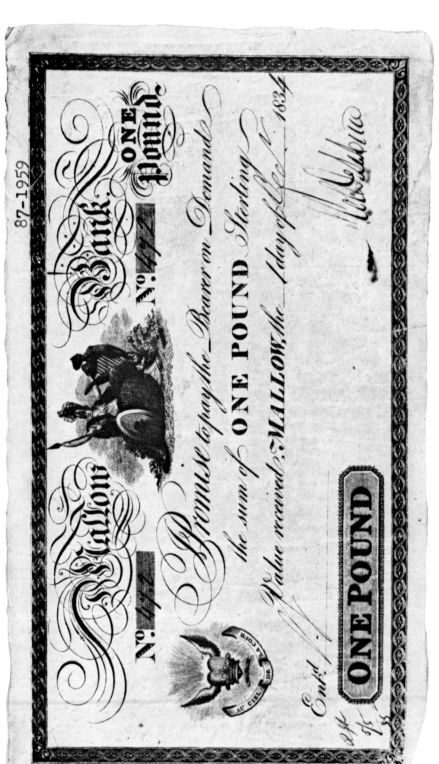

PLATE 14

A £1 note issued by Delacour's of Mallow on 1 December 1834. This was the last private bank to issue notes and it failed the following year, so this must be one of the last private bank notes ever issued in Ireland. (National Museum.)

PLATE 15

The old lady of College Green. A thirty shillings note of the Bank of Ireland issued in 1830. Bank of Ireland notes continued to be the most important element in Irish circulation throughout this period. Notes including fractions of a pound such as this were made illegal by the 1845 act.

(Old Dublin Society.)

PLATE 16

An unsuccessful attempt by the Hibernian Joint Stock Company to find a way round the ban on a Dublin bank issuing notes. A token for thirty shillings with no promise to pay.

(Institute of Bankers, London.)

The promoters may then be acquitted of fraudulent misrepresentation but it is harder to defend their record of management. Of the consulting committee only James Dwyer, a barrister who had been for two years secretary of the Hibernian Bank,[62] had any previous banking experience. This would not have mattered greatly if the bank had had competent staff but initially, to save expense, no general manager was appointed and the duties were performed either by the secretary or by one of the directors.[63] A fulltime general manager was only appointed early in 1836, in the person of William Mitchell, a bank official from Scotland of whom the directors seem to have had a high opinion,[64] but who had just been dismissed as manager of the Western Bank of Scotland in Glasgow.[65] The post of general inspector of branches—the key to the success of the Provincial—was held from July to September 1836 by John Crosse who, as a witness before the 1837 committee, showed little understanding of his job; his previous banking experience had been as cashier in a bank in Wells for an unspecified period that ended in 1823. In the brief life of the bank before his appointment there had been two or three other holders of the post.[66]

Banking expertise was a scarce commodity in the 1830s. The main source of supply was Scotland and the demand from England and Wales, where over forty new joint banks were formed between 1826 and 1834,[67] must have been intense.[68] Ultimately the Agricultural did employ a fair number of Scots,[69] but from the recorded facts they must have been too few, been lacking in the necessary qualities or have been given insufficient chance to use them.

Staff was one difficulty; the deed of settlement was another. The principles of the prospectus as approved by the shareholders were embodied in a deed dated 1 December 1834.[70] It described the company as already constituted by the members of the consulting com-

---

62 His evidence before the 1837 committee covers sixty pages; Q.2453-61 deal with his own position. *F.J.*, 18, 23 June 1827, reports his resignation from the Hibernian and the public dinner given for him at which O'Connell was vice-chairman.
63 *1837 committee*, Q.3086, evidence of Dwyer.
64 *Ibid.*, Q.2781; *F.J.*, 20 Apr. 1836, report of general meeting.
65 *1858 committee*, report para. 47, deals with this bank which failed in 1857. See also C. A. Malcolm, *The Bank of Scotland*, p. 105. The records of the Commercial Bank of Scotland contain details of Mitchell's varied career—he ended life as a preacher in Australia—which have kindly been supplied to me by Mr R. N. Forbes of the Royal Bank of Scotland.
66 *1837 committee*, Q.3608-15, evidence of Crosse.
67 *Ibid*, app. II-1.
68 *Ibid.*, Q.4329, evidence of Marshall.
69 *F.J.*, 2 Jan. 1837, report of dinner given by his fellow officers to John M'kenzie, the resigning accountant general.
70 *F.J.*, 10 Oct. 1834, reports the meeting at which the principles were approved. R.I.A., Haliday 1629, has a copy of the deed; there is a summary of its main points in *Origins and principles of the Agricultural and Commercial Bank of Ireland*, a pamphlet published by the bank in 1835 (N.L.I., P. 641).

E

mittee signing the heads of the prospectus and the purpose of the deed as 'more fully and precisely' to establish it. As a constitution for the bank it would have proved adequate but for the reluctance of members to sign it. Dwyer attributed this to the alarm caused by 'public contention with another bank'.[71] O'Connell's warnings about liability had evidently struck home. When in July 1835 Reynolds charged that it was operating without a deed the committee gave the equivocal reply that the deed had been signed by all the committee members resident in Dublin before the opening of the first branch, that copies had been sent to all branches for signature and that it was binding on all members who had joined subsequently.[72]

Though few had signed the deed the members' names were duly registered at the Stamp Office. In December 1834 a certified copy of two extracts from the register dated 28 October and 7 November was published, evidently on O'Connell's instructions with intent to expose the weakness of the bank's backing. There were 374 names, a few of them from England but the great bulk from different parts of Ireland.[73] The consulting committee promptly commented that the total should have been 471.[74] By June 1835 it was stated to be 800,[75] and by April 1836 over 3,000.[76] O'Connell's notice promised a similar list in respect of the National as soon as its deed had been signed but this never seems to have been published.

Another difficulty was over capital. There was no legal minimum at this date for either subscribed or paid-up capital before a bank might open.[77] Between £20,000 and £40,000 was subscribed before the opening of the first branch but not more than £3,000 was paid-up.[78] To meet the consequent shortage of liquid funds the committee decided to look to England and in November 1835 they made a new issue, specifically for English subscribers, of 10,000 shares of £25, £10 to be paid up. The shares were issued largely through the Northern & Central, and Herbert Hardie, one of its directors, described by Dwyer as 'a great speculator in banking', became the largest shareholder with £20,000 paid up. He was nominated as corresponding director for Lancashire. In April and May 1836 a further issue of £10 shares was made to Irish subscribers, followed by another of £25 with provision for consolidation of the original £5 shares into £25.[79] All these shares

71 *1837 committee*, Q.2565, 2597.
72 *F.J.*, 8 July 1835.
73 *F.J.*, 11 Dec. 1834; the names of Mooney and Chambers were both on this list with their correct addresses.
74 *F.J.*, 12 Dec. 1834.
75 *F.J.*, 13 June 1835, notice by the bank.
76 *F.J.*, 20 Apr. 1836, report of general meeting.
77 *1836 committee*, report, p. viii.
78 *1837 committee*, Q.2477, evidence of Dwyer.
79 *Ibid.*, Q.2551-62, evidence of Dwyer; the National Museum has a certificate for twenty £25 shares held by a Cork member.

were part of the capital of £5 million. By October 1836 the total paid up was £375,000.[80]

All this was a departure from the original plan for small shares and Irish capital. A new deed was therefore drawn up to incorporate the necessary amendments, and was dated 10 June 1836.[81] Its preamble stated that 'several wealthy merchants and traders and other persons resident in Great Britain' had subscribed to the new 'British stock' and that 'a large and influential proprietary' had subscribed in Belfast, and its main purpose was to provide for these two groups. A British proprietor was to be nominated as corresponding director, and Herbert Hardie was confirmed in this position for the current year. A board of correspondence and consultation was to be appointed from proprietors resident in London, and in Belfast members were authorized to elect a committee of audit to perform functions similar to those of the advisory committees of the Northern and the Belfast Banks. For the rest the deed repeated the provisions of the 1834 deed with some tightening up.

But once again the bulk of the members, evidently including the new English shareholders,[82] refused to sign. Ultimately some six hundred signed, said to be a majority in value but only a fraction of the total number of over three thousand.[83] Crosse seems to have spent much of his time as general inspector in taking this deed round the branches trying to collect signatures. The precise facts and obligations under these two deeds were later the subject of intense argument and litigation, but one thing is clear—in a well-managed bank the rights and obligations of all concerned should be beyond dispute; by this criterion the Agricultural was not a well-managed bank.

If the legal position was unsatisfactory the accounting position was no better. The general meeting in March 1837 appointed four auditors to report on the accounts.[84] They included William Goodier, manager of the National Provincial Bank in Manchester, and George Dundas, the Agricultural's manager in Belfast, both of whom gave evidence before the 1837 committee. They visited fifteen (out of forty-five) branches, obtained full access to the books and were able to interrogate the staff.[85] Their report runs to thirteen pages in the appendix of the 1837 committee report.[86] Its general finding was that

> there is no efficient control over the branches and that the system of inspection was most imperfect; a complete absence of plan for

80 *F.J.*, 18 Oct. 1836, report of general meeting.
81 There is a copy of this deed in R.I.A., Haliday 1681.
82 *Cases with opinions . . . exemplified by the facts stated in respect of the Agricultural and Commercial Bank of Ireland*, p. 33.
83 *1837 committee*, Q.2604-8, evidence of Dwyer.
84 *F.J.*, 21 Mar. 1837, report of general meeting.
85 *1837 committee*, Q.3341-2, evidence of Goodier.
86 *Ibid.*, app. I-no. 107.

checking the accounts existed at the head office in Dublin; and the book-keeping had been so faulty that we are convinced that no accurate balance sheet could at any time have been constructed.

Several schemes to improve the accounts had been attempted but none completely carried through.

Dwyer admitted that the books were not kept 'in that regular state which bankers or merchants would wish', for which he blamed the precipitation with which the bank had been pushed forward and the confusion which followed a run prompted by the National in June 1835.[87] According to Gresham there was no register of note issues and the books in general were four months behind,[88] while Goodier complained that there was no detailed stock account either, that overdue bills and unsecured overdrafts were included as good assets, and that some shares had been paid for by bills constantly renewed, such capital being therefore a complete illusion.[89] In October 1838 the board reported that nearly all the overdue bills had then been paid,[90] but this does not answer the charge that they were not good liquid assets in 1836.

These and many more criticisms only came to light after the crisis of November 1836, and may in part be discounted by hostility of the speakers to the directors, but there can be no doubt that the accounting system was quite inadequate for the scale on which the bank tried to operate—and the keeping of proper accounts is the very substance of good banking.

Despite all this the bank made rapid progress. The first meeting to form a branch was held at Roscrea on 7 August 1834, just ahead of the National's first at Waterford on 16 August. Over the next two years reports and notices of meetings and branch openings of the two banks pursue each other through the pages of the press as one can picture their emissaries pursuing each other round the coach roads of Ireland. The procedure was fairly uniform—a local personality in the chair, a speech explaining the bank's objectives normally from one of the consulting committee, resolutions of confidence in Ireland's ability to run her own banks without being beholden to Englishmen or Scotsmen, and finally the election of a local committee to receive applications for shares with 1s equipment fee per share to be forwarded to Ball's bank in Dublin. By the end of September twenty important towns and districts had held meetings approving the bank.[91]

The first branch was opened at Nenagh on 1 November 1834, and

87 *1837 committee*, Q.3084-5, app. I-no. 107.
88 *Ibid.*, Q.3243.
89 *Ibid.*, Q.3313-607.
90 *F.J.*, 16 Oct. 1838, report of general meeting; see also report of general meeting of October 1837 in *F.J.*, 20 Oct. 1837.
91 *F.J.*, 1 Oct. 1834, report of general meeting.

was followed by Ennis and Bandon in December and Castlebar in January 1835,[92] all before the first branch of the National.[93] Details of later openings are less clear. The Drummond report on the development of railways lists forty-five but one of these is the administrative headquarters in Dublin; of the other forty-four three are shown as opened in 1834, twenty-two in 1835 and nineteen in 1836.[94] Where notices were published in the press they normally agree with these years.

The head office was in Dublin at 63 Fleet Street, behind the Bank of Ireland who in fact owned the building.[95] It was the seat of the consulting committee (or board of directors) but it could not legally transact any banking business with the public. Agents were therefore employed for the payment of notes in Dublin, as permitted by the 1830 act—first R. S. Guinness, then from November 1835 Gray's and finally from July 1836 the new Royal Bank.[96] The London & Westminster were agents in London, and allowed the Agricultural discounts on good bills up to £30,000 plus another £30,000 without cover in time of pressure. Similar arrangements were later made in addition with three other London firms.[97] In the rest of Britain notes and drafts could be paid at any of the thirty-five branches of the Northern & Central or the forty-one of the Commercial Bank of Scotland.[98]

The Agricultural undoubtedly received wide support, from landlords and merchants as well as the small men to whom its appeal was particularly directed. After the run for gold in July 1835 a letter of support commending the manner in which it had been met was addressed to the committee by fifty-three noblemen, gentlemen, traders and farmers of Kerry headed by the earl of Kenmare.[99] Catholic priests were prominent at meetings, a curate named James Bermingham being a frequent and eloquent speaker,[100] but the bank was careful to emphasize its freedom from sectarian ties. The committee comprised equal numbers of catholics and protestants,[101] and the report of the general meeting in April 1836 notes particularly the presence of representatives of all sects including the Society of Friends.[102]

But the bank's special appeal was to the small tenant farmers, 'the

92 *Origins and principles; F.J.*, 15 Jan. 1835.
93 Below, p. 124.
94 *Drummond report*, app. B 16.
95 Leased since 1824 to Leland Crosthwaite & Sons, sugar merchants and millers, who sub-leased to the Agricultural (B. of I. Mins., 22 Apr. 1824, 19 Nov. 1850). Leland Crosthwaite was governor 1808-10; his son was a director in 1834 and remained so until 1869 (Hone, in Hall, *Bank of Ireland*, pp. 484-5).
96 *F.J.*, 6 Dec. 1834, 21 Nov. 1835, 4 July 1836.
97 *1837 committee*, Q.2831-5, evidence of Dwyer.
98 *F.J.*, 16 July 1835, public notice.
99 *F.J.*, 17 July 1835.
100 *F.J.*, 8 July 1835.
101 *F.J.*, 20 Apr. 1835, letter from clerk of consulting committee.
102 *F.J.*, 20 Apr. 1836, report of general meeting.

frieze-coated men', as both shareholders and customers. 'We are the poor man's bank', as Thomas Mooney put it at Boyle in December 1835. The bank habitually discounted bills of £5 and £10 for poor farmers but, he declared, had never lost on them—though he did not say how often it had avoided such loss by the facile method of renewing the bills. The same meeting was told how the nearby branch in Strokestown, opened the previous August, had made it possible for tenants to pay their rents without having to sell their crops at the prevailing low prices. By discounting bills at the Agricultural for three months at 3d in the £ (the equivalent of 5 per cent per annum) they had been able to wait for a better market—and received 75 per cent more.[103]

As in so many things in Ireland of this period we are never far from the land question. Mahony, in his 1837 evidence, explained in reply to leading questions from O'Connell that rents were normally due on 29 September and landlords began to press for payment early in October, but produce, notably pork, was not usually marketed for another two months. He argued that the discounting of bills by tenants to carry them over these months merely transferred the losses from the landlords to the banks while increasing local prices, but he agreed that this was a criticism of the land system as much as of the Agricultural Bank. Before the establishment of the banks—he seems to have been referring to pre-1825—usurers had been accustomed to charge over 15 per cent for loans, while butter merchants who had secured a monopoly position made advances to their suppliers at effective rates of 60 per cent. The solution he considered suitable for 'the humbler class of person' was relief by charitable loans rather than through the banks.[104]

But however helpful small charitable loans might be they were quite inadequate to the massive problem of rural Irish poverty. The Agricultural Bank's scheme, on the other hand, was one of mutual self-help. At the Boyle meeting already referred to, Mooney pointed out that the Boyle Savings Bank had £14,000 on deposit in the names of 4,000 persons, mainly artisans and labourers. This, from one small town, was evidence of the existence of capital in plenty in Ireland but instead of being used for local circulation it was invested through the savings banks in government stock. Much of it did not even get as far as the savings banks. By mobilizing the people's savings and monetizing the produce of the country before it was sold—by the discounting of farmers' bills—the Agricultural Bank would break the vicious circle of an underemployed population destitute for lack of things it could produce or buy with its own labour.

In May 1837 in a long letter to 'The farmers of Ireland' Mooney

103 *F.J.*, 10 Dec. 1835.
  04 *1837 committee*, Q.3997-4013.

developed this theme.[105] In Ireland, he pointed out, unlike England and Scotland, the one great branch of employment was 'the tillage of the earth'. In case of crop failure this led to misery, starvation and emigration. And he continued,

> You are poor because you are obliged to sell to the busy inhabitants of England and Scotland your provisions the moment they are raised to pay your rent and other charges which take away the power because it takes away the 'capital' or subsistence necessary to maintain men for a considerable time before your production can be brought to a distant market, and therefore a return can be had for your productions; and you are poor because you have little else to occupy you but the raising of provisions.

With working capital manufacturing could be developed which would increase the demand for produce and so raise farmers' incomes which in turn would increase the demand for manufactures. 'You are poor because you have no trade and you have no trade because you are poor' was how Mooney summed up the dilemma.

The key was the expansion of banking. It was pure nonsense to say that the greater prosperity of Scotland was due to their having capital where Ireland had none; 'their capital consists in their extended and matured banking institutions'. Irish poverty sprang from artificial causes, the lack of artificial institutions called banks and its cure lay in their creation. He recognized the danger of inflation from too much easy money but in an economy suffering from extreme deflation this could be contained. As Keynes would have put it a century later, a deficiency in effective demand could be made good by the expansion of bank credit. In the light of the disaster that was to sweep rural Ireland in the next decade from the lack of a developed exchange economy the scorn with which Mooney's ideas were greeted in orthodox circles rings a little hollow.

Where the Agricultural Bank went wrong was not in theory but in practice. It expanded too fast for its managerial capacity. Up to the spring of 1836 the flood of competitive branch openings had covered most of Munster and Connacht and the fringes of Leinster. In Ulster the only Agricultural branch by 1835 was at Strabane in the extreme west of Tyrone, while the National, after a brief foray at Belfast,[106] kept out of the province altogether. Then in the spring of 1836 the Agricultural launched itself into the north-east, and sixteen of the nineteen branches opened that year were in Ulster. By October 1836 a large part of the £375,000 paid-up capital was held there, £62,000 of it in Belfast alone.[107] The northern openings increased note issues by some £150,000

105 *F.J.*, 20 May 1837; R.I.A., Haliday 1685.
106 Below, p. 129.
107 *F.J.*, 18 Oct. 1836, speech by Dwyer at general meeting.

but they also brought competition with the Belfast banks who commonly allowed large cash credits and overdrafts. This led to what Dwyer described in 1837 as great difficulties between the board and the northern subscribers.[108] By then the difficulties had broken into open conflict.

The Agricultural's purpose was the reflation of a depressed economy by supplying the banking services and credit for which there was a demand. This demand existed in the south and west but not in the north-east, already well served by the Northern and the Belfast and by the branches of the Bank of Ireland and the Provincial. If economic growth called for more the Ulster Banking Company, which commenced business in July 1836, was better placed to supply them than the Agricultural with its resources already fully stretched. In November 1836 this over-expansion, and the internal conflict which it set up, was to prove fatal.

The National Bank of Ireland

As the Agricultural grew so did the National. The initial meeting of the promoters was held on 21 June 1834 at 53 Old Broad Street, London, with O'Connell in the chair,[109] and the prospectus was published in London and Dublin at the beginning of July.[110] It held out to investors the attractions of the higher rate of interest in Ireland (6 per cent as against 5 in Britain), the lower level of competition and the scope for wider circulation of paper and credit. It praised the Provincial but pointed out that in nine years it had reached only twenty-one towns, a consequence of the defective principle of too great centralization. The National would avoid this by making each branch a separate company in which the main company would hold half the shares; this would make it possible both to absorb rivals and to expand without extra overheads.

The scheme originated, according to the deed of settlement, with T. Lamie Murray, a former associate of Joplin's.[111] The system of branch companies was the same as that incorporated by Joplin in the initial plan for the Provincial,[112] and proposed by him for the National Provincial Bank of England in 1833.[113] but in neither case adopted. The branches were to be self-supporting, employing the money they borrowed locally, while the London company's capital was kept free as security behind them.[114] To validate the claims for the London link

108 *1837 committee*, Q.3156-65.
109 *F.J.*, 28 June 1834.
110 *The Times*, 14 July 1834; *F.J.*, 1 July 1834.
111 Robert White papers (N.L.I., MSS 8856-7) show Murray in a most unfavourable light as promoter of an unsound mining venture in Brittany in 1838-41.
112 Above, p. 78.
113 Gregory, *Westminster Bank*, i, 337-9; Gilbart, *Practical treatise*, p. 633.
114 *F.J.* 5 Dec. 1834, speech by Murray at Corn Exchange, Dublin.

it was necessary to emphasize central control but at the same time each branch was projected as a local institution.

Perhaps only O'Connell's great popular standing in Ireland could have overcome this contradiction, but at the same time his position in the bank added a conflict of its own. His personal finances, despite a large income at the bar, seem to have been in an almost perpetual state of embarrassment. This is clear from his papers,[115] though the suggestion of one of his biographers that the bank was founded for the purpose of bringing them relief[116] seems to be without foundation. But the conflict arose not so much from this as from his previous policy of inciting runs on the banks for gold with intent to bring pressure on the government. In June 1830 a run in the Waterford area followed a letter in which he wrote:[117]

> Is it not foolish for any man to take or keep a scrap of paper when he can easily have a piece of gold? The bank note may possibly be worth nothing; the piece of gold must be worth twenty shillings always, and I think will be worth much more. Let me therefore strongly urge every sensible and rational man to turn his bank notes into gold.

This was in retaliation for the imposition of new stamp and spirit duties. In January 1831, in protest against a threatened attack on the freedom of the press, he varied the emphasis a little:[118]

> It is essentially necessary for the permanent good of Ireland that the present anomalous state of the currency be corrected, and that England should not have the advantage over Ireland of a gold circulation when Ireland has only paper.

These appeals met with considerable response and were a better testimony to O'Connell's influence over the holders of small notes than to his perception of the country's economic needs. He seems to have realized this, for in February 1833, when urging a vigorous campaign against a new coercion bill, he concluded:[119]

> Let me implore you not to injure commercial credit by calling for a run on the bank for gold. That run will take place of itself, to the last bank note, if the atrocious Algerine code be enacted.

The run duly occurred, but on a small scale, and O'Connell could blame it on the action of the government rather than take credit for it himself

---

115 See especially letters from his brother James, U.C.D., MSS 47.5, 48.6, 50.15, 55.6; accounts, N.L.I., MSS 13641.
116 M. MacDonagh, *Life of Daniel O'Connell*, p. 243.
117 *F.J.*, 26 June 1830.
118 *F.J.*, 17 Jan. 1831.
119 *F.J.*, 21 Feb. 1833.

as he had in 1830.[120] His change of attitude in 1833 was adopted with great reluctance, evidently on the advice of his former close associate, F. W. Conway of the *Dublin Evening Post*.[121] This paper ran a series of articles bitterly attacking the policy which it described as 'the O'Connell cholera'; the banks, it pointed out, were in no danger and the only effect was to hamstring trade to the general impoverishment of the community.[122]

The main burden of these runs fell on the Provincial whose capacity to bear it owed a great deal to its London connection[123]—now quoted to justify a similar connection for the National.[124]

The metamorphosis of the inciter of these runs into the orthodox head of a note-issuing bank was surprising but in political terms comprehensible. O'Connell's purpose was to eradicate all vestiges of ascendancy power and to this end it was reasonable to incite runs on protestant-controlled, government-supported banks. It was equally reasonable to launch a rival bank free from sectarian taint. His aim was to crush the monopoly of banking in Ireland as Andrew Jackson had recently crushed it in America[125]—a reference to Jackson's withdrawal of all public deposits from the Bank of the United States and his refusal to renew its charter which was due to expire in 1836. On a later occasion O'Connell spoke of the National as 'a great means of breaking down the Orange faction'.[126]

By this last remark he meant that the National would give no preference on grounds of religion or politics but would judge its customers solely by the security they had to offer. If the grand master of the Orange Lodge of Ireland himself applied to have a bill discounted the bank would look only to the security he had to offer. Any banker would doubtless echo this sentiment, but with sectarian feeling running high—particularly at this moment over the tithe war and municipal reform[127]—it would be naïve to think that it had no influence, even subconscious, on banking decisions. In the Bank of Ireland the directors had, since 1829, dropped the anti-popery declaration but it was still inscribed in the charter, a tacit confirmation of O'Connell's charge of bias. In fighting to remove such bias O'Connell

---

120 F. W. Fetter, *The development of British monetary orthodoxy*, pp. 134-5, discusses O'Connell's political use of runs for gold. W. Fagan, *Life and times of Daniel O'Connell*, ii, 499-504, written by a supporter immediately after his death, deplores O'Connell's involvement in banking as depriving him of this political weapon.
121 W. J. Fitzpatrick, *Correspondence of Daniel O'Connell*, i, 338-9.
122 *Dublin Ev. Post*, 7-19 Mar. 1833.
123 *Provincial Bank annual reports 1830/1, 1832/3; 1837 committee*, Q.4430-9, evidence of Marshall.
124 Below, p. 123.
125 *F.J.*, 24 Nov. 1834, speech at Tralee. See also *F. J.*, 21 Aug. 1834, letter to Waterford meeting with a definition of the bank's aims.
126 *F.J.*, 27 Jan. 1836, speech at Tuam.
127 A. MacIntyre, *The Liberator*, pp. 157-200, 227-61, gives a good account of these two problems.

claimed to be taking politics out of banking; to his opponents it appeared just the opposite.

The National soon became known in Ireland as The Liberator's bank, and it certainly owed much of its popular support to O'Connell, but the deed of settlement makes it clear that the scheme originated not with him but with Lamie Murray. This may lie behind the assertion by the Agricultural Bank that O'Connell was no more than a figurehead for some London financiers. But the point is not of lasting importance; the essence of the project was the marriage of O'Connell's popular standing with the security of London capital and management.

The main work of propaganda fell to John Reynolds who was appointed in August 1834 as secretary and agent for Ireland.[128] He addressed most of the public meetings and his persistent theme was that a bank headed by O'Connell must be worthy of support.[129] At the same time he emphasized the practical value of the London connection. In Waterford he pointed out how the similar link had enabled the Provincial to meet the recent run there without any extra call on its members. Far from being unpatriotic such a system brought the benefits of English capital to Ireland with a £1 million reserve (the capital of the London company) to guarantee the bank's security and the entire property of the London subscribers to protect the Irish shareholders.[130] O'Connell declared his preference for having the bank's management in Ireland but emphasized that for the present control from London would avoid local jealousies and ensure effective inspection.[131]

The deed of settlement was signed in London on 6 January 1835 by 249 members. Supplementary deeds of 15 February and 6 July 1836 brought in a further 35 and 22 members respectively.[132] As no addresses are given it is not possible to estimate the division between England and Ireland but the impression is that the bulk of the original proprietary was English while Irish subscriptions were mainly to the branch companies.[133] The deed had only five articles. The first declared the name of the society to be The National Bank of Ireland. The second stated its purpose as the establishment of branch banks, agencies and banks in copartnership with local shareholders in any cities, towns and places in Ireland or in Great Britain, Jersey, Guernsey

---

128 *F.J.*, 13 Aug. 1834, report of committee meeting; Reynolds, recently bankrupt, had just broken with the Hibernian with a press attack on its management—see *F.J.*, 26 July, 19, 25 Aug. 1834.
129 See especially report of meeting at Roscrea in *F.J.*, 8 July 1835, and subsequent correspondence in *F.J.*, 28 Nov. 1835.
130 *F.J.*, 21 Aug. 1834, report of Waterford meeting.
131 *F.J.*, 5 Dec. 1834, 27 Jan. 1836, speeches in Dublin and Tuam.
132 The originals of the deeds are in the National Bank in London.
133 By far the largest subscriber was the Reverend Horace G. Cholmondeley of Tunbridge Wells with 2,105 shares.

or the Isle of Man; this inclusion of Britain was to be important later but not at this date. The third article fixed the capital at £1 million in 20,000 shares of £50. The fourth nominated the first directors— ten English with subscriptions ranging from thirty shares to three hundred and totalling 1,340, and four Irish, O'Connell, his son Maurice and his son-in-law Christopher Fitzsimon with thirty shares each and Cornelius O'Brien with fifty—and appointed Lamie Murray as managing director.

The fifth article signified agreement to the general regulations, un-numbered but grouped under five heads, which took up the bulk of the deed. They vested control in the court of directors operating through the managing director. It was empowered to organize local branch companies and to fix their capital and the terms of their deeds. No copies of these deeds appear to be extant but they presumably provided for control by the court in London. The co-partnership could be dissolved at any time by a simple recommendation of the directors confirmed by two special general meetings, and if 25 per cent of the capital were lost the directors were required to take such action unless three-quarters of the proprietors agreed to continue, in which case the dissidents were to be bought out.

In consideration of his services in founding the bank Murray was to be paid £500 a year for life if the dividend was 5 per cent, plus £300 for every point by which it exceeded that, plus one-tenth of the value of any bonus paid. These payments were to cease if he acquired an interest in any other bank. He could be removed by the court but otherwise was to hold office without need for re-election.

Public meetings of the National were very similar to those of the Agricultural, the main difference being the undertaking by the London directors to subscribe shares equal to the number taken locally. Between August and October 1834 Reynolds held a series of meetings in the south and west,[134] and in November on returning from a visit to London he announced plans for the first branch at Carrick-on-Suir.[135] This opened for business at the end of January 1835.[136] The notice, typical of others to follow, is headed by a list of the fifteen directors of the National Bank of Ireland, followed by the names of the correspondent banks at which notes would be paid, and then by the five directors of the 'Bank of Carrick-on-Suir'. The London directors included five O'Connellite M.P.s, three of them catholics and two protestants.[137] The correspondent banks included the Hibernian, Ladbroke's in London and ten others all in Lancashire and Yorkshire.

134 *F.J.*, 21 Aug.-31 Oct. 1834, reports of meetings in Waterford, Carrick-on-Suir, Enniscorthy, Ballinasloe, Limerick and Tralee.
135 *F.J.*, 20 Nov. 1834.
136 *F.J.*, 4 Feb. 1835, public notice dated 26 Jan. 1835 that the branch 'has opened'; the first annual report gives the date as 28 Jan.
137 The catholics were the two O'Connells and Fitzsimon, the protestants Cornelius O'Brien and David Roche (MacIntyre, *The Liberator*, pp. 303-6).

Later notices added fourteen branches of the National Provincial in different parts of England.

The first annual report in May 1836[138] included a list of branches at that date—seven full and twelve sub opened in 1835, six full and seven sub in the early months of 1836.[139] Cork is unaccountably omitted, though press notices show it as open in December 1835,[140] and the bank's records give its opening as October. The second annual report in May 1837 shows only one more full branch, at Ballina.[141] The introduction of sub-branches and agencies leads to some confusion in the early records. The first annual report makes no distinction but the second shows twenty-one sub-branches and seven agencies. With one exception[142] the sub-branches were all later converted to full. The last of the agencies seems to have been closed in 1839.[143]

To get round the ban on operations in Dublin the National proposed to form a branch company there on similar lines to the others but with no more than six partners. It would be a bank of issue with branches in the monopoly zone and possibly at Liverpool. O'Connell announced the plan at a meeting in December 1834 at the end of which Reynolds produced a book with the names of many wealthy and influential individuals who had already subscribed £100,000 of stock—but he failed to explain how these 'many' could belong to a bank of only six partners.[144] No more was heard of the scheme during 1835. The Hibernian continued to act as paying agent in Dublin until March 1836 when the National opened its own office at 53 Dame Street. It was specifically for payment of notes and orders as authorized by the 1830 act, and the agent was Charles Copland who later became general manager of the Royal Bank.[145] Then in May 1836 the plan was revived under the title of the Metropolitan Bank of Dublin; its capital was to be £2 million and applications to be made to Copland.[146] By July the scheme seemed well advanced, and in September 40,000 shares were allotted.[147]

---

138 Reprinted in R. Gordon, *A review of trade and banking in Ireland and England*, pp. 76-9 (R.I.A., Haliday 1681).
139 Enniscorthy opened as an independent branch in August 1835 but was subordinated to Wexford when the latter opened in March 1836.
140 *F.J.*, 12 Dec. 1835, public notice including list of branches.
141 *F.J.*, 30 May 1837; *Drummond report*, app. B 16, shows it opened in 1837.
142 Castlebar opened as a full branch (*F. J.*, 14 Oct. 1836), subordinated to Ballina 1837, then closed and transferred to Westport (bank records).
143 *F.J.*, 27 May 1839, fourth annual report; bank records.
144 *F.J.*, 5 Dec. 1834, report of meeting; 30 Dec. 1834, prospectus of 'The Dublin Bank'.
145 *F.J.*, 25 Feb. 1836.
146 *F.J.*, 23 Apr., 4 May 1836, notice and prospectus.
147 *F.J.*, 23 July, 26 Sept. 1836.

In the meantime another project had appeared, centred on Drogheda. According to a critical letter addressed by 'a shareholder' to the rest of the shareholders in August 1836 this bank, with the clumsy title of the Drogheda, Dundalk, Meath and Louth Joint Stock Banking Company, was to have a capital of £1 million, and 40,000 shares had already been subscribed, but the promoters had resolved to remain inactive pending new legislation.[148] Obviously they deemed it unwise to proceed until they could issue notes—an understandable decision despite the writer's scoffs. His letter can hardly have been unconnected with a meeting just held in Drogheda on behalf of the Metropolitan. It was addressed by Reynolds and resolved, in view of the decision of the 'Drogheda local bank' to remain inactive and the urgent need for a bank in the town, that a branch of the Metropolitan should be established. A committee was appointed and applications were invited for shares.[149]

But as long as the exclusive privileges of the Bank of Ireland remained, inactivity was the only lawful condition for projected joint stock banks of issue within fifty miles of Dublin, and in time the Metropolitan's promoters too were obliged to bow to this fact. The National's annual report in May 1836 spoke optimistically of the scheme but a year later it had been abandoned by reason of 'numerous difficulties presenting themselves'.[150] It seems that the project looked to the early ending of the monopoly and when this failed to materialize it was dropped. A full branch in Dublin had to wait till 1845.

The system of subsidiary branch companies soon proved too cumbersome and difficult to control, and in 1838 all but two were absorbed into the main company.[151] In 1836, 1837 and 1838 separate National Banks of Ireland were registered in nine different towns but in 1839 they were all merged in the National Bank of Ireland with the exception of Carrick-on-Suir and Clonmel,[152] which continued as separate companies until 1856.[153] The sub-branches were all subordinate to the branch companies and their upgrading to full branches took place at this time. Lists of branches for payment of dividends appear in the press regularly in the third week of June and December, from December 1839 onwards, and they make no distinction between full and sub-branches. In Appendix 3 below the dates are those of the first opening in whichever form.

By May 1837 the initial growth was over and O'Connell told the

---

148 *F.J.*, 9 Aug. 1836.
149 *F.J.*, 8, 12 Aug. 1836.
150 *F.J.*, 30 May 1837, second annual report.
151 *F.J.*, 27 May 1839, 30 May 1840, fourth and fifth annual reports.
152 *Account of the number of private and joint stock banks registered in Ireland 1820-44*, H.C. 1844 (232), xxxii, 445.
153 *F.J.*, 29 May 1857, twenty-second annual report.

general meeting that no more branches were planned until the board decided that the time was ripe for expansion into the north.[154] Two new branches were in fact opened in 1839,[155] but there were then no more until 1844-5 when six were opened in the south-west.[156] With the Dublin office converted to a full branch this brought the total at the end of 1845 to forty-four, six more than the Provincial. Nine were in Leinster, twenty-five in Munster, ten in Connacht and none in Ulster.

In circulation the National soon approached the same level as the Provincial, and for the second half of 1837 paid composition duty on £663,300 compared to the Provincial's £668,000.[157] By 1845 the difference had widened again; for the twelve months to 1 May 1845 the Provincial's average was £927,667 against the National's £852,269.[158] It was the early 1850s before the National overtook the Provincial in circulation,[159] but by 1845 it was firmly established as one of the main suppliers of banking services to the south and west.

The early capital history of the National is a little hard to unravel. Subscriptions to the deed totalled 18,499 shares but by 1837 this had risen to 19,999, only one short of the authorized 20,000 shares of £50. £12 10s 0d per share had by then been called. Total paid-up capital should therefore have been almost £250,000 but with forfeits and defaults it was only £245,575 10s 0d. This was the capital of the London company. In addition local capital had been created by the branch companies totalling £818,900; of this £665,060 had been issued in £10 shares on which £2 10s 0d had been called, giving a total branch capital of £166,262.[160] Assuming, as seems to be the case, that this did not include the capital held in the branches by the London company, the total paid-up capital of the group was nearly £412,000. The second annual report refers to a call of £5 by the London company to meet the crisis of November 1836, but it does not seem to have been included in the above figures. It would have left the shares £17 10s 0d paid, or a total of £350,000 on the full 20,000, and this is the capital indicated by subsequent profit statements which show 5 per cent dividends totalling £17,500 and 6 per cent totalling £21,000. At the end of 1845 a further call of £5 to provide for expansion into the former monopoly area brought the total to £450,000.[161]

The procedure by which the branch companies were absorbed is not quite clear but no new capital was issued. By 1843 the members

154 *F.J.*, 30 May 1837.
155 *F.J.*, 27 May 1839, Kanturk; 21 Nov. 1839, Banagher.
156 *F.J.*, 30 May 1845, tenth annual report.
157 *Drummond report*, app. B 16.
158 *Dublin Gaz. 1845*, pp. 512-4.
159 *Dublin Gaz., passim*, quarterly returns under 1845 act.
160 *1837 committee*, app. I-no 102.
161 *F.J.*, 29 June 1846, eleventh annual report; also in *B. Mag.*, v, 238-40.

were predominantly Irish,[162] a marked change from the original signa-tories of the deed. It seems therefore that the 1838-9 exchange was effected by transferring shares from English members of the main com-pany to Irish members of the branch companies in exchange for their local shares which were then extinguished.

The directors were required by the deed to submit a statement to the general meeting in 1836 covering transactions to the end of 1835, and annual statements to subsequent meetings. The first annual report consequently included the following statement:

Balance sheet as at 31 December 1835

	£		£
Investments	155,741	Capital	374,141
Securities	826,638	Circulation	521,745
Specie and cash	166,472	Deposits	256,638
Preliminary expenses:		Undivided fund	14,521
London company	8,547		
Branches	9,647		
	1,167,045		1,167,045

Profits for the year, including premium on shares, came to £25,568, with charges of £3,728 and dividends of £7,319, leaving £14,521 undivided.[163]

No accounts of such detail were published again until 1851. None at all seem to be extant issued in 1837 or 1838 but in 1839 and sub-sequent years a brief profit statement gave the undivided balance at the opening of the year, the total paid in dividends and the undivided balance at the close. On 31 December 1837 the balance was £406, a fall of over £14,000 from that of two years before in the above state-ment. Even if preliminary expenses had all been written off, the profits for these two years had certainly been slim. In 1838 the net profits were £22,800, from which they rose steadily to £28,800 in 1841, dropped to £18,200 in 1843 and rose to £24,600 in 1845. The average over the eight years was just over £24,000 and the reserve at the end of 1845 stood at just over £40,000.[164] Dividends were paid at 5 per cent each year to 1839 when the rate was raised to 6 per cent.[165]

O'Connell's foundation of the National Bank has received surpris-

162 *Annual reports* from 1843 held by the bank include lists of members with their addresses and number of votes. *Dublin Gaz. 1846*, pp. 157-71, shows the partners in February 1846, of whom 788 were resident in Ireland and only 96 in Britain.
163 Reprinted in Gordon, *Trade and banking* (R.I.A., Haliday 1681).
164 Annual reports in *F.J.*, at the end of May each year 1839-46.
165 Dividend notices in *F.J.*, 16 Mar., 1 July 1836, 31 Jan. 1837, 5 Feb., 26 July 17 Dec. 1838, 21 June 1839, 16 June, 15 Dec. 1840, etc.

ingly little attention from his biographers, due perhaps to the paucity of references to it in his surviving papers. Of those writing in the present century MacDonagh makes one brief reference,[166] O'Faolain makes an even briefer one to the fact that O'Connell was a banker,[167] MacIntyre notes in passing that he was a shareholder and governor of the National Bank,[168] Gwynn makes no reference at all.[169] The essays marking the centenary of O'Connell's death ignore the subject entirely.[170] The *Dictionary of National Biography* in a sixteen page article mentions the bank only as owner of a portrait. It is hard to say how big a part O'Connell played in the running of the bank but he nearly always presided at general meetings and his standing with the Irish public was certainly of the greatest value. Among his services to Ireland this was certainly not the least.

The Ulster Banking Company

The National Bank made only one serious attempt to move into Ulster in this period. In November 1835 a meeting was held in Belfast and addressed by Lamie Murray; it endorsed a scheme for a Belfast National Bank of Ireland on lines similar to the others,[171] but the Belfast promoters soon had second thoughts. After studying the draft deed they found that the bulk of the money deposited would be diverted to England, that all profits on English business and half those on Irish would go to the English partners and that the transfer of shares by Irish residents was restricted. They resolved therefore, at a meeting on 22 February 1836, that since the deed was 'incompatible with our views of a liberal and reciprocal connection we decline establishing a bank on the terms therein proposed'. They decided instead to form a bank of their own under the name of the Ulster Banking Company.[172]

The new bank's capital, £1 million in shares of £10, would all be raised locally. Only 80,000 shares were in fact issued and after two calls totalling 25 per cent the total paid up was £204,000.[173] With this, business commenced on 1 July 1836 in Waring Street, Belfast.[174]

The deed of settlement is dated 1 April 1836. Despite the initial contacts with the National it conforms closely to those of the Northern and the Belfast.[175] Management was vested in permanent directors and

166 Above, p. 121.
167 Sean O'Faolain, *King of the Beggars,* p. 303.
168 MacIntyre, *The Liberator,* pp. 22, 74, 304.
169 Denis Gwynn, *Daniel O'Connell.*
170 Michael Tierney (ed.), *Daniel O'Connell: nine centenary essays.*
171 *F.J.,* 12 Dec. 1835, prospectus and report of meeting at Royal Hotel, Belfast.
172 *Decades of the Ulster Bank,* pp. 12-3; Gregory, *Westminster Bank,* pp. 20-2. The head office of the bank has a copy of the prospectus.
173 *1837 committee,* app. I-no 79.
174 *Decades,* pp. 14-5.
175 The original deed is held in the head office of the bank in Belfast.

an annually elected committee. The first four directors were nominated in the deed, two to be managing directors who must devote their full time to the bank, two to be assistant directors who must attend daily for as long as the managing directors required them. Only the managing directors were debarred from engaging in other business but no partner in any other bank in Ireland was qualified for election as either kind. Directors held office until they died, retired or were removed by a vote of two-thirds in number and value of the proprietors. The seven committee members, on the other hand, were to be elected annually by the general meeting. They were to meet monthly and their duties were similar to those in the other two banks. They became known as the advisory committee.

The initial shareholders numbered about 830 of whom over 90 per cent gave addresses in Ulster, about equally divided between the Belfast area and the rest of the province. There were 40 from Liverpool, a reflection presumably of trading links, and a few from other parts of England and Ireland but none from Scotland. All the first directors and committee members were resident in or near Belfast, so the object stated in the prospectus that the bank should be 'under the sole control of resident proprietors' was effectively achieved.

The deed provided for the establishment of branches and the first was opened at Enniskillen on 3 August following approval by a public meeting there. Nine more followed before the end of the year, two in 1837 and one in 1838. In only one case, Armagh, was a local director appointed but he resigned in 1837 when his salary was cut from £100 to £50 and he was not replaced.[176]

Up to 1845 all the branches were in Ulster. A part-time agency in Newry brought protests from the Bank of Ireland and had to be withdrawn in 1841.[177] The Hibernian was appointed paying agent in Dublin but during the pressure of November 1836 it had to refuse payment of a draft on the Ulster of £2,940 for want of funds, whereupon the Ulster made temporary arrangements with Boyle's and then transferred the agency to the new Royal Bank. During the pressure £80,000 of Ulster notes were presented within fifteen days, a severe test on so new an institution, but all were paid and no customers lost.[178]

No profit figures were issued for the first year but over the next eight they averaged £16,000. A dividend of 5 per cent was paid in 1837 from which it was raised by half a point each year to 7 per cent in 1840 and lowered again to 5 per cent in 1843.[179]

A truer measure of the bank's services to the public was the total of liabilities, that is of deposits and notes in circulation. This rose steadily from £160,500 on 1 September 1837 to £626,600 on 1 September

176 *Decades*, pp. 22-39.
177 B. of I. Mins., 8 Dec. 1840-7 Dec. 1841.
178 F.J., 11 Nov. 1836; *Decades*, pp. 15-6.
179 *Decades*, pp. 17, 44-6; Advisory committee minute book.

1845.[180] For the six months ending 31 December 1837 the Ulster's circulation was £133,400 compared to £167,400 for the Belfast and £136,600 for the Northern.[181] By 1845 the Ulster had moved in front with an average circulation of £311,079 compared to £281,611 for the Belfast and £242,440 for the Northern.[182]

The Ulster Banking Company clearly filled a gap in the expanding economy of the north-east. By 1845 it had fifteen branches compared with the Northern's twelve and the Belfast's eighteen. All three were still confined to Ulster where to some extent their services overlapped. Four towns had branches of all three, nine of two and another fifteen had one each. In addition there were four branches of the Bank of Ireland and sixteen of the Provincial in the province. The density of banks in Ulster was therefore greater than in any other part of Ireland. This was both cause and effect of its greater economic development.

The Royal Bank of Ireland

A joint stock bank in Ireland in the 1830s had to choose between issuing notes and operating in the Dublin area; it could not do both. The next bank to be formed chose, like the Hibernian, to operate in Dublin. The prospectus appeared in April 1836;[183] it was to be styled the Royal Bank of Ireland and, though not so stated, it was floated to take over Shaw's in Foster Place. Its capital was £1,500,000 in 30,000 shares of £50 of which some 20,000 were issued with £10 called per share, giving a total paid-up capital of about £200,000.[184] The first directors were elected in May, the deed of settlement was signed, by 309 members, on 1 September and the bank opened for business on 26 September.[185]

The stock exchange year book states, under the heading of the Royal Bank of Ireland, that it was established under a special act of 13 September 1836 but this is incorrect. Unlike the Hibernian the Royal had no special act and therefore no right to take legal actions by a public officer, a privilege for which it had to wait until the act of 1845.

Like the Hibernian, the Provincial, the Agricultural and the National, the Royal relied to a large degree on English subscribers for its initial capital.[186] The deed gave their representatives an entrenched position on the board. Management was entrusted to a general board of thirteen, seven of them resident in Dublin or its vicinity and six in Great Britain. Of the first appointments the latter comprised two

---

180 Dillon, *Banking in Ireland*, p. 67, has a table of these figures.
181 *Drummond report*, app. B 16.
182 *Dublin Gaz. 1845*, pp. 512-4.
183 F.J., 15 Apr. 1836, has the full prospectus.
184 *1837 committee*, app. I-no 97.
185 K. Milne, *The Royal Bank of Ireland*, pp. 24-5.
186 Shareholders' minute book, 11 May 1836, committee report.

each from Manchester, Liverpool and London, and it seems to have been intended that this arrangement continue. The original proprietary was almost equally divided in value between England and Ireland,[187] but the largest shareholders were English. The top holding was that of Herbert Hardie with 1,000 shares, followed by James Hardie, Elizabeth Hardie (possibly the wife of one of them) and James Heyworth with 500 each, then William Smith with 300 and Henry Moult with 280. The two Hardies were the Manchester directors and were connected with the Northern & Central Bank, of which Moult, a witness before the 1837 committee, was chairman. Heyworth and Smith were the Liverpool directors. The two London directors had smaller holdings and clearly owed their position to their connection with the London & Westminster Bank.[188] The latter was appointed London agent for the Royal,[189] and in December 1836 agreed to relax its usual terms since 'it did not appear that the state of the account warranted rigid application of the rules'.[190]

The Royal had no share transactions with the Northern & Central as such, the shares being allocated to its directors as individuals. Moult explained that he took his 'under the spirit of the share mania', and because he 'thought it would be good for Ireland to have joint stock banks'.[191]

Rather different was the Royal's connection with the Agricultural. One of the first Dublin directors was James Dwyer, and he assured shareholders that no conflict would arise from his election since the two banks operated in different spheres. He appeared at the same time to claim to have been the original projector of the Royal, and certainly to have secured the interest of the Hardies and others from Manchester.[192] When the Agricultural closed in 1836 its assets included £14,000 of Royal stock which Dwyer described as having been taken as an investment with a view to uniting the two banks. He did not explain how this could have been done under the existing law but he may have been looking, like O'Connell with the Metropolitan, to the day when the law would be changed. The shares were paid for by the Agricultural and held in trust by the directors individually. The cashier had custody of the certificates—all except that in the name of Thomas Mooney who had managed to get hold of his and sell the shares. It was the voting power of these shares that put Dwyer onto the board of the Royal.[193]

187 Shareholders' minute book, 13 Nov. 1844, annual report 1844.
188 The deed of settlement, held at the head office, gives the number of shares held by each signatory but no addresses; the shareholders' minute book, 12 May 1836, gives the names of the directors.
189 Gregory, *Westminster Bank*, p. 304, gives details of the agreement.
190 *Ibid.*, p. 241.
191 *1837 committee*, Q.715-38.
192 *F.J.*, 12 May 1836, report of general meeting.
193 *1837 committee*, Q. 2675-7, evidence of Dwyer.

In passing it is interesting to note that both Thomas Mooneys were candidates for election to the first board of the Royal; the ironmonger of Pill Lane received 578 votes and was elected, the baker of Francis Street received 17 and was not.[194] Mooney of Pill Lane continued as a director until 1848 when he failed for some £27,000, including an unsecured loan of £15,000 from the Royal.[195]

To the Royal Bank the directors of the Agricultural were individual shareholders. If the board knew of their take-over plans—if such they were—it does not appear in the records. In May they accepted appointment as the Agricultural's Dublin agent,[196] and on 6 June resolved, on Dwyer's motion, to open a branch in Dundalk to issue Agricultural notes—a dubious move within fifty miles of Dublin. The resolution was amended the next day to cover branches in general issuing notes of all banks.[197] There is no further mention of the plan, and the first branches were not in fact opened until the 1860s and then only in Dublin, but the incident suggests that the other directors were chary of Dwyer's ideas.

Another concern with which the Royal was involved was the proposed Union Bank of Ireland, promoted by one W. C. Gillam. It was to be the same type of bank and a notice promising its prospectus was published in April 1836 two days after a similar notice for the Royal.[198] After negotiations with Gillam the Royal's board agreed to issue shares both to him and to the other subscribers and the plan for the Union Bank was dropped.[199] Another Union Bank of Ireland was founded in 1862 but seems to have had no connection with this one.

The Royal's deed, unlike those of the Northern and the Belfast, made no provision for control by the partners of the private bank being taken over. Sir Robert Shaw took 150 shares but had no part in the management. The second partner, Thomas Richard Needham, took 195, was elected to the first board and became the first chairman.

Day-to-day functions were entrusted by the deed to a committee of management, later known as the Bills Committee, of one English and three Irish directors, the latter to attend daily to examine bills, fix discount rates, deal with staff matters and to prepare a weekly abstract of operations for the full board.[200] Dealings with the public were to be through a general manager to which post Charles Copland,

194 Shareholders' minute book, 12 May 1836.

195 F.J., 12, 19 June, 9 Nov. 1848.

196 Board minutes, 21 May 1836, record the appointment; it was not publicly announced until July—see notice in F.J., 4 July 1836.

197 Board minutes, 6, 7 June 1836.

198 F.J., 11 Apr. 1836.

199 Board minutes, 4 June 1836; F.J., 6 June 1836.

200 Milne, Royal Bank, p. 34.

then Dublin agent for the National, was appointed.[201] Much of the early success of the Royal seems to have been due to his ability.[202]

The first annual general meeting was held on 8 November 1837 when the board reported a successful first year, thanks to what it called without explanation a 'new mode of business'.[203] The terms of business approved in August 1836 would have applied in general to the Hibernian or any of the Dublin private banks,[204] so one suspects that this was no more than bankers' sales talk.

Needham, in evidence in 1838, summarized the Royal's business as the discounting of bills, the taking of deposits and the keeping of accounts. It suffered, he said, from two inconveniences, the inability to take actions by a public officer or to draw or accept bills of less than six months' tenure, and if these were removed its position would be the same as that of the Bank of Ireland apart from the issue of notes.[205] Despite much lobbying the Royal had to wait till 1845 for their removal.

The issue of notes was authorized by the deed if permitted by law. There is frequent comment on it in the annual reports but Shaw's had latterly made no use of the right and Needham said that the Royal had no intention of availing itself of it if granted. He also denied that any injurious monopoly arose from the Bank of Ireland's privileges or that mercantile men offering good security had the least difficulty in obtaining accommodation in Dublin.[206] He at least seems to have appreciated that with the growth of cheque-operated accounts the issue of notes was no longer an essential feature of banking. Like the Hibernian, the Royal clearly managed quite satisfactorily with Bank of Ireland notes.

A weakness in the law at this date, demonstrated in the case of the Agricultural Bank, was that actions between shareholders and directors could only be taken by filing a bill in equity with the names of all the partners. The Royal tried to obviate this by a clause in the deed that in suits between shareholders and the company no objection was to be taken on the grounds that all the shareholders' names had not been included; the deed was to be read in evidence and this article to be taken as an admission by all the members. It may have been modelled on a similar article in the deed of the London & Westminster.[207] As no such suit seems to have occurred we cannot say whether it would have been effective. In 1838 an act was passed to remedy this defect by authorizing members of banking partnerships in

---

201 *F.J.*, 28 May 1836, has the advertisement for a general manager; it was repeated in papers all over England, Scotland and Ireland.
202 Milne, *op. cit.*, p. 32.
203 Shareholders' minute book, 8 Nov. 1837.
204 Milne, *Royal Bank*, pp. 33-4, gives the full text of these terms.
205 *1838 committee*, Q.1644-9.
206 *Ibid.*, Q.1677-89.
207 Gregory, *Westminster Bank*, p. 92.

England and Ireland to sue or be sued by their companies in the name of a public officer in the same manner as strangers.[208] This would not have applied to the Royal since it had no power to sue by a public officer, but it does not seem to have been much used in any case and after 1842 was allowed to lapse. In 1845 the Agricultural had to sponsor special legislation to enable it to take action against some of its members.[209]

The Royal's profits during its first ten years ranged from just under £13,000 in 1837-8 to a little over £20,000 in 1845-6, almost the same range as those of the Ulster in the same period on a similar capital. A dividend of 5 per cent was paid each year, which took just over £10,000. The balance was paid to the reserve which by 1846 totalled a little over £40,000, while the premises had been written down from £16,000 (the price paid to Shaw's) to £5,000.[210]

The English directors took little part in the management. They were rarely able to attend meetings and their main contribution was their financial backing and contacts with English banks. More and more shares passed in time into Irish hands, and by 1843, with only a few thousand pounds of stock still held by Englishmen the appointment of English directors had become 'inconvenient and difficult to accomplish'.[211] The next year the deed was amended to vest the entire management in a board of seven resident in or near Dublin. This transfer of capital and control to Ireland was hailed as a sign of increased Irish capacity for money investment and of public confidence in the Royal Bank.[212] By 1846 out of 483 members only 31 were resident in Britain; of the other 452 the bulk were from the Dublin area.[213]

Up to 1845 the Royal's business was carried on in Shaw's old premises at 3-4 Foster Place, beside the Bank of Ireland. The next year these were extended by the acquisition of the adjoining building from the Hibernian United Service Club, and this block, with later additions, still houses the head office. No. 4 Foster Place was acquired by Shaw's in 1799 and No. 3 added to it in 1832. No. 4 is therefore the oldest bank building in Dublin, or indeed in Ireland, still in use as such.

208 1 & 2 Vic., c. 96, extended to 1842 by 3 & 4 Vic., c. 111.
209 Below, p. 155.
210 Shareholders' minute book, *passim.*
211 *F.J.,* 9 Nov. 1843, chairman's speech at annual general meeting.
212 Shareholders' minute book, 22 Nov. 1844, report of special general meeting to amend the deed; 13 Nov. 1844, annual general meeting.
213 *Dublin Gaz. 1846,* pp. 197-205.

6

The System Shaken Out

The Crisis of November 1836

The expansion of banking in Ireland in the mid-thirties—from thirty-nine branches at the end of 1833 to one hundred and seventy-five in October 1836[1]—was parallel to and in some degree an extension of a similar movement in England where sixty-two new banking companies were formed during the same period.[2] While this was going on there was a steady external drain of funds for investment in America, by the sale of American securities in London and the export of gold, and this was aggravated by the efforts of President Jackson to replace notes by gold coin as the currency of the United States.[3] The Atlantic community, with its financial centre in London, was trying to invest more money than it had readily available, and this was the basic cause of the crisis in the autumn of 1836.

Conditions in London inevitably affected Ireland.[4] The liabilities of Irish banks were backed in the first instance by their London funds, and if they needed extra gold in time of pressure the ultimate source was the Bank of England. The Bank of Ireland tried to keep such imports under its own control and preferred that other banks depend on it rather than import direct, but it was not always possible to enforce this on the new banks, particularly the Provincial and the National with their London head offices. In February 1836 the Bank of Ireland was complaining to the Bank of England that gold had been imported by an Irish bank from Liverpool, probably from the Bank of England's branch.[5] A few days later it announced its own readiness to supply gold to other banks, but in the middle of April this was withdrawn.[6]

During the first half of 1836 money was still flush in London and the Bank of England's discount rate was kept at 4 per cent, as it had been since 1827.[7] The market rate fell in March to 3½ per cent and in April and May to 3¼.[8] The Bank of Ireland's rate on English bills

1 Below, Appendix 3, 4, for their distribution.
2 *1837 committee*, app. II-1.
3 Thomas Tooke, *History of prices*, ii, 284-5; R. C. O. Matthews, *A study in trade cycle history*, pp. 43-69, 91-3, analyses the fluctuations in the United States; *Dublin Ev. Post*, 10, 12 Nov. 1836, gives a Dublin view.
4 *1837 committee*, Q.4475, evidence of Marshall, shows how this was appreciated by the Provincial Bank.
5 B. of I. Mins., 24 Feb. 1836.
6 *Ibid.*, 1 Mar., 16 Apr. 1836.
7 Clapham, *Bank of England*, ii, 150-3.
8. *1857 committee*, pp. 463-4, gives ten London market rates foreach month 1824-56 supplied by the managing partner of Overend & Carney.

normally followed the Bank of England's but on 10 March, as part of a move to recover some of the business lost to the new banks, the court reduced it from 4 to $3\frac{1}{2}$ per cent. At the beginning of April other measures followed to the same end, both improved services such as the free supply of cheque books and easier credit on overdrafts and promissory notes, while the rate on Irish bills, which had been 4 per cent on bills payable in Dublin and 5 on those payable elsewhere, was unified at 4 per cent on all bills.[9]

These expansionary moves were in line with conditions in England. Their effect is evident in the monthly discount figures; from January to March they were lower than at the same period in any year going back to 1826, but in April they rose sharply and remained above the level of earlier years until November.[10]

By 21 July the Bank of England had taken alarm at the drain to America and raised its rate to $4\frac{1}{2}$ per cent but the Bank of Ireland made no move to follow. Its rate thus remained a full point below the Bank of England's, and also below the London market rate which rose to 4 per cent in June and July, $4\frac{1}{2}$ per cent in August and 5 in September. The governor, Isaac D'Olier, subsequently defended this policy on the grounds that the bank's own liabilities were unusually moderate,[11] its gold and securities fully adequate and the bills it held of the very best quality. The only unsatisfactory item in its balance sheet was its overdraft at the Bank of England. This was never intended to be large or of long duration but exceptional government transfers and unusually low return payments had pushed it to the excessive figure of £200,000.[12]

On 1 September, with gold still draining to America, the Bank of England again raised its rate, to 5 per cent, and at the same time called on the Bank of Ireland to repay the overdraft, adding the awkward rider that the sale of exchequer bills held as security would be possible only at a serious loss. This is the first indication in the Bank of Ireland's court minutes of the need to tighten credit. The rate on English bills was promptly raised to 4 per cent, and three days later that on Irish bills to $4\frac{1}{2}$. To clear the overdraft the court instructed the Bank of England to sell exchequer bills on its behalf as far as this could be done without serious loss; if this were not possible it asked to be allowed to continue the overdraft until the end of the month when over £600,000 of exchequer bills would fall due and could be taken in cash rather than the normal exchange for new bills.

But again there was a difficulty. To take exchequer bills in cash meant to increase the liquidity of the system, the exact opposite of

9 B. of I. Mins., 1 Mar.-2 Apr. 1836.
10 *1837 committee*, app. III-23.
11 *Ibid.*, app. III-2, twice-monthly circulation figures confirm this.
12 D'Olier to Pattison, governor of the Bank of England, 29 Nov. 1836 (B. of I. Mins., 29 Nov. 1836).

what the Bank of England was endeavouring to do. It was therefore most unwilling to comply, and the Bank of Ireland authorized it instead to sell stock, some of which was transferred from Dublin for the purpose. In addition, in reluctant response to a request from the Bank of England, it shipped £100,000 in sovereigns to Liverpool on 17 September. This, with some £45,000 from exchequer bills which the Bank of England had succeeded in selling, proved sufficient with other receipts to put the account back in credit.[13]

The Bank of England followed up this improvement with an inquiry whether the Bank of Ireland, whose discount rate was still 1 per cent below its own, would take up some of the large quantity of commercial bills that were pressing on the London market, but this the Bank of Ireland refused.[14] With pressure beginning to be felt in Ireland it could not afford to tie up its resources; it began instead to take restrictive measures of its own. The general limit on the period that bills must have left to run when taken by the bank was sixty-four days—that is sixty-one days plus three days grace. On 29 September this was cut to twenty-one in the case of bankers, and on 1 October the rate on Irish bills was raised to 5 per cent.[15]

But this did not prove sufficient. Towards the end of September the court found that some £70,000 in gold had been withdrawn for transmission to Liverpool, attracted presumably by the higher rates ruling in England. At the same time the operations of some of the new banks were causing it increasing concern. On 26 October therefore it finally brought the rate on English bills into line with the Bank of England's at 5 per cent, the rate now also ruling in the London market; simultaneously it reduced the period for drawing bills on England from twenty-one days to ten and ordered further sales of exchequer bills and stock to strengthen the account at the Bank of England.[16]

In his evidence in 1838 James Pim, one of the partners in Boyle's, described these restrictions as the first cause of the panic. Banks in difficulties in Lancashire, particularly the Northern & Central, had been sending bills to Dublin which were discounted, not at the Bank of Ireland but elsewhere for its notes which were then used to draw gold. The bank, he said, was unaware of this, and when it found out became alarmed, raised its discount rate and almost ceased discounting, particularly for banks connected with others.[17]

This was an oversimplified but essentially correct account of what happened. As Thomas Wilson put it to the same committee, it was the bank's principle to be slow in making changes; had it known the

13 B. of I. Mins., 3-19 Sept. 1836.
14 *Ibid.* 27 Sept. 1836.
15 *Ibid.,* 29 Sept., 1 Oct. 1836.
16 D'Olier to Pattison, 26 Oct. 1836 (B. of I. Mins., 26 Oct. 1836).
17 *1838 committee,* Q.378-80.

true state of the English markets and the American transactions it would have raised the rate sooner. It 'followed the footsteps of the Bank of England but at a measured pace'.[18] A month earlier, on 29 September, the court had resolved to restrict discounts for bankers but it was certainly the outflow of gold to Liverpool that prompted the final tightening. On 29 October the bank's agents were all instructed to reduce their discounts, especially on Irish bills, and all bills with over sixty-one days to run were to be considered out of course.[19] The latter ruling only confirmed existing practice but its formal announcement evidently created some alarm.[20]

Simultaneously the bank was faced with a demand from the treasury for the transfer of £200,000 that month to the Bank of England to the credit of the paymaster of exchequer bills, and a further £200,000 the next month. This was totally unexpected, and the £400,000 was rather more than the balance in the government account, but as a loyal banker, the Bank of Ireland made preparations to comply. The transfers would have to be made from the account at the Bank of England which was still in process of being restored to balance. To provide another £400,000 further sales of stock and exchequer bills would be urgently needed, and the court sent instructions to the Bank of England to undertake them on its behalf.[21]

It was part of the process of tightening credit that the bank was obliged to sell its holdings of government stock so as to mop up money from the public to provide funds for the government to pay off the exchequer bills falling due, the same which the bank had itself wished to take in cash. Such sales could only have been made at a loss, that is by pushing up the rate of interest, and, quite apart from this, the Bank of England was most reluctant to press sales that might alarm the market. Pattison, the governor of the Bank of England, explained these difficulties to the treasury in London, and a few days later a deputation from the Bank of Ireland waited on Spring Rice, the chancellor, who was on a visit to Dublin, and he agreed to suspend the warrant for the £400,000 for the present.[22]

The reason for Spring Rice's consent was the increasingly dangerous situation among the Irish joint stock banks. On 29 October, only six weeks after shipping £100,000 to Liverpool, D'Olier warned Pattison that the operation of several of the banks might shortly oblige the Bank of Ireland to import gold again, and on 5 November he wrote again that there was delay in the discharge of notes by certain banks and that they were pressing more English bills on the Dublin market than it could absorb. He expected calls for help, and

18 *1838 committee*, Q.875, 935.
19 B. of I. Mins., 29 Oct. 1836, circular to agents.
20 *F.J.*, 3 Nov. 1836.
21 B. of I. Mins., 28, 29 Oct. 1836.
22 *Ibid.*, 1, 5 Nov. 1836.

asked for £100,000 in sovereigns to be placed at the bank's disposal in Liverpool immediately and another £100,000 as soon as convenient. On the seventh he reported that all the banks were paying promptly and that the only substantial withdrawal of gold from the Bank of Ireland had been £10,000 to La Touche for the Provincial, who had previously had £30,000 on the fifth. These withdrawals were against Bank of Ireland notes presented for payment.[23]

On the eighth the exchanges were larger than usual, particularly on notes of the National and the Agricultural, but all had been discharged. Then on the ninth came the first open sign of trouble when the Hibernian refused the draft on the Ulster.[24] At the same time it evidently refused payment on notes of the Belfast Bank for whom it was also agent. A report of this refusal in the *Dublin Evening Mail* caused a run on some of the Belfast's branches to meet which it had to appeal for help from the Bank of Ireland.[25] Both banks removed their agencies from the Hibernian, the Ulster to Boyle's and then to the Royal, and the Belfast back to Solomon Watson.[26]

The Hibernian's spokesman before the 1838 committee blamed the Bank of Ireland for these refusals. It had submitted good English bills for discount on behalf of the Ulster and the Belfast, they asserted, and the secretary thought refusal so unlikely that he did not send for an answer in the usual way at one o'clock and only heard at four o'clock that the bills had been refused. This left the Hibernian unable to pay the notes and bills of the two northern banks. Later the Bank of Ireland gave the accommodation but by then it was too late.[27]

A strong defence of the Bank of Ireland's conduct in this crisis appeared in the *Dublin University Magazine* in 1840-1 in a series of four articles on banking written anonymously by Mountifort Longfield, formerly professor of political economy and subsequently of law.[28] Their main theme was the need for a strong central bank to control the currency, and the experience of 1836 was cited in support. The Bank of Ireland had then been able to help because it had not over-discounted itself. It did not normally rediscount for banks of issue since their paper would not be for real transactions and attempts by them to rediscount must indicate overtrading, but 'as an extraordinary exertion for the public interest' it did help them in time of panic, just when it was most inconvenient to itself. Such last resort loans must be

23 Below, p. 143.
24 Above, p. 130.
25 *Dublin Ev. Mail*, 9-14 Nov. 1836; B. of I. Mins., 12 Nov. 1836.
26 Above, p. 130; below, p. 207.
27 *1838 committee*, Q.1222-5, evidence of Ignatius Callaghan; 1324-35, of Jeremiah Dunne.
28 'Banking and currency', in *Dublin University Magazine*, xv, xvi (1840, 1841), especially xv, 226-30; R. D. C. Black, *Economic thought and the Irish question*, p. 151, n. 2, identifies Longfield as author; see above, p. 74, for his criticism of Callaghan.

on terms that would put a stop to the overtrading, and the Hibernian had failed to allow for this; its rediscounts were for banks of issue but had been submitted in the ordinary way and were refused because they were not ordinary.

By refusing to discount for banks of issue in normal times the Bank of Ireland left itself able to help when pressure reached the point of crisis. The court evidently did not yet think that this point had been reached on 8 November when it refused an application from the National to open an account with a deposit of £40,000 English bills and £60,000 Irish as security. Its stated reason was its concern at the state of the circulation due to the operations of the new banks, and it doubted whether the Bank of England would approve giving them indirect help through the Bank of Ireland. The court was particularly unhappy about the National in which the division of responsibility between the centre and the branches was obscure and the quality of securities on which notes were sometimes issued was open to question.[29]

Pattison gave full support to this policy which accorded with the long-established principle of the Bank of England that banks of issue should always 'depend for the support of their circulation on the public market' by selling securities to obtain 'money already in existence' rather than new money issued to them.[30] But before this letter had reached the Bank of Ireland, before even it had been written, the court had decided, on 9 November after the Hibernian's default, that the time had come to intervene. It resolved to discount short English bills for banks provided they stated the whole amount needed to meet the pressure on them—in other words it would give help to set matters right but not to continue overissues.[31] This was its traditional policy in time of pressure.[32]

An application for discount of £10,000 already received from the Agricultural was approved, and applications followed quickly from all the other joint stock banks except the Provincial and the Northern. Wilson's evidence in 1838 gave the total help granted as:[33]

	£
Belfast Bank	103,000
Ulster Bank	60,000
Hibernian Bank	21,000
Agricultural Bank	19,600
National Bank	42,600
Total	246,200

29 D'Olier to Pattison, 8 Nov. 1836 (B. of I. Mins., 8 Nov. 1836).
30 Pattison to D'Olier, 11 Nov. 1836 (B. of I. Mins., 14 Nov. 1836).
31 B. of I. Mins., 9 Nov. 1836.
32 Above, pp. 18-9.
33 *1838 committee*, Q.891; Wilson had been deputy governor in 1836.

The court minutes do not give full details, but sufficient to show that these figures may be taken as accurate. £10,000 was also approved for Ball's but never used while an application from Boyle's was rejected as they were not regarded as bankers. At the end of the crisis, on 21 November, an additional £70-75,000 was agreed to for the National but was not needed.[34]

The advances were mainly on bills or letters of credit drawn by the banks on their correspondents in England, with some Irish bills, and the Bank of Ireland gave credit for their value less the discount. The credit was drawn on as needed, sometimes in Bank of Ireland notes but chiefly in gold.[35]

Since the middle of 1833 the Bank of Ireland had let its specie fall well below the normal level of over £1,000,000, and by the end of 1835 it was only £702,500, the lowest half-yearly figure in the series running back to 1808.[36] By the end of June 1836 it had risen to £746,000 but by November it must have fallen again after the shipment of £100,000 to Liverpool and the withdrawal of £70,000 for the same destination. During the crisis a total of £400,000 was imported by the bank from Liverpool[37] where, in the words of the Bank of England agent, it had 'a large margin allowed for gold'[38]—a great convenience but no saving on cost since the charge included transport from London.[39] The gold was needed only to help other banks. The Bank of Ireland itself was under no pressure and during the crisis it paid out only £2,000 more gold to the public than it received back. Some was paid to other banks against Bank of Ireland notes but there is no record of how much. The only gold paid to the Provincial seems to have been £40,000 in this way.[40] On the other hand, at one stage the National deposited £40,000 in sovereigns in exchange for Bank of Ireland notes which it used to pay off its own liabilities.[41]

The Bank of Ireland's efforts to keep the import of gold in its own hands were not wholly successful. The Provincial imported £400,000 on its own account[42] and the National evidently imported £200,000.[43] The Northern also imported some but there is no record of how much.[44] To minimize imports the court agreed, early in the crisis, to

34 B. of I. Mins., 10-21 Nov. 1836; *1838 committee*, Q.690-1, evidence of Wilson. Hall, *Bank of Ireland*, pp. 162-3, gives rather higher figures but without citing his authority; his inclusion of £100,000 to the Provincial is certainly wrong.
35 *1838 committee*, Q.894-900, evidence of Wilson.
36 *1837 committee*, app. III-2.
37 D'Olier to Pattison, 28 Nov. 1836 (B. of I. Mins., 28 Nov. 1836).
38 *1838 committee*, Q.300, evidence of Samuel Turner.
39 *Ibid.*, Q.728-31, evidence of Wilson.
40 B. of I. Mins., 8 Nov. 1836.
41 *Ibid.*, 14 Nov. 1836.
42 *1837 committee*, Q.4442, evidence of Marshall.
43 *1838 committee*, Q.1072, evidence of Wilson, who agreed to figures stated in the question; the figure of £700,000 stated there for imports by the Provincial refers to 1828 not 1836.
44 *Ibid.*, Q.366, evidence of James Pim.

pay gold to any bank in Dublin against deposits made at the Bank of England, at a charge to cover the cost of transport.[45] This seems to have been little used but while the Bank of Ireland's agreement to it was still in the post Pattison suggested that such deposits be taken in London for repayment in Dublin not in gold but in Bank of England notes. In anticipation of the Bank of Ireland's consent he accepted a number of such deposits, issued letters of credit against them payable in Dublin and dispatched £300,000 of Bank of England notes to the Bank of Ireland with which to meet them.

The notes were intended for settlement of balances between the Irish banks, to economize gold, but Pattison's letter, received by the Bank of Ireland at the height of the crisis on Sunday 15 November, far from bringing relief caused consternation. The bank charter act of 1833 had declared Bank of England notes to be legal tender[46] but the Bank of Ireland, with strong legal backing, denied that this applied to Ireland since, among other things, it would contravene the act of 1821.[47] The Provincial, with equal legal backing, took the opposite view, and now accepted some Bank of England notes in settlement of the balance due to it from another bank. The Bank of Ireland decided not to refuse them for the same purpose but expressly stated that this was as a convenience to other banks not as a right.[48] This was the point that Pattison took up, quoting further legal opinion that the notes were legal tender in Ireland. At the same time the treasury informed the Bank of Ireland that it took the same view and called on the directors to 'govern yourselves accordingly in receipt and transmission of revenue'.[49]

Without waiting for the meeting of the court on Monday D'Olier wrote urgently to Pattison to suspend the scheme since it would be 'little short of an admission that the Bank of Ireland is unable to meet its engagements and calculated to excite an alarm of the most formidable nature'. After consideration by the court the next day he wrote again at some length. Most Irish circulation, he pointed out, was in small notes which Bank of England notes (of minimum value of £5) would be little use in paying; banks who received them would instead present them for gold at the Bank of Ireland who would therefore be obliged to send them back to England to exchange for gold itself.

It turned out just as D'Olier had feared. When the letters of credit were presented the bank handed over parcels of Bank of England notes to the stated amounts. £25,000 was so paid to the National and the manager promptly tendered the notes back again to be lodged

45 D'Olier to Pattison, 10 Nov. 1836 (B. of I. Mins., 10 Nov. 1836).
46 3 & 4 Will. IV, c. 98, s. 6.
47 *1838 committee*, Q.949-63, evidence of Wilson.
48 B. of I. Mins., 9 Nov. 1836.
49 *Ibid.* 14 Nov. 1836.

to his credit. He offered to pay the transport of any gold drawn against the credit but the Bank of Ireland refused to take any of the notes except in discharge of balances from the exchange of notes at the branches. The manager then asked for £25,000 against a draft on London, stating that he would send the notes there to provide for it, but the bank again refused. It agreed finally to take the notes 'under the urgency of the case', and the manager promptly drew out £10,000 in gold. D'Olier described the incident to Pattison as 'a painful transaction but unavoidable on our part'.

The Provincial's case was a little different. It received £30,000 of Bank of England notes in the same way, and the following day La Touche on its behalf paid in £60,000 in Bank of England notes as revenue receipts. In the light of the treasury instruction the Bank of Ireland could hardly refuse them, but on examination the notes were found to include the identical £30,000 just paid out. This, as D'Olier duly pointed out to Pattison, showed the power given to banks receiving revenue; they could hold all the Bank of Ireland notes received from the collectors (and demand gold for them at will) and pay in the revenue in Bank of England notes. The Bank of Ireland objected not so much to the cost as to the risk of unpredictable demands.[50]

In the face of this reaction Pattison dropped the scheme, with assurances that he never doubted the Bank of Ireland's ability to meet its own obligations in gold but only feared that there might not be enough in Ireland to cover inter-bank exchanges. This was the beginning of a long correspondence between him and D'Olier on the topic of bank reserves; Pattison urged both that joint stock banks be encouraged to hold more themselves and that the Bank of Ireland hold enough to give necessary help in emergency; D'Olier in reply pointed out the difference in Irish conditions both from the circulation of small notes and from demand being much more for drafts on London than for gold, the Bank of Ireland being able to provide for the one only at the expense of its ability to provide the other. No formal conclusion was reached but both sides agreed that the exchange had been useful.[51]

In practice the Bank of Ireland did increase its gold stocks. By 31 December they were up to £887,700 and from 1837 onwards were normally well over £1,000,000, as they had been up to 1832,[52] but they never approached the level of one-third of the bank's liabilities 'in time of full currency' which Pattison had urged, an application of the

50 B. of I. Mins., 14-19 Nov. 1836.
51 *Ibid.*, 21-29 Nov., 20 Dec. 1836. Hall, *Bank of Ireland*, pp. 167-9, reprints the two final letters, but his account of this correspondence and of the crisis in general in the previous pages is incomplete and at times most inaccurate.
52 *1837 committee*, app. III-2; below, Appendix 6.

F

Palmer rule which would have been quite unsuited to the circumstances of the Bank of Ireland.

Annual figures of gold supplied to and received from Ireland by the Bank of England show that from 1833 to 1835 the total shipped to Ireland was £410,000 while almost £900,000 was received back. This was the normal pattern with little demand for gold in Ireland. It made it all the more difficult to meet the demand when it came, as it did in 1836 when £926,000 was supplied as against about £240,000 received back, these figures referring to the whole year not just the crisis period.[53]

By 28 November D'Olier was able to write to Spring Rice that the run had completely subsided and the bank could now begin the transfers to London on treasury account whose suspension at the beginning of the month had been 'most useful and timely'. The same day he wrote to Pattison that gold had not yet started to flow back into the Bank of Ireland but he hoped that it would shortly. Large sums were being invested by the public in government stock which indicated excessive circulation. The bank proposed to enter the market itself to mop this up and he asked for stock to be sent from London for the purpose. The next day he wrote that 'the storm has blown over leaving our mercantile and manufacturing interest with very trifling exceptions unshaken'. Pressure had been confined to the banks, and the only casualty had been the Agricultural.[54]

The Agricultural Bank Suspension

The 1836 pressure in London would not have had the effect it did in Ireland had the new banks not been overextended. In his evidence in 1838 Wilson described the crisis as a banking not a commercial one; mercantile transactions were 'in a very regular state' with no overtrading but there was distrust of the new banks and, in consequence of the Agricultural's discounts in particular, there must have been 'a greater plenty of money' than usual amongst the farming community.[55]

The purpose of both the Agricultural and the National—indeed to some degree of all banks—was to provide the financial means of greater production and employment by increasing the supply of money in the form of their own notes and deposits. Sound banking required

---

53 *1837 committee*, app. 5, 6, returns submitted by the Bank of England. Hall, *Bank of Ireland*, p. 166, quotes figures for gold imports and exports by the bank which are quite wrong; they refer in fact to government remittances by banking transfers and have nothing to do with gold—D'Olier to Spring Rice, 21 Nov. 1836 (B. of I. Mins., 21 Nov. 1836).

54 B. of I. Mins., 28, 29 Nov. 1836. Clapham, *Bank of England*, ii, 154, refers to Irish 'failures' but this is an error; there was only one and it was a suspension not a failure, and occurred in the middle of November not the end as stated.

55 *1838 committee*, Q.839-51.

that the volume of such liabilities on which payment would be demanded at any one time be balanced by the volume of assets then available in liquid form. A sudden extraordinary increase in demand for payment beyond the level of liquid assets on hand would leave the bank dependent for its survival on its ability to borrow enough to make up the difference until sufficient assets matured. In the nature of banking, demand liabilities were balanced by assets due at a later date; the gap was bridged by public confidence, and this is what the Agricultural Bank lost.

The rapid expansion of the banking system had aroused alarm in orthodox circles for some time. The Provincial, for instance, had anticipated trouble since the previous year and had been exercising restraint.[56] But the final break came as a result of three separate incidents. The first was the publication at the general meeting on 17 October of the following balance sheet:[57]

	£		£
Paid-up capital	375,030	Bills on hand	902,457
Notes in circulation	421,597	Government and other	
Deposit and current		securities	20,607
accounts	366,182	Property	28,500
		Credit accounts	93,732
Total liabilities	1,162,809	Cash on hand	134,892
Surplus assets	17,379	Total assets	1,180,188
Dividend for half year	9,375		
Reserve fund	8,004		

These figures were later questioned but it is not their accuracy that is at issue here; it is the figures themselves that are said to have aroused distrust, with only £135,000 cash to meet liabilities of nearly £1,163,000. Pierce Mahony spoke at length about this with no hint that he realized that it was nonsense,[58] while Ignatius Callaghan declared that the account showed that the Agricultural had not 'anything like a sum at its command to meet its issues'.[59] Ignorant noteholders may then really have believed that their paper would be worthless unless they could exchange it before the £135,000 cash was exhausted.

But in fact cash represented some 32 per cent of the circulation, approximately the same proportion as in the National's balance sheet

56 *1837 committee*, Q.4458-62, evidence of James Marshall.
57 *F.J.*, 18 Oct. 1836, report of general meeting.
58 *1837 committee*, Q.4021.
59 *1838 committee*, Q.1366.

of 31 December 1835[60] and as the average gold cover held by the Provincial over the years 1831-41,[61] and well above the 20 per cent required by that bank's agreement with the treasury. The Agricultural's cash presumably included other bank notes, as did that of the National, but by any normal banking standards the proportion was adequate. Taking notes and deposits together cash represented about 17 per cent, again quite enough in normal circumstances. To relate cash on hand to the balance sheet total, including the bank's own capital, was patently ridiculous.

The key items were the £902,457 of bills on hand and the £93,732 of credit accounts. If these were of good quality and appropriate maturity dates the bank was in a perfectly sound condition. If there were doubts about them they were quite independent of the balance sheet. By later standards more of the assets should have been in government stock on which to raise money in emergencies, but this was still far from general practice. Publication of balance sheets was rare at this date; what the incident really showed was the need for it so that they might be better understood.

The second event, blamed by Dwyer for increased pressure on the bank all over Ireland,[62] was the appearance a week later of a letter to the shareholders from Thomas Mooney.[63] In emotional terms he wrote of the bank which he had founded as 'a great local establishment' not subject to 'the caprice of a distant proprietary and directory'. It had brought benefit especially to the humbler classes but now, he warned, it was about to be handed over to a London board. The pretended reason was that the capital was insufficient, yet there was some £375,000 paid up, and only a dozen of the eighty-six joint stock banks in England had as much.

The letter was promptly disavowed by the consulting committee who denied any plans for a London board; all that was proposed was a shareholding connection with several London capitalists. The notice was signed by John Chambers as chairman and by all the members of the committee except Mooney.[64]

The bank's liquid resources were clearly under strain. The general meeting of 17 October had approved a third call of 10 per cent. Its stated purpose was to expand the business and bring the paid-up capital to the Provincial's level of £500,000,[65] but Dwyer revealed the next year that the money had been urgently needed to avoid legal action by an English banker to whom the bank owed £200,000.[66]

60 Above, p. 128.
61 Below, Appendix 9.
62 *1837 committee*, Q.2871-7.
63 *F.J.*,24 Oct. 1836, has the letter itself.
64 *F.J.*,25 Oct. 1836; see also 17 Oct. 1837, report of general meeting.
65 *F.J.*,18 Oct. 1836, report of general meeting; notices of the call are in *F.J.*, 20 Oct., and *London Gazette,* 18 Oct. 1836.
66 *F.J.*,17 Oct. 1837, speech at general meeting.

Proposals to relieve the pressure included the introduction of some wealthy new partners from London[67] and some form of link with the Minerva Insurance Company.[68] It was this that sparked the breach between Mooney and the rest of the board.

On 7 November the annual election of directors took place. Mooney was not re-elected. The new board, or committee, had ten Dublin members and five representing the districts.[69] No sooner were they elected than the third blow fell in the form of an anonymous placard circulated among Dublin tradesmen on 8 November warning that the bank was in an unsound state and advising them to demand payment of its notes.[70] The board offered a reward of £200 for the conviction of the author of 'this false and malicious placard',[71] but to no avail. A run ensued on the Agricultural and also on the National but as neither of them issued notes in Dublin it can hardly have been on a major scale. Both paid with promptitude and the next day confidence was said to have been restored.[72] But the respite was only momentary for the same day saw the Hibernian's refusal of the draft on the Ulster which brought the general crisis to a head.

On 9 November Thomas Michael Gresham, newly elected to the board of the Agricultural, was persuaded by his fellow directors to lend the bank £8,000 as a matter of urgency, and was only able to do so by a hurried sale of government stock. The next day, after being convinced that the financial safety of the country depended on it, he agreed to endorse bills for £10,000 to cover an advance from the Bank of Ireland.[73] This must be the £10,000 which the bank's minutes show as applied for against English bills on the ninth and approved on the tenth. The total help to the Agricultural was £19,600, but a further request on the twelfth for £20,000 to be secured in the first place on the bank's own retired notes pending the receipt of local bills from the branches, was rejected, as were frantic appeals for help on the fourteenth.[74] The Agricultural's efforts to get help from various banks in England and Scotland fared no better—the Northern & Central in particular was unable to help as it was in trouble itself—and no alternative remained but to stop payment. This it did on 14 November.[75]

67 *1837 committee*, Q.2854, evidence of Dwyer.
68 *B. Mag.*, iii, 65-70.
69 *F.J.*,8 Nov. 1836, report of general meeting.
70 *1838 committee*, Q.846, evidence of Wilson; no copy of the placard appears to be extant.
71 *F.J.*,9 Nov. 1836, advertisement by consulting committee.
72 *F.J.*,10 Nov. 1836, news report including quotation from *Dublin Ev. Mail*.
73 *1837 committee*, Q.3228-32, evidence of Gresham.
74 B. of I. Mins., 9-14 Nov. 1836. Dwyer told the *1837 committee* (Q.2885-90) that the Bank of Ireland refused an advance of £20-30,000 on local bills and then granted £20,000 on bills personally endorsed by two directors—but this seems to have reversed the order of events.
75 *1837 committee*, Q.2899-906, evidence of Dwyer.

The public notice of suspension stated that the bank had paid out £537,000 since 3 October and was now presented with demands for £11,000 from the Provincial and £10,000 from the Bank of Ireland on its notes and orders. Assets were 'abundantly ample to pay all demands and leave the capital untouched', but a lapse of a month would be necessary to collect bills falling due. Members were urged to pay the third call promptly and so enable the company to resume business within cautious limits.[76] A statement a few days later showed assets on 5 November to have exceeded liabilities by over £381,000, some £6,000 more than the paid-up capital. This was certified as correct by two Belfast shareholders who had 'minutely investigated the books and accounts'. The bank added a note that half of these liabilities had since been paid off—but without pointing out that this must mean a similar reduction in the assets.[77]

Payment of notes in Dublin was a matter of convenience not of right but the pressure reached its climax there by reason of the inter-bank exchange system. When excessive issues by the Agricultural were accompanied by restraint on the part of the Bank of Ireland and the Provincial more Agricultural notes came into the hands of those two banks than vice versa, and the branch managers had to give drafts on Dublin to settle the differences. The demands mentioned in the suspension notice must have been in the form of such drafts. Regular exchanges were considered a useful means of keeping mul-tiple issues under control,[78] but their restraining influence only operated on presentation of the drafts in Dublin and depended for its efficacy on each bank's internal system of control.[79]

The suspension strictly speaking referred only to Dublin.[80] The only branch suspension was at Galway on 11 November, three days earlier, the result apparently of unnecessary nerves on the part of the manager.[81] On 17 November all branches were reported to be open and 'promptly exchanging notes for gold'. On the nineteenth 'most of the country branches' continued to discharge their engagements.[82] Reports in the press tell of meetings up and down the country which expressed confidence in the bank, deplored the hostile efforts of un-specified 'interested parties' and promised to accept its notes on all occasions. Some landlords virtually insisted on rents being paid in bank notes, while tradesmen published special advertisements under-taking to accept Agricultural notes for their goods. On 20 November,

76 *F.J.*,16 Nov. 1836, has the notice in full.
77 *F.J.*,18 Nov. 1836.
78 Above, pp. 97-8.
79 *1837 committee*, Q.4485, evidence of Marshall; see also Q.4041-4, evidence of Mahony.
80 *1838 committee*, Q.1667-70, Thomas Needham pointed this out.
81 *1837 committee*, Q.2872-82, evidence of Dwyer.
82 *Dublin Ev. Post*, 17, 19 Nov. 1836.

the Sunday after the crisis, the spiritual arm gave support with admonitions from the altar on the folly of pressing for gold.[83]

Initially the run seems to have affected the National almost as much as the Agricultural, and resolutions of confidence often coupled the two together. No figures are available for the National's issues at this time. The Bank of Ireland, as we have noted, had doubts about its stability but its resources were certainly greater than those of the Agricultural. It was able to give the Bank of Ireland good security for advances of £42,600 plus stand-by facilities for a further £70-75,000, whereas the Agricultural, relying mainly on local bills, could only obtain £19,600. In addition the National imported gold on its own account—apparently £200,000 worth.[84] The influence of the London board must have been important in this connection, and the efforts of the Agricultural to form links in London had a similar purpose.

A particular strength of the National was the standing of O'Connell. On 21 November at a personal interview with directors of the Bank of Ireland he arranged the final advance of £75,000, promising to go to London himself if need be to see to its repayment. From the anxiety expressed by the governors of both the Bank of England and the Bank of Ireland and that shown by O'Connell himself, the position of the National had until then been far from assured.[85] The extra accommodation was never in fact used; it was intended to be effective and final, and the fact that it was available seems to have been just that. O'Connell's record of hostility to the Bank of Ireland must have made the negotiations quite delicate, but the suggestion that the advance was obtained by political threats was firmly denied by Thomas Wilson in his 1838 evidence.[86]

Two days later, with his bank secure, O'Connell made his first public statement. In an open letter he explained that he had kept silent to give time for the National to prove its soundness. He now appealed for support for all the banks; the Agricultural, he was convinced, would pay every single note in full and no one should part with any at a loss, the Provincial's shareholders were extremely opulent and it was perfectly safe to hold their notes, the Bank of Ireland's directors deserved thanks for their liberality in sustaining public credit. The run would only keep down prices and curtail trade and employment. 'As a friend of the people,' he wrote, 'I call on them to allow the banks to do them good.'[87] O'Connell's monetary ideas had certainly progressed since 1830.[88]

83 *F.J.*, 17-26 Nov. 1836.
84 *1838 committee*, Q.1072, as stated in the question; Q.281, the Bank of England's Liverpool agent mentioned £100,000 supplied one day as a matter of urgency.
85 B. of I. Mins., 21, 24 Nov. 1836.
86 *1838 committee*, Q.690-2, answering questions from O'Connell.
87 *F.J.*, 23 Nov. 1836.
88 Above, pp. 121-2.

Before the end of November the run had altogether ceased.[89] In Dublin the Agricultural had to wait to collect maturing bills and on 29 December announced that payment would be resumed on 23 January 1837.[90] In March it reported that all debts on notes and letters of credit had been fully discharged out of the produce of bills held on 14 November. This included amounts to three London correspondent banks who had been 'most liberal and considerate' in allowing payment by instalments, the London & Westminster having commended the Agricultural in its recent report for paying in full with only the delay 'necessarily incidental to the collection of assets'; the Northern & Central had been paid in full from bills previously deposited with it, and the Agricultural was now free from all liabilities and its shareholders protected.[91]

There was some dispute as to the accuracy of the figures in this report but on the fact of payment in full there is no doubt. Within three months of the suspension £788,000 was paid out—which Dwyer cited as proof of the soundness of the assets.[92] Gresham was fully repaid the advances that he personally had made to the bank.[93] Moult confirmed that the Northern & Central would sustain no loss; £35,000 of the £40,000 due to it had been paid by May 1837 and other assets held would cover the rest.[94] The same month O'Connell told the National's annual general meeting that the Agricultural had 'satisfied the public in all the demands that had been made upon them'.[95]

The Agricultural Bank was thus proved by the event to have been perfectly solvent. Where it failed was in liquidity; its readily available assets were insufficient to meet unanticipated demands. This indicated a failure of management, a failure to foresee what was foreseeable and to be as ready as a good bank should for what was not, but not the irresponsible conspiracy to defraud the public that has so often been alleged.

The Agricultural Bank After the Crisis

The Agricultural's suspension became inevitable when its members failed to pay the third call—out of £157,000 due only £23,000 was paid.[96] Reports of the spate of meetings held after the suspension are punctuated with appeals for payment and at the beginning of January a peremptory demand was issued,[97] but evidently to little effect. The

89 *F.J.*, 29 Nov. 1836, quoting 'the entire provincial press'.
90 *F.J.*, 31 Dec. 1836.
91 *F.J.*, 25 Mar. 1837, report of general meeting of 20 Mar.
92 *1837 committee*, Q.2696.
93 *Ibid.*, Q.3303-4, his own evidence.
94 *Ibid.*, Q.746-7, evidence of Moult.
95 *F.J.*, 30 May, 1837.
96 *1837 committee*, Q.3051-2, evidence of Dwyer.
97 *F.J.*, 2 Jan. 1837, notice by consulting committee.

bank now began to pay the price of earlier equivocation over share-holders' liabilities and signature of the deed, as well as of its reliance on large numbers of small shareholders of limited means.

The proprietors were in three distinct groups: the supporters of the board (mainly the original subscribers from the south and west), its Irish critics (mainly the recently joined members from the north) and the small group of large shareholders from England. The last came chiefly from Lancashire and Yorkshire and were interested in the bank as an investment; many of them were connected with the Northern & Central which was also in trouble. Dwyer was the leader of the management, while the leadership of the other two groups quickly passed into the hands of the indefatigable Pierce Mahony was was engaged, reluctantly as he alleged, as legal representative of the two groups of dissidents.[98]

The full story of the struggle between these three groups, the efforts to refloat the bank and the final winding up is too long to tell here. Two stormy meetings were held in Dublin on 20 March and 17 April 1837.[99] At the first four auditors were appointed and their highly critical report was presented to the second.[100] Its reliability was much disputed, and on some points such as the value of the assets it was certainly misleading, but its general picture of faulty accounting and inadequate control is irrefutable.

The meeting of 17 April degenerated into a general mêlée with rival factions operating at each end of the room. From it a resolution emerged to suspend the principal directors but the disorder had been such that the directors were able to resist it as illegal.[101] A bill in chancery to enforce the resolution was later dismissed with costs,[102] and a private bill in parliament to dissolve the bank failed for lack of support.[103]

The directors were therefore successful in frustrating the attempts to dislodge them but getting the bank back into business proved a harder task. All debts owing at the time of suspension had been paid off but this left the coffers empty. Little of the third call had been paid but in 1837 and 1838 new funds were raised by an issue of debentures, evidently in London.[104] With their liabilities paid off most branches had simply ceased to function but with this help twenty were reopened.

---

98 *F.J.*, 30 Mar. 1837, open letter from Mahony to the board.
99 *F.J.*, 21 Mar.-22 Apr. 1837, has a blow by blow account of these two meetings and other events. A report of the second meeting from the viewpoint of the dissidents is in R.I.A., Haliday 1685.
100 Above, pp. 115-6.
101 *1837 committee*, Q.3822, 3860, evidence of Mahony who tried to enforce the resolution on behalf of the dissidents.
102 *F. J.*, 16 Oct. 1838, report of general meeting at which a vote of thanks to the judge was proposed but withdrawn to avoid bitterness.
103 *F.J.*, 4 May-29 June 1837, reports its progress and petitions about it.
104 *F.J.*, 1 Feb., 19 Nov. 1844, law reports of White v Woodall and Taylor v Hughes.

A new issue of notes was printed of a different design,[105] and by April 1838 the company was reported to have been restored to credit in both the London and Dublin markets.[106]

But in the end all the board's efforts proved unavailing. It was still moderately optimistic in April 1840[107] but by June it was in trouble. An urgent appeal to the Bank of Ireland for help to meet pressure in Dublin was rejected as the security offered was inadequate, and on the nineteenth payments were again suspended in Dublin.[108] This time, despite a confident promise of resumption, it was for good. Assets were stated to exceed liabilities by some £200,000 compared with stock on the books valued £247,500[109]—which indicated some loss to the shareholders but no need for further calls.

A winding-up committee was appointed in October 1840 and its report, presented in September 1844, gives the best account of events after the closure.[110] The original figures of assets and liabilities proved to be too optimistic and in March 1841 a further call was made of £5 per share on British shares and 10s per share on Irish. The committee tried to persuade creditors to give time for it to be paid but without success. Among others the Provincial Bank obtained judgement for £2,400 and its right to recover it from individual members was confirmed by the court.[111] This led to the formation of one and then another shareholders' committee, and the bulk of the liabilities soon passed into their hands.

Once again Pierce Mahony appeared on the scene, this time as solicitor to some of the principal creditors. He agreed with the committee that they would supply him with the names of shareholders in default on the call and after obtaining judgement against the bank he would enforce it against them only. Some three or four hundred suits were cleared off in this way,[112] and in one such enforcement action in 1843 the court both rejected the plea that this arrangement amounted to collusion and commended the committee for having secured payment of so large a part of the company's debts.[113]

105 *F.J.*, 3 Oct. 1837, report of opening of Tuam branch; £1 notes issued in Londonderry, Enniscorthy, Nenagh, Tralee and Kanturk in 1838-40 are in various collections. See plates 6 and 7.
106 Report of chairman's speech at meeting of 16 Apr. 1838 included in letter from the bank's parliamentary agent to Spring Rice, in Monteagle papers (N.L.I., MSS 13,388). This view is confirmed by the La Touche letter book (Munster & Leinster Bank), especially letter of 17 Oct. 1838.
107 *Dublin Ev. Post*, 28 Apr. 1840, half-yearly report.
108 B. of I. Mins., 23 June 1840; *F.J.*, 20 June 1840, notice of suspension.
109 *Dublin Ev. Post*, 30 June 1840, letter to the shareholders from the board.
110 There is a copy of this report in R.I.A., Haliday 1898; other information is in *F.J.* and *Dublin Ev. Post*, 1840-4, *passim*.
111 *F.J.*, 13 Nov. 1841; *Limerick Chronicle*, 20 Nov. 1841, rolls court, Agricultural Bank v Provincial Bank.
112 *F.J.*, 21 Nov. 1844, court of chancery, Taylor v Hughes.
113 *F.J.*, 3 July 1843, queen's bench, White v Dowling.

The committee's task was greatly complicated by the state of the accounts and records. Many transfers were found to have been irregularly executed, and in 1843 the committee, on counsel's advice, reinserted the names of all such transferors on the register. The list filed at the Stamp Office in 1843 included in consequence some 2,400 names formerly omitted. Many had sold their shares to the company under a resolution of October 1837 which the committee was now advised was invalid. The inclusion of these people on the list would have made them liable as contributories but when a creditor sought to enforce a judgement against one of them the court ruled that the committee had no authority to reinsert his name. This was accepted as relieving all 2,400 of liability.[114]

By 1844 only about £40,000 was still due to outsiders, mainly holders of the debentures issued in 1837-8, but the state of the law made it almost impossible to disentangle the claims among the shareholders. The committee therefore applied for a special act of parliament, and it was passed with little debate in 1845.[115] Its stated purpose was to facilitate actions through the court of chancery, to dispense with the need to make all shareholders parties to actions and to remove doubts about the application of the 1825 act. Creditors might sue either the public officer or the committee, and the omission of any shareholder's name could not be pleaded as a defect. The committee might similarly sue any five or more shareholders in a representative capacity to ascertain liability. Cross-bills by members not included as defendants were debarred without the court's leave, which would be granted only to ensure justice and fair trial.

The master in chancery was appointed to supervise the winding up,[116] and in May 1847 his list of defaulting shareholders was confirmed by the court and they were ordered to pay within four months.[117] In 1850 a further call was made of 16s per share, bringing the total called to £3 7s 0d.[118] The *Belfast Newsletter* described this sum as a dead loss incurred by those who had paid but it was in fact their contribution to the bank's capital out of a total liability of £5 per share which they had accepted. How much, if any, was repaid in the final liquidation is not known. By March 1851 liabilities were reported to be down to £4,100 of which £600 was due to the Bank

---

114 *F.J.*, 19, 21 Nov., 3 Dec. 1844, court of chancery, Taylor v Hughes; also reported in *B. Mag.*, ii, 220-2. Hall, *Bank of Ireland*, p. 159, describes this judgement as relieving all who had not signed the deed, but this is incorrect.
115 8 & 9 Vic., c. 147, local & personal; *B. Mag.*, ii, 172, reports the decision to apply for it. Hall, *op. cit.*, p. 161, cites this act incorrectly as 8 & 9 Vic., c. 98 which is a public act for the winding up of joint stock companies in Ireland in general.
116 *B. Mag.*, v, 60.
117 *Saunders' Newsletter*, 22 June 1847.
118 *F.J.*, 2 Oct. 1850, extract from *Belfast Newsletter*.

of Ireland for the Fleet Street premises. The committee had more than that on hand and the winding up was described as virtually complete.[119]

The Southern Bank of Ireland

From the wreckage of the Agricultural two new banks emerged during 1837, both short-lived. One was the Southern Bank of Ireland in Cork, the other the Provident Bank of Ireland in Dublin.

The founders of the Southern were William Mitchell, former general manager, John M'kenzie, former accountant general, and William Bennett, former Cork manager, of the Agricultural.[120] A return at the end of February 1837 stated its capital to be £500,000 in shares of £25 of which 10,000 had been issued with the first instalment of £5 in course of payment; no business had yet been transacted.[121] Earlier that month Bennett, described as 'banker of this city', had been appointed manager in Cork.[122] It is not clear when business commenced but by April the bank was issuing notes.[123]

Statements before the 1837 committee, which sat from February to July, may well have undermined confidence in this bank.[124] In any case in September a letter in the *Cork Southern Reporter* attacked it as a 'swindling bubble' with no capital, operating on fraudulent bills of exchange; two or three clerks were said to have been arrested and a deputation sent to London and Edinburgh in search of more capital.[125] At about the same time Bennett and M'kenzie were arrested in London. It is not clear what they were charged with, and there was some inconclusive correspondence in the press as to whether they had been in flight or on lawful business for the bank.[126] The last information on the case is that the evidence had been submitted to the crown solicitor.[127] As there is no further reference in the press we may assume that the case was dropped but we cannot say whether the project was in truth a swindling bubble or an honest if mismanaged attempt to expand banking in the Cork area.

119 *F.J.*, 31 Mar. 1851, commercial intelligence; *B. Mag.*, xi, 290, report of meeting of shareholders in Belfast 1 Apr. 1851.
120 *1837 committee*, Q.2781, evidence of Dwyer, 3408, of Goodier, 3872-8, of Mahony; *F.J.*, 2 Jan. 1837, reports a farewell dinner given for M'kenzie by the staff of the Agricultural.
121 *1837 committee*, app. I-no 22.
122 *F.J .*, 8 Feb. 1837.
123 Notes of £1 issued on 5 Apr. 1837 and signed by Bennett are in the National Museum, the Institute of Bankers in Ireland and the Cork Public Museum. See plate 12.
124 Dillon, *Banking in Ireland*, p. 79, attributes the bank's failure to this; the evidence referred to is that of Goodier and Mahony—see n. 120 above.
125 *F.J.*, 28 Sept. 1837, extract from *Cork Southern Reporter*.
126 *F.J.*, 7, 12 Oct. 1837.
127 *F.J.*, 5 Oct. 1837.

The Provident Bank of Ireland

Rather more is known about the Provident, a brainchild, like the Agricultural, of Thomas Mooney. In his letter of May 1837 to the farmers of Ireland he wrote that the Agricultural would have continued until doomsday had it remained true to its principles of local capital and local control.[128] The next month he followed this with a second letter to the farmers of Ireland which embodied a prospectus for the Provident Bank of Ireland to put these principles into practice.[129] Its capital would be £500,000 divided, not into small shares like the Agricultural's, but into shares of £2,000; in addition it would issue £5 debentures carrying 5 per cent interest but no liability.[130] Though not so stated, this would enable the bank to confine itself to six partners and so be able to operate in Dublin and yet to draw capital from a wider field. Once the Bank of Ireland's monopoly had ended, Mooney explained later, the intention was to offer shares in exchange for the debentures and so convert the Provident into a normal joint stock bank. In any case, he maintained, it was a sound principle to have the capital divided between loan and equity—in this way 'the capital of the timid and the retiring would be brought to mingle with the capital of the enterprising and the bold'.[131]

Like many of Mooney's ideas this scheme, sound in theory, failed in execution. Instead of the wealthy proprietary subscribing half a million in shares of £2,000 that the prospectus implied, the only shareholders were Mooney himself and W. H. Holbrooke, a retail trader and engraver, who printed the bank's notes. The prospectus stated that the shares would be fully paid but when the bank closed in 1840 only £310 had been paid by Mooney and £501 by Holbrooke.[132]

The Provident opened for business in Dublin at the beginning of July 1837[133] and for the second half of 1837 paid duty on a circulation of £6,000.[134] Its notes have been described as deliberate copies of the Provincial's, to such a degree that a Provincial clerk was said to have taken one in error.[135] Surviving notes are undoubtedly similar in design, but hardly justify this description.[136]

128 Above, pp. 118-9.
129 *F.J.*, 8 June 1837.
130 The National Museum has a £5 debenture issued 13 Nov. 1838; it is redeemable by notice after five years, failing which it would be extended for another five, and so on *ad infinitum*, but the bank had the right to pay it off at any time on three months notice. See plate 9.
131 *F.J.*, 21 Aug. 1838, letter from Mooney to *Saunders' Newsletter*.
132 *F.J.*, 3 Apr. 1841, report of bankruptcy proceedings.
133 *F.J.*, 3 July 1837; the premises were at 4 College Green.
134 *Drummond report*, app. B16.
135 *1838 committee*, Q.629, evidence of George Matthews.
136 The National Museum has two Provident Bank notes dated 1 Mar. 1837; this was four months before the opening, which suggests that the initial plans were delayed. They may be compared with two notes of the Provincial of 1825 and 1833 held in that bank's head office in Dublin. See plates 1 and 8.

A particular feature of the Provident was to be the making of loans of under £10 to tradesmen, farmers and others. This brought it into conflict with the Loan Fund Board set up in 1836 to supervise societies making such small loans in Ireland. The board's secretary George Matthews, in evidence in 1838,[137] told how he had heard that the Dublin Provident Loan Society, enrolled in 1837, was doing business as a joint stock bank, and on investigating he had found it to be virtually identical with the Provident Bank, both being, as he put it, a speculation of Thomas Mooney. Loans were made through loan societies in Carlow, Athy, Mullingar, Strabane and elsewhere in the bank's notes and repaid by instalments in silver. He had warned Mooney that the board would not allow the funds of a loan society to be used for banking, and when Mooney refused to desist the board issued a notice depriving the society of the benefits of registration.[138]

This view was in fact the reverse of the truth. It was the funds of the bank, raised mainly on its debentures, which were used by the society to make small loans—on the face of it a useful and perfectly legitimate proceeding. In a published reply Mooney stated that neither bank nor society had received any funds from the board and were therefore under no obligation to permit it to examine their affairs.[139]

Closely linked to the Provident was another creation of Mooney's, the Commercial Assurance Company of Ireland, launched in August 1837 with a proposed capital of £1 million and an imposing list of aristocratic patrons; the public were invited to transfer their insurance to it and so 'retain and employ the capital of the country for the benefit of the inhabitants'.[140] But in less than a year it had come to an end. It was wound up with heavy losses and its life policies were taken over by the Scottish Union Insurance Company.[141] It had upwards of two hundred shareholders but Mooney admitted that the paid-up capital was only some £1,500—a position, he asserted, similar to that in many insurance companies.[142]

Mooney at this time was playing a leading role in the agitation against the Bank of Ireland's monopoly,[143] which was expected to end in 1838. The persistence of the monopoly and the hostility to Mooney that undoubtedly pervaded orthodox circles may have played some part in preventing the Provident from growing into a fully fledged joint stock bank, but, like the Agricultural, the bank itself seems to have had weaknesses enough to explain its own collapse.

137 *1838 committee*, Q.607-31.
138 *F.J.*, 4 Oct. 1837, has the notice.
139 *F.J.*, 7 Oct. 1837; this was part of a long correspondence divided between the
  F.J., Dublin Ev. Post and *Dublin Ev. Mail*.
140 *F.J.*, 10 Aug. 1837.
141 *F.J.*, 15, 25 May 1838.
142 *F.J.*, 1 Feb. 1841, report of Holbrooke's bankruptcy proceedings.
143 Below, p. 168.

On 4 December 1839 Mooney called on all holders of notes to present them for payment.[144] A week later, as a baker and flour factor, he was adjudged bankrupt.[145] By the end of June 1840 his case was concluded with a first and final dividend of 11¼d in the £.[146] Holbrooke carried on the business for a time but Mooney could not be granted his discharge until the affairs of the bank had been settled, and on 14 October 1840 the two partners were jointly adjudged bankrupt as bankers, traders and chapmen.[147] The reported proceedings deal only with Holbrooke.[148] Mooney appeared as a witness but after paying his 11¼d he had nothing left to adjudicate.

The proceedings against Mooney and Holbrooke were started by Despard Taylor, a former director of the Agricultural and himself closely associated with the Provident.[149] According to Holbrooke he used to preside at board meetings, arranged the rediscount of bills on commission, was a partner in the Commercial Assurance Company, appointed staff of the bank and was generally regarded by the public as a partner. Counsel for the debenture holders said that he was regarded as the principal partner and had by his actions rendered himself liable for the bank's debts.[150] He never appeared himself so it is not possible to disentangle his position, but the commissioner evidently did not hold him liable as a partner.

The management was clearly in a most unsatisfactory state. Holbrooke said he knew little about the bank's affairs, and his understanding of accounts seems to have been shaky. Mooney excused himself from knowledge of details by not having the books to hand.[151] The last information is that in April 1841 the notes had almost all been paid off but some £14,000 was still outstanding on debentures; even on the most optimistic valuation the assets covered little more than half this sum.[152] At Holbrooke's final examination the commissioner exonerated him as an innocent victim of others and described the bank as 'bottomed in fraud'.[153] This is the reputation that has attached to it but the evidence is insufficient to say whether it is justified.

With the end of the Provident Bank Thomas Mooney passes out of Irish banking history. In June 1841 he left for America whence he

---

144 *F.J.*, 30 Nov. 1839.
145 *Return of banks in Ireland which have become bankrupt since 1825,* H.C. 1845 (334), xxviii, 213.
146 *Dublin Ev. Post,* 25 May 1840; *F.J.,* 1 July 1840.
147 *Return of banks in Ireland which have become bankrupt since 1825,* H.C. 1845 (334), xxviii, 213.
148 *Dublin Ev. Post,* 14 Nov. 1840; *F.J.,* 12 Dec. 1840-3 Apr. 1841 *passim,* 2 Apr. 1842.
149 He was also creditor-plaintiff in Taylor v Hughes (above p. 155, n. 114) and was a partner in the Southern Bank (B. of I. Mins., 6 Mar. 1838).
150 *F.J.,* 3 Apr. 1841, report of bankruptcy proceedings.
151 *F.J.,* 1 Feb. 1841.
152 *F.J.,* 3 Apr. 1841, assignee's balance sheet.
153 *F.J.,* 2 Apr. 1842.

sent back a series of reports, chiefly on the prospects for emigrants, which appeared first in the *Pilot* and then in the *Nation*.[154] He returned to Dublin in 1850 and gave some lectures on the same topic at the Mechanic's Institute,[155] the substance of which is to be found in a book published the same year.[156] In May 1850 he was instrumental in founding the Board of Irish Manufactures and Industry, a private body for the promotion of Irish industry of which he became secretary,[157] but after a stormy couple of years, not unlike his banking career, he resigned and left for Australia.[158] There, according to Dillon, he built a theatre and a hotel in Melbourne on borrowed money[159]—a method of building finance not so common in the mid-nineteenth century as today, but not necessarily dishonest.

Before leaving Mooney it is worth noting a scheme for banking reform which he put forward in 1837.[160] He proposed that issues for the whole United Kingdom be concentrated in a government-appointed board of trustees who would issue notes to all banks in proportion to their holdings of government stock. Each bank would make periodic returns of its capital, issues, deposits and assets, and the trustees would have power to withhold notes from any whose management was unsatisfactory and to issue extra in case of need against suitable securities. Every bank being thus under the protection of government would 'proceed quietly and steadily in the administration of credit as a trade and not as a mysterious science'. These ideas were not original—Joplin had proposed something similar in 1823[161]—but they do clash with Mooney's charlatan reputation. The pinkeen baker of Francis Street may have had his failings in bank management but his ideas embraced many elements that were subsequently to be embodied in the banking system.

The Tipperary Joint Stock Bank

With the disappearance of the Agricultural, the Southern and the Provident, Irish banking, apart from the private banks in Dublin was left in the hands of eight banks who, with the Munster & Leinster (founded in 1885), made up the Irish commercial banking system until the 1960s. But towards the end of our period two other banks were founded, the Tipperary and the London & Dublin, which lasted respectively till 1856 and 1848.

A third new bank, the Dublin Banking Company, was promoted in

154 *Pilot*, 28 Aug. 1841 *et seq.*; *Nation*, 11 Mar. 1843 *et seq.*
155 *F.J.*, 8 Feb. 1850.
156 T. Mooney, *Nine years in America* (Dublin 1850).
157 *F. J.*, 25 May 1850 *et seq.*; Barrow, 'Thomas Mooney', in *Dublin Hist. Rec.*, xxiv no 1 173-88.
158 *F.J.*, 21 Aug., 8 Oct. 1852.
159 Dillon, *Banking in Ireland*, p. 78.
160 *F.J.*, 15 Mar. 1837, reprinted from *The Constitutional* (London), 21 Jan. 1837.
161 *B. Mag.*, vi, 70-80, Memoir of Thomas Joplin.

1842.[162] The manager was John Reynolds, formerly of the National,[163] and it was stated to have branches in Dublin, Banagher, Gort and Loughrea.[164] If it in fact ever opened for business it was not for long. A case in the rolls court in 1844 shows it to have been a fraudulent flotation,[165] and it was finally wound up as a company in 1856.[166]

The Tipperary Joint Stock Bank seems to have been a revival of Scully's[167] whose surviving partner, James Scully, was, on the testimony of his son, another James, 'the principal person in establishing the bank'.[168] The managing director was his nephew, James Sadleir,[169] in whose name nearly all the bank's transactions were conducted. His younger brother John was a Tenant League politician who achieved notoriety after the 1852 election by accepting office, as junior lord of the treasury, in direct disregard of his election pledges. Later he became fatally prominent in London financial circles, being among many other things chairman of the London & County Bank, but he was never a director of the Tipperary and his link with it was always through his brother James who was managing director for its whole life. Another Sadleir, Richard, was the first chairman but by 1842 he had been replaced by James Scully. In July of that year a new deed of partnership nominated Scully, James Sadleir and Wilson Kennedy, a Clonmel solicitor, as the three directors.[170]

The distinctive feature of the Tipperary was the agreement it made with the Bank of Ireland in October 1838 to issue its notes exclusively in return for discount facilities at 1 per cent below the normal rate and the right to draw letters of credit to specified limits on the bank's agencies.[171] This was modelled on similar agreements made by the Bank of England since 1830 and it made the Tipperary a virtual extension of the Bank of Ireland in its operations, though not in its management. Thomas Wilson in 1841 described the establishment of the Tipperary as coincidental with and dependent on this agreement. As a result of it Bank of Ireland circulation had become 'very current in a part of the country where formerly there was not a Bank of

162 *Return of private and joint stock banks registered in Ireland 1820-44*, H.C. 1844 (232), xxxii, 445; this shows the partners as nine in 1842 rising to twenty-eight in 1844.
163 *P. O. Directory 1843*, p. 589.
164 *B. Mag.*, i, 314-7; Provincial Bank Galway, outgoing letter book has references in 1843 to this bank being about to open in Loughrea and Gort.
165 *Limerick Chronicle*, 6 July 1844, Lambert v Dublin Banking Company.
166 *F.J.*, 30 June, 8 July 1856.
167 Below, p. 211 J. F. McCarthy, 'The story of Sadleir's Bank', in *Clonmel Hist. & Arch. Soc. Jn.*, i, no 3, and Dillon, *Banking in Ireland*, pp. 80-1, both treat of this bank, but inaccurately.
168 *F.J.*, 5 Mar. 1856, rolls court, Rafferty *ex parte* The Tipperary Joint Stock Bank.
169 Tenison, in *Inst of Bankers in Irel. Jn.*, xii, 11, describes their relationship.
170 No copy of this deed (nor of that of 1838) appears to be extant but details of it may be deduced from court proceedings in 1856—see especially *F. J.*, 13 May 1856, Master Murphy's office.
171 B. of I. Mins., 25 Oct., 6 Nov. 1838; *F.J.*, 13 Dec. 1838, report of governor's speech to general court of proprietors.

Ireland note to be seen'. The agreement was terminable at three months' notice and the quantity of notes supplied was at the Bank of Ireland's discretion.[172]

In 1845 the Irish Banking Act specifically confirmed this agreement until 1 January 1856.[173] If the Bank of Ireland terminated it before then it must pay the Tipperary 1 per cent of the average amount of Bank of Ireland notes it kept in circulation, provided it continue to issue them exclusively. This section was added to the bill at the request of the Tipperary, with the consent of the Bank of Ireland; it was designed to compensate the former for the loss of the right of issue which it would have enjoyed under the act but for this agreement, it being the only bank in Ireland with over six partners which could lawfully have issued but did not. The maximum on which the Bank of Ireland would be liable to pay the 1 per cent composition fee was agreed at £60,000, the approximate level of notes kept in circulation by the Tipperary at that date.[174]

This privileged position naturally roused hopes of similar treatment in others. An application from the Royal was rejected by the Bank of Ireland as its circumstances were held to be 'perfectly dissimilar' to those of the Tipperary, and another from the Agricultural was dismissed even more brusquely. In 1841 the District Bank of Ireland was promoted in Dublin to open branches in several districts issuing Bank of Ireland notes only, but when the Bank of Ireland refused support the scheme was dropped.[175] Wilson spoke of a similar request from an institution about to be formed in Belfast which was refused 'because we thought that banking accommodation there was sufficient';[176] he did not give its name and there is no reference to it in the court's minutes.

The Tipperary's capital was £500,000 in 10,000 shares of £50 but only 4,055 shares seem to have been issued; £10 per share was paid making the total paid-up capital a little over £40,000.[177] It was registered for the first time in August 1839, a formality not legally necessary for a non-issuing bank but desirable as carrying the right to conduct proceedings in the name of a public officer. From 1840 to 1844 the partnership varied a little either side of fifty.[178] At the beginning of 1846 there were fifty-three partners, all Irish and mainly from the area of the bank's operations.[179]

172 *1841 committee*, Q.2669-94.
173 8 & 9 Vic., c. 37, s. 31.
174 Sadleir to Goulburn, 30 May 1845; governor to Goulburn, 31 May 1845 (B. of I. Mins., 19 June 1845).
175 B. of I. Mins., 18 Dec. 1838, 14 May 1839, 25 May 1841.
176 *1841 committee*, Q.2693.
177 *F.J.*, 21 June 1856, rolls court, in re Ginager.
178 *Return of private and joint stock banks registered in Ireland 1820-44*, H.C. 1844 (232), xxxii, 445.
179 *Dublin Gaz. 1846*, pp. 206-7.

The head office initially was in Tipperary, possibly in Scully's old premises. The Bank of Ireland seems to have envisaged the bank's activities being confined to that locality where the directors had local influence and could exercise control. Between 1839 and 1841 five branches were opened, all in County Tipperary except for one just outside.[180] The Bank of Ireland acquiesced in these but objected to a proposal in 1841 to open in Gorey in County Wexford, which was consequently but reluctantly dropped.[181] It objected even more strongly, and again effectively, when the Tipperary started discounting through an agent in Belfast.[182] In July 1842 the head office was moved to Clonmel as being both the county town of the south riding of Tipperary and a better centre for communications. It was also the site of a Bank of Ireland agency. For this reason it was proposed to confine the office to management but there was a strong local demand for it to conduct all banking business and the Bank of Ireland finally gave its consent.[183] Two more branches were opened in 1845 at Carlow and Athy; they were the only ones within fifty miles of Dublin and were intended to forestall any issuing bank that might plan to open there after the 1845 act came into force.[184] This brought the total branches to nine.[185]

The Tipperary is the only bank outside Ulster to have operated successfully on a local basis in this period. There can be little doubt that it owed its success to its links with the Bank of Ireland, but the latter might well have done better both for the country and for itself had it opened its own branches in the area instead. The difficulties of keeping control over such a bank, dependent on it yet not subject to its regulations, are very evident in the court's minutes. The Tipperary finally crashed in 1856 because James Sadleir lent too much of its money to his brother John who employed it in railway speculation on the continent. When his speculations failed he took his own life leaving the shareholders and depositors to fight a ruinous legal battle over who should bear the loss. This financial recklessness on top of his earlier political villainy has earned him a place in the Irish rogues' gallery, but it all lay in the future. Up to the end of our period the bank played a valuable role in providing the Tipperary area with banking services.

The London & Dublin Bank

The London & Dublin differed from the Tipperary in that it was specifically planned to operate within fifty miles of Dublin, and so with

180 B. of I. Mins., 8 Jan. 1839, 11 Aug. 1840, 11 May 1841; *F.J.*, 6 June 1841. Appendix 3 below gives the branches' locations.
181 B. of I. Mins., 14-28 Sept. 1841.
182 *Ibid.*, 23 July-27 Aug. 1844.
183 *Ibid.*, 4 Nov. 1841, 22 June-20 Sept. 1842.
184 *Ibid.*, 6 Aug.-7 Oct. 1845.
185 See also dividend notices in *Limerick Chronicle*, 14 Feb. 1844, *Tipp. Free Press*, Feb. 1844, *Tipp. Vindicator*, 14 Feb. 1846.

no right to issue notes of its own. The scheme was launched at a meeting in November 1841 and the prospectus was issued in July 1842.[186] There were seven peers as honorary directors and fourteen ordinary directors of whom the only Irish one seems to have been Robert Rundell Guinness of Guinness & Mahon. The bank was to be managed by a board in London aided by a committee in Dublin, and its freedom from sect or party was emphasized. The capital was £1 million in shares of £50 of which £10 was to be paid on application. As a non-issuer the bank was not required to register, and did not do so until 1842 when its partnership was 250.[187]

A deputation of directors toured Ireland in September-October 1842 to arrange for the branches,[188] and the first seven, including Dublin, were opened during 1843. The first seems to have been Dundalk, taken over from the National who had planned to open there issuing Bank of Ireland notes only but had been forced to drop the project as illegal for an issuing bank.[189] Another three branches were opened before the end of 1845,[190] making a total of ten, of which seven were within fifty miles of Dublin.

The bank was debarred from issuing its own notes and so could only operate by issuing those of some other bank. Within the monopoly zone this could only be the Bank of Ireland. Some proposals were put to the Bank of Ireland in June 1843 on this subject but they were so vague that the court replied asking for more information. It was not till the end of 1844 that an agreement was signed, to take effect from 1 January 1845.[191] It was almost identical with that between the Bank of Ireland and the Tipperary—the London & Dublin had to deposit £25,000 security and was allowed to discount bills at 1 per cent below the current rate (with a minimum of 3 per cent), and its Dublin office could draw letters of credit on any of the agencies of the Bank of Ireland; no branch was to be opened where the Bank of Ireland had one, nor was the bank to act as agent for any Irish bank or for any bank of issue whatsoever.

During its short career the London & Dublin issued only two financial statements, covering the years 1844 and 1845.[192] In 1844 gross profits were £6,829, total expenditure £4,524 and net profits £2,305. In

186 *F.J.*, 13 Nov. 1841, describes the meeting as held in Dublin but the *Dublin Ev. Post*, 6 Nov. 1841, in a fuller account puts it in London; possibly meetings were held in both. *Limerick Chronicle*, 15 June 1842, has the prospectus; it is also reproduced, with comments, in R.I.A., Haliday 1834.
187 *Return of private and joint stock banks registered in Ireland 1820-44*, H.C. 1844 (232), xxxii, 445.
188 *F.J.*, 8 Oct. 1842.
189 *B. Mag.*, i, 41-2, annual report 1844.
190 *F.J.*, 14 Mar. 1845, report of general meeting notes opening at Carrickmacross; *F.J.*, 24 Aug. 1845, dividend notice has one more at Athy; B. of I. Mins., 14 Oct. 1845, records opening at Kinsale. *Dublin Gaz. 1846*, p. 262, gives the full list.
191 B. of I. Mins., 27 June 1843, 3 Dec. 1844.
192 *F.J.*, 14 Mar. 1845, 20 Mar. 1846; also in *B. Mag.*, iii, 117-8, v, 140-1, 241.

1845 gross profits had almost doubled to £13,385, expenditure more than doubled to £9,254 and net profits in consequence rather less than doubled to £4,131. A dividend of 4 per cent was paid each year. At the end of 1845 the capital was £58,900 and total liabilities to the public were £166,495.

The Bank of Ireland complained repeatedly of the way that the London & Dublin was conducted;[193] control was lax, the division of authority between London and Dublin unsatisfactory, the limit on discounts at the Bank of Ireland was normally exceeded while the cash balance was frequently inadequate and sometimes overdrawn, bills were often of poor quality and the court had several times to demand additional security to cover advances. At the end of 1845 there were some critical discussions and during 1846 matters improved, but in 1847 complaints were renewed. During the pressure of that year the court urged the London & Dublin to reduce its discounts but with little effect. It evidently lacked the resources to withstand the pressure and at the end of the year approached the National with an offer to sell its assets. The National accepted and in January 1848 a special general meeting of the London & Dublin resolved on dissolution.[194]

The National paid off the Bank of Ireland's advances and took over seven of the ten branches while some of the directors joined its board.[195] This is the only instance to this date of one Irish joint stock bank absorbing another. It gave the National six branches within fifty miles of Dublin where till then it had none. The winding up nevertheless was not easy. By the end of 1849 liabilities were reported down to £12,000 with assets said to be worth a little more,[196] but even this proved too sanguine and in 1851 a call had to be made of £2 per share.[197] It was poorly paid and action had to be taken against defaulters. By March 1853 liabilities were down to £3,300 but exceeded assets by over £2,200. The bulk were now owing to the National Bank and the issue lay therefore between it and the defaulting shareholders.[198] The final winding up seems to have taken place in 1857.[199]

193 B. of I. Mins., 19 Aug. 1845-1 Feb. 1848 *passim.*
194 *Dublin Gaz. 1848,* p. 53.
195 *B. Mag.,* viii, p. 392, National Bank thirteenth annual report.
196 *B. Mag.,* x, 338-9.
197 *B. Mag.,* xi, p. 290.
198 *B. Mag.,* xiii, 694-5.
199 *F.J.,* 6 Feb. 1857, notice of petition.

The System Consolidated

The Bank of Ireland Monopoly

Up to 1845 the Bank of Ireland, part central bank, part commercial, continued to dominate the Irish banking scene, and the issue of the monopoly to possess the public mind. This had three distinct but commonly confused aspects. The first was the charter, the bank's corporate constitution, which, by the act of 1808, could be abrogated by the government any time after 1 January 1837 on twelve months' notice and repayment of all sums due. This would mean the dissolution of the bank, but it was entirely at the government's option and there was no provision for automatic termination at any time.

Secondly there was the matter of the bank's exclusive privilege as a note-issuing bank of over six members within fifty miles of Dublin. This was what aroused public interest. It entailed some restraint on the expansion of joint stock banks but it depended, not on the charter, but on section 14 of the act of 1782. Parliament had modified this section in 1821 and could repeal it altogether but had promised that it would not before 1 January 1838 grant any further power, privilege or authority to any partnership or society contrary to the laws in force in 1821 relating to the bank.

Thirdly there were the capital loans made by the bank to the government. The two loans of £600,000 and £500,000 under the acts of 1782 and 1797 need only be repaid on the bank's dissolution, but those of £1,250,000 of 1808 and £500,000 of 1821 were due for repayment on 1 January 1838.[1] This was regardless of what happened to the charter and regardless too of any consent to postponement by the bank. It was a matter of parliamentary control of public funds and could only be avoided by legislation.

From the beginning of 1838 therefore the government was free to withdraw the charter or to promote legislation to abolish the special privileges but was under no obligation to do anything about either. It was, on the other hand, under a statutory obligation to repay the equivalent of £1,750,000 Irish on 1 January 1838. To avoid this an act of 1837 postponed the date for one year, all related powers and privileges being similarly extended,[2] and in 1838 another act postponed it again to 1 January 1840.[3]

One petition from a public meeting in Dublin in June 1838 was

1 See Appendix 1 below.
2 7 Will. IV. & 1 Vic., c. 59.
3 1 & 2 Vic., c. 81.

almost the only comment on these acts.[4] The bank's critics were evidently awaiting the outcome of the parliamentary committee then in session. But in 1839 the government proposed a wider measure designed to bring the Bank of Ireland's dates into line with those of the Bank of England. Its main provision was to extend the date after which the charter might be terminated to 1 August 1844,[5] and this was generally regarded as an extension of the monopoly for another five years.

The bill was sponsored by Spring Rice as chancellor. He had negotiated its terms with the bank but to the evident surprise of both it evoked a storm of protest. There was a vigorous campaign in Dublin with Thomas Mooney of Francis Street as its principal and most eloquent speaker—he addressed successive meetings of business-men, of trade unionists, of the gentry and landowners of the county and even of the court of proprietors of the Bank of Ireland itself to which he gained access by the purchase of £35 of stock[6]—and a number of petitions were presented to parliament.[7] The opposition in parliament was led by O'Connell and Joseph Hume, the English radical who had been given a safe seat in Kilkenny by O'Connell.[8] The bill was introduced late in the session when many of the Irish members had gone home. The government secured majorities on the early stages but by fighting every procedural point O'Connell and Hume were able to prevent completion before the end of the session. Complaining bitterly of this abuse of procedure Spring Rice finally withrew the bill and brought in another which simply postponed repayment of the two loans again to 1 January 1841, and it was rushed through all its stages without opposition.[9]

The next year, 1840, the new chancellor, Francis Baring, brought in another bill to regulate the capital loans. Existing provisions on the charter and the bank's privileges were specifically left untouched and the bill was passed with little discussion.[10] The annuities totalling £125,000 Irish (5 per cent on the first two loans of £600,000 and £500,000 and 4 per cent on the last two of £1,250,000 and £500,000) were consolidated into one annuity of the equivalent sum of £115,384 12s 4d British, to be paid in two annual instalments. It could be reduced with the Bank of Ireland's consent and could be

4 *F.J.*, 12, 13 June 1838.
5 The full text of the bill is in H.C. 1839 (485), i, 55; the form as amended in committee is in H.C. 1839 (557), i, 79.
6 *F.J.*, July-Aug. 1838, *passim*.
7 *F.J.*, 9, 21 Aug. 1839, parliamentary reports.
8 MacIntyre, *The Liberator*, p. 87; he had just lost his own seat at Middlesex.
9 2 & 3 Vic., c. 91; the debates are reported in *Hansard 3*, xlix, 1; and more fully in *F.J.*, 29 July-28 Aug. 1839.
10 3 & 4 Vic., c. 75. Hall, *Bank of Ireland,* pp. 189-90, has an account of these acts which is confused by the omission of any reference to the bill that was passed, as distinct from the one that was abandoned, in 1839.

redeemed on six months' notice by the treasury by repayment of the principal sum of £2,630,769 4s 8d British.

The position after this act was therefore that the charter could be withdrawn on twelve months' notice and the repayment of all debt by the government, the capital loan could be repaid at six months' notice without affecting the charter, and the monopoly could be legislated out of existence any time that parliament so decided. That this left the Bank of Ireland very much at the government's mercy was demonstrated in 1841 when the chancellor proposed to reduce the annuity to $3\frac{1}{2}$ per cent, or £92,076 18s 5d. This had been a provision of the abandoned bill of 1839 when it would have been compensated for by the extension to 1844 of the date before which the bank could not be dissolved. This time there was no quid pro quo and the bank had to accept under threat of repayment of the entire loan and the cancellation of the annuity.[11] There was one small sop—under an act of 1796[12] the sum of £2,067 13s 6d had been deducted from the annuity each year to cover the Bank of Ireland's contribution to certain legal salaries in connection with the suitors' funds which it held; the treasury was now authorized to cancel this, which it did.[13] The full annuity was therefore paid in future, which made the net reduction in the bank's income just over £20,000.

The main effect of the Bank of Ireland's special privileges was that joint stock banks might not operate within fifty miles of Dublin if they issued notes, or issue notes if they operated within fifty miles of Dublin. This placed a special obligation on the bank towards this area, and a common criticism was that it failed to meet it. In a report on banking drawn up by John Reynolds in 1844 O'Connell's Repeal Association complained that only six of the Bank of Ireland's thirty-three branches were within fifty miles of Dublin, which left the area seriously underbanked.[14]

This criticism ignores the domination of the area by Dublin. With its suburb of Kingstown it had a population of 240,000 in 1841 and only six other towns within fifty miles had more than 5,000. Of these Newry had one of the first branches in 1825, Carlow and Drogheda received branches in 1834, Dundalk and Tullamore in 1836. Only Navan, seventeen miles from Drogheda, had no branch by 1845. One smaller town, Mountmellick, had one from 1836. In addition the London & Dublin, closely linked to the Bank of Ireland, had six branches within the area. The Bank of Ireland's policy was to confine

11 *Copies of treasury warrants authorising the reduction of the annuity granted to the Bank of Ireland from 8 July 1841*, H.C. 1841 (20), xiii, 197; see also *F.J.*, 2 Feb. 1841, governor's speech to general court of proprietors.

12 36 Geo. III, c. 1, s. 6.

13 B. of I. Mins., 13, 26 Jan. 1841.

14 Loyal National Repeal Association, *Parliamentary committee reports*, i, 28-33.

itself to the larger centres, and outside the zone only three of the seventeen branches were in towns of less than 5,000 population.

A return to parliament of applications for branches received by the Bank of Ireland from 1833 to 1844 shows that five out of seven from inside the zone were agreed to but only four out of nineteen from outside it[15]—which hardly supports the charge that it neglected the area where it was sheltered from competition in favour of that where it was not. Wilson told the 1838 committee that the bank followed precisely the same principles in regard to branches within fifty miles of Dublin as beyond it; if there were any difference it would be a greater liberality in discounting within the the fifty miles.[16] The court minutes certainly support this view.[17]

Circulation, Exchanges and Reserves

Events since 1821 had in some respects reduced the Bank of Ireland to a level with the other banks, but with its surviving privileges and its status as government banker it still dominated the system. Its share of total circulation was about three-quarters in September 1833, dropped sharply in 1835, and from then to 1845 remained fairly steady between one half and two-thirds.[18]

The only other bank for which we have individual figures is the Provincial a summary of whose circulation for 1831-41 was handed in to the 1841 committee.[19] This gives figures for each quarter day whereas official figures are monthly averages, but it is possible to compare general trends. The Provincial's share in the circulation of 'other banks' dropped from some 85 per cent in September 1833 to under 40 per cent at the end of the decade. This was a natural consequence of the rise of the new banks, but the figures show the fall to have been absolute as well as relative, the highest in the series being for the quarter days from Michaelmas 1834 to Midsummer 1835. The Provincial was the only bank under any formal restraint—by its agreement with the treasury to maintain gold stocks equal at least to one-fifth of its circulation[20]—but the statement shows that its gold was always well above the required level, and over the whole period averaged nearly one-third of the circulation. The fall in the Provincial's circulation must be attributed less to this than to its caution when others were expanding.

Though under no such formal restraint the other banks all had

15 *Return of the number of applications made to the Bank of Ireland for the establishment of a branch*, H.C. 1844 (350), xxxii, 265.
16 *1838 committee*, Q.768-9.
17 For example, B. of I. Mins., 2 Apr. 1836, report of sub-committee on branch policy.
18 Below, Appendix 10.
19 Below, Appendix 9.
20 Above, p. 94.

the general contractual liability to pay gold on demand for their notes By the act of 1828 this meant at the branch of issue, a requirement that did not exist in Britain except for the Bank of England. Its intro- duction in Ireland had been largely in response to pressure from the Provincial in its early rivalry with the Bank of Ireland but its views had now changed. With the expansion of branches its spokesmen argued that it would be sufficient if payment were obligatory at three or four only.[21]

Keeping branches supplied with gold entailed some inconvenience but it is doubtful if it had much restrictive effect on circulation. In normal times they suffered from a surplus of specie rather than a shortage. Little gold was withdrawn except by emigrants, while there was a steady flow into the banks. Some of this was gold taken from hoards and deposited to earn interest as confidence grew, some was coin brought back from England either by returning harvest labourers or by cattle and pig dealers and other small traders who exchanged it for notes on arrival.[22] The Bank of Ireland received some £150,000 a year in sovereigns by the latter means and shipped the surplus back for payment to its account at the Bank of England.[23] The Provincial too received a good deal; it found itself 'much encumbered' by the silver which neither the Bank of Ireland nor the Bank of England would take from it, but it had been able to get rid of some to Scotland.[24]

Gold held was only relevant to circulation as a precaution against panic. What mattered more was the availability of funds in London. The Bank of Ireland's practice, as described by Wilson in 1841, was virtually the same as described by Guinness in 1826.[25] Bills on England were taken by the bank and offered for sale to anyone who required to remit funds there. Those not sold were sent to the Bank of England to collect when due. Monies thus accumulated in London at particular periods were invested in further bills which were sent to Dublin for sale as required. The only charge was discount for the period left to run. The Bank of Ireland also gave cash orders on London at a charge of $\frac{1}{8}$ per cent or drafts at ten days at par.[26]

The Bank of Ireland was therefore under a necessity to keep a proper balance between its London funds and its total liabilities, since the latter could always be converted into demands for payment in

21 *1837 committee*, Q.3945, evidence of Mahony; *1841 committee*, Q.3039-42, of Murray.
22 *1838 committee*, Q.732-7, evidence of Wilson; *1841 committee*, Q.3031-7, 3059, of Murray.
23 *1841 committee*, Q.2640, evidence of Wilson.
24 *Ibid.*, Q.2933, evidence of Murray; app. 21, memorandum from the Bank of Scotland, which gives the cost of such shipments from Londonderry to Glasgow as 7s per £100.
25 Above, pp. 44-5.
26 *1841 committee*, Q. 2612, 2616-20.

London. These funds were made up of balances at the Bank of England, English bills of exchange, exchequer bills and government stock, and were available at need for conversion into specie. Tightness in the London market, Wilson explained, would increase demand for English bills in Dublin and so cause tightness there with more demand for accommodation from the Bank of Ireland. At such times the bank would sell public securities, either in Dublin to draw in its own notes and reduce its deposits, or in London to increase its cash balance at the Bank of England. In the opposite case, when money was plentiful, the bank could afford to increase its liabilities and, if good bills offered were insufficient for it to do so by increased discounts, it would buy government stock and so expand its circulation.[27]

These market operations, Wilson emphasized, were for purposes of exchange control not profit. In addition two other factors helped to hold the exchanges steady. The first was the active market in Dublin in Bank of England post bills, really a special part of the market in bills of exchange; the second was the transfer of government stock between the two countries.

Bank of England post bills came to Dublin either for payments due or as speculative transfers by brokers or as imports by banks for exchange purposes. Murray explained that when money was easy in London a cornfactor would pay his Irish suppliers with post bills whereas when money was tight he would ask them instead to draw on him at sixty or ninety days, and conversely in the case of payments by Irish importers. Equally when large blocks of stock were sold in Dublin, where the market was limited, it would be purchased by a broker for transfer to London and remittance of the proceeds in post bills. By whatever means the post bills came to Dublin they were sold there to persons with payments to make in England. Normally they bore a small premium but sometimes the supply was excessive and they went to a discount.[28]

James Pim, whose firm dealt extensively in this market, explained that the exchange limits between Dublin and London were extremely narrow, the average charge on post bills being only 2s 6d or 3s per cent, the equivalent of ten days interest.[29] Needham mentioned that the Royal Bank's manager attended the exchange regularly to buy post bills for use in remittances to England; the discount on them could never exceed the cost of freight and insurance on bullion, and between harvests when Irish imports exceeded exports they were always at a premium.[30]

The second factor, arbitrage dealings in government stock, has been

27 *1841 committee*, Q. 2788-805, 2850.
28 *Ibid*, Q.2951, 2962.
29 *1838 committee*, Q.407-10.
30 *Ibid*, Q.1702-8.

discussed above.[31] From 1839 to 1848 the net movement of stock was from England to Ireland each year, rising to over £1 million annually from 1843 to 1847; in the case of long annuities there were large transfers from England to Ireland in the two years 1844 and 1845 but only negligible amounts in the other years.[32] The money paid for this stock was the residual transfer from Ireland to England to keep the exchange rate steady after all other transactions. It represented a decrease in Irish circulation and an increase in English. Wealth which, in the form of notes and deposits, would have exerted much-needed reflationary pressure in Ireland was held instead in government securities yielding an income to the holders but no benefit to the rest of the community.

What was happening was that Irish savings were being withdrawn from circulation and exported to Britain to buy stock. To achieve a Keynesian equilibrium this monetary drain should have been made good by a similar surplus of government payments over receipts, but in fact the opposite occurred. From 1830 to 1845 exchequer remittances from Dublin to London totalled £9,745,000 with only £180,000 the other way.[33] The balance of £9,565,000, an average of £600,000 per year, may be seen as Ireland's contribution to the central expenses of the United Kingdom government. The surplus of government receipts over payments initially withdrew money from circulation into public deposits at the Bank of Ireland, and when the transfer took place the bank would debit the government account in its Dublin books and pay out the same amount to the treasury from its account at the Bank of England. This reduction in its London funds had a deflationary effect similar to that of payments for stock, but where the latter were balanced by an increase in investments held in Ireland the drain through the exchequer was balanced only by the invisible benefits from the overhead expenditure of the central government—a point not lost on those who held such benefits to be negative.

Among the more important holders of government stock were the banks, and the transfer facility made it effectively part of their London funds. The Bank of Ireland, when short of liquid funds in London, commonly procured more by sale of stock.[34] It seldom sold in Dublin where the market was too limited, an immediate sale of £100,000 of stock being impossible,[35] but when it did the effect was to reduce its London funds (the stock sold) and its circulation in Ireland (the pay-

31 Above, pp. 48-50. 58.
32 *Return of the amounts of stock transferred between England and Ireland 1837-47*, H.C. 1847-8 (196), xxxix, 571.
33 *Account of the balances arising from the remittance of public money to and from the British and Irish exchequers 1796-1855*, H.C. 1864 (569), xxxiv, 153; this consolidates earlier returns. See also above, pp. 46-7.
34 *1838 committee*, Q.1057, evidence of Wilson; the bank court's minutes have frequent references to such transactions.
35 *1838 committee*, Q.1016-8, evidence of Wilson.

ment for it in Dublin) by the same amount. Excess circulation was thus absorbed by the Bank of Ireland and transferred to England as exported capital.[36]

Operations by other banks were presumably similar to those of the Bank of Ireland but on a smaller scale. The Provincial, as Murray explained, would help a customer in time of pressure by selling securities rather than by increasing its circulation but tried to avoid doing either by watching the exchanges and restricting its issues if pressure were foreseen. In Dublin, he asserted, it would not be possible to realize £50,000 of consols in two weeks, and even the reserve which the Provincial kept there on loan at three, seven or ten days against stock was difficult to get back when needed. Large sales were therefore made either to brokers in Dublin who transferred the stock to London, or by the bank itself in London.[37]

It was the Provincial's uniform practice to invest its surplus funds in government stock, exchequer bills and Bank of England stock. The view, expressed by Marshall in 1837,[38] that a banking system with its capital all in commercial bills would certainly not be safe was coming to be accepted as sound banking practice but it was still far from universal. The 1836 committee called attention to the absence of any statutory requirement for such a reserve.[39] From the lack of one the Agricultural was unable either to raise money by sale of stock or to borrow it by offering the stock as security. The Hibernian did not hold any securities, but it did hold an adequate reserve of the Bank of Ireland notes in which it operated;[40] from a monetary point of view therefore its transactions were an extension of those of the Bank of Ireland.

The question of bank investments was part of the conflict between security and expansion which had always lain at the heart of banking. The more a bank held in reserve the less it had available for profitable employment; the more it expanded its discounts and loans the greater its profits but the greater too the potential demand on its reserves. Reserves in government stock at least earned some interest but they did not earn as much as discounts, and even Callaghan had to admit that the Bank of Ireland could not fairly be accused of preferring its own profits to public accommodation by holding public securities instead of commercial bills.[41]

What the Bank of Ireland was doing was to put monetary stability before short-term profit. Had it sold the stock and used the proceeds to increase discounts it would have inflated the Irish circulation with

36 One such instance in 1836 is discussed above, p. 146.
37 *1841 committee*, Q.2954-72, evidence of Murray.
38 *1837 committee*, Q.4401-9.
39 *1836 committee*, report p. ix.
40 *1838 committee*, Q.1128-32, evidence of Callaghan.
41 *Ibid* , Q.1196.

consequent pressure on its London funds. Any real demand for more money in circulation could have been met without risk to the stability of the banks if private holders of stock sold it in London and employed the money in Ireland. The fact that they did not suggests that the return they anticipated from investing in Ireland was less than they received on the stock. This may be because they set too high a value on their own security, but it does suggest that what was lacking was not money but business opportunities or the initiative and confidence to grasp them.

The Bank Charter Act, 1844

The effect of all these arrangements was that the Irish money supply, while distinct from the English, was closely linked to it. Its regulation depended therefore on the regulation of the English circulation, and so on the Bank Charter Act of 1844.[42] This act is important in Irish banking history as the precursor of the Irish Banking Act the following year, but except for two sections it did not apply to Ireland, nor to Scotland.

The principle underlying the act, as described by the London banker Lord Overstone (formerly S. Jones Loyd) to the 1857 committee, was that 'a certain portion of the precious metals is the proper money of this country, and that paper notes are merely a mechanical contrivance to be used for convenience in lieu of that metal'.[43] This was the so-called currency principle. To put it into effect the Bank of England was divided into the issue department (to be responsible under specified conditions for the issue of notes) and the banking department (to operate on the lines of a normal bank). Its note issues were limited to the value of bullion and government securities held by the issue department, not more than one-fifth of the bullion to be silver and the securities to total not more than £14 million. The latter, the amount by which the Bank of England's issues might exceed its bullion, was known, though not so described in the act, as the fiduciary issue. Notes to that value were to be transferred by the issue department to the banking department in exchange for securities. For the rest the bank might only issue notes in exchange for gold and silver or for old notes paid in. It was obliged to issue to all persons who tendered gold at the rate of £3 17s 9d per standard ounce—which complemented its obligation to pay gold for notes tendered at the mint price of £3 17s 10½d per ounce.

Other banks in England and Wales which issued notes on 6 May 1844 might continue to issue up to the maximum of their average circulation over the twelve weeks to that date, but if any ceased the Bank of England might apply to increase its fiduciary issue by up

42 7 & 8 Vic., c. 32.
43 *1857 committee*, Q. 646.

to two-thirds of the abandoned amount. This was designed to keep total circulation roughly unchanged, such a bank being assumed to hold a reserve of about one third of its permitted issue in cash which would then either go into circulation or be exchanged for notes at the Bank of England. Any bank that ceased issuing could not later resume, and any issuing bank of not more than six partners lost its right of issue if its partners increased above six. The purpose and the effect of these provisions was gradually to concentrate all note issues in England and Wales in the issue department of the Bank of England where, apart from the fiduciary issue, they would be covered by precious metal.

The act was widely criticized at the time and later as too restrictive.[44] Circulation could only rise with the flow of bullion into the Bank of England and must fall when it flowed out. If the economy needed more than the flow of bullion justified, nothing could lawfully be done about it. In practice, as the crises of 1847, 1857 and 1866 were to prove, the only recourse was for the government (illegally) to authorize the Bank of England to break the law. If money meant only the precious metals and the strictly limited fiduciary issue it was fortunate for the British economy that its operators were learning so rapidly to do without it by the use of bank deposits instead.

The two sections of the 1844 act which applied directly to Ireland and Scotland were section 10 which prohibited the issue of bank notes in any part of the United Kingdom by any person other than a banker who had lawfully been issuing on 6 May 1844, and section 12 which prohibited any banker in the United Kingdom who ceased issuing notes from resuming 'at any time hereafter'. In other words there could be no new banks of issue nor old banks revived. This applied both to new banks and to old banks which had not issued previously. Repeated appeals were made both in and out of parliament to have this relaxed in favour of the Hibernian and the Royal, but Peel refused.[45]

Peel's policy on note issues was set out in a memorandum to the cabinet early in 1844.[46] The solution he would have preferred would have been to concentrate all issues in the United Kingdom in the hands of the government in exercise of its sovereign right and duty to provide a currency, but he recognized that conditions did vary in the three kingdoms and that such a breach with existing practice might destroy confidence in the system in Scotland and Ireland. As a compromise he proposed the creation of the issue department of the Bank of England in the likeness, on paper at least, of a government agency. In practice

44 F. W. Fetter, *The development of British monetary orthodoxy 1797-1875*, pp. *186-94*, gives a good summary of the literature on the 1844 act.
45 *F.J.*, 27 May-19 June 1845 *passim*, reports numerous such appeals.
46 C. S. Parker, *Sir Robert Peel from his private papers*, pp. 134-9, gives this memorandum in full.

it never existed except on paper,[47] but it was the formal device by which the Bank of England was made responsible for the English currency. It would, Peel hoped, regulate its issues by gradual contraction and expansion according to the flow of bullion, and so keep the circulation in line with the state of the foreign exchanges.

The Irish Banking Act, 1845

In 1845 Peel proceeded to apply the same principles to the other two kingdoms. Seeking leave to introduce two bills for that purpose he explained that parliament, in passing the 1844 act, had assumed the standard of value to be 'a certain quantity of gold definite in point of weight and definite in point of fineness' and a promissory note to be a promise to deliver a certain quantity of such gold. Despite local differences he was convinced that the same system could be applied to Scotland and Ireland. Banks in both countries were protected by the 1844 act against new competition and enjoyed the right, denied to English banks, of issuing notes under £5. In deference to what he described as the prejudices and universal scruples prevalent in Scotland and Ireland he now formally agreed not to interfere with the latter right. The banks in return must accept restrictions like those in England.[48]

English banks were allowed to issue up to their average circulation over the selected period of twelve weeks. In Scotland and Ireland the average was taken over twelve months, the reason being the recent sharp rise in Irish circulation which would have unduly inflated the figures over the twelve-week period alone. This was a minor difference in treatment. More important was that in respect of bullion. English banks other than the Bank of England were confined to their certified circulation only but in Scotland and Ireland all banks of issue were to be allowed to issue against bullion over and above their certified totals. The rationale of this was that Bank of England notes, which in England would provide circulation against bullion, did not circulate in Scotland or Ireland—were in fact by these acts declared not to be legal tender there. English banks could exchange their bullion for legal tender notes at the Bank of England; Scottish and Irish banks could not and so were allowed to issue their own notes instead against the bullion. For the same reason the Bank of England could not take over lapsed rights in Scotland and Ireland. Amalgamating banks were therefore allowed to issue the combined total of their former certified issues, the intention being that a bank expecting to fail would quickly sell its business to another which would thus acquire its issuing rights.

There was considerable consultation between the government and the Bank of Ireland both before and after the introduction of the bill,

47 Clapham, *Bank of England* ii, 193.
48 *Hansard 3*, lxxix, 1321-55.

G

but it is clear that only matters of detail were open to discussion. The governor, Thomas Crosthwaite, and two directors, Thomas Wilson and George Carr, crossed to London in April at the chancellor's request and, after an interview with Peel on the twenty-first, Crosthwaite wrote back that 'he is *quite decided against* our continuing our privileged distance'. He went on to outline Peel's proposals, and these were identical with the main provisions of the bill as passed into law. The only real issue still open was whether the interest on the capital loan should be cut to 3 per cent with a specific management fee for the government account and the national debt in addition, or whether the rate should be left at $3\frac{1}{2}$ per cent, the extra $\frac{1}{2}$ being considered a substitute for such a fee.

The day after this interview the chancellor, Goulburn, wrote to Crosthwaite giving the formal government view. The exclusive privileges, which he described as 'practically of little value' since the 1844 act's ban on new banks of issue, were to be terminated but no payment or loan was to be demanded, as on previous occasions, for the renewal of the charter. The bank's relations with the government would be unchanged and the interest rate would be left at $3\frac{1}{2}$ per cent, which he considered 'a liberal but not excessive remuneration' for its services. For circulation purposes the Bank of Ireland would be treated on the same footing as other Irish banks but it was proposed to require returns from it analogous to the more detailed ones made by the Bank of England under the 1844 act.

In their reply the delegation expressed 'considerable alarm' at the effect of the removal of the Bank of Ireland's privileges on the circulation, but there was little they could do except agree. This they did in the conviction that the change would be accompanied by practical measures to ensure a sound currency. A week later the court of proprietors gave formal approval.[49]

During the bill's passage through parliament the court continued to press for amendments. It secured the insertion of two clauses to permit issuing banks to surrender their rights to the Bank of Ireland and an amendment to put the bank on the same footing as others in the matter of returns. But it failed to get any modification of the 1782 act's ban on taking security by mortgage of land; this applied only to the Bank of Ireland but the chancellor insisted on its retention as a principle of sound banking which should not be abandoned by the government banker. The court also tried in vain to have the section about Bank of England notes amended by cutting out the declaration that their circulation in Ireland was 'not prohibited'.[50]

Peel acknowledged in parliament the liberal and reasonable attitude

49 B. of I. Mins., 24-30 Apr. 1845, reproduce these letters in full; Hall, *Bank of Ireland*, pp. 202-4, gives the full texts of Goulburn's letter of 22 Apr. and the deputation's reply.
50 B. of I. Mins., 10 May-19 June 1845.

of the Bank of Ireland's directors and their willingness to co-operate with the government. The governor, addressing the proprietors just after the third reading of the bill, put this co-operation another way when he said that it was useless for them to contend against the ending of the bank's privileges. One stockholder aptly spoke of the bill as 'really the best bill they could obtain'.[51]

The Irish and Scottish bills passed through parliament together and both received the royal assent on 21 July 1845.[52] The Scottish act[53] need not concern us further; its main difference from the Irish arose from the absence of any monopoly to abolish. The Irish act[54] opened with the abolition of the Bank of Ireland's special privileges. Section 1 repealed entirely the 1782 act's ban on issuing banks of over six partners and authorized them to do business within fifty miles of Dublin in the same manner as beyond it. The 1844 act had, by contrast, done nothing to abolish the Bank of England's note-issuing monopoly but was rather aimed at its full restoration. Banks of issue wishing to operate within sixty-five miles of London were therefore obliged to give up their issuing rights while new banks or non-issuing banks within the sixty-five miles radius would not be allowed to issue in any event. In Ireland there was no similar intention to concentrate issues in the Bank of Ireland, all existing banks being treated on the same footing. Peel was able therefore, with a fair grace, to meet the persistent demands for abolition of the monopoly.

Section 2 of the act provided that the capital debt to the Bank of Ireland continue as a charge on the consolidated fund of the United Kingdom with the annuity at $3\frac{1}{2}$ per cent, while section 3 required the bank to continue to manage the public debt without charge for the duration of the charter. Section 4 provided for the dissolution of the Bank of Ireland on twelve months notice by the lord lieutenant any time after 1 January 1855 on repayment of the capital debt and any arrears of the annuity. From the circulation point of view the bank was losing its privileges but its special position as a chartered bank operating the government account and managing the national debt was unaffected.

The next three sections dealt with sundry matters. Section 5, added in committee, repealed the 1760 act's ban on public officers being partners in banks, an anachronism in the joint stock age. Section 6 cleared up the doubts about Bank of England notes by declaring that they were not legal tender in Ireland but at the same time that their circulation was not prohibited. Section 7 abolished the anti-popery

51 *F.J.*, 20 June 1845.
52 The Irish bill as introduced is in H.C. 1845 (281), i, 89, and as amended in committee in H.C. 1845 (345), i, 109. *Commons' Jn.*, c, 242-708 *passim; Lords' Jn.*, lxxvii, 495-689 *passim; Hansard 3*, lxxxi *passim*, report its progress through parliament.
53 8 & 9 Vic., c. 38.
54 8 & 9 Vic., c. 37.

declarations prescribed in the charter of the Bank of Ireland—done, as Peel explained with some emphasis, at the request of the protestant members of the court.

The core of the act was in section 8 which dealt with note issues. Bankers who claimed the right of issue were required to notify the commissioner of stamps and taxes who would then, on the basis of their returns, issue a certificate of their average circulation over the twelve months to 1 May 1845. After 6 December 1845 bankers would be allowed to issue up to this certified total plus the value of their bullion holdings. No other note issues in Ireland would be lawful. Banks amalgamating were entitled, by section 11, to a certificate for the aggregate of their certified issues and any bank was permitted, by sections 12 and 13, to relinquish its rights in favour of the Bank of Ireland. Section 15 required all notes in future to be in pounds sterling without fractions.

Publicity on note issues was considered an essential counterpart to their regulation, and section 16 required weekly returns to the Stamp Office of both the volume of notes in circulation on the previous Saturday, distinguishing large from small, and the volume of gold and silver held on each day of the week. The Stamp Office was required, by section 18, to publish a four-weekly summary of these returns in the *Dublin Gazette*. Section 17 defined notes as being in circulation from the time of issue to the time of return to the banker, his servant or agent, and section 19 defined how the average was to be calculated. Section 20 laid down that the only coin to be counted was that held at the head offices or places of issue not exceeding four, of which not more than two might be in the same province, and limited the silver coin that might be included to one quarter of the gold held, that is to one-fifth of the total bullion. Section 21 authorized the commissioner to inspect books and bullion stocks, and section 22 required annual returns for publication in the *Gazette* of members and places of business from all banks except the Bank of Ireland.

Penalties were imposed by section 23 on banks exceeding their permitted limits (they were to forfeit a sum equal to the excess), and by sections 26 and 27 on anyone issuing notes under £5 without authority or uttering or negotiating notes so issued (the penalty was £20 per note). No specific penalty was prescribed in respect of large notes; their issue was simply unlawful under section 8 except in accordance with the act.

Section 28, which was added in committee, declared that nothing in the act prohibited

> any draft or order by any person on his banker or any person acting as such banker for the payment of money held by such banker or person to the use of the person by whom such draft or order shall be drawn.

This cumbersome phraseology meant that cheques were unaffected by the act; whether or not they or the deposits which they transferred were money, their use was lawful.

Finally there were two sections added during the passage through parliament: section 30 which cleared up a legal doubt by permitting banking companies within fifty miles of Dublin to sue and be sued in the names of their public officers in the same manner as banks elsewhere, a right for which the Royal Bank had long been pleading; and section 31 which required the Bank of Ireland to continue its note-issuing agreement with the Tipperary Bank until 1 January 1856,[55] a contrast to the 1844 act which required such agreements by the Bank of England to be terminated.

The act came into effect on 6 December 1845. The Provincial promptly converted its Dublin office to a full branch.[56] The National presumably did the same; it had recently erected a new building in the city centre but it is not clear just when it was made a full branch.[57] The only other opening within fifty miles of Dublin before the end of the year was by the Belfast in Newry; the Bank of Ireland, no longer able to prevent this, sold its original premises to the Belfast for the purpose.[58] The Provincial opened branches early in 1846 in Newry, Drogheda, Dundalk and Carlow, but of these Carlow closed later in the year and Dundalk in 1849, and no others were opened until 1856. The National opened no new branches until 1848 when it took over seven branches of the London & Dublin, six of them within fifty miles of Dublin.

Even in Dublin the three northern banks did not think it worth their while to open branches at this date.[59] This lack of branch openings in the late 1840's is of course partly accounted for by the depression of the famine. As far as Dublin banks were concerned their hopes had centred on the right of issue and this was still denied them. Their position on branches was unaltered. The Hibernian in fact opened three more by 1850; the Royal did not open any until the 1860s and then only in Dublin.

The ending of the Bank of Ireland's monopoly was however only incidental to the main purpose of the act, the regulation of issues. Peel, when introducing the bill, pointed out that there had been a recent rapid rise in Irish circulation and the act would allow further increases to the extent of the specie held by each bank, so it could not, he argued, be called unduly restrictive. But it was so described by many since it checked the expansion of circulation that the economy

55 Above, p. 162.
56 *B. Mag.*, v, 173-4, Provincial Bank annual report 1845/6.
57 *B. Mag.*, iii, 234, National Bank tenth annual report.
58 B. of I. Mins., 2 Sept. 1845; its own agency had moved into new premises.
59 The Ulster opened in Dublin in 1862, the Northern in 1888 (by taking over Ball's) and the Belfast in 1892.

needed. A meeting of merchants in Belfast protested strongly that it would restrain the growth of the linen trade.[60] The *Banker's Magazine* pointed out that it authorized banks to expand into the richest part of Ireland without permitting the increased circulation necessary to do so.[61] Peel's reply to such criticisms, in his speech on the third reading, was that the permanent benefit of Ireland depended much more on the stability of the banking system than on any amount of circulation.[62]

The reaction of the banks may be typified in the report of the committee of the Northern to its general meeting in September 1845. They did not anticipate *much* inconvenience *in favourable times,* but the act's restrictions might tend to diminish to some extent the accommodation they could afford customers. The ban on new banks of issue might favour existing establishments and the abolition of the monopoly might enlarge their field of activity but the committee doubted if these benefits were worth the price that had been paid for them.[63] But by 1848 all three Irish witnesses before the committee on commercial distress agreed that the act in practice had had no material effect on monetary conditions.[64] This view was reiterated in 1858.[65]

The first four-weekly summary by the Stamp Office appeared in the *Dublin Gazette* in January 1846 and covered in effect the month of December 1845.[66] It forms the basis of Appendix 11 below. The column of certified circulation shows the amounts certified under section 8 of the act as each bank's average circulation for the twelve months to 1 May 1845. The total of this and their bullion holdings was the maximum circulation permitted over the four weeks. The table shows that this total was over £8,800,000 but that the actual circulation was only £7,400,000. All six banks were well below their permitted limits though December was normally the seasonal peak. This pattern of aggregate circulation well short of the permitted total was to continue for as long as the act endured. It was not always true of individual banks but in the face of it the argument that the act kept circulation down loses much of its force.

What it did tend to do was to freeze the distribution between the banks. The Bank of Ireland still had the dominant share with some 59 per cent of the certified total, followed at a distance by the Provincial with some 15 per cent and the National with 13, while the

60 *F.J.*, 4 June 1845, report from *Northern Whig*.
61 *B. Mag.*, iv, 73-7.
62 *Hansard 3*, lxxxi, 623.
63 Hill (ed.), *Northern Banking Company*, pp. 125-6.
64 *1848 committee* (C), Q.6612, evidence of John M'Donnell, governor of the Bank of Ireland; 7227, of James Bristow of the Northern Bank; *ibid.* (L), Q.4244, of Robert Murray of the Provincial.
65 *1858 committee*, Q.3820, 5176, evidence of Charles Haliday and John Barlow of the Bank of Ireland, and Bristow for the three northern banks.
66 *Dublin Gaz. 1846*, p. 35.

remaining 13 was divided fairly equally between the three northern
banks. Small notes made up over 60 per cent of the total—46 per cent
for the Bank of Ireland, about 70 per cent for the Provincial and
National and around 90 per cent for each of the northern banks.

Holdings of gold and silver equalled about a third of the total
circulation but here again there was wide variety, from the Bank of
Ireland and the Ulster with about 29 per cent of their issues covered
to the Belfast with 47 per cent. Provided the certified circulation was
not exceeded there was nothing in the 1845 act to oblige a bank to hold
any specie at all, but its contractual liability to pay gold for its notes
on demand remained. The 1828 act required this to be at the branch of
issue.[67] Every branch must therefore hold specie but only that in the
four main offices, not more than two of them in one province, was
counted for purposes of the return. The Bank of Ireland named Dublin,
Cork, Belfast and Galway as its main offices and made each responsible
for supplying up to £10,000 on demand to any other agency in its
province. The other twenty agencies were each to hold £5,000, making
a total of £100,000 of gold above the amount shown in its official
returns.[68] In the Provincial and the National the number of branches
may well have made the discrepancy even greater, as it would in the
three northern banks whose branches were all in the same province so
that only the specie held in two of them could be counted. In some
circumstances this anomaly might oblige banks either to restrict their
issues unduly or to import gold which they did not really need.[69]

The Dublin Clearing House

The removal of all legal distinctions between banks of issue and the
coming of the Provincial and the National to Dublin showed up the
need for a more formalized system of inter-bank exchanges. Formerly
Bank of Ireland notes were the only ones legally payable in Dublin.
Other banks were allowed by the 1830 act to pay there as a convenience and were always willing to do so, but the Bank of Ireland
stood on its legal rights and insisted on their notes being exchanged at
the branches where they were issued; the balances were then settled
by drafts on Dublin.

The Scottish banks had operated a clearing house in Edinburgh
since 1752, and since 1835 they had settled their balances by exchequer
bills held specially for the purpose.[70] In October 1845 Robert Murray
of the Provincial approached the Bank of Ireland with proposals for
something similar in Dublin and a scheme was worked out which was
adopted by the Bank of Ireland on 2 December and accepted by

67 9 Geo. IV, c. 81; this act was only repealed in 1920 by 10 & 11 Geo. V, c. 24.
68 B. of I. Mins., 28 Oct. 1845.
69 *1848 committee* (C), Q.6721, 7267-8, evidence of Murray and Bristow.
70 *1841 committee*, app. 21, gives the full regulations agreed in 1835; see also
   Graham, *One pound note*, pp. 310-5.

the three northern banks a few days later. It is not clear when the National came in but on 8 December the scheme went into operation. It was primarily for the exchange of notes but seems from the first to have embraced the clearance of cheques and other claims as well.[71]

Premises and staff were provided by the Bank of Ireland but without liability and evidently without charge. Each day the banks delivered statements of their claims on each other and at 2 p.m. were advised of the balance due. Apart from fractions of £500 (which could be settled in the debtor's notes) these were settled by transfer of exchequer bills valued at par plus the interest accrued.

Exchequer bills, to be marked 'Dublin exchange bills', were to be held solely for this purpose and quotas totalling £330,000 were apportioned between the banks on the basis of their circulations.[72] As the bills approached maturity they were returned to the original holder for renewal. Holdings fluctuated daily with the settlements but the banks agreed to maintain them within a third of their quotas. Any bank whose holding fell below this must buy bills from others, paying at the seller's option in letters of credit on London or gold in Dublin. Otherwise no bank was to demand gold from or pay gold to any other, and if requiring to import or export gold must bear the cost itself. This provision was held so important that violation of it would be treated as withdrawal from the agreement. The Scottish banks' agreement had no such provision and, unlike the Irish, allowed settlement in Bank of England notes. The three northern banks stipulated that they be allowed pay gold in Belfast, but they were ready to receive it in either Belfast or Dublin.

The four non-issuing banks were not members of the clearing house but all came into it through agreements with the Bank of Ireland. In July 1845 the Hibernian in return for an advance of £150,000 at 1 per cent below the public rate (with a minimum of 3 per cent) and the right to discount English bills on the same terms agreed to issue Bank of Ireland notes exclusively and, if it ever wished to rediscount mercantile bills, to do so at the Bank of Ireland.[73] In September 1846 this agreement was renewed with some modifications and a similar one was made with the Royal.[74] The terms were essentially the same as those agreed by the Bank of Ireland with the Tipperary and with the London & Dublin.[75] All four non-issuing

---

71 B. of I. Mins., 30 Oct., 2, 9 Dec. 1845; Gilbart, *Practical treatise* (5th ed. 1849), pp. 662-4, gives the text of the agreement. See also W. A. Craig, 'The clearing system', in *Inst. of Bankers in Ire. Jn.*, i, 249-50; *1848 committee (C)*, Q7312-5, evidence of Bristow.

72 The quotas were: Bank of Ireland £134,000 ,Provincial £58,000, National £48,000, Belfast £30,000, Northern £30,000, Ulster £30,000; they were adjusted from time to time—in 1858 the total was £370,000 (*1858 committee* Q.3738), in 1865 £402,000 (Gilbart, *op. cit.* 1865 ed., p. 605).

73 B. of I. Mins., 15 July 1845.

74 *Ibid.*, 15-29 Sept. 1846.

75 Above, pp. 161-2, 164.

banks were therefore virtual extensions of the Bank of Ireland as far as issues were concerned.

The three northern banks operated in the clearing house through their agents, initially Boyle's for the Northern, Solomon Watson for the Belfast and the Royal for the Ulster, each with authority to draw on London agents in payment for exchequer bills.[76] In May 1846, as part of an agreement covering all aspects of its business, the Northern transferred its agency to the Bank of Ireland which then added the Northern's quota to its own.[77] In November 1847 an identical agreement was made between the Belfast and the Bank of Ireland.[78]

The effect of the clearing house scheme was that any bank which overextended its issues or deposits had to transfer exchequer bills to redeem the consequent surplus of claims against it; if this reduced its holding below two-thirds of its quota it must buy back bills to make good the deficiency, paying out of its London funds except in the unlikely event that the creditor bank preferred gold in Dublin. Similarly a bank which underissued had to accept exchequer bills in settlement of its surplus claims; if this raised its holding to more than four thirds of its quota it must sell the excess for drafts on London or gold in Dublin. The bills thus provided a cushion for day-to-day fluctuations in bank liabilities while major changes were settled by transfers between the London funds of the different banks. As one Irish banker put it in 1849, the arrangement had 'made London the actual and final place of settlement, through machinery working in Dublin'.[79]

Bank Deposits

Initially the clearing house seems to have dealt mainly with notes, but as time went on note issues were increasingly overshadowed by deposits. To Peel and the currency school deposits like notes were no more than statements of claims to money, but in practice, just as notes were generally preferred to gold, so a bank's promise inscribed in its books and transferred by cheque was for many purposes preferred to notes. In both cases, as Peel insisted, acceptability depended on the security of the banks, but once this was established it was pedantic to argue that either notes or deposits were not money. Yet the 1845 act, which so precisely regulated the issue of notes, left deposits quite uncontrolled—a difference in treatment which the governor of the Bank of Ireland in 1858 described as 'extraordinary'.[80]

The preoccupation with note issues means that quite good statistics

76 B. of I. Mins., 9 Dec. 1845, reproduce letters from all three banks.
77 *Ibid.*, 12 May 1846.
78 *Ibid.*, 30 Nov. 1847.
79 Gilbart, *Practical treatise* (5th ed.), pp. 661-2, quoting a letter from an Irish banker.
80 *1858 committee*, Q.4010-1, evidence of Haliday.

of circulation are available from 1833, and even better ones from 1845, but information on deposits is most inadequate. Yet their importance is beyond dispute.[81] As Pierce Mahony put it in 1837, 'a very large circulation exists through cheques which go from hand to hand and by orders from bank to bank which is never represented in what is called the note currency'.[82] Murray told the 1841 committee that changes in the linen trade over the previous dozen years meant that cloth formerly bought for small notes by bleachers from individual weavers in the markets was now mostly bought in large quantities from mills and paid for by bills cleared against bank accounts.[83] In the Bank of Ireland cheques down to £5 had been allowed since 1834; this meant that they replaced large notes rather than small. It was not till 1858 that they were allowed down to £1.[84]

Annual averages of deposits in the Bank of Ireland are summarized in Appendix 8 below. Comparison with Appendix 10 shows that from 1837 to 1845 the total of deposits and sundry balances was roughly equivalent to circulation, but these include public deposits which are more properly treated as money withdrawn from circulation. Annual averages of private deposits are available up to 1836 but from then on the best figures are those for private deposits and sundry balances from the twice-yearly statements of assets and liabilities.[85] They include unspecified amounts of sundry balances but do give an idea of the scale of private deposits. For 1845 they must have been something over £2,000,000, compared with circulation that December of £2,000,000 small notes and £2,350,000 large. Deposits probably had a lower velocity than notes but they certainly formed a substantial portion of the money made available by the Bank of Ireland.

There are no individual figures for other banks but from 1840 there is an official series of aggregate figures based on confidential returns. In 1870 the totals at the end of each year from 1840 to 1869 were published over the signature of W. Neilson Hancock,[86] and the series was carried on to 1902 in the volumes of banking, railway and shipping statistics. These figures are frequently cited as statistics of bank deposits but their meaning in the early years is not clear. Hancock describes them as the aggregates of private balances in the Bank of Ireland and deposits in the Belfast, Hibernian, National, Northern, Provincial, Ulster and Royal banks at the end of each year, but in a footnote he states that some banks (unspecified) were

81 Above, pp. 34-6.
82 *1837 committee*, Q.4092; see also *1838 committee*, Q.792-807, evidence of Wilson.
83 *1841 committee*, Q.2928-9, evidence of Murray.
84 B. of I. Mins., 6 May 1834; *F.J.*, 5 July 1858, commercial intelligence.
85 Below, Appendix 7, column 2.
86 W. N. Hancock, *Report on deposits and cash balances 1840-69;* Hancock was professor of political economy at Trinity College, Dublin; the figures were published by the Statistics Office in the form of a report by him to the under-secretary.

found in 1863 to have been including cash balances as well but that, as this had been done throughout, it did not affect the year-to-year comparison. From 1864 cash balances of all banks were included, but before that the figures were evidently intended to cover permanent deposits only but included some current (or cash) accounts inadvertently. Bank deposits are treated as a form of investment analogous to government stock and deposits in saving banks, and the emphasis throughout is on annual variations as indications of saving and investment.

As evidence of the significance of deposits as part of the money supply these figures, up to 1863, are therefore subject to two weaknesses of opposing tendencies. The totals are understated by the omission of part, possibly the greater part, of the current accounts in the banks listed and of all deposits in the Tipperary, the London & Dublin and the private banks, while their significance as money is reduced by the extent to which the deposits were held for investment rather than for current use. The latter could be measured if we had some idea of the turnover but we have none. All the banks except the Bank of Ireland paid interest on deposits,[87] which presumably encouraged holders to leave them undisturbed. Current deposits obviously had a higher velocity of circulation than permanent, but it is not possible to say more.

Subject to these uncertainties the figures show deposits on 31 December 1840 to have totalled £5,568,000, just less than total note circulation. They then rose each year to £8,000,000 in 1845 and £8,442,000 in 1846, and were always well above circulation totals. A comparison with Appendix 8 below suggests that a little over one third of the total were private deposits in the Bank of Ireland. Its circulation by contrast was always well over half the total, but this included notes in government hands—analogous to public deposits which were not included in the deposit figures. The difference also reflects the special prestige of Bank of Ireland notes and their status in the monopoly area, but this relatively low share of deposits must have been partly due to the fact that the Bank of Ireland alone paid no interest.

Looking ahead over the rest of the century, the total of bank deposits fell sharply in 1847, then rose, with some fluctuations, over the next thirty years, passing £10 million in 1852, £20 million in 1866 and £30 million in 1874. After steadying out for the next twenty years it resumed its upward trend in the late nineties and passed the £40 million mark in 1899.[88] During the same period total circulation

87 *1841 committee*, Q.2701-3, evidence of Wilson.
88 Hancock, *Deposits and cash balances; Report on certain statistics of banking in Ireland 1859-85* (C. 4681), H.C. 1886, lxxi, 141; Department of Agriculture and Technical Instruction for Ireland, *Banking and railway statistics, Ireland, December 1900* (Cd. 342), H.C. 1900, ci, 573.

varied little, being seldom above the 1845 level and normally well below it. Even if a large portion of the deposits were short-term investments their steady increase in volume must have included a considerable element of current money supply. It was here rather than in the issue of notes—restricted by the 1845 act—that the future development of Irish banking lay.

The Joint Stock Banking Code

After 1845 no new bank appeared in Ireland until the 1860s. New banks of issue had been prohibited by the 1844 act but of even more effect was another of Peel's acts, known as the Joint Stock Banking Code, which was enacted for England and Wales in 1844[89] and applied to Scotland and Ireland by a brief act of 1846.[90] Its purpose was to check the abuses and weaknesses of joint stock banking such as came to light in the Agricultural. Any firm of over six partners carrying on business as a bank was required first to obtain letters patent. The conditions laid down for their issue were so rigorous that very few banks were formed under the code in England and none in Ireland. It was finally repealed in 1857.[91]

The code followed in the main the criticisms of the 1836 committee. To a modern eye the matters prescribed for inclusion in the deed of partnership and for the general regulation of the banks seem perfectly reasonable, and for the most part were embodied in later company legislation, but at the time they were regarded as an intolerable interference with commercial freedom.

As far as Ireland was concerned it is doubtful whether any new banks would have been founded in any event in these years of famine and its aftermath. Already in 1841 Thomas Wilson had described the country as overbanked[92]—for which he was severely taken to task by the Repeal Association.[93] He argued that the higher price of public funds normally prevailing in Dublin than in London and the demand in Dublin for English money and bills were evidence of excess circulation, and therefore of too many banks. In other words he considered the supply of money to be excessive relative to the demand for it. This might have been rectified by increasing the demand, that is by economic expansion, rather than by holding back the supply, but it does suggest that there was no need for more banks until those in existence were more fully utilized.

89 7 & 8 Vic., c. 113,
90 9 & 10 Vic., c. 75.
91 20 & 21 Vic., c. 49.
92 *1841 committee*, Q.2695-7.
93 Loyal National Repeal Association, *Report of committee on banking*, pp. 38-44.

Conclusion

As 1845 ended, with the blight already on the potatoes, the Irish banking system had reached maturity, just twenty-one years from the opening of the first joint stock bank. One hundred and seventy-three branches in ninety towns covered the country, with the main concentrations in north-east Ulster and eastern Munster. There were still few banks in Leinster outside Dublin, and the area west of the Londonderry-Cork line was poorly served, but the change since 1820 had been remarkable.[1]

In 1820 the Bank of Ireland's supremacy had been unchallenged, thanks in part to its central banking functions but even more to its privileged status as a commercial bank. This had established its notes as a stable currency, not merely as good as gold but generally preferred. The price of this was excessive restraint on the expansion of banking. Without competitive pressure the Bank of Ireland itself remained immobile in Dublin while the two dozen private banks, kept small by law, provided an auxiliary service in Dublin, in north-east Ulster and in parts of the south.

By 1845 with the rise of joint stock banks, the expansion of the Bank of Ireland and the growth of co-operation between them, a system had emerged which was described twenty-five years later by Hancock as providing a currency and discount facilities 'as perfect and convenient as exists in England, so that Irish trade enjoys to the full all the banking and monetary arrangements it requires and can widen them as new necessities spring up'.[2] There was now a branch for every 48,000 of the population as a whole—for every 36,000 in Ulster, every 48,000 in Munster, 52,000 in Leinster and 79,000 in Connacht. On a county basis the population per branch ranged from under 30,000 in Derry, Antrim and Armagh to over 150,000 in Leitrim and Queen's County and 184,000 in Meath. There were banks in all eighteen towns of over 10,000, in twenty-seven of the thirty-two towns between 5,000 and 10,000 and in forty-four towns of under 5,000.

As far as we can tell from the statistics this expansion had not been accompanied by a proportionate rise in note circulation. After allowing for private bank issues in the earlier years the net change between 1820 and 1845 seems to have been small.[3] Deposits, on the other hand, had undoubtedly increased, though it is not possible to distinguish between those which should be treated as current money and those that were short-term investments. What had been achieved was a

1 See appendix 3 for the location of these branches.
2 Hancock, *Deposits and cash balances*, p. 8.
3 Above, pp. 32-4; below, Appendices 8, 9, 10.

much wider geographical spread of banking services and an enormous improvement in their quality and in the soundness of bank money. The banks had created a mechanism; the use that was made of it depended on conditions beyond their control.

Banking is essentially an adjunct of trade and industry. Its steadiest development in these years was therefore in the north-east where the linen industry provided both the demand for banking services and the security on which to base them. Elsewhere the first branches of the Bank of Ireland and the Provincial in the mid-1820s were in the larger market towns and operated mainly through the discount of bills for merchants.[5] The effect on the rural economy was indirect, by the increased capacity of merchants to buy produce, rather than direct by advances to farmers.

The second wave of expansion in the mid-1830s bore more directly on the rural community. The Agricultural and National Banks in particular spread into many small country towns and by the end of 1845, even after the closure of the Agricultural, there were forty-four branches in towns of under 5,000, of which only one dated from before 1830. These new banks did much of their business direct with farmers by discounting their bills. In the nature of farming such bills were less secure than those drawn by merchants or manufacturers for definite commercial transactions and many were accommodation bills to raise money for rent. Evidence before the Devon commission showed the latter to have been quite common, often with the encouragement of landlords seeking rent from impoverished tenants. Rates were normally 5 or 6 per cent but drawers unable to meet the bills frequently renewed them, adding 4 per cent or more over the years in stamps and commission.[6]

This was nevertheless cheaper than the alternative of borrowing from local usurers who charged effective rates of from 25 to 100 per cent, supposedly to protect themselves against the risks involved. The government tried to encourage small loan funds to remedy this situation but they met with the same difficulties as the banks—their efficacy depended on regular repayments which the small tenant farmers were rarely in a position to make. Delays and fines so increased the cost that such loans were only 'less immediately ruinous' than dealing with private usurers.[7]

These difficulties reflected the basic weaknesses of the economy which banking improvements might alleviate but could not cure. Evidence on the economic condition of Ireland in the years leading to

5 *1833 committee,* Q.4288-98, evidence of Joseph Sandars, a Liverpool corn merchant dealing with Ireland; 8931-7, 8970-1, of Edward Roberts, a land agent in Waterford.
6 J. P. Kennedy (ed.), *Digest of evidence before the Devon commission on land tenure in Ireland 1844,* pp. 202-5.
7 *Ibid.,* pp. 194-6.

the famine is voluminous,[8] and it is remarkable how little the picture had changed from that painted in the evidence before the 1823 committee.[9] The exhaustive reports of the poor inquiry commission of 1835-6 and of the Devon commission on land tenure of 1844 describe the same paradox of great numbers of the rural population, particularly in the south and west, living in extreme degradations of poverty, pressing desperately on the available land, avid for employment but unable to move off the land for the lack of any alternative means of livelihood. Visiting observers such as H. D. Inglis, an experienced English traveller who toured Ireland in 1834,[10] or the *Times* special commissioner, T. Campbell Foster, whose detailed if unsympathetic reports date from 1845-6,[11] tell the same story.

Without land there was for many literally no life. The first claim on their money was therefore to pay the rent. Outside Ulster there was neither security of tenure nor a claim on the value of improvements made, and therefore little incentive to make any. The landlords and middlemen had the first call on whatever money was available but they too put little of it back into their estates. On a short-sighted view there was no need to; population pressure would keep rents up without additional investment and a better return could normally be obtained by buying government stock. Many estates were in any case so encumbered that the owners could afford no investment. As the Society of Friends put in their report on famine relief in 1846-7, 'the nominal owner has often been in reality only a trustee for others'.[12] There was intense pressure on tenants to get money for their rent but once paid much of the money went, not into consumption or investment by the landlord on the spot, but out of the rural economy altogether into the hands of his creditors or parasite relatives.

It is hard to tell how significant this leakage of money was but that it occurred at all was the reverse of what such a depressed economy needed. In 1836 the masters of the court of chancery estimated the gross rental of Ireland at something under £10 million; out of this some 10 per cent would go in expenses and losses while annuities and interest charges were reckoned to take at least £3 million, leaving net income at under £6 million.[13] Some of this would have been spent on local consumption but much leaked away in expenditure on such things as imported luxuries, foreign travel or rents to absentees. What

8 T. W. Freeman, *Pre-famine Ireland*, gives the best summary of the economic background at this date.

9 Above, pp. 53-9.

10 H. D. Inglis, *A journey throughout Ireland 1834*.

11 T. Campbell Foster, *Letters on the condition of the people of Ireland*, reprinted from *The Times*, Aug. 1845-Feb 1846.

12 Society of Friends, *Transactions during the famine in Ireland*, p. 113.

13 *Poor inquiry, third report 1836*, p. 28.

was left as savings after this was more likely to have been invested in the funds or in railway or mining speculations than in local improvements.

One way in which the landlords' money was fed back into the rural economy was through rates paid under the poor law of 1838.[14] This act was based on the same principle as the recent poor law in England that local poverty should be relieved at the expense of local property. In 1833 the poor inquiry commission had been appointed to look into the condition of the poorer classes in Ireland with a view to the introduction of a poor law, and in their third report in 1836 they pointed emphatically to the need for a different approach to that adopted in England. For an equivalent quantity of cultivated land there were five labourers in Ireland for every three in Britain. The difficulty was not 'to make the able-bodied look for employment but to find it profitably for the many who seek it'. For thirty weeks of the year some 585,000 were normally out of work, making with about 1,800,000 dependants a total of 2,385,000 persons in need of relief. What was required was employment for these people. To provide workhouse relief for so large a part of the population by the collection of rates on local property was bluntly stated by the commission to be impossible.[15]

They proposed instead that workhouse relief be confined to the sick and infirm and that the needs of the destitute unemployed be met by a scheme of land reclamation, agricultural education and public works, to be financed partly from local rates and partly from advances by the Board of Works to be repaid from the increased value of the property improved.[16] Such reflation was just what the depressed economy needed but the plan was thrust aside by Melbourne's Whig government in favour of a scheme on the English model devised after a brief visit to Ireland by George Nicholls, a poor law commissioner of great industry and ability but little imagination.[17]

The Nicholls plan was embodied in the 1838 act, and its effect was to encumber local property yet further with rates for the support of the local poor. The poorer the area the higher the rates had to be. To keep them down landowners were expected to provide work for the paupers, but in practice, particularly in the poorer areas where the need was greatest, they were seldom in a position to do so. Instead of reflation there was more deflation. Landlords, as the quaker report put it, were 'almost ruined by the taxation required for supporting pauper labourers in the workhouses while millions of acres are wholly waste or imperfectly cultivated, and millions of money are

14 1 & 2 Vic., c. 56.
15 *Poor inquiry, third report 1836*, pp. 3-5.
16 *Ibid.*, pp. 17-33.
17 R. B. McDowell, *The Irish administration*, pp. 175-99.

lying at a low rate of interest in the funds'.[18] Investment which might have taken the form of land improvements took instead the form of building workhouses where paupers could be housed in conditions deliberately designed to discourage resort to them. Discouraging conditions were successfully produced but the intention that this would drive paupers to find employment failed—such employment just did not exist.

If there was any expansion of the economy it was certainly not on the scale to provide for the rising population. The 1821 total, possibly an underestimate, was 6,800,000; by 1841 it was 8,175,000, a rise of some 20 per cent in twenty years. About one in five of this population lived in towns and villages, something over one in ten in towns of over 5,000.[19] Outside Dublin and the linen towns of Ulster they were mainly market centres with small patches of industry. But their size did not indicate their economic importance for they included many migrants from the surrounding country who had been unable to secure or retain even the smallest potato patch on which to subsist, yet lacked the will or the means to move on to Britain or America. As Freeman has pointed out, 'it was among them that human misery reached its depths'.[20] Their share in the economy as either producers or consumers was slight, but the failure of the community to provide for them in either capacity was living evidence of economic debility.

It was widely agreed nevertheless that the economy was improving, even if on an inadequate scale. The poor inquiry commissioners spoke of 'a rising spirit of improvement in Ireland' which must be stimulated by sound legislation to 'relieve the country from the lingering effects of the evil system of former times'.[21] Bank reports and evidence of bankers before select committees frequently refer to such a spirit but the facts tabulated in the 1841 census report[22] testify to its inadequacy even before the devastating proof of the Famine.

The banks played their part in this improvement by making credit more easily available either to merchants and manufacturers or direct to farmers, but once the money came into the hands of the farmers the first claim on it was for rent. Any left in their hands would tend to be invested, wherever possible, in the extension of holdings by the purchase of goodwill or the payment of further rent, or be put aside for future rent. In 1820 such saving would have been by the hoarding of coin but by the 1840s it would more commonly be by deposit in a savings bank or joint stock bank or, in the case of larger farmers, by the purchase of government stock. Since savings banks invested all their funds in government stock this withdrew money

18 Society of Friends, *Transactions*, p. 110.
19 Freeman, *Pre-famine Ireland*, p. 27.
20 *Ibid.*, p. 5.
21 *Poor inquiry, third report 1836*, p. 34.
22 Connell, *Population of Ireland*, pp. 248-50, gives a good analysis of this.

from the rural economy just as if the stock had been bought direct. In the case of deposits in the joint stock banks, if a corresponding quantity of good bills were offered for discount or sound applications made for loans the money would be fed back into local circulation but if not the banks had little choice but to buy stock with it themselves.

In the rural economy therefore savings tended to outrun investment, while demand from the urban areas was insufficient to make up the difference. To keep the system in equilibrium the surplus of total income over total consumption should have been spent on physical investment; instead it was converted into less liquid form by the purchase of stock. Some of the stock may then have been monetized by being pledged as collateral for loans from the banks but the net effect was certainly deflationary.

The urgent need for reflationary investment to create employment and improve the economy was emphasized repeatedly by commentators. We have already noted the poor inquiry commission's proposals of 1836. Two years later the Drummond commission on railway development took a similar line with a massive scheme for a government-supported programme of railway building.[23] It was widely welcomed in Ireland, with some misgivings lest it turn into a political job, but it clashed with orthodox ideas of *laissez-faire* and the government's approach was hesitant. It proposed to raise £2,500,000 on treasury bills to finance the suggested line from Dublin to Cork but this met strong opposition in the Commons led by Sir Robert Peel and when there was further opposition in the Lords it was dropped. Railway development was left instead to small scale speculators. By 1846 various acts had authorized some 1,500 miles but of these only 123 had been completed, with a further 164 in hand.[24]

Railway investment had not gone far by 1845 either to improve communications or to reflate the economy, but it had absorbed a considerable volume of savings. Some one hundred and forty companies had been floated for railway construction in Ireland and the ninety-eight for which details are available had an issued capital of almost £60 million of which £3½ million was paid up.[25] Some of this money was undoubtedly English but, allowing for the large amount of Irish money invested in railway speculations in Britain and America, it gives some idea of the volume of investible funds diverted into this channel. Had the money been used to construct an efficient railway system it would have served just the purpose envisaged by the Drummond commission but as yet there was little to show for the

---

23 *Drummond report*, especially pp. 79-85.
24 J. C. Conroy, *Railways in Ireland*, p. 12; Black, *Economic thought and the Irish question*, pp. 191-5.
25 *F.J.*, 20 Nov. 1845, has a table of the financial position of Irish railway companies at that date.

investment. The bulk of the money had gone in legal expenses or speculators' profits, or was lying unused in the companies' hands.

Industrial development as a means of reflation had many exponents, the most eminent being Sir Robert Kane whose classic work on industrial resources was published by the Royal Dublin Society in 1845,[26] but the years leading up to the famine, far from witnessing a rise in industrial activity, saw a decline in much that existed.

This arose paradoxically from a great beneficial source, the temperance campaign of Father Mathew which opened in 1838 and swept the country. His followers were said at one time to number about half the adult population and the result was a dramatic fall in the consumption of liquor. Spirits charged to duty for consumption in Ireland fell from almost 12,300,000 gallons in 1838 to under 5,300,000 in 1842,[27] while production of beer halved from a little over a million gallons in 1837 to just over half a million in 1843.[28] In the long run the increase in sobriety and thrift and the diversion of both consumption and production into more useful channels might be of great economic as well as moral benefit but in the short run the spread of temperance brought distress to the brewers and distillers, to the farmers from whom they bought their grain and to the publicans who controlled much of the trade in general retail goods as well as liquor. Whatever the long-term benefits the immediate effect was another twist to the deflationary spiral.[29]

The economy was therefore in no fit state to meet the crisis of the famine, the almost inevitable outcome of the conditions we have been discussing. The partial failure of the potato crop of 1845 led to some food shortage in 1846; the total failure of the 1846 crop brought general famine in 1847; after a respite the next year the failure of the 1848 crop brought famine again in 1849.[30] The blight was a visitation of nature which struck Britain and parts of Europe as well, but only in Ireland did so large a part of the population depend on the potato for survival. They lived on the potatoes they grew, with an element of barter to the extent that they met their rent and other essential payments with their own labour.[31] Money, obtained by sale of produce, by wages for local work, by harvest labour in Britain or from any other source, was jealously guarded to secure the land on

26 R. Kane, *The industrial resources of Ireland;* see especially pp. 389-410

27 *Return of the total number of gallons distilled and charged with duty . . . in England, Scotland and Ireland 1820-45,* H.C. 1846 (361), xliv, 427.

28 Lynch and Vaizey, *Guinness's brewery,* pp. 78-80.

29 *Provincial Bank annual reports 1839/40, 1840/41; Dict. of Nat. Biog.,* Father Theobald Mathew.

30 C. Woodham Smith, *The great hunger,* gives the most vivid account of the famine.

31 Above, p. 54; W. N. Hancock, 'On the variation of the supply of silver coin in Ireland', in *B. Mag.,* vii, 340-8.

which life depended. In the fullest sense this was true only of the people, labourers or small farmers, at the bottom of the economic ladder, but that was where much of the Irish population was to be found in the 1840s and it was this section that was virtually wiped out by the famine.

The limitations of the monetary exchange economy were what turned the potato failure from distress to disaster. Official relief, designed for an English type economy, was aimed at stimulating the flow of normal trade, but normal trade was export-oriented, to provide farmers with cash for rent. Internal trade in food, particularly in imported food, was limited by the lack of money among so many potential consumers. They relied for food on the potatoes they grew, and when those potatoes failed they starved. It was then too late to develop the channels of trade to supply an alternative diet.[32]

The ability of the banks to remedy this money shortage was strictly limited. The exchange system tied the value of the currency to that of England on lines that later developed into the sterling exchange standard.[33] The effect was that the external account was balanced by movements of capital rather than by changes in the rate of exchange. Ireland was in the anomalous position of earning a current surplus while suffering from internal deflation, and this left little scope for benefit from a different exchange rate. A higher rate would have absorbed the surplus but aggravated the deflation whereas a lower rate would have increased the surplus and so required greater capital exports to balance it. Under a single political authority and an increasingly unified fiscal regime the conditions for a different exchange rate were lacking, but even had they existed it is hard to see how it could have helped. Equally there was little scope for variations in interest rates. The free flow of money through the banking system kept rates in Ireland closely in line with those in London.[34]

The fact that capital was exported rather than imported must be attributed to the owners of the money rather than to the banks. Economic pressures placed a large share of the national income in the hands of the rich who lacked the will or the understanding to invest it in Ireland. As Kane put it, when money was made in Ireland it was used to buy stock or land which yielded a small return but 'one with the advantage of not requiring intense exertion or intelligence

32 T. P. O'Neill, 'The organisation and administration of relief 1845-52', in R. D. Edwards and T. D. Williams (eds.), *The great famine*, pp. 209-59; Barrow, 'Use of money in mid-nineteenth century Ireland', in *Studies*, lix, no 233 (Spring 1970) 81-8.

33 W. T. Newlyn and D. C. Rowan, *Money and banking in British colonial Africa*, especially pp. 154-63, 188-201, describes the working of this system a century later.

34 *1848 committee* (L), Q.4127-62, evidence of John M'Donnell, governor of the Bank of Ireland.

and free from serious risk'.[35] The theory that a greater share of income for the rich means higher savings and investment was true in Ireland in this period as far as the savings were concerned, but if invested in Ireland at all they tended to be placed for safety not growth.[36]

If Ireland is treated as part of the single economy of the United Kingdom the export of funds to England may be seen as the flow of savings to the centre whence they would flow out again to where opportunity beckoned. It was the tragedy of nineteenth-century Ireland that opportunity did not beckon there with enough vigour or conviction either to retain the savings of her own people or to attract those of others. Why this was so and whether public expenditure could or should have made good the failing of private are questions fundamental to the history of Ireland, political and social as well as economic, but they cannot be fully answered within the limits of a history of banking.

35 Kane, *Industrial resources*, p. 408.
36 J. Lee, 'Capital in the Irish economy', in L. M. Cullen (ed.), *Formation of the Irish economy*, pp. 53-4, describes this as a shortage of risk capital—another way of saying the same thing.

Appendix 1

BANK OF IRELAND CAPITAL

1782 Act—21 & 22 Geo. III, c. 16 (Ir.)
Provided for the raising of the initial capital of £600,000 Irish to be paid either in cash or by the surrender of 4 per cent government debentures. The government expected payment to be entirely in debentures, which were standing at a discount,[1] and so it turned out.[2] The debentures were then cancelled and an annuity of £24,000 (4 per cent of £600,000) was created for payment to the bank in twice-yearly instalments, to be passed on to the members in proportion to their holdings. The effect of this was

(a) from the stockholders' point of view, that they exchanged 4 per cent debentures for the same amount of bank stock on which 4 per cent interest was in effect guaranteed by government;
(b) from the government's point of view, that its liability to the debenture holders was replaced by a similar one to the bank;
(c) from the bank's point of view, that its liability to its members, created by their subscriptions, was balanced by an asset which was in effect, though never so called in the act, a loan to government of £600,000 at 4 per cent.

1791 Act—31 Geo. III, c. 22 (Ir.)
Authorized an increase of capital to £1,000,000, the additional £400,000 to be raised by subscriptions from the stockholders; the limit on borrowing would then be raised to £1,000,000. The new capital was to be left with the bank but it was required to pay the government a sum agreed with the lord lieutenant; the amount was not specified but was in fact £60,000.[3] During the negotiations it was agreed that if the rate at which the government could raise money on debentures in 1795 had risen to $4\frac{1}{4}$ per cent or fallen to $3\frac{3}{4}$ the rate on the capital loan would be altered similarly.[4]

1796 Act—36 Geo. III, c. 1 (Ir.)
Increased the rate of interest on the £600,000 capital loan to $4\frac{1}{4}$ per cent in accordance with the 1791 agreement.

1797 Act—37 Geo. III, c. 50 (Ir.)
Authorized an increase in capital to £1,500,000 by raising a further £500,000 from the stockholders, this to be lent to government and employed to discharge treasury bills held by the bank. Wartime pres-

1 *Parl. Reg. Ire.*, i, 295-7, speech by the chief secretary, William Eden.
2 *Charter of the Bank of Ireland*, preamble.
3 B. of I. Mins., 22 Mar. 1791; *1837 committee*, app. III-1.
4 B. of I. Mins., 8 Feb., 26 Apr. 1791, describe the negotiations; Hall, *Bank of Ireland*, pp. 61-2, has an account which is somewhat inaccurate.

sures, which had just forced the suspension of cash payments, had left the government unable to meet any of its short-term debt to the bank of over £700,000.[5] This was therefore a funding operation to relieve the exchequer. Interest on the new loan was to be 5 per cent with an additional annuity of £3 12s 6d per cent for nineteen years. The rate on the original £600,000 was raised again to 5 per cent, and in the event of dissolution the new £500,000 was to be repaid in the same manner as the £600,000. The borrowing limit was raised again to £1,500,000.

1808 Act—48 Geo. III, c. 103

Authorized a further increase in capital of £1,000,000 to make £2,500,000, with the borrowing limit raised to the same figure. The new £1,000,000 was to be raised from the stockholders at a premium of 25 per cent and the whole £1,250,000 lent to government at 5 per cent. The lengthy correspondence preceding the act shows that the bank, anxious to push the date of its possible demise further into the future, was this time in the weaker position.[6] The government side was formally in charge of John Foster, chancellor of the Irish exchequer, but the letters leave no doubt that the reality of power in financial matters lay with the chancellor of the British exchequer, Spencer Perceval. When in reply to his insistence on more favourable terms the court cited the numerous advantages that the government enjoyed from the bank, Perceval merely reminded them that the nearer they got to 1816 the higher the price that parliament would demand for any further extension of the charter, and they had no choice but to make an offer which he would accept. The final capital arrangement was nevertheless as proposed by the court, and Perceval's suggestion that only the £1,000,000 capital be treated as a loan and the extra £250,000 be 'sunk entirely to the use of government' had been dropped. By a provision inserted over the court's protest the treasury was authorized to repay the £1,250,000 loan at any time on six months' notice, in which case the money had to be invested in government securities for the bank's use. The significance of this became evident in 1822 when the treasury proposed to reduce the rate of interest to 4 per cent and the bank was obliged to agree under threat of having the loan repaid.[7]

1821 Act—1 & 2 Geo. IV, c. 72

Authorized an increase in capital to £3,000,000 by a bonus issue of £500,000 to the stock-holders, with a loan of the same amount to

5 *Commons' Jn. Ire.*, xvii, app., ccxxxvi-ix, reprints the letters between the bank and the treasury, Apr. 1794 to Jan. 1797, which show the treasury repeatedly pressing for short-term advances. B. of I. Mins., 31 Mar. to 27 Apr. 1797, reproduce the letters leading to the act.

6 B. of I. Mins., 21 Apr., 8, 28 May 1808, reproduce the relevant letters; *ibid.*, 16 Sept. 1806, shows that an earlier attempt by the court to open negotiations had been rejected as premature by the government.

7 *Ibid.*, 23 Mar. 1822.

government. The loan was used to discharge treasury bills held by the bank and was to be repaid by the government by 1 January 1838. It brought the total loan to £2,850,000.

1822 Act—3 Geo. IV, c. 26
Reduced to 4 per cent the rate of interest on the loan of £1,250,000 under the 1808 act, required that it be repaid by 1 January 1838 in the same manner as the loan under the 1821 act and repealed the provision giving the treasury an option of earlier repayment.

1837 Act—7 Will. IV & 1 Vic., c. 59
Extended to 1 January 1839 the date by which the government must repay the £500,000 under the 1821 act and the £1,250,000 under the 1822 act.

1838 Act—1 & 2 Vic., c. 81
Extended the above date again to 1 January 1840.

1839 Act—2 & 3 Vic. c. 91
Extended the above date again to 1 January 1841.

1840 Act—3 & 4 Vic., c. 75
Consolidated the annuities due by the government, totalling £125,000 Irish, into one annuity of the equivalent amount of £115,384 12s 4d British, and provided for redemption at the treasury's option on six months' notice by repayment of the capital sum of £2,630,769 4s 8d, the equivalent of £2,850,000 Irish. The treasury was also authorized to reduce the annuity with the bank's consent, which it did in 1841 making it £92,076 18s 5d (or $3\frac{1}{2}$ per cent).[8]

1845 Act—8 & 9 Vic., c. 37
Confirmed the provisions of the 1840 act charging the repayment of the £2,630,769 4s 8d capital loan and the payment of the annuity of £92,076 18s 5d on the consolidated fund. This position continued unaltered until 1965 when, at the bank's request, the entire loan was repaid and the annuity cancelled.

8 *Copies of treasury warrants of 8 July 1841,* H.C. 1841 (20), xiii, 197; *F.J.,* 2 Feb. 1841, governor's speech to court of proprietors.

Appendix 2

THE PRIVATE BANKS IN 1820

An initial difficulty in any study of the private banks is to identify them. Registration was first required by the Stamp Act of 1799, but only for firms wishing to pay a composition fee in lieu of stamps on their notes. Only firms so registered were to be treated as bankers for purposes of law.[1] The Stamp Act of 1803 continued this[2] but it was repealed the next year.[3] An act of 1815 was more clearcut in forbidding the issue of notes by anyone not registered at the Stamp Office in Dublin,[4] but no details of registrations under it seem to have been officially published. *Watson's Almanack* each year gives a list of banks registered in Ireland, which refers to the same year in the case of Dublin banks and to the year before in the case of others. Though not so stated these may refer to registrations under this act. Evidence from surviving notes sometimes shows the almanack entries to have been inaccurate.[5]

A much used source on private banks is a series of articles in the *Journal of the Cork Historical and Archaeological Society*, 1892-5, repeated with additions in the *Journal of the Institute of Bankers in Ireland*, 1900-10. The author was Charles McCarthy Tenison, formerly a bank official in Cork but at the time of writing employed by a bank in Tasmania.[6] He deals more with personal history than business, his sources are seldom stated and he is far from reliable. By his previous name of Collins he wrote *The law and practice of banking in Ireland*, the historical section of which is, and admits to being, of similarly doubtful authority.

On banks in Cork and Limerick much fuller and more reliable information is to be found in *The old private banks and bankers of Munster* (Cork 1959) by Eoin O'Kelly, but the statement in its foreword, by Professor James Busteed, that the thesis on which it is based contains further material on the rest of Munster, is misleading; the thesis, in the library of University College, Cork, is substantially the same as the book. Unfortunately nothing comparable exists for the rest of Ireland, but some information on particular banks is to be found in various articles referred to below.

1 39 Geo. III, c. 5, ss. 51-2 (Ir.).
2 43 Geo. III, c. 21, ss. 125-6.
3 44 Geo. III, c. 68, s. 6; *1804 committee*, app. I, gives details of the small number of agreements made; these were mainly by the Bank of Ireland for whom the right was restored in 1806 (46 Geo. III, c. 35).
4 55 Geo. III, c. 100.
5 There are large collections of notes in the National Museum, the Institute of Bankers, the Institute of Bankers in Ireland, the Ulster Museum, the Cork Public Museum, the Royal Irish Academy and in private hands.
6 *Cork Hist. Soc. Jn.*, xxi, 198; *Inst. of Bankers in Ire. Jn.*, ii, 163.

THE DUBLIN BANKS

LA TOUCHE'S, in Castle Street.[7] Originated as an off-shoot of the poplin manufactory set up in 1693 in High Street by David Digues La Touche, a huguenot who came from Holland with William of Orange and fought at the Boyne. He died in 1745 and was succeeded by his son David who in turn, on his death in 1785, was succeeded by his son, yet another David. This third David, the first governor of the Bank of Ireland, was a member of the Irish Privy Council and is often referred to as the Right Honourable David La Touche. From 1758 the partners seem to have been all members of the family.[8]

La Touche's clientele were principally the landed rich, and with the union many of them moved to London. Despite this, or maybe thanks to the increased business of transferring their money, it was still the leading private bank in Dublin twenty years later. It operated mainly by the clearance of drafts and bills against accounts, and made considerable loans against deposit of stock or on personal bonds with sureties.[9] Up to 1797 it issued notes for £5 and over but ceased when it became impossible to pay them in gold; it continued to issue post bills as low as £3 but they were discontinued about 1820.[10] As a non-issuer it was able to ride out all the financial storms until 1870 when it finally succumbed to joint stock competition and was taken over by the Munster Bank. When the latter failed in 1885 the Munster & Leinster was formed to take over the assets and in consequence now hold sundry account books and records of La Touche's.

NEWCOMEN'S, in Castle Street. Traced its origin to Swift's Bank founded in 1722,[11] which was taken over on the death of its founder in 1745 by the new firm of Thomas Gleadowe & Co.[12] In 1772 Thomas's son William married the heiress of Charles Newcomen of Carrickglass in Longford,[13] and taking both her money and her name the firm became William Gleadowe-Newcomen & Co. By 1800 William was a

---

7 A. M. Fraser, 'David Digues La Touche, banker, and a few of his descendants', in *Dublin Hist. Rec.,* v, no 2, gives a good account of this bank in the eighteenth century. G. L. Barrow, 'Some Dublin private banks', in *Dublin Hist. Rec.,* xxv, no 2, discusses this and other Dublin banks in greater detail than here.

8 *Watson's Almanack* shows repeated changes from 1758 onwards, but always La Touches; the style is sometimes David La Touche & Co., which may include outsiders, but it seems unlikely.

9 Bond register 1750-1868, in Munster & Leinster Bank.

10 *1826 committee* (L), p. 63, evidence of Peter La Touche; the National Museum has a £3 post bill of 1812, the Royal Irish Academy has others of 1814.

11 J. Busteed, 'Irish private banks', in *Cork Hist. Soc. Jn.,* liii, 32.

12 *Watson's Almanack 1746,* p. 61; *1747,* p. 62; Tenison, in *Inst. of Bankers in Ire. Jn.,* v, 282-5.

13 *F.J.,* 4 Feb. 1825, social column, describes this lady's distressing experience of the life of an eighteenth-century heiress; the King Harmon papers (P.R.O.I.) include deeds of purchase and mortgage of Newcomen lands by Sir William.

baronet and an M.P. and voted for the Union—for which he was rewarded with a viscountcy for his wife. Sir Jonah Barrington also rakes up spurious evidence of a cancelled debt to government which he put at £20,000; his grounds for this do not stand up to examination[14] but the 'bribe' is nevertheless commonly cited as a fact. Sir William died in 1807 and his wife in 1817 when their son Thomas succeeded to the title. In 1820 the firm was known as Newcomen & Co., the only partners being the viscount and James Evory, an employee since 1780 who had been taken into partnership in 1806 on a salary of £600 and no share in the profit or loss.

Viscount Newcomen evidently suffered from poor health but his death on 17 January 1825 came as a complete surprise and the bank promptly closed. Rumours that he had shot himself were quickly denied,[15] but the facts subsequently revealed suggest that there may have been more truth in the report than in the denial. Evory at once lodged the bank's cash, £38,500, in the Bank of Ireland. A further £7,000 was due in good debts, but liabilities amounted to £206,500. This left a shortage of £161,000 and the only source from which it could be met was Lord Newcomen's private property, valued at just over £120,000 which his representatives declared to be a serious underestimate.[16]

A creditors' committee found that for some years the bank had done no more than cover its expenses. There were 'considerable defalcations' arising from the cost of educating Lord Newcomen's daughters and meeting his living expenses as a nobleman, and the committee described the whole conduct of his affairs as 'slovenly and wasteful'. He owed the bank a total of £118,000, including £74,000 due from Sir William on his death. His private debts, evidently including this figure, totalled £281,000, against which his property was valued at £279,000 plus £15,000 good debts.[17] Some of the property was sold by court order but by October 1828 no dividend had yet been paid. £154,000 was then on hand with some property still to be realized,[18] so it is possible that the creditors did in the end receive a fair part of what was due to them.

Much sympathy was expressed for Evory whose forty-six years of service to the firm had left him with property worth only £5,603. Though supposedly having no share in the loss any more than in the profit he was legally liable for all the firm's debts. Bankruptcy

14 Sir J. Barrington, *The rise and fall of the Irish nation*, pp. 562-4; the debt in question was one of £5,000 owed in 1786 by Lord Naas, Sir William being concerned solely as executor for one of the sureties.
15 *F.J.*, 18, 19 Jan. 1825.
16 *F.J.*, 24, 25, 27 Jan. 1825.
17 *F.J.*, 5, 7 Feb. 1825.
18 *F.J.*, 9, 11 Oct. 1828.

proceedings were begun against him at once; they were unfinished at his death in 1832 and were still before the courts in 1839.[19]

Newcomen's is mainly remembered today for the elegant bank house designed for it by Thomas Ivory at the gates of Dublin Castle across the street from La Touche's.[20] *Watson's Almanack* shows the bank removed to Mary's Abbey from 1777 to 1788, presumably the period when the new building was under construction. It was purchased in the bankruptcy by the Hibernian Bank who moved into it in 1831 and who extended it between 1856 and 1858.[21] It is now occupied by Dublin Corporation.

FINLAY'S, in Jervis Street. Founded apparently in 1754.[22] According to Tenison it had the mercantile and trading business as distinct from La Touche and Gleadowe whose clientele was aristocratic and professional.[23] From 1799 to 1803 its note issues were considerable,[24] and in 1815 a report on a forgery prosecution stated that Finlay's 'notoriously discounts more for the citizens of Dublin than all the other private banks combined'.[25] In 1819 its notes were still worth forging,[26] but by 1826 they were being withdrawn.[27]

Tenison states that Finlay's collapsed in 1835 but this is an error. In February 1829 it was described at a meeting of Hibernian Bank shareholders as being 'about to discontinue business in a way highly creditable to itself'.[28] Two months later when a national tribute to O'Connell was being collected it was the only Dublin bank omitted from the list of those to whom payments might be made.[29] It was also omitted from the list in an appeal by a Dublin charity, the Stranger's Friend Society, at the end of 1829, having been included in an otherwise identical list at the beginning of the year.[30] *Watson's Almanack* shows it for the last time in 1829 and we may conclude that it closed during that year and paid in full.

BALL'S, in Henry Street. Originally Beresford's founded in 1793 in Beresford Place by John Claudius, son of John Beresford the powerful

19 *Return of banks in Ireland which have become bankrupt since 1825*, H.C. 1845 (334), xxviii, 213; *F.J.*, 26 Jan. 1825, 24 Apr. 1832; *Saunders' Newsletter*, 11 May 1839.
20 M. Craig, *Dublin 1660-1860*, p. 220.
21 *F.J.*, 2 Dec. 1856, 7 Dec. 1858.
22 *Watson's Almanack 1754*, p. 64, shows it for the first time.
23 *Inst. of Bankers in Ire. Jn.*, v, 186-91.
24 *1804 committee*, app. D-H.
25 *F.J.*, 29 Mar. 1815.
26 The National Museum has two forged notes of 1819.
27 *1826 committee (C)*, p. 86, evidence of J. R. Pim; *ibid. (L)*, p. 44, of Newport. See plate 4; this must be among the last notes printed by the firm.
28 *F.J.*, 7 Feb. 1829.
29 *F.J.*, 11 Apr. 1829.
30 *F.J.*, 1 Jan., 29 Dec. 1829.

chief commissioner of revenue.[31] By 1803 it had the largest circulation of any private bank in Ireland.[32] In about 1808 it moved to Henry Street and in 1810 J. C. Beresford withdrew on account of private financial troubles. The three remaining partners, led by Benjamin Ball, obtained £150,000 of help from the Bank of Ireland to tide them over any consequent public alarm, and continued business as Ball's at the same premises in Henry Street.[33]

Ball's agents used to visit the linen markets in the north to discount for traders,[34] and in 1826 Mahony included six of its agencies in towns from Dundalk to Londonderry in his list of banks operating in Ireland before the opening of the Provincial.[35] The same year Benjamin Ball died suddenly on a visit to London but this had no effect on the stability of the bank[36]—a marked contrast to the fate of Newcomen's the year before. His son took his place and business continued under the same name. In 1837, with a circulation of £16,500, it was the only one of the old private banks still issuing notes.[37] It carried on until 1888 when it was taken over by the Northern as its Dublin branch.

SHAW'S, in Foster Place. Formerly Lighton's founded in 1797 by Sir Thomas Lighton, Thomas Needham (both of whom had just withdrawn from Beresford's) and Robert Shaw.[38] The last named was the son of a prosperous flour merchant, also Robert, who had come to Dublin from Kilkenny,[39] and who carried on a large discount business tied in with his trading.[40] The bank opened in his premises in Fleet Street but moved in 1799 to Foster Place. After Lighton's death in 1805 it became known as Shaw's and in 1820 the partners were Shaw (who became a baronet the next year), Needham's son Thomas Richard Needham, and Shaw's brother Ponsonby.[41] Like Ball's it sent agents to the northern linen markets[42] but it is not clear whether it was still doing so by 1820. In 1826 in refutation of Mahony's evidence it

31 *Watson's Almanack 1794*, p. 7, shows it for the first time; the tale of the Dublin populace burning its notes in 1798 to bring ruin on the hated Beresfords seems, alas, to be apocryphal—see *Dublin Hist. Rec.* xxv, No. 2, pp. 44-5.
32 *1804 committee*, app. H.
33 B. of I. Mins., 4, 5 Dec. 1810; *Dublin Ev. Post*, 6 Dec. 1810; *Watson's Almanack 1811*, p. 176; *1812*, p. 155. Tenison deals with both banks (*Inst. of Bankers in Ire. Jn.*, v, 260-1; vi, 12-3) but was unaware of any link between them.
34 *1826 committee (L)*, pp. 12, 27, evidence of Dobbin and Houston.
35 *1826 committee (C)*, pp. 252-3.
36 *F.J.*, 4, 5 Apr. 1826; he collapsed in a box at Drury Lane Theatre.
37 *Drummond report*, app. B 16. See plate 5.
38 B. of I. Mins., 15 Aug. 1797, has letters from both firms explaining the split; see also *Watson's Almanack 1797*, p. 7; *1798*, p. 99.
39 *Burke's Peerage, baronetage and knightage*, p. 2265.
40 Cullen, *Anglo-Irish trade*, pp. 202-3.
41 A. M. Fraser, 'The romance of the house of Lighton', in *Dublin Hist. Rec.*, vii, no 3, 112-9; this relates the tale of how Lighton acquired his fortune as a result of earlier adventures in India.
42 *1826 committee (L)*, pp. 12, 27, evidence of Dobbin and Houston.

issued a denial that it had agents in Ulster or anywhere else.[43] In 1836 the Royal Bank of Ireland was floated to take over Shaw's, and Thomas Richard Needham became its first chairman.[44]

ALEXANDER'S, in Sackville Street. Founded in 1810 by Sir William Alexander, a linen factor from Londonderry.[45] He had been lord mayor of Dublin in 1787,[46] and was first cousin of the earl of Caledon.[47] In 1820 the partners were Sir William and four of his family headed by his eldest son Robert, a director and former governor of the Bank of Ireland.[48] Its connections were largely with the north and its notes were in general circulation in Cavan.[49] In June 1820 it failed with liabilities of £175,000, against which it had assets of only £134,000 plus personal property of the partners valued at £36,000.[50] Much of the latter was sold by auction,[51] but the final outcome is not known. Lord Caledon and other relatives had advanced £25,000 on mortgage just before the closure but waived any right to priority for this debt.[52] The creditors started proceedings under the 1760 act but in September 1820 they resolved to avoid litigation[53]—a sensible decision but frustrating for the historian. A first dividend of 2s 6d in the £ was paid in October 1821,[54] but there is no record of anything more.

BANKS IN THE NORTH

GORDON'S, of Belfast. Founded in 1808 and known as the Belfast Bank. In 1820 the partners were David Gordon, Narcissus Batt and John Holmes Houston. In 1822 Robert Batt joined the firm and in 1824 Gordon withdrew, after which it was known as Batt's. Its notes were payable by its Dublin agent, Solomon Watson, and this was said to increase their circulation.[55] Houston supplied the 1826 committee with annual figures of circulation for 1811-25.[56]

43 *F.J.*, 15 Aug. 1826.
44 Above, p. 131.
45 *Watson's Almanack 1810*, p. 170, shows it for the first time; E. Wakefield, *Ireland statistical and political*, ii, 171, mentions it in 1812.
46 *Calendar of the ancient records of Dublin*, xiv, p. xxxi.
47 *Burke's Peerage*, pp. 52, 412.
48 Hone, in Hall, *Bank of Ireland*, pp. 479-80.
49 *Annual Register 1820*, p. 230; *F.J.*, 20 June 1820. See plates 2 and 3 for a note of 1819 much endorsed.
50 *F.J.*, 13, 28 June 1820, reports of closure and creditors' meeting.
51 *F.J.*, 22 July, 4, 13 Sept. 1820, auction notices.
52 *F.J.*, 13 July 1820, law report, court of chancery.
53 *F.J.*, 20 Sept. 1820, report of creditors' meeting.
54 *F.J.*, 30 Aug. 1821, has the trustees' notice which does not state the amount but *F.J.*, 2 Oct. 1821, reports it to have been 2s 6d.
55 *1826 committee (L)*, p. 25.
56 Above, p. 33, n. 65.

TENNENT'S, of Belfast. Founded in 1809 and known as the Belfast Commercial Bank. In 1827 it amalgamated with Batt's and promoted the Belfast Banking Company to take over the combined business.[57]

MONTGOMERY'S, of Belfast. Founded in 1809 and known as the Northern Bank. In 1824 the Northern Banking Company was promoted by the partners to take it over.[58]

MALCOLMSON'S, of Lurgan. Founded in or before 1804 by Joseph Malcolmson and three others.[59] Shortly afterwards it seems to have merged with William Brownlow & Co. of Lisburn to form a new firm in Lurgan with Brownlow as the first partner and Malcolmson as the second. This continued to 1815 when Brownlow died and Malcolmson became senior partner.[60] A local directory shows Malcolmson's as the only bank in Lurgan in 1819.[61] Its notes were payable by its Dublin agent, originally Jonas Stott in Dominick Street, then Willcocks & John Phelps in Capel Street.[62] The bank seems to have come to an end in 1820 but it is not clear how.

BANKS IN THE SOUTH

PIKE'S, of Cork. Founded by the descendants of a Cromwellian corporal who came to Ireland in 1648, turned quaker after the wars and settled as a merchant in Cork. The family was linked by marriage and partnership with the Hoares who founded a bank in Cork in 1680 which was almost certainly the first in Ireland. It was apparently wound up in 1740 and Pike's was opened, possibly in the same house, in 1770-1. The partners had always been members of the family, and since 1801 there had been only one, Joseph Pike.[63] The bank survived a politically inspired run in 1812 and the crisis of 1820 and only closed on Joseph's death in 1826.[64] Its gold stocks were then transferred to the newly opened Bank of Ireland agency which paid off all its liabilities.[65]

LESLIES', of Cork. Formerly Roberts' founded in or before 1789.[66] The last Roberts, Sir Walter, retired in 1819 leaving the brothers Charles

57 Above, p. 81.
58 Above, p. 66.
59 A note of this firm of 1804 is in the collection of Mr F. E. Dixon in Dublin.
60 *Watson's Almanack 1805*, p. 112; *ibid. 1806*, p. 118; *ibid. 1816*, p. 246.
61 T. Bradshaw, *General directory of Newry, Armagh et. al. for 1820*. Hall, *Bank of Ireland*, p. 126, shows both Brownlow's and Malcolmson's in Lurgan in 1820, but this cannot be right.
62 The National Museum has a forged note of 1805 payable by Stott; *Watson's Almanack 1807*, p. 123, shows the change to Willcocks & Phelps.
63 *Watson's Almanack 1776-1820, passim*.
64 O'Kelly, *Munster banks*, pp. 38-44.
65 *1826 committee (C)*, pp. 264-5, evidence of John Cotter.
66 O'Kelly, *op. cit.*, pp. 61-79; *Watson's Almanack 1790*, p. 7, shows it for the first time.

Henry and John Leslie as the two partners. It suspended payments during the 1820 crisis. Investigation by a creditors' committee produced a rather shaky balance sheet but with the backing of local guarantors led by the earl of Shannon, brother-in-law of John Leslie's wife, a loan of £80,000 was obtained from government and the bank reopened in 1822.[67] But it never regained public confidence and when Pike's closed in 1826 it did so too. Fifty thousand pounds still owing on the loan took priority over other debts, which left little for the other creditors. There was some resentment at the failure of the guarantors to repay the loan and then claim rateably with the rest, but only Lord Shannon offered to. A dividend of 10s in the £ was forecast in 1827[68] but it is not known what was finally paid. Estates belonging to the partners were sold in 1828,[69] and the case was still proceeding in 1831.[70]

ROCHES', of Cork. Founded in 1800 by the brothers Stephen and James Roche of a wealthy catholic family of produce merchants from Limerick. Two other brothers founded Roches' Limerick bank the next year but there was no formal link between the firms. To comply with the 1756 act the brothers had first to sever their connection with the family business. The Cork bank did well in the wartime produce boom but the post-war fall in prices, and consequently in the value of land on which it had made mortgage loans, brought on difficulties from which it never fully recovered.[71] It was finally forced to close on 25 May 1820 and this was what precipitated the 1820 crisis. Its liabilities were £258,000, its good assets only £105,000. The bankruptcy proceedings were marked by unusual expressions of esteem and sympathy for the partners but produced only 4s in the £ for the creditors. James Roche subsequently became commercial and parliamentary agent in London for Cork, Youghal and Limerick, a position he held when he appeared before the 1823 and 1826 committees. He ended his life as a local director of the National Bank.[72]

NEWENHAM'S, of Cork. First registered in 1799.[73] It seems to have closed in 1816, reopened late in 1820 and closed again in 1823 or 1824 when it paid in full.[74] It was of little importance.

MAUNSELL'S, of Limerick. Founded in 1789 and known as the Bank of Limerick, the only bank of which there is any record there before

67 Above, pp. 22-3; B. of I. Mins., 2 Jan 1822, records payment of the loan.
68 *Limerick Chronicle*, 29 Aug. 1827.
69 *Cork Mercantile Chronicle*, 2 Jan. 1828, *et seq.*
70 *Limerick Chronicle*, 2 July 1831.
71 *1826 committee (L)*, p. 52, evidence of James Roche.
72 O'Kelly, *Munster banks*, pp. 84-94, quoting from *Limerick Chronicle*, 31 May-25 Nov. 1820, 25 Oct. 1826.
73 *1804 committee*, app. K.
74 O'Kelly, *op. cit.*, pp. 80-2; *Watson's Almanack* includes it 1800-16. omits it 1817-20 and includes it again 1821-5.

H

1800. When news of the Cork suspensions reached Limerick on 27 May 1820 it closed its doors with liabilities of £265,000 and good assets of only £194,000. In addition the partners had unsettled property worth £20,000 and life interests of £2,200 per annum. After a stormy meeting the creditors appointed trustees under the 1760 act to liquidate the firm. They accepted payment of debts due to the bank 'one sixth in Bank of Ireland notes and the remainder in engagements of the bank at 15s in the £',[75] but it is not known how much was finally paid. In 1827 the premises were leased to the Bank of Ireland for a short time for its Limerick agency.[76]

ROCHE'S, of Limerick. Founded in 1801 by Thomas and William Roche. It enjoyed a quick success, thanks doubtless to the family's commercial standing. When Maunsell's closed in 1820 the Roches arranged for publication of a notice of confidence in their own bank signed by sixty-one merchants and others, followed a few days later by another signed by thirty-six landed proprietors of the district—a common practice when a private bank was in danger. A run on Roches' duly occurred but it not only survived but was able to relieve pressure on others by accepting a proportion of their paper in payment of bills due, a courageous acknowledgement of the interdependence of the banking system. With the passing of the crisis the bank reduced its activities and finally closed in 1825 when its premises and business were taken over by the Provincial of which the two Roches became local directors.[77]

BRUCE'S, of Limerick and Charleville. Successor to Evans's founded in Charleville, twenty-four miles south of Limerick, in 1803 and in Limerick itself in 1808. The links between the firms are a little obscure,[78] but by 1820 the partners were George Evans Bruce and his two nephews (or possibly his brother and nephew). Business seems to have been small in Limerick, somewhat larger in Charleville. After Maunsell's closure in May both branches closed but with the sale of some property all debts seem to have been paid in full. O'Kelly's account shows Bruce as a dissolute and rapacious character[79] but this is hard to reconcile with this satisfactory liquidation. Pending the

75 O'Kelly, *op. cit.*, pp. 98-107, quoting from *Limerick Chronicle*, 27 May 1820-7 Mar. 1821.
76 B. of I. Mins., 3 Apr. 1827, 5 Feb. 1828.
77 O'Kelly, *Munster banks*, pp. 120-5; *1837 committee*, Q.4340, evidence of Marshall; *F.J.*, 19 Aug. 1825.
78 *1804 committee*, app. K, shows Evans, Bruce & Roberts in Charleville registered in 1803; *Watson's Almanack* includes it there 1804-16, and Evans & Co. in Limerick 1809-17, after which it disappears and Bruce's is shown in Limerick but not in Charleville. The National Museum has a note issued by Bruce's in Charleville in 1806.
79 O'Kelly, *op. cit.*, pp. 114-8.

realization of its securities the Charleville branch obtained some bridging help from the Bank of Ireland.[80]

DELACOUR'S, of Mallow. First registered in 1801. There were two partners in 1820, Robert Delacour and Richard T. Cuthbert, but the latter retired in 1823. Delacour was sole partner for the rest of the bank's life.[81] It continued paying promptly during the crisis—for which the populace demonstrated their thanks by hauling Delacour's carriage through the streets.[82] Several witnesses in 1826 mentioned it as one of the two private banks still issuing in the south—the other was Redmond's of Wexford—but it could not survive the rise of the joint stock banks. In 1835, the last private bank outside Dublin, it went into liquidation and Robert Delacour was bankrupted.[83] The same year the Provincial opened in Mallow. By 1841 15s in the £ had been paid and total property distributed was reported to be £46,000.[84] The case was still uncompleted in 1845.[85]

SCULLY'S, of Tipperary. Founded in 1803 by James Scully who died in 1816, after which the partners were his two sons Denis and James junior.[86] During the 1820 crisis it continued 'to transact business upon its usual limited but secure scale without the interruption of an instant'.[87] What happened to it after this demonstration of stability is not clear but it may have closed in 1827.[88] In 1838 its assets seem to have been taken over by the Tipperary Bank of which James Scully was a founding director.[89]

RIALL'S, of Clonmel. Traced its origin to Phineas Riall who made loans to Clonmel town council early in the eighteenth century, but it does not seem to have been established as a bank until 1754.[90] The partners were always Rialls—since 1800 William, Charles and Arthur. After the 1820 failures in Cork and Limerick James La Touche noted in his diary that the stability of Riall's 'seemed to tranquillize the public mind and to guard Dublin from the evil'[91]—but this did not

80 Above, p. 19.
81 *Watson's Almanack 1820-34, passim.*
82 *F.J.*, 5 June 1820; *Leinster Journal,* 14 June 1820.
83 *Return of all banks in Ireland which have become bankrupt since 1825,* H.C. 1845 (334), xxviii, 213; *F.J.*, 17 June 1836, bankruptcy notice.
84 *Dublin Ev. Post,* 29 May 1841; *F.J.*, 6 June 1841.
85 *Limerick Chronicle,* 24 May, 10 Sept. 1845.
86 *1804 committee,* app. K; *Watson's Almanack 1817,* p. 235.
87 *F.J.*, 16 June 1820.
88 Tenison, in *Inst. of Bankers in Ire. Jn.,* xii, 10-1.
89 Above, p. 161.
90 W. P. Burke, *History of Clonmel,* pp. 188-90; Tenison, in *Inst. of Bankers in Ire. Jn.,* vi, 170-2. *Saunders' Newsletter,* 12 June 1820, refers to it as then 98 years in being, but this may relate to the earlier activities of Phineas. *Watson's Almanack 1771,* p. 67, includes it for the first time.
91 Urwicke, *James D. La Touche,* p. 265.

last long. On 7 June Newport's failed in Waterford and Riall's, linked to it by marriage as well as business, closed the next day. Good assets just exceeded liabilities but after a few months delay the firm went into liquidation. With the help of a loan of £33,000 from government all creditors were paid in full and after the sale of some family estates the loan was repaid.[92] In 1825 when the Provincial opened in Clonmel it was in Riall's premises.

(WATSON'S, of Clonmel. Founded in 1800 and had a note issue similar to Riall's from then to 1803.[93] It is sometimes said to have survived till 1820,[94] but this is an error. It closed about 1809.[95])

SAUSSE'S, of Carrick-on-Suir. Founded in 1804 by Richard Sausse, brother-in-law of James Scully of Tipperary.[96] In 1820 it paid promptly at first but when liquid resources grew strained it adopted the device of paying 10s on each £1 and endorsing the note to be re-presented a week later for the other 10s.[97] It may have closed for a short time and reopened.[98] It finally went into liquidation in 1823 or 1824[99] having obtained a loan of £20,000 from government. With this help the creditors were all paid but by 1838 half the loan was still outstanding. It was probably repaid in the end from the sale of estates.[100]

NEWPORT'S, of Waterford. Founded some time before 1760 by Simon Newport of a family of Walloon weavers who had been settled in Carrick by the duke of Ormonde in 1760. His wife was a daughter of William Riall of Clonmel, and Sir John Newport, the prominent Whig politician, was their eldest son. He left the firm in 1803 on entering politics, and at the beginning of 1820 the senior partner was his younger brother William, with a cousin Samuel and his own son John. The bank seems to have stood up well to the news of the failures in Cork and Limerick but on 7 June William Newport died suddenly and it closed. With liabilities of £224,000 against assets of only £218,000 its affairs were administered in bankruptcy.[101] A first dividend of 6s 8d

92 Above, p. 23.
93 *1804 committee*, app. K, E-H.
94 Tenison, in *Inst. of Bankers in Ire. Jn.*, vi, 172; Hall, *Bank of Ireland*, p. 126.
95 Burke, *Clonmel*, p. 188, puts its failure in about 1809; *Watson's Almanack* shows it for the last time in 1811.
96 Tenison, in *Inst. of Bankers in Ire. Jn.*, vi, 167-8; *Watson's Almanack* shows it for the first time in 1805, then every year to 1825. The name is sometimes spelt Sause or Sauce.
97 *F.J.*, 17 June 1820.
98 *1826 committee (C)*, p. 73, evidence of Henry Hunt of Waterford; *Saunders' Newsletter*, 14 June 1820, denies reports that it had closed, but on 20 June states that it is about to.
99 *Watson's Almanack 1825* shows it for the last time, registered in 1824.
100 Above, p. 23.
101 W. P. Burke, 'Newport's bank', in *Cork Hist. Soc. Jn.*, iv (1898), 278-86; this gives Newport's death as suicide, which may be true, but there is no other evidence for it.

in the £ was paid in Samuel Newport's bankruptcy in January 1821, and by 1844 a total of 12s had been paid in John Newport's,[102] but the final result is not known.

(HAYDEN & RIVERS, of Waterford. Founded in about 1776 and the only bank in Waterford before 1797. It is sometimes said to have lasted till 1820,[103] but a letter from Rivers's heir in 1856 gives circumstantial details of its failure in 1793.[104])

SCOTT'S, of Waterford. A small firm, properly Scott, Ivie and Scott, founded in 1816 by Thomas Scott who had formerly been a partner in Newport's.[105] It remained open during the crisis of 1820 and a report after Newport's closure stated that trade would suffer little inconvenience since Scott's was continuing to discount all approved bills on Dublin and London with Bank of Ireland notes.[106] After the crisis a branch was opened in Clonmel.[107] In October 1824 the Bank of Ireland agreed to open an account for Scott's—an unusual concession for a private bank—on condition that it discontinue the issue of its own notes. The next year Thomas Scott and his two sons were jointly appointed as agents for the Bank of Ireland in Waterford and Clonmel. The private bank was wound up.[108]

REDMOND'S, of Wexford. Founded about 1770 by a prominent County Wexford family.[109] Another Redmond had a bank in Enniscorthy in 1803[110] but it did not exist by 1820. Redmond's met the pressure in May-June by paying off the bulk of its notes after which the alarm subsided; it never closed.[111] Shortly after the crisis, on 16 June, it received a loan of £11,900 from the Bank of Ireland;[112] this may be what enabled it to resume issues. By 1826 it and Delacour's were the only two private banks still issuing in the south. In February 1829 when the Bank of Ireland opened in Wexford John E. Redmond, the

102 *F.J.*, 18 Jan. 1821, 11 Dec. 1844.
103 e.g., Hall, *Bank of Ireland,* p. 126; this mistake derives from an incoherent Hayden family memoir written years later and quoted by Tenison in *Inst. of Bankers in Ire. Jn.,* xi, 13.
104 *F.J.*, 16 Oct. 1856; *Watson's Almanack 1797* shows it for the last time.
105 Tenison, in *Inst. of Bankers in Ire. Jn.,* xii, 14, 18; Burke, in *Cork Hist. Soc. Jn.,* iv, 280; *Watson's Almanack 1818,* p. 238, shows it registered for the first time in 1817; Scott appears as a partner in Newport's 1811-6; he was joint proprietor of the *Waterford Mirror*—as stated in its typehead.
106 *Saunders' Newsletter,* 20 June 1820, quoting from *Waterford Chronicle.*
107 Henry Scott, *Letter (1840),* in R.I.A., Haliday 1762.
108 B. of I. Mins., 5 Oct. 1824, 15 Apr. 1825.
109 Tenison, in *Inst. of Bankers in Ire. Jn.,* xii, 118; *1804 committee,* app. K, shows it registered in 1799; *Watson's Almanack* does not include it until 1801, but for a provincial bank this is not significant.
110 *Watson's Almanack 1804,* p. 99; it does not appear again.
111 *F.J.*, 13 June 1820.
112 Above, pp. 19-20.

senior partner, was appointed agent jointly with his elder brother Patrick (not a member of the firm).[113] The bank was wound up and its premises and much of its business taken over. Tenison dates the firm's voluntary liquidation as 1834, which may be when it was completed.

LOUGHNAN'S, of Kilkenny. A small bank first registered in 1800 whose sole proprietor in 1820 was James Loughnan.[114] On 3 June it succumbed to the crisis and closed, but efficient publicity by the creditors' committee averted any panic. The local paper attributed the closure to a deficiency of small Bank of Ireland notes, but as the firm's liabilities proved to be £63,000 against assets of only £25,600 this was obviously not the primary cause.[115] The only dividend seems to have been 7s 6d in the £ paid in 1822; by 1834 some creditors had still not collected it. The case was still before the courts in 1842.[116]

(WILLIAMS & FINN, of Kilkenny. Founded in 1800 with a branch in Dublin for a short time, and sometimes wrongly described as failed in 1820.[117] The *Leinster Journal* from 1818 onwards has no reference to it and mentions only Loughnan's in its account of the 1820 crisis in Kilkenny (where it was published). The most likely date for its failure seems to be 1805.[118] By 1816 bankruptcy proceedings were well under way.[119] Sir John Newport in 1826 cited Williams & Finn as an example of an irresponsibly managed private bank, having an issue of £200,000 to £300,000 though 'it was perfectly known afterwards that the partners had never possessed of £1,000'[120]—an oft-quoted comment but with no more authority than the popular hearsay on which it was based. He made no reference to the date of failure.)

113 B. of I. Mins., 24 Feb. 1829.
114 *1804 committee*, app. K; *Watson's Almanack 1820*, p. 210; Barrow, 'Kilkenny private banks', in *Old Kilkenny Review*, xxiii (1971), 36-40.
115 *Leinster Journ.*, 7, 17 June 1820; *F.J.*, 17 June 1820, quoting from *Kilkenny Moderator*, 13 June.
116 *F.J.*, 8 Mar. 1822, 15 May 1834, 20 July 1835, 5 July 1842.
117 Tenison, in *Inst. of Bankers in Ire. Jn.*, xi, 108-9.
118 *Watson's Almanack 1805*, p. 112, shows it for the last time. The National Museum has three notes issued in Dublin that year; there are others elsewhere but all of the same year.
119 *F.J.*, 9 Dec. 1816, advertisement for the sale of debts due to Williams & Finn, bankrupts.
120 *1826 committee (L)*, p. 47.

Appendix 3

BANK BRANCH OPENING DATES

Town populations are shown to the nearest thousand by the 1841 census. All towns of over 5,000 are included; those under 5,000 only if they had a bank.

Towns of over 10,000 are given in order of population, the rest in alphabetical order in two groups, over and under 5,000. Towns within 50 Irish miles (65 statute miles) of Dublin are marked*. Dates refer to the opening of full or sub-branches, not to agencies, except in the Bank of Ireland, whose agencies were really branches. Where two dates are shown the second is the date of closure. The branches of the Agricultural and Commercial Bank had all closed by 1840, but dates are not known.

Town	Co.	Pop.	Bank of I	Prov Bk	Natl Bk	Hibn Bk	Royl Bk	Nthn Bk	Belf Bk	Ulst Bk	Lond & Dub	Tipp Bk	Ag & Comm
Dublin*	Dub	233,000	1783	1845	1845	1825	1836				1843		
Cork	Crk	81,000	1825	1825	1835								1835
Belfast	Ant	75,000	1825	1826				1825	1827	1836			1836
Limerick	Lim	48,000	1827	1825	1835								1835
Waterford	Wat	23,000	1825	1826	1835								1836
Kilkenny	Klk	19,000	1835	1827	1836								1835
Galway	Gal	17,000	1830	1826	1836								1835
Drogheda*	Lth	16,000	1834			1843							
Londonderry	Lry	15,000	1825	1825	1825			1835	1833	1840			1836
Clonmel	Tip	13,000	1825	1825	1835							1842	
Sligo	Sli	12,000	1828	1826	1836								1835
Newry*	Dwn	12,000	1825						1845				

Town	Co.	Pop.	Bank of I Bk	Prov Bk	Natl Bk	Hibn Bk	Royl Bk	Nthn Bk	Belf Bk	Ulst Bk	Lond & Dub	Tipp Ag & Bk Comm
Tralee	Ker	11,000	1835	1828	1835							1836
Wexford	Wex	11,000	1829	1826	1836							
Carrick-on-Suir	Tip	11,000		1835	1835						1841	
Dundalk*	Lth	11,000	1836								1843	
Carlow*	Car	10,000	1834									1845
Armagh	Arm	10,000	1827	1827				1836	1835	1836		1836
Athlone	Wth	6,000		1827	1836							1835
Ballina	May	7,000		1828	1837							1834
Bandon	Crk	9,000		1834				1835	1834			1836
Ballymena	Ant	5,000		1833					1834	1838		
Cashel	Tip	7,000			1836							
Castlebar	May	5,000			1836-7							1835
Coleraine	Lry	6,000		1827				1835	1828			1836
Cove	Crk	5,000										
Dungarvan	Wat	9,000		1835	1835							1834
Ennis	Cla	9,000		1835	1836							1835
Enniscorthy	Wex	7,000		1841	1835							1836
Enniskillen	Fer	6,000		1831						1836		
Fermoy	Crk	6,000		1844	1835							1835
Killarney	Kry	7,000			1845							1835
Kilrush	Cla	5,000		1838	1835							1835
Kingstown*	Dub	7,000									1845	
Kinsale	Crk	7,000										
Lisburn	Ant	6,000						1835				
Loughrea	Gal	5,000			1836							
Mallow	Crk	7,000		1835	1845							1835

Town	Co.	Pop.	Bank of 1	Prov Bk	Natl Bk	Hibn Bk	Royl Bk	Nthn Bk	Belf Bk	Ulst Bk	Lond & Dub	Tipp Bk	Ag & Comm
Navan*	Mth	6,000											
Nenagh	Tip	9,000			1836							1839	1834
New Ross	Wex	7,000	1840		1835								1835
Newtownards	Dwn	8,000							1836				
Parsonstown	Kgs	6,000		1833							1843		1836
Roscrea	Tip	5,000			1835							1842	1835
Strabane	Tyr	5,000		1835					1835				1835
Thurles	Tip	8,000			1835							1840	1836
Tipperary	Tip	7,000			1835							1838	1835
Tuam	Gal	6,000			1836								1835
Tullamore*	Kgs	6,000	1836										
Youghal	Crk	9,900	1834	1831									
Antrim	Ant	3,000								1836			
Athy*	Kld	5,000											
Ballinasloe	Gal	5,000	1836		1836						1845	1845	1836
Ballymoney	Ant	2,000							1834	1836			
Ballyshannon	Don	4,000		1835	1839				1836				
Banagher	Kgs	3,000											
Banbridge	Dwn	3,000		1833	1836					1837			
Boyle	Ros	3,000											1836
Carrickfergus	Ant	4,000						1836					
Carrickmacross*	Mon	2,000									1844		
C-on-Shannon	Lei	2,000									1843		
Castlerea	Ros	1,000			1836								
Cavan	Cav	4,000		1834									1836

Town	Co.	Pop.	Bank of I Bk	Prov Bk	Natl Bk	Hibn Bk	Royl Bk	Nthn Bk	Belf Bk	Ulst Bk	Lond & Dub	Tipp Bk	Ag & Comm
Charleville	Crk	4,000			1835								
Clonakilty	Crk	4,000			1844								
Clones	Mon	3,000						1840					1836
Comber	Dwn	2,000							1835	1836–7			
Cookstown	Tyr	3,000								1841			
Cootehill	Cav	2,000		1837						1837			
Dingle	Kry	3,000											1836
Downpatrick	Dwn	5,000		1834				1835	1835	1836			
Dungannon	Tyr	4,000		1834									1836
Kanturk	Crk	4,000			1839								1835
Kells*	Mth	4,000									1843		
Larne	Ant	3,000							1836				
Letterkenny	Don	2,000						1835	1835				
Limavady	Lry	3,000							1835				
Longford	Lng	5,000	1834		1836			1835		1836			1835
Lurgan	Arm	5,000		1834				1835	1835				1836
Magherafelt	Lry	2,000			1845								
Midleton	Crk	4,000			1835								
Mitchelstown	Crk	4,000			1836								
Moate	Wth	2,000											
Monaghan	Mon	4,000		1832					1835	1840			
Moneymore	Lry	1,000		1835-43									
Mountmellick*	Qus	5,000	1836										
Mullingar*	Wth	5,000									1843		
Omagh	Tyr	3,000		1834						1845			1836
Portadown	Dwn	3,000							1835	1836			
Rathkeale	Lim	4,000			1845								

Town	Co.	Pop.	Bank of I	Prov Bk	Natl Bk	Hibn Bk	Royl Bk	Nthn Bk	Belf Bk	Ulst Bk	Lond & Dub	Tipp Bk	Ag & Comm
Roscommon	Ros	3,000			1836								1836
Skibbereen	Crk	5,000		1839	1844								1835
Strokestown	Ros	2,000											1835
Tallow	Wat	3,000			1836								
Tanderagee	Arm	2,000							1835	1836-44			
Thomastown	Klk	2,000										1841	1835
Westport	May	4,000	1825		1837								
Wicklow*	Wic	3,000									1843		

Sources:

Bank of Ireland: Hall, *Bank of Ireland*, app. L.
Provincial Bank: Annual reports, summarized in Dillon, *Banking in Ireland*, p. 53.
National Bank: Annual reports, bank records, notices in *F.J.*
Hibernian Bank: Annual reports in *F.J.*
Royal Bank: Minute book of shareholders' meetings.
Northern Bank: *Northern Banking Company centenary volume*, p. 249.
Belfast Bank: Bank records.
Ulster Bank: *Decades*, pp. 22-39, 47-50.
London & Dublin Bank: Annual reports in *B. Mag.*; notices in *F.J.*
Tipperary Bank: B. of I. Mins.; *1841 committee*, Q.2681; notices in *Limerick Chronicle* and *Tipperary Vindicator*.

Agricultural Bank: *Drummond report*, app. B16; notices in *F.J.*

Appendix 4

BANK BRANCHES OPEN AT THE END OF EACH YEAR
(including head offices)

Year	Bank of I	Prov Bk	Natl Bk	Hibn Bk	Royl Bk	Nthn Bk	Belf Bk	Ulst Bk	Lond & Dub	Tipp Bk	Total	Ag & Comm
1824	1										1	
1825	8	4		1		1					14	
1826	8	9		1		1					19	
1827	10	13		1		1	1				26	
1828	11	15		1		1	2				30	
1829	12	15		1		1	2				31	
1830	13	15		1		1	2				32	
1831	13	17		1		1	2				34	
1832	13	18		1		1	2				35	
1833	13	21		1		1	3				39	
1834	17	27		1		1	5				51	3
1835	19	33	16	1		9	15				93	25
1836	23	33	34	1	1	11	17	11			131	44 (Oct.)
1837	23	34	35	1	1	11	17	11		1	133	20 (?)
1838	23	35	35	1	1	11	17	12		2	136	20 (?)
1839	23	36	37	1	1	11	17	12		3	140	20 (?)
1840	24	36	37	1	1	12	17	14		5	145	
1841	24	37	37	1	1	12	17	15		7	149	
1842	24	37	37	1	1	12	17	15		7	151	
1843	24	36	37	2	1	12	17	15	7	7	158	
1844	24	37	39	2	1	12	17	14	8	7	161	
1845	24	38	44	2	1	12	18	15	10	9	173	

Sources: as for Appendix 3.

Appendix 5

Map of Ireland showing provincial boundaries and towns with a popluation of 10,000 or more in 1841.

Appendix 6

BANK OF IRELAND ASSETS 1817-45

(Figures all in British currency, converted from Irish for 1817-25)

Year	Public securities	Private securities	Total Securities	Specie	Total assets
1817	4,154,900	1,578,600	5,733,500	1,439,800	7,173,300
1818	4,246,900	1,707,600	5,954,500	1,264,400	7,218,900
1819	3,949,400	1,861,200	5,810,600	1,080,300	6,890,900
1820	4,111,300	1,963,400	6,074,700	1,225,700	7,300,400
1821	5,174,700	944,300	6,119,000	1,524,300	7,643,300
1822	5,132,000	915,600	6,047,600	1,298,600	7,346,200
1823	5,039,800	1,168,600	6,208,400	1,424,800	7,633,200
1824	5,822,900	1,494,300	7,317,200	1,443,000	8,760,200
1825	5,441,300	3,110,750	8,552,050	1,310,400	9,862,450
1826	3,498,600	3,583,600	7,082,200	999,300	8,081,500
1827	4,128,000	3,192,000	7,320,000	916,000	8,236,000
1828	4,045,350	3,859,300	7,904,650	1,137,600	9,042,250
1829	3,284,200	3,507,800	6,792,000	1,772,500	8,564,500
1830	3,913,550	3,449,250	7,362,800	1,178,100	8,540,900
1831	4,001,300	3,107,600	7,108,900	1,177,400	8,286,300
1832	4,471,050	2,812,100	7,283,150	1,152,400	8,435,550
1833	4,604,000	2,860,300	7,464,300	917,500	8,381,800
1834	4,882,350	2,784,900	7,667,250	782,700	8,449,950
1835	4,693,900	2,640,100	7,334,000	711,800	8,045,800
1836	3,902,800	3,016,900	6,919,700	816,800	7,736,500
1837	3,827,100	2,267,050	6,094,150	1,255,150	7,349,300
1838	4,393,850	2,210,850	6,604,700	1,356,400	7,961,100
1839	3,652,450	2,539,400	6,191,850	1,315,650	7,507,500
1840	2,863,750	3,252,050	6,115,800	1,108,250	7,224,050
1841	2,953,450	3,235,850	6,189,300	1,025,950	7,215,250
1842	2,842,250	3,301,000	6,143,250	1,000,350	7,143,600
1843	3,791,700	2,957,250	6,748,950	1,021,600	7,770,550
1844	4,694,200	2,947,950	7,642,150	1,047,150	8,689,300
1845	4,582,400	3,471,000	8,053,400	1,159,950	9,213,350

Sources: 1817-36, *1837 committee*, app. III-2.
1837-9, *1840 committee*, app. 32.
1840, *1841 committee*, app. 17.
1841-5, *1848 committee (C)*, app. 42.

All figures are the average of those for 30 June and 31 Dec. or the nearest dates thereto in each year.

Appendix 7

BANK OF IRELAND DEPOSITS 1817-45

(Figures all in British currency, converted from Irish for 1817-45)

Year	Public deposits	Private deposits	Total deposits	Deposits and sundry balances
1817	712,700	596,900	1,309,600	2,064,000
1818	960,700	565,000	1,525,700	2,041,100
1819	850,900	556,000	1,406,900	2,012,600
1820	609,700	480,400	1,090,100	1,802,400
1821	717,100	694,700	1,411,800	1,673,200
1822	697,000	762,200	1,459,200	1,534,300
1823	765,700	726,800	1,492,500	1,649,500
1824	1,128,500	867,300	1,995,800	2,217,800
1825	1,115,400	930,800	2,046,200	2,669,300
1826	885,300	943,400	1,828,700	2,250,700
1827	1,123,300	1,142,200	2,265,500	2,608,550
1828	1,426,300	1,347,700	2,774,000	3,121,400
1829	1,620,600	1,324,200	2,944,800	3,191,650
1830	1,689,900	1,432,900	3,122,800	3,378,700
1831	1,486,600	1,430,200	2,916,800	3,234,350
1832	1,534,500	1,492,900	3,027,400	3,128,200
1833	1,362,700	1,662,500	3,025,200	3,289,100
1834	1,495,600	1,550,900	3,046,500	3,530,900
1835	1,351,500	1,547,900	2,899,400	3,406,800
1836	1,205,600	1,476,000	2,681,600	3,151,950
1837	1,111,150	2,004,850		3,116,000
1838	1,297,850	2,265,200		3,563,050
1839	1,286,600	1,939,900		3,226,500
1840	1,190,450	1,849,000		3,039,450
1841	1,104,700	1,851,300		2,956,000
1842	1,153,450	1,870,550		3,024,000
1843	1,174,550	2,218,100		3,392,650
1844	1,464,400	2,451,700		3,916,100
1845	1,575,600	2,452,650		4,028,250

Sources:
1817-36, col. 1, *1837 committee*, app. III-20, average aggregate amount of all public monies in the hands of the bank.

col. 2, *ibid.* app. III-21, average aggregate amount of all private deposits in the hands of the bank.

col. 3, the sum of cols. 1 and 2.

col. 4, *ibid.,* app. III-2, average of deposits and sundry balances on 30 June and 31 December.

1837-9, *1840 committee*, app. 32, averages of public deposits (col. 1), private deposits and sundry balances (col. 2) and total deposits and sundry balances (col. 4) on 30 June and 31 December.

1840, *1841 committee*, app. 17, the same.

1841-5, *1848 committee (C)*, app. 42, the same.

223

Appendix 8

BANK OF IRELAND CIRCULATION 1817-36

Annual averages

Year	Large notes	Small notes	Total notes	Post bills	Total
1817	1,729,000	1,052,300	2,781,300	1,271,700	4,053,000
1818	1,788,700	1,058,000	2,846,700	1,244,700	4,091,400
1819	1,695,400	1,116,600	2,812,000	1,154,300	3,966,300
1820	1,555,800	1,221,000	2,776,800	1,138,400	3,915,300
1821	1,713,700	1,461,400	3,175,100	1,608,800	4,783,900
1822	1,781,000	1,289,800	3,070,800	1,657,900	4,728,700
1823	1,687,100	1,277,200	2,964,300	1,716,100	4,680,400
1824	1,789,100	1,339,000	3,128,100	2,022,300	5,150,500
1825	1,817,800	1,548,500	3,366,300	2,457,700	5,824,000
1826	1,502,700	1,644,200	3,146,900	1,758,000	4,905,000
1827	1,460,300	1,491,800	2,952,100	1,411,300	4,363,400
1828	1,540,200	1,668,800	3,209,000	1,375,900	4,585,000
1829	1,615,200	1,459,300	3,074,500	1,362,700	4,437,300
1830	1,541,800	1,385,100	2,926,900	1,147,700	4,074,700
1831	1,488,600	1,399,300	2,887,900	1,025,000	3,913,000
1832	1,534,400	1,519,600	3,054,000	1,028,900	4,083,000
1833	1,600,600	1,472,300	3,072,900	943,400	4,016,400
1834	1,608,400	1,363,300	2,971,700	862,700	3,834,400
1835	1,623,400	1,249,800	2,873,200	763,600	3,636,900
1836	1,708,500	1,087,400	2,795,900	633,200	3,429,200

Source: 1837 committee, app. III-4.

Appendix 9

PROVINCIAL BANK OF IRELAND CIRCULATION 1831-41

Figures are all to the nearest thousand pounds. Percentages show the proportion which Provincial Bank circulation, as in this table, forms of the total circulation of private and joint stock banks in the corresponding month in Appendix 10.

Year	Lady Day (25 March)	Midsummer (24 June)	Michaelmas (29 September)	Christmas (25 December)
1831		640,000	794,000	1,065,000
1832	1,085,000	899,000	995,000	1,218,000
1833	926,000	785,000	947,000 85%	1,126,000 76%
1834	1,123,000 74%	898,000 76%	1,024,000 82%	1,280,000 76%
1835	1,171,000 73%	900,000 68%	946,000 67%	1,050,000 54%
1836	1,008,000 48%	798,000 41%	745,000 36%	752,000 41%
1837	752,000 38%	570,000 37%	701,000 42%	790,000 35%
1838	854,000 35%	691,000 34%	748,000 38%	999,000 34%
1839	1,009,000 37%	798,000 35%	770,000 38%	912,000 34%
1840	922,000 35%	711,000 40%	776,000 36%	866,000 36%
1841	863,000 37%			

Average circulation over whole period	898,000
of which one fifth	180,000
Average gold held	282,000
Average total cash held	383,000

Source: 1841 committee, evidence of Robert Murray, inspector of branches of the Provincial Bank; figures summarized from confidential returns submitted quarterly to the chancellor of the exchequer showing notes in circulation, gold and other notes held on each quarter day.

Appendix 10

NOTE CIRCULATION—ALL IRISH BANKS 1833-45

**September 1833 to June 1841: average circulation during calendar month.
September 1841 to December 1845: average during nearest four weeks.**

		Bank of Ireland	Private and joint stock banks	Total	Bank of Ireland as % of total
1833	September	3,678,950	1,112,155	4,791,105	77
	December	4,024,750	1,489,292	5,514,042	73
1834	March	3,964,020	1,521,952	5,485,972	72
	June	3,704,325	1,184,280	4,888,605	76
	September	3,521,425	1,250,122	4,771,547	74
	December	3,911,825	1,684,038	5,595,863	70
1835	March	3,858,300	1,600,586	5,458,886	71
	June	3,525,425	1,329,633	4,855,058	73
	September	3,265,375	1,405,321	4,670,696	70
	December	3,526,375	1,957,512	5,483,887	64
1836	March	3,513,375	2,090,775	5,604,150	63
	June	3,367,675	1,948,532	5,316,207	63
	September	3,136,750	2,060,958	5,197,708	60
	December	3,572,040	1,813,509	5,385,549	66
1837	March	3,345,750	1,997,905	5,343,655	63
	June	3,160,700	1,540,909	4,701,609	67
	September	2,981,780	1,650,042	4,631,822	64
	December	3,274,060	2,247,541	5,521,601	59
1838	March	3,359,620	2,408,358	5,767,978	58
	June	3,289,040	2,055,041	5,344,081	62
	September	3,054,260	1,953,172	5,007,432	61
	December	3,488,640	2,972,118	6,460,758	54
1839	March	3,531,260	2,758,517	6,289,777	56
	June	3,330,720	2,257,674	5,588,394	60
	September	2,960,725	2,000,016	4,960,741	60
	December	3,215,625	2,686,900	5,902,525	54
1840	March	3,132,500	2,663,925	5,796,425	54
	June	2,985,350	1,790,963	4,776,313	63
	September	2,801,600	2,133,223	4,934,823	57
	December	3,198,175	2,382,124	5,580,299	57

		Bank of Ireland	Private and joint stock banks	Total	Bank of Ireland as % of total
1841	March	3,164,250	2,314,169	5,478,419	58
	June	3,065,050	1,984,751	5,049,801	61
	September	2,877,925	1,929,906	4,807,831	60
	December	3,205,875	2,515,677	5,721,552	56
1842	March	3,074,125	2,259,556	5,333,681	58
	June	2,901,525	1,769,184	4,670,709	62
	September	2,806,025	1,663,012	4,469,037	63
	December	3,112,950	2,099,641	5,212,591	60
1843	March	3,085,400	2,019,740	5,105,140	60
	June	3,105,150	1,734,730	4,839,880	64
	September	2,975,950	1,699,946	4,675,896	64
	December	3,489,650	2,361,189	5,850,839	60
1844	March	3,573,100	2,424,072	5,997,172	60
	June	3,488,300	2,080,277	5,568,577	63
	September	3,359,150	2,052,262	5,411,412	62
	December	3,917,800	3,065,751	6,983,551	56
1845	March	3,946,625	3,105,552	7,052,177	56
	June	3,882,600	2,736,432	6,619,032	59
	September	3,907,025	2,926,265	6,833,290	57
	December	4,351,200	3,053,166	7,404,366	59

Source: 1857 committee, app. 15; figures to June 1841 also appear in *1841 committee*, app. 23.
Bank of Ireland figures include post bills whose use was steadily declining in these years (see Appendix 8); *1875 committee*, app. 12, shows their total as £386,300 in Nov. 1845.

Appendix 11

	Certified circulation	Gold/Silver holdings	Total permitted
Bank of Ireland	3,738,428	1,247,955	4,986,383
Provincial Bank	927,667	502,576	1,430,243
National Bank	852,269	345,221	1,197,490
Ulster Bank	311,079	100,868	411,947
Belfast Bank	281,611	178,090	459,701
Northern Bank	243,440	114,544	357,984
Total	6,354,494	2,489,254	8,843,748

| | Actual circulation | | |
	£5 & over	Under £5	Total
Bank of Ireland	2,351,100	2,000,100	4,351,200
Provincial Bank	346,011	807,713	1,153,725
National Bank	251,911	645,473	897,385
Ulster Bank	28,120	316,559	344,679
Belfast Bank	38,605	342,094	380,699
Northern Bank	24,107	252,570	276,678
Total	3,039,854	4,364,509	7,404,366

Source: Dublin Gaz. 1846, p. 35, return by commissioner of stamps and taxes under the Irish Banking Act (8 & 9 Vic., c. 37); see above, pp. 182–3.

Appendix 12

LIST OF STATUTES CITED

Year	Number	Subject
1703	2 Anne, c. 6 (Ir.)	Penal code
1708	7 Anne, c. 30 (formerly c. 7)	Bank of England monopoly
1709	8 Anne, c. 11 (Ir.)	Bank notes
1731	5 Geo. II, c. 7 (Ir.)	Usury
1756	29 Geo. II, c. 16 (Ir.)	Irish bankers—restrictions
1759	33 Geo. II, c. 4 (Ir.)	Malone's bank
1760	33 Geo. II, c. 14 (Ir.)	Irish bankers—insolvency, etc.
1772	11 & 12 Geo. III, c. 8 (Ir.)	Bankruptcy
1774	13 & 14 Geo. III, c. 35 (Ir.)	Catholic oath
1777	17 Geo. III, c. 30	Small notes (England)
1782	21 & 22 Geo. III, c. 16 (Ir.)	Bank of Ireland—foundatic₆
1782	21 & 22 Geo. IᴵI, c. 46 (Ir.)	Anonymous partnershipꜱ
1787	27 Geo. III, c. 16	Small notes (England)
1791	31 Geo. III, c. 22 (Ir.)	Bank of Ireland—capitaᴵ
1793	33 Geo. III, c. 21 (Ir.)	Catholic relief
1796	36 Geo. III, c. 1 (Ir.)	Bank of Ireland—interesᴛ raᴄᴇ
1797	37 Geo. III, c. 45	Restriction of cash payments (England)
1797	37 Geo. III, c. 50 (Ir.)	Bank of Ireland—capital
1797	37 Geo. III, c. 51 (Ir.)	Restriction of cash payments (Ireland)
1797	37 Geo. III, c. 54 (Ir.)	Management of Irish national debt
1799	39 Geo. III, c. 5 (Ir.)	Stamp duties and bank registration
1799	39 Geo. III, c. 48 (Ir.)	Small notes (Ireland)
1803	43 Geo. III, c. 21	Stamp duties and bank registration
1804	44 Geo. III, c. 68	Stamp duties and bank registration
1804	44 Geo. III, c. 71	Bank of Ireland tokens
1804	44 Geo. III, c. 91	Small notes (Ireland)
1805	45 Geo. III, c. 41	Small notes (Ireland)
1805	45 Geo. III, c. 42	Bank of Ireland tokens
1806	46 Geo. III, c. 35	Bank of Ireland composition fee
1808	48 Geo. III, c. 103	Bank of Ireland—capital, etc.
1812	52 Geo. III, c. 157	Silver tokens prohibition
1814	54 Geo. III, c. 83	Government accounts (Ireland)
1815	55 Geo. III, c. 100	Bank registration and composition
1816	56 Geo. III, c. 96	Bank of England—capital
1816	56 Geo. III, c. 98	Amalgamation of exchequers
1817	57 Geo. III, c. 34	Distress loans
1817	57 Geo. III, c. 48	Deficiency bills
1817	57 Geo. III, c. 79	Stock transfers
1818	58 Geo. III, c. 23	Stock transfers
1818	58 Geo. III, c. 80	Stock transfers
1819	59 Geo. III, c. 23	Cash payments (England)
1819	59 Geo. III, c. 24	Cash payments (Ireland)
1819	59 Geo. III, c. 49	Cash payments (England)
1819	59 Geo. III, c. 99	Cash payments (Ireland)
1820	1 Geo. IV, c. 39	Distress loans
1821	1 & 2 Geo. IV, c. 26	Cash payments (England)
1821	1 & 2 Geo. IV, c. 27	Cash payments (Ireland)

Year	Number	Subject
1821	1 & 2 Geo. IV, c. 72	Bank of Ireland—capital, monopoly, etc.
1821	1 & 2 Geo. IV, c. 73	Stock transfers
1822	3 Geo. IV, c. 17	Stock transfers
1822	3 Geo. IV, c. 22	Distress loans
1822	3 Geo. IV, c. 26	Bank of Ireland—capital loan
1822	3 Geo. IV, c. 56	Irish treasury offices
1822	3 Geo. IV, c. 70	Small notes (England)
1822	3 Geo. IV, c. 118	Distress loans
1823	4 Geo. IV, c. 42	Distress loans
1824	5 Geo. IV, c. 53	Stock transfers
1824	5 Geo. IV, c. 73	Joint stock banking (Ireland)
1824	5 Geo. IV, c. 159, local & personal	Hibernian Joint Stock Company
1825	6 Geo. IV, c. 42	Joint stock banking (Ireland)
1825	6 Geo. IV, c. 79	Assimilation of currencies
1825	6 Geo. IV, c. 98	Bank of Ireland tokens
1826	7 Geo. IV, c. 6	Small notes (England)
1826	7 Geo. IV, c. 46	Joint stock banking (England)
1828	9 Geo. IV, c. 65	Scottish and Irish bank notes in England
1828	9 Geo. IV, c. 80	Stamp duties and licences (Ireland)
1828	9 Geo. IV, c. 81	Payment of bank notes (Ireland)
1829	10 Geo. IV, c. 7	Catholic emancipation
1830	11 Geo. IV & 1 Will. IV, c. 32	Payment of notes in Dublin
1833	3 & 4 Will. IV, c. 83	Circulation returns
1833	3 & 4 Will. IV, c. 98	Bank of England charter
1837	7 Will. IV & 1 Vic., c. 59	Bank of Ireland loans
1838	1 & 2 Vic., c. 56	Irish poor law
1838	1 & 2 Vic., c. 81	Bank of Ireland loans
1838	1 & 2 Vic., c. 96	Actions by bank partners
1839	2 & 3 Vic., c. 91	Bank of Ireland loans
1840	3 & 4 Vic., c. 75	Bank of Ireland loans
1840	3 & 4 Vic., c. 111	Actions by bank partners
1841	4 & 5 Vic., c. 50	Circulation returns
1844	7 & 8 Vic., c. 32	Bank of England charter
1844	7 & 8 Vic., c. 113	Joint stock banking code
1845	8 & 9 Vic., c. 37	Irish banking
1845	8 & 9 Vic., c. 38	Scottish banking
1845	8 & 9 Vic., c. 147, local & personal	Agricultural & Commercial Bank of Ireland—winding up
1846	9 & 10 Vic., c. 75	Joint stock banking code—application to Scotland and Ireland
1857	20 & 21 Vic., c. 49	Joint stock banking code—repeal
1920	10 & 11 Geo. V, c. 24	Repeal of 9 Geo. IV, c. 81

Bibliography

I. MANUSCRIPT MATERIAL

(*a*) DUBLIN

Bank of Ireland
  Charter 1783
  Minute books of court of directors 1783–1860

Dixon, F. E.
  Collection of notes and other paper issued by Irish banks

Hibernian Bank
  Deed of settlement, 11 April 1825
  Minute books of general assembly 1825-59

Institute of Bankers in Ireland
  Collection of notes and other paper issued by Irish banks

Munster & Leinster Bank
  La Touche's Bank, outgoing letter books 1835-9, 1838-61
  La Touche's Bank, bond register 1750-1868
  La Touche's Bank, sundry account books

National Library of Ireland
  Crofton estates, Cos. Cavan and Monaghan—rent accounts
    (MS 8150/6)
  Crofton estates, Co. Cork —rent accounts (MSS 8150/8-9)
  Crofton estates, Co. Wicklow—wage accounts (MS 2065)
  Mahon estates, Co. Roscommon—accounts and papers (MS 10,154)
  Monteagle (Spring Rice) papers (MS 13,388)
  Mount Trenchard estate, Co. Limerick—accounts (MS 515)
  Mullins Mills, Kells, Co. Kilkenny—accounts (MS 5219)
  O'Connell papers (various)
  Paul estates, Waterford—rent accounts (MS 12,982)
  Slator Mills, Edgeworthstown, Co. Longford—accounts (MS
    12,150)
  Townley Hall, Co. Louth—
    Slane Mills accounts (MSS 9525; 9526; 10,273)
    Estate accounts (MSS 9538; 9604; 11,924)
  Robert White papers (MSS 8840-58)

National Museum of Ireland
  Collection of notes and other paper issued by Irish banks

Provincial Bank of Ireland
  Prospectus, 18 August 1824 (printed)
  Deed of settlement, 1 August 1825
  Annual reports 1826-50 (printed)

Public Record Office of Ireland
  Bateman estates, Tralee—rent accounts (1a/37/51)
  McKenzie's brewery, Dungannon—deeds (D.17421, 17427)
  King Harmon estates—accounts and deeds

Royal Bank of Ireland
  Deed of settlement, 1 September 1836
  Minute book of board of directors 1836
  Minute book of shareholders' meetings 1836-45

Royal Irish Academy
Collection of notes and other paper issued by Irish banks

State Papers Office
Chief secretary's office—abstract of outgoing correspondence
Chief secretary's office—registered papers
Irish office—incoming correspondence

Stock exchange
Daily price lists 1820-45

University College
O'Connell papers

(*b*) BELFAST

Belfast Bank
Deed of settlement, 2 July 1827 (printed)

Public Record Office of Northern Ireland
Annesley papers (D 1150/1/16,/17,/19,/20,/37)
Sir George Hill papers (DOD 642)
James Sloane, merchant, Moy—papers (D 1767/1/2)
R. A. L. Taylor, merchant, Coleraine—accounts (D 1435/2)
A. A. Watt, wine merchant, Londonderry—accounts (D 1506/2/1,
/11)

Ulster Bank
Prospectus, undated (printed)
Deed of settlement, 1 April 1836
Minute book of advisory committee 1836-50

Ulster Museum
Collection of notes and other paper issued by Irish banks

(*c*) CORK

Cork Public Museum
Collection of notes and other paper issued by Irish banks

(*d*) GALWAY

Provincial Bank of Ireland
Outgoing letter book 1828-44

(e) KINGSTON-ON-THAMES

Surrey County Record Office
Goulburn Papers

(f) LONDON

British Museum
Peel papers (Add. MSS 40329-455)
Ripon papers (Add. MSS 40862)
Vansittart papers (Add. MSS 31232)

Institute of Bankers
Collection of notes and other paper issued by Irish banks

National Bank
Deed of settlement of National Bank of Ireland, 6 January 1835
Supplementary deeds, 15 February and 6 July 1836
Annual reports 1843-50 (printed)

Public Record Office
Treasury out letters, Ireland (T. 14)
Treasury minutes (T. 29)
Treasury accounts—Ireland (T. 37)

II. PRINTED ORIGINAL SOURCES

a) Statutes

Statutes at large passed in the parliaments held in Ireland 1310-1800
(20 vols. Dublin 1786-1801)
Public general statutes of the parliament of the United Kingdom 1801-69 (74 vols. London 1801-69)
Local and personal statutes of the parliament of the United Kingdom 1801-47 (London 1801-47)

(b) *Parliamentary proceedings*	Abbreviations in footnotes
Journal of the House of Commons	*Commons' Jn.*
Journal of the House of Lords	*Lords' Jn.*
Journal of the Irish House of Commons 1613-1800 (19 vols. Dublin 1796-1800)	*Commons' Jn. Ire.*
Journal of the Irish House of Lords 1634-1800 (8 vols, Dublin 1779-1800)	*Lords' Jn. Ire.*

Irish Parliamentary register 1781-97 (17 vols, Dublin 1782-1801) *Parl. reg. Ire.*

Cobbett's parliamentary debates 1803-20 (41 vols, London 1804–20) *Hansard 1*

Hansard's parliamentary debates, new series, 1820-30 (25 vols, London 1820-30) *Hansard 2*

Hansard's parliamentary debates, third series 1830-46 (88 vols, London 1831-46) *Hansard 3*

(c) *Reports of parliamentary committees and commissions*

Select committee of the House of Commons on the circulating paper, the specie and the current coin of Ireland; and also on the exchange between that part of the United Kingdom and Great Britain 1804, H.C. 1826 (407), v, 461 *1804 committee*

Select committee of the House of Commons to inquire into the high price of gold bullion 1810, H.C. 1810 (349), iii, 1 *1810 committee*

Select committee of the House of Commons on the expediency of the Bank resuming cash payments 1819, H.C. 1819 (202, 282), iii, 1 *1819 committee (C)*

The same of the House of Lords 1819, H.C. 1819 (291), iii, 363 *1819 committee (L)*

Select committee of the House of Commons on the condition of the labouring poor in that part of the United Kingdom called Ireland . . . 1823, H.C. 1823 (561), vi, 331 *1823 committee*

Select committee of the House of Commons to inquire into the state of the circulation of promissory notes under the value of £5 in Scotland and Ireland . . . 1826, H.C. 1826 (402), iii, 257 *1826 committee (C)*

The same of the House of Lords 1826, H.C. 1826-7 (245), vi, 377 *1826 committee (L)*

Select committee of the House of Commons to inquire into the present state of agriculture and persons employed in agriculture in the United Kingdom 1833, H.C. 1833 (612), v, 1 *1833 committee*

Select committee of the House of Commons to inquire into the operation of the act of 7 Geo. IV, c. 46 permitting the establishment of joint stock banks . . . 1836, H.C. 1836 (591), ix, 411 *1836 committee*

Select committee of the House of Commons to inquire into the operation of the acts permitting the establishment of joint stock banks in England and Ireland . . . 1837, H.C. 1837 (531), xiv, 1   *1837 committee*

Select committee of the House of Commons appointed the following session to consider the same subject 1838, H.C. 1837-8 (626), vii, 1   *1838 committee*

Select committee of the House of Commons to inquire into the effects produced on the circulation of the country by the various banking establishments issuing notes payable on demand 1840, H.C. 1840 (602), iv, 1   *1840 committee*

Select committee of secrecy of the House of Commons appointed the following session to consider the same subject, 1841, H.C. 1841 (366, 410), v, 1, 5   *1841 committee*

Select committee of the House of Commons on commercial distress 1848, H.C. 1847-8 (395, 584), viii pts I & II   *1848 committee (C)*

The same of the House of Lords 1848, H.C. 1847-8 (565, 565-II), viii pt III   *1848 committee (L)*

Select committee of the House of Commons to inquire into the operation of the bank act of 1844 (7 & 8 Vict., c. 32) and of the bank acts for Scotland and Ireland of 1845 (8 & 9 Vict., c. 37 & 38) . . . 1857, H.C. 1857 (220-session 2), x pts I & II   *1857 committee*

Select committee of the House of Commons appointed the following session to consider the same subject 1858, H.C. 1857-8 (381), v   *1858 committee*

Select committee of the House of Commons upon the restrictions imposed and the privileges conferred by law on bankers authorised to make and issue notes in England, Scotland and Ireland 1875, H.C. 1875 (351), ix, 1   *1875 committee*

Commission of inquiry into the condition of the poorer classes in Ireland 1835-6, three reports,
  first report H.C. 1835 (369), xxxii pt I, 1
  second report H.C. 1837 (68), xxxi, 587
  third report H.C. 1836 (43), xxx, 1
  appendices H.C. 1835 (369), xxxii pts
  I & II; 1836 (35), xxx, (36), xxxi, (37),
  (38) xxxiii, (39-42), xxxiv   *Poor inquiry*

Commissioners appointed to consider and recommend a general system of railways for Ireland,
    first report 1837, H.C. 1837 (75), xxxiii, 283
    second report 1838, H.C. 1837-8 (145), xxxv, 469   *Drummond Report*
Commission of inquiry into the law and practice in respect of the occupation of land in Ireland 1845, H.C. 1845(605, 606), xix,(616), xx, (657), xxi, (672, 673), xxii   *Devon report*

(*d*) *Other parliamentary papers*

Correspondence with the Bank of Ireland respecting an advance of £500,000, H.C. 1821 (450), xix, 163

Abstract of the population of Ireland according to the late census 1813 and 1821, H.C. 1822 (36), xiv, 737

Account of the total amount of debt due to the Bank of Ireland 3 April 1822, H.C. (210), xviii, 391

Return of coals imported into the different ports of Ireland 1821, H.C. 1822 (48), xviii, 481

Correspondence with the Bank of England on the subject of the charter 1822, H.C. 1822 (316), xxi, 35

Bank of Ireland accounts 1823, H.C. 1823 (323), xvi, 61

Letter . . . respecting a loan to Nowlan Shaw & Co in 1821, H.C. 1823 (414), xvi, 69

List of all advances made by the commissioners under 1 Geo. IV, c. 39 and subsequent acts, H.C. 1823 (415), xvi, 81

Account of the quantity of butter exported from each port of Ireland 1806-23, H.C. 1826 (338), xxiii, 291

Account of the number of country bank notes stamped in Ireland 1825-7, H.C. 1828 (91), xxii, 81

Account of the amount of stock transferred between England and Ireland 1826-30, H.C. 1830-1 (250), v, 353

Return of all banking establishments in Ireland 1826 and 1836, H.C. 1836 (346), xxxvii, 373

Return of the sums advanced for the relief of commercial credit in Ireland, H.C. 1837-8 (723), xlvi, 407

Copies of treasury warrants authorising the reduction of the annuity granted to the Bank of Ireland from 8 July 1841, H.C. 1841 (20), xiii, 197

Account of the amount of stock transferred between England and Ireland 1831-40, H.C. 1841 (361), xiii, 219

Report of the commissioners appointed to take the census of Ireland for the year 1841, H.C. 1843 (504), xxiv, 1

Account of the number of private and joint stock banks registered in Ireland 1820-44, H.C. 1844 (232), xxxii, 445

Return of the number of applications made to the Bank of Ireland for the establishment of a branch, H.C. 1844 (350), xxxii, 265

Return of all banks in Ireland which have become bankrupt since 1825, H.C. 1845 (334), xxviii, 213

Return of the total number of gallons of spirits distilled and charged to duty . . . in England, Scotland and Ireland 1820-45, H.C. 1846 (361), xliv, 427

Return of the amounts of stock transferred between England and Ireland 1837-47, H.C. 1847-8 (196), xxxix, 571

Account of the balances arising from the remittances of public money to and from the British and Irish exchequers 1796-1855, H.C. 1864 (569), xxxiv, 153

Report on certain statistics of banking in Ireland 1859-85 (C. 4681), H.C. 1886, lxxi, 141

Department of Agriculture and Technical Instruction for Ireland, Banking and railway statistics, Ireland, December 1900 (Cd. 342), H.C. 1900, ci, 573

(e) Newspapers and journals

Annual Register (London)
Banker's Magazine (London)
Cork Mercantile Chronicle (Cork)
Dublin Evening Mail (Dublin)
Dublin Evening Post (Dublin)
Dublin Gazette (Dublin)
Freeman's Journal (Dublin)
Leinster Journal (Kilkenny)
Limerick Chronicle (Limerick)
London Gazette (London)
Northern Whig (Belfast)
Saunders' Newsletter (Dublin)
Times (London)
Tipperary Free Press (Clonmel)
Tipperary Vindicator (Nenagh)
Waterford Mirror (Waterford)

(f) Pamphlets

Agricultural & Commerical Bank of Ireland deed of settlement, 1 December 1834 (R.I.A., Haliday 1629)

Agricultural & Commercial Bank of Ireland deed of settlement, 10 August 1836 (R.I.A., Haliday 1681)

Cases, with the opinion of the attorney general of England and others, on the law regulating joint stock banks as exemplified by the facts *in respect of the Agricultural & Commercial Bank of Ireland* (London 1837) (N.L.I., P799)

Extract of a letter to the right honourable the chancellor of the exchequer dated London 28th April 1824 . . . and a copy of a letter dated 20th May 1824. (Northern Bank Ltd, Belfast)

Gordon, Richard, *A review of trade and banking in Ireland and England* (Dublin 1836) (R.I.A., Haliday 1681)

Joplin, Thomas, *An essay on the general principles and present practice of banking in England and Scotland* (Newcastle-upon-Tyne 1822) (R.I.A., Haliday 1224)

Observations on the bill for the regulation of banking partnerships in Ireland. . . . 1825. (Northern Bank Ltd, Belfast)

Origins and principles of the Agricultural & Commercial Bank of Ireland (Dublin 1835) (N.L.I., P799)

Proceedings at the meeting of shareholders of the Agricultural & Commercial Bank of Ireland, 17, 18, April 1837 (Dublin 1837) (R.I.A., Haliday 1685)

Proceedings of special general meeting of the Agricultural & Commercial Bank of Ireland, 12 September 1844 (Dublin 1844) (R.I.A., Haliday 1898)

Scott, Henry, *Letter* (1840) (R.I.A., Haliday 1762)

Statement by the directors of the Bank of Ireland and observations in answering thereto (undated, 1825?) (Northern Bank Ltd, Belfast)

(g) *Other contemporary sources*

Dutton, Hely, *Statistical survey of County Galway* (Dublin 1824)

Fagan, William, *Life and times of Daniel O'Connell* (2 vols. Cork 1848)

Fitzpatrick, W. J. (ed.), *The correspondence of Daniel O'Connell* (2 vols. London 1888)

Foster, T. Campbell, *Letters on the condition of the people of Ireland* reprinted from *The Times* 1845-6 (London 1846)

Gilbart, J. W., *A history of banking in Ireland* (London 1836)

Gilbart, J. W., *A practical treatise on banking* (5th ed. London 1849)

Hancock, W. N., *Report on deposits and cash balances in joint stock banks in Ireland 1840-69* (Dublin 1870)

Inglis, H. D., *A journey throughout Ireland 1834* (London 1835)

Kane, Sir Robert, *Industrial resources of Ireland* (Dublin 1845)

Kennedy, J. P. (ed.), *Digest of evidence before the Devon commission on land tenure in Ireland 1844* (Dublin 1847)

(Longfield, Mountifort), 'Banking and currency', in *Dublin University Magazine*, xv (1840), 3-15, 218-33; xvi (1841), 371-89, 611-20

Loyal National Repeal Association, *Reports of parliamentary committee* (Dublin 1840-5)

Marmion, Anthony, *The ancient and modern history of the maritime ports of Ireland* (London 1856)

Parker, C. S., *Sir Robert Peel from his private papers* (London 1899)

Parnell, Sir H., *Observations on paper money, banking and overtrading* (London 1827)

Ricardo, David, *Works,* ed. P. Sraffa (10 vol. Cambridge 1951)

Society of Friends, *Transactions during the famine in Ireland 1846 and 1847* (Dublin 1852)

Thornton, Henry, *Paper credit of Great Britain* (1802), ed. Hayek (London 1962)

Tooke, Thomas, *A history of prices and the state of the circulation from 1793 to 1837* (London 1838)

Wakefield, Edward, *An account of Ireland statistical and political* (2 vols. London 1812)

III SECONDARY SOURCES

(a) Ireland—banking and finance

Barrow, G. L., 'Justice for Thomas Mooney', in *Dublin Hist. Rec.,* xxiv, no 1 (December 1970), 173-88

Barrow, G. L., 'Kilkenny private banks', in *Old Kilkenny Rev.,* xxiii (1971), 36-40

Barrow, G. L., 'Some Dublin private Banks', in *Dublin Hist. Rec.,* xxv, no. 2 (March 1972), 38-53

Barrow, G. L., 'The use of money in mid-nineteenth century Ireland', in *Studies,* lix, no 233 (Spring 1970), 81-8

Burke, Rev. W. P., 'Newport's Waterford bank', in *Cork Hist. Soc. Jn.,* iv (1898), 278-86

Busteed, J., 'Irish private banks', in *Cork Hist. Soc. Jn.,* liii (1948), 32-8

Collins, Charles McCarthy, *The law and practice of banking in Ireland* (Dublin 1880) (The author subsequently changed his name to Tenison—see below)

Craig, W. Alexander, 'The clearing system', in *Inst. of Bankers in Ire. Jn.,* i (1899), 249-50

Decades of the Ulster Bank 1836 to 1964 (Belfast 1965)

Dillon, Malcolm, *The history and development of banking in Ireland* (London & Dublin 1889)

Dunraven, Earl of, *The finances of Ireland* (London 1912)

Fetter, Frank W., *The Irish pound 1797-1826* (London 1955)

Fetter, Frank W., 'Legal tender during the English and Irish bank restriction', in *Journal of Political Economy,* lviii, no 3 (June 1950), 241-53

Fraser, Mrs A. M., 'David Digues La Touche, banker, and a few of his descendants', in *Dublin Hist. Rec.,* v, no 2 (December 1942), 55-68

Fraser, Mrs A. M., 'The romance of the house of Lighton', in *Dublin Hist. Rec.,* vii, no 3 (June 1945), 112-9

Hall, F. G., *The Bank of Ireland 1783-1946,* with an architectural chapter by C. P. Curran and biographical notes by Joseph Hone (Dublin & Oxford 1949)

Hall, F. G., 'The trend of banking in Ireland since 1800' (unpublished Ph.D. thesis in the library of Trinity College, Dublin)

Hill, E. D. (ed.), *Northern Banking Company centenary volume* (Belfast 1925)

McCarthy, J. F., 'The story of Sadleir's bank', in *Clonmel Hist. & Arch. Assn. Jn.,* i, no. 3 (1954-5), 3-7

Milne, Kenneth, *A history of the Royal Bank of Ireland* (Dublin 1964)

Nolan, Rev. Dom Patrick, *The history and mystery of banking in Ireland and elsewhere* (Bruges 1923)

O'Brien, George, 'The last years of the Irish currency', in *Economic History,* ii (1927), 249-58

O'Kelly, Eoin, *The old private banks and bankers of Munster* (Cork 1959)

Tenison (formerly Collins), C. McC., Various papers on Irish private banks in *Cork Hist. Soc. Jn.,* i-iii (1892-5), and in *Inst. of Bankers in Ire. Jn.,* ii-xii (1900-10)

Urwick, W., *Biographical sketches of James D. La Touche* (Dublin 1868)

(b) Ireland—economic and general

Beckett, J. C., *The making of modern Ireland 1603-1923* (London 1966)

Black, R. D. C. *Economic thought and the Irish question 1817-70* (Cambridge 1960)

Brocker, Galen, *Rural disorder and police reform in Ireland 1812-36* (London 1970)

Burke, Rev. W. P., *History of Clonmel* (Waterford 1907)

Coe, W. E., *The engineering industry of the north of Ireland* (Newton Abbott 1969)

Connell, K. H., *The population of Ireland 1780-1845* (Oxford 1950)

Connell, K. H., 'Some unsettled problems in English and Irish population history 1750-1845', in *I.H.S.,* vii (1950-1), 225-34

Connolly, James, *Labour in Irish history* (Dublin 1910)

Conroy, J. C., *A history of railways in Ireland* (London 1928)

Craig, E. T., *An Irish commune, a history of Ralahine* (Dublin 1920)

Craig, M. J., *Dublin 1660-1860* (London 1952)

Cullen, L. M., *Anglo-Irish trade 1660-1800* (Manchester 1968)

Cullen, L. M., 'Irish history without the potato', in *Past and Present,* xl (July 1968), 72-83

I

Cullen, L. M. (ed.), *The formation of the Irish economy* (Cork 1969)

Delaney, V. T. H. and D. R., *The canals of the south of Ireland* (Newton Abbott 1966)

Drake, Michael, 'Marriage and population growth in Ireland 1750-1845', in *Econ. Hist. Rev.*, 2nd series xvi, no 2 (December 1963), 301-13

Edwards, R. D. and Williams, T. D. (eds.), *The great famine* (Dublin 1956)

Freeman, T. W., *Pre-famine Ireland* (Manchester 1957)

Gill, Conrad, *The rise of the Irish linen industry* (Oxford 1925)

Green, E. E. R., *The Lagan valley 1800-50* (London 1959)

Gribben, H. D., *The history of water power in Ulster* (Newton Abbott 1969)

Gwynn, Denis, *Daniel O'Connell* (Cork 1947)

Jones, Emrys. *A social geography of Belfast* (Oxford 1960)

Kerr, Barbara M., 'Irish seasonal migration to Great Britain 1800-38', in *I.H.S.*, iii (1942-3), 365-80

Lee, J., 'Money and beer in Ireland 1790-1875', in *Econ. Hist. Rev.,* 2nd series xix, no 1 (April 1966), 183-90

Lee, J., 'The dual economy in Ireland 1800-50', in T. D. Williams (ed.), *Historical Studies,* viii, (Dublin 1971), pp 191-201

Lynch, Patrick, and Vaizey, John, *Guinness's brewery in the Irish economy* 1759-1876 (Cambridge 1960)

McCutcheon, W. A., *The canals of the north of Ireland* (Newton Abbott 1965)

MacDonagh, Michael, *Life of Daniel O'Connell* (Dublin 1929)

McDowell, R. B., *Public opinion and government policy in Ireland 1801-46* (London 1952)

McDowell, R. B., *The Irish administration 1801-1914* (London 1964)

MacIntyre, Angus, *The Liberator* (London 1965)

Maxwell, Constantia, *Dublin under the Georges 1714-1830* (London 1936)

Maxwell, Constantia, *Country and town in Ireland under the Georges* (London 1940)

Monaghan, J. J., 'A social and economic history of Belfast 1801-25' (unpublished Ph.D. thesis in the library of Queen's University, Belfast)

Monaghan, J. J., 'The rise and fall of the Belfast cotton industry', in *I.H.S.*, iii (1942-3), 1-17

O'Brien, George, *Economic history of Ireland from the Union to the Famine* (London 1921)

O'Connor, Ulick, *The Gresham Hotel 1865-1965* (Dublin 1965)

O'Donovan, J., *Economic History of livestock in Ireland* (Cork 1940)

O'Faolain, Sean, *King of the beggars* (London 1938)

Pomfret, J. E., *The struggle for the land in Ireland 1800-1923* (Princeton 1930)

Rebbeck, D., 'A history of iron shipbuilding on the Queen's Island up till 1874' (unpublished Ph.D. thesis in the library of Queen's University, Belfast)

Woodham Smith, Mrs Cecil, *The great hunger* (London 1962)

(*c*) *Great Britain—banking and general*

Ashton, T. S., and Sayers, R. S. (eds.), *Papers in English monetary history* (Oxford 1953)

Clapham, J. H., *An economic history of modern Britain,* i (Cambridge 1959)

Clapham, J. H., *The Bank of England 1694-1914* (2 vols. Cambridge 1958)

Crick, W. F. and Wadsworth, J. E., *A hundred years of joint stock banking* (London 1936)

Feavearyear, A. E., *The pound sterling,* 2nd ed. revised by E. Victor Morgan (Oxford 1963)

Fetter, Frank W., *The development of British monetary orthodoxy 1797-1875* (London 1966)

Gourvish, T. R., 'The Bank of Scotland 1830-45', in *Scottish Journ. of Polit. Econ.,* xvi, no 3 (November 1969), 288-305

Graham, William, *The one pound note in the history of banking of Great Britain* (Edinburgh 1911)

Gregory, T. E., *The Westminster Bank through a century* (London 1936)

Malcolm, C. A., *History of the Bank of Scotland* (London 1936)

Marwick, W. H., *Scotland in modern times* (London 1964)

Thomas, S. Evelyn, *The rise and growth of joint stock banking* (London 1934)

(*d*) *General*

Keynes, J. M., *The general theory of employment, interest and money* (London 1936)

Matthews, R. C. O., *A study of trade cycle history* (Cambridge 1954)

Mints, Lloyd W., *A history of banking theory in Great Britain and the United States* (Chicago 1945)

Newlyn, W. T., and Rowan, D. C., *Money and banking in British colonial Africa* (Oxford 1954)

Smith, Adam, *The wealth of nations* (1776), Seligman ed. (London 1910)

Tobin, J., 'Money, capital and other stores of value', in *American Economic Review,* li, no 2 (May 1961), 26-56

(e) *Works of reference*

Bradshaw, Thomas, *Belfast general and commercial directory for 1819* (Belfast 1819)

Bradshaw, Thomas, *General directory of Newry, Armagh et al. for 1820* (Newry 1819)

Burke's Peerage, baronetage and knightage (London 1912)

Calendar of the ancient records of Dublin

Dictionary of national biography

Parliamentary gazetteer of Ireland 1844-5 (Dublin, London & Edinburgh 1846)

The gentleman and citizen's almanack (*Watson's almanack*) (Dublin 1733-1842)

Wilson's Dublin directory (Dublin 1751-1837)

Index